1992 Supplement

to

CIVIL RIGHTS ACTIONS:

SECTION 1983 AND RELATED STATUTES

By

PETER W. LOW

Hardy Cross Dillard Professor of Law
University of Virginia

and

JOHN C. JEFFRIES, JR.

Emerson Spies Professor of Law
and Horace W. Goldsmith Research Professor
University of Virginia

Westbury, New York
THE FOUNDATION PRESS, INC.
1992

COPYRIGHT © 1988 through 1991 THE FOUNDATION PRESS, INC.

COPYRIGHT © 1992
By
THE FOUNDATION PRESS, INC.
All rights reserved
ISBN 0–88277–994–X

PREFACE

This Supplement covers five terms of the Supreme Court, from 1987 through 1992, and the scholarship published during that period. It includes two new main cases. The first is the Fourth Circuit's decision in *National Organization for Women v. Operation Rescue*, page 145. The case has been scheduled for reargument in the Supreme Court this term. The second new main case is ***Burlington v. Dague***, page 185, which replaces *Pennsylvania v. Delaware Valley Citizens' Council for Clean Air* on the use of a multiplier to increase attorney's fees for having run the risk of not prevailing on the merits. *Delaware Valley* resulted in a virtual non-decision of this question, while in *Burlington* a significantly changed Supreme Court resolved the issue against risk enhancement.

The other main cases in this Supplement are noted below:

City of St. Louis v. Praprotnik, page 12, and ***City of Canton v. Harris***, page 30, are the Court's latest pronouncements on the "official policy or custom" requirement for municipality liability under § 1983. The issue has two aspects: first, when the act of a government agent can be attributed to the government; and second, when the government can be held liable for failure to train its employees. *Praprotnik* deals with the first question, and *Harris* addresses the second.

Will v. Michigan Department of State Police, page 42 confirms that a state is not a "person" within the meaning of § 1983. For those who do not wish to cover this issue at length, the alternative of a four-paragraph summary of the decision is included at page 4.

Zinermon v. Burch, page 62, concerns the enforcement of due process violations under § 1983. This decision features competing analyses of *Parratt v. Taylor* (1981) and *Hudson v. Palmer* (1984). We therefore have omitted *Parratt* as a main case and substituted *Zinermon*.

Patterson v. McLean Credit Union, page 96, is the Court's decision not to overrule *Runyon v. McCrary* on the construction of § 1981 to reach private discrimination. *Patterson*, however, raised an issue of equal controversy by construing that statute not to apply to on-the-job racial harassment, as distinct from racial discrimination in employment contracts. This limiting construction was overturned by the Civil Rights Act of 1991. It is doubtful, therefore, that *Patterson* will long survive as a main case, but we include it in this Supplement for the benefit of those who wish to review the controversy.

PREFACE

Jett v. Dallas Independent School District, page 121, was a suit by a white teacher who alleged racial discrimination against him. The teacher sued under § 1981, hoping thereby to avoid the *Monell* limitation of governmental liability under § 1983 to acts constituting "official policy or custom," but the Court held, five-four, that § 1981 carries the same restriction.

Felder v. Casey, page 159 disapproved application of Wisconsin's notice-of-claim statute to § 1983 claims heard in state court.

Missouri v. Jenkins and ***Spallone v. United States***, pages 205 and 226 respectively, involve controversial enforcement of judicial decrees. *Jenkins* is the Kansas City desegregation case where the District Court raised local property taxes to pay for improvements to the city's schools. The Justices voted five-four to uphold judicial authority to increase taxes but said that the court should have ordered the local officials to set the increased tax rate. *Spallone* is the Yonkers housing case, in which the Court ruled, again five-four, that the District Court erred in holding local legislators personally in contempt for failing to implement the desegregation order. The two cases make an interesting comparison, so we present them together under the heading of Enforcing Structural Reform Decrees.

Pennsylvania v. Union Gas Company, page 242, resolves the question whether Congress can override the 11th amendment by exercising its power over interstate commerce. The case is more interesting than *Welch v. State Department of Highways*, which it accordingly replaces.

Many other decisions have been noted where appropriate, sometimes at some length. Additionally, we have updated references to the literature to take account of recently published scholarship.

PERMISSION TO DUPLICATE

There are many intersections between Civil Rights Actions: Section 1983 and Related Statutes and its companion volume, Federal Courts and the Law of Federal-State Relations (Second Edition, 1989). Occasionally, a teacher using one book may wish to use material from the other annual supplement.

We wish to facilitate such borrowings whenever they would be useful. To that end, we authorize teachers who have adopted either book to duplicate limited portions of the other or its annual supplement for distribution to their students.

PREFACE

We are grateful to Foundation Press, Inc., for agreeing to make this option available.

PWL
JCJjr

Charlottesville, Virginia
July, 1992

TABLE OF CONTENTS

Numbers on the left indicate where the new materials fit into the casebook. Numbers on the right indicate the page in this Supplement where the new materials can be found. Cases set out at length are in **bold face**. New main cases are set out in **BOLD CAPS**.

	Page
PREFACE	iii
TABLE OF CASES	xiii
TABLE OF SECONDARY AUTHORITIES	xvii

CHAPTER I: 42 U.S.C. § 1983

Casebook Page		Supplement Page
	Section 1: "Under Color of" Law	
13	Additional Citation	1
16	Addition to Note 3	1
16	Additional Citation	1
18	*Pennsylvania v. Union Gas Company*	2
20	Substitute a Paragraph of Text	2
	Section 2: Official Immunities	
28	Additional Citation	2
28	*Forrester v. White*	2
28	**Burns v. Reed**	3
32	Additional Citation	3
36	Additional Citations	3
39	Additional Citation	3
41	Additional Citation	4
43	Additional Citation	4
51	Additional Citation	4
	Section 3: Governmental Liability	
80	**Will v. Michigan Department of State Police**	4
105	**American Trucking Associations, Inc. v. Smith**	5
105	Substitute for Pages 105–24:	
	Introductory Notes on Determining "Official Policy"	7
	1. Introduction	7
	2. *Pembaur v. City of Cincinnati*	8
	CITY OF ST. LOUIS v. PRAPROTNIK	12
	Note on *Praprotnik*	29
	CITY OF CANTON v. HARRIS	30
	Notes on "Official Policy" and Failure to Train	39
	1. Questions and Comments on *Harris*	39

TABLE OF CONTENTS

Casebook Page		Supplement Page
	2. Bibliography	40
126	Additional Citations	41
128	Add new Case: **WILL v. MICHIGAN DEPARTMENT OF STATE POLICE**	42
	Notes on *Will v. Michigan Department of State Police*	54
	1. Questions and Comments	54
	2. Territories as "Persons": *Ngiraingas v. Sanchez*	54
	3. State Officials as "Persons" When Acting in Official Capacity: **Hafer v. Melo**	55

Section 4: For What Wrongs?

145	Additional Citation	58
145	*Siegert v. Gilley*	58
145	***Deshaney v. Winnebago County Dept. of Social Services***	59
146	Substitute for Pages 146–64: **ZINERMON v. BURCH**	62
	Additional Notes on Constitutional Rights Enforceable Under § 1983	83
	1. ***Parratt v. Taylor***	83
	(i) Mental Elements of § 1983	83
	(ii) Negligence Deprivation of Due Process	84
	(iii) The Process Due	85
	2. ***Hudson v. Palmer***: Application of *Parratt* to Intentional Wrongs	86
	3. ***Daniels v. Williams***: *Parratt* Overruled on Meaning of "Deprivation"	87
	4. ***Davidson v. Cannon***	89
	5. Questions and Comments on *Parratt* and Its Progeny	90
	6. Bibliography	92
183	*Wilder v. Virginia Hospital Association*	93
188	Omit Note 9 and Add Three New Notes:	
	9. ***Jett v. Dallas Independent School District***: Relation Between § 1981 and § 1983	93
	10. ***Golden State Transit Corp. v. Los Angeles***: § 1983 Actions to Enforce Federal Preemption of State Law	94
	11. ***Dennis v. Higgins:*** § 1983 Actions to Enforce Negative Commerce Clause Claims	94

viii

TABLE OF CONTENTS

CHAPTER II: ADDITIONAL RECONSTRUCTION LEGISLATION

Section 2: 42 U.S.C. § 1981

Casebook Page		Supplement Page
231	Additional Citation	96
256	Add new Cases:	
	PATTERSON v. McLEAN CREDIT UNION	96
	Notes on *Patterson v. McLean Credit Union*	119
	1. The Order for Reargument	119
	2. The Decision	120
	3. The Overruling	120
	4. Bibliography	121
	JETT v. DALLAS INDEPENDENT SCHOOL DISTRICT	121
	Notes on *Jett v. Dallas Independent School District*	143
	1. Background	143
	2. Questions and Comments	144

Section 3: 42 U.S.C. § 1985(3)

290	Additional Citation	144
291	Additional Text	144
291	Add New Materials:	
	NATIONAL ORGANIZATION FOR WOMEN v. OPERATION RESCUE	145
	Notes on the "Operation Rescue" Cases	148
	1. The Supreme Court's Deposition of the Fourth Circuit Decision	148
	2. The District Court Decision	148
	3. The Second Circuit Decision	151
	4. Comments and Questions	156

CHAPTER III: ADMINISTRATION OF THE CIVIL RIGHTS ACTS: INTERSECTIONS OF STATE AND FEDERAL LAW

Section 1: Res Judicata

315	Additional Citations	158

Section 3: Statutes of Limitations

338	Additional Citations	158
338	*Owens v. Okure*: Choice Between Personal Injury Statutes	158

Section 4: Exhaustion of Remedies

360	*McCarthy v. Madigan*	159
364	*FELDER v. CASEY*	159

TABLE OF CONTENTS

Casebook Page		Supplement Page
	Section 5: Relation of § 1983 to Federal Habeas Corpus	
380	Substitute for Notes 1–2, Pages 380–81:	
	1. Questions and Comments on the Relation of § 1983 and Habeas Corpus	175
	2. Relation of *Younger* and *Preiser* to § 1983 Actions for Damages	176
	3. *Guerro v. Mulhearn*	176
	4. *Deakins v. Monaghan*	177
	(i) Justice Blackmun's Opinion	177
	(ii) Justice White's Concurrence	179
	5. Questions and Comments on *Guerro* and *Deakins*	180
	Section 7: Release Dismissal Agreements	
431	Bibliography	181

CHAPTER IV: ATTORNEY'S FEES

Section 1: Determining Fee Awards

451	*Kay v. Ehrler*	182
451	*Rhodes v. Stewart*	182
451	*Blanchard v. Bergeron*	182
451	*Venegas v. Mitchell*	182
451	**Texas State Teachers Assoc. v. Garland Independent School District**	183
452	West Virginia University Hospitals, Inc. v. Casey	183
455	Additional Citations	183
456	Substitute for pages 456–74:	
	Section 1A: Risk Enhancement	
	Introductory Note on Risk Enhancement	184
	CITY OF BURLINGTON v. DAGUE	185

CHAPTER V: ABSTENTION IN CIVIL RIGHTS CASES

Section 2: *Younger* Abstention

545	Cross Reference	197
547	Additional Citations	197
555	Additional Citations	197
583	Substitute for Note 3, pages 583–84:	
	3. *New Orleans Public Service, Inc. v. Council of City of New Orleans*	198
	4. Questions and Comments on the Extension of *Younger* to Civil Proceedings	200
585	Additional Citation	200

x

TABLE OF CONTENTS

CHAPTER VI: SELECTED PROBLEMS IN STRUCTURAL REFORM LITIGATION

Casebook Page		Supplement Page
593	Additional Citations	202
593	Additional Citations	202

Section 1: Structural Reform and Standing
613	Additional Citation	202
632	Additional Citation	202

Section 4: Structural Reform and the Definition of Rights
685	*Wilson v. Seiter*	203
685	Additional Citation	205
686	Additional Citation	205

Section 5: Enforcing Structural Reform Decrees
686	Add a new Section:	
	MISSOURI v. JENKINS	205
	Notes on *Missouri v. Jenkins*	220
	1. Introduction to Desegregation Strategies	220
	2. History of the *Jenkins* Litigation	223
	3. Questions and Comments on *Jenkins*	225
	SPALLONE v. UNITED STATES	226
	Note on *Spallone v. United States*	237

CHAPTER VII: STATE SOVEREIGN IMMUNITY AND THE 11TH AMENDMENT

Section 1: Origins
697	Additional Citation	238
700	Additional Citations	238
701	Additional Citations	238

Section 2: Suits Against State Officers
727	*Port Authority Trans-Hudson Corp. v. Feeney*	239
735	*Missouri v. Jenkins*	239
736	*Will v. Michigan Department of State Police*	239
737	*Dellmuth v. Muth; Hoffman v. Connecticut Dept of Income Maintenance*	239
737	Substitute for Pages 737–52:	
	5. *Welch v. Texas Department of Highways and Public Transportation*	239
	PENNSYLVANIA v. UNION GAS COMPANY	242
	Note on *Pennsylvania v. Union Gas Company*	258

xi

TABLE OF CONTENTS

Casebook Page		Supplement Page
	Section 3: The *Pennhurst* Problem	
773	Additional Citation	258

APPENDIX B: SELECTED FEDERAL STATUTES

B–3	Amended Statute	259
	(§ 1981)	259
B–5	Amended Statute	259
	(§ 1988)	259

TABLE OF CASES

Principal cases are in italic type. Non-principal cases are in roman type. References are to Pages.

Adickes v. S. H. Kress & Co., 16, 20, 38
Alabama v. Pugh, 51
Alyeska Pipeline Service Co. v. Wilderness Soc., 110
American Trucking Associations, Inc. v. Scheiner, 5, 6, 7
American Trucking Associations, Inc. v. Smith, 5
Anderson v. Creighton, 3, 4
Arizona v. Rumsey, 98
Arlington Heights, Village of v. Metropolitan Housing Development Corp., 84
Armstrong v. Manzo, 85
Atascadero State Hosp. v. Scanlon, 2, 5, 44, 48, 239, 240, 243, 248

Bass, United States v., 44
Bivens v. Six Unknown Named Agents of Federal Bureau of Narcotics, 58, 134, 143, 159
Blanchard v. Bergeron, 182
Blum v. Stenson, 187
Board of Regents of State Colleges v. Roth, 61
Boys Markets, Inc. v. Retail Clerk's Union, Local 770, p. 93
Brown v. Board of Education of Topeka, Shawnee County, Kan., 109, 219, 220, 221, 223, 224
Brown v. General Services Admin., 133, 140
Brown v. Western Railway of Alabama, 162, 168, 169, 173
Burford v. Sun Oil Co., 198, 200
Burlington, City of v. Dague, 185
Burnett v. Grattan, 166, 167, 174
Burns v. Reed, 3
Buschi v. Kirven, 147, 149

California, State of, United States v., 48
Cannon v. University of Chicago, 132, 137
Canton, Ohio, City of v. Harris, 8, 30, 39, 40, 41
Carey v. Piphus, 72
Chapman v. Houston Welfare Rights Organization, 129, 131
Chevron Oil Co. v. Huson, 6
Chisholm v. State of Georgia, 254
City of (see name of city)

Cody v. Union Elec., 114
Coffin v. Coffin, 231
Colorado River Water Conservation Dist. v. United States, 178, 179, 180
Conklin v. Lovely, 153
Conroy v. Conroy, 147, 153
Consumer Product Safety Com'n v. GTE Sylvania, Inc., 142
Cooper v. Aaron, 237
Cort v. Ash, 137, 143

Daniels v. Williams, 62, 68, 69, 78, 87, 88, 89, 90
Davidson v. Cannon, 62, 89, 90
Deakins v. Monaghan, 177, 180, 181
Della Grotta v. State of R.I., 51
Dellmuth v. Muth, 2, 239
Dennis v. Higgins, 94
DeShaney v. Winnebago County Dept. of Social Services, 59, 62
District of Columbia v. Carter, 127
Doe v. Bolton, 146, 150, 155
Dollar Sav. Bank v. United States, 48

Edelman v. Jordan, 52, 249
Erie R. Co. v. Tompkins, 168, 174
Evans v. Buchanan, 223

Felder v. Casey, 44, *159*
Fitzpatrick v. Bitzer, 2, 5, 43, 241, 243, 244, 247, 256
Flood v. Kuhn, 110
Forrester v. White, 2
Friends of the Earth v. Eastman Kodak Co., 196
Frontiero v. Richardson, 153
Furnco Const. Corp. v. Waters, 106

General Bldg. Contractors Ass'n, Inc. v. Pennsylvania, 106, 127, 128
Golden State Transit Corp. v. City of Los Angeles, 110 S.Ct. 444, p. 94
Golden State Transit Corp. v. City of Los Angeles, 106 S.Ct. 1395, pp. 94, 95
Goodman v. Lukens Steel Co., 101, 115, 119
Great American Federal Sav. & Loan Ass'n v. Novotny, 151
Green v. County School Bd. of New Kent County, Va., 221

xiii

TABLE OF CASES

Grier v. Specialized Skills, Inc., 114
Griffin v. Breckenridge, 149, 150, 152, 154
Griffin v. County School Bd. of Prince Edward County, 210, 216, 225
Griswold v. Connecticut, 151
Guaranty Trust Co. of New York v. York, 168, 169, 174
Guerro v. Mulhearn, 176, 179, 180

Hafer v. Melo, 55
Hagans v. Lavine, 43
Hall v. Bio–Medical Application, Inc., 114
Hall v. Pennsylvania State Police, 114
Hans v. State of Louisiana, 238, 241, 243, 245, 247, 248, 249, 250, 251, 252, 253, 254, 257
Harlow v. Fitzgerald, 3, 4, 58
Harris v. Reed, 250
Hensley v. Eckerhart, 183, 189, 190
Hicks v. Miranda, 200
Hobson v. Wilson, 153
Hoffman v. Connecticut Dept. of Income Maintenance, 2, 239
Howard Sec. Services, Inc. v. Johns Hopkins Hospital, 114
Howlett By and Through Howlett v. Rose, 1
Hudson v. McMillian, 204
Hudson v. Palmer, 63, 67, 70, 71, 73, 74, 75, 76, 77, 78, 79, 80, 81, 86, 87, 88, 89, 92
Huffman v. Pursue, Ltd., 198
Hunt v. Weatherbee, 150
Hurd v. Hodge, 126, 127, 138, 139, 141
Hutto v. Finney, 5, 53, 239

Imbler v. Pachtman, 3

Jenkins by Agyei v. Missouri, 855 F.2d 1295, p. 223
Jenkins by Agyei v. Missouri, 807 F.2d 657, pp. 220, 224, 225, 226, 237
Jett v. Dallas Independent School Dist., 93, *121*, 143, 144
J. I. Case Co. v. Borak, 143
Johnson v. Railway Exp. Agency, Inc., 103, 114, 115
Johnson v. Transportation Agency, Santa Clara County, Cal., 99
Jones v. Alfred H. Mayer Co., 127, 138
Juidice v. Vail, 198

Kay v. Ehrler, 182
Keating v. Carey, 153
Kentucky v. Graham, 47, 52
Keyes v. School Dist. No. 1, Denver, Colo., 221

Lake Country Estates, Inc. v. Tahoe Regional Planning Agency, 230

Life Ins. Co. of North America v. Reichardt, 147, 153
Logan v. Zimmerman Brush Co., 64, 87, 92

Maine v. Thiboutot, 1, 5, 43, 131, 140, 143
Martinez v. California, 172
Mathews v. Eldridge, 69, 70, 75, 78, 81, 82, 83
McCarthy v. Madigan, 159
McDonnell Douglas Corp. v. Green, 106, 107
McLean v. International Harvester Co., 153
Memphis, City of v. Greene, 112
Memphis Community School Dist. v. Stachura, 4
Meritor Sav. Bank, FSB v. Vinson, 102, 113
Merrill Lynch, Pierce, Fenner & Smith, Inc. v. Curran, 137
Middlesex County Sewerage Authority v. National Sea Clammers Ass'n, 93
Milliken v. Bradley, 97 S.Ct. 2749, pp. 53, 210, 212, 229, 249
Milliken v. Bradley, 94 S.Ct. 3112, p. 222
Mississippi Women's Medical Clinic v. McMillan, 147, 156
Missouri v. Jenkins, 205
Missouri v. Jenkins by Agyei, 184, 190, 239
Mitchum v. Foster, 129, 172, 197
Monaco v. State of Mississippi, 245
Monell v. New York City Department of Social Services, 4, 7, 10, *11*, 14, 15, 19, 20, 25, 26, 27, 32, 33, 35, 36, 37, 39, 40, 41, 42, 43, 45, 46, 49, 50, 52, 93, 110, 125, 126, 130, 131, 134, 140, 141, 252
Monroe v. Pape, 1, 4, 43, 46, 67, 68, 75, 83, 91, 141
Moor v. Alameda County, 132
Moses H. Cone Memorial Hosp. v. Mercury Const. Corp., 180
Mt. Healthy City School Dist. Bd. of Ed. v. Doyle, 46

National Abortion Federation v. Operation Rescue, 149
National Cable Television Ass'n, Inc. v. United States, 215
National Organization for Women v. Operation Rescue, 914 F.2d 582, p. *145*
National Organization for Women v. Operation Rescue, 726 F.Supp. 1483, pp. 145, 148
National R. R. Passenger Corp. v. National Ass'n of R. R. Passengers, 132
Nevada v. Hall, 53
Newburg Area Council, Inc. v. Board of Ed. of Jefferson County, Kentucky, 223
New Orleans Public Service, Inc. v. Council of City of New Orleans, 198, 200

TABLE OF CASES

Newport, City of v. Fact Concerts, Inc., 14, 20, 21, 45, 128
Newton, Town of v. Rumery, 181
New York State Nat. Organization for Women v. Terry, 886 F.2d 1339, pp. 147, 150, 151, 156
New York State Nat. Organization for Women v. Terry, 704 F.Supp. 1247, p. 150
Ngiraingas v. Sanchez, 5, 54
Novotny v. Great American Federal Sav. and Loan Ass'n, 147, 153

O'Connor v. Donaldson, 72
Oklahoma City, City of v. Tuttle, 14, 28, 34, 39, 41
Owen v. City of Independence, Mo., 6, 7, 11, 14, 21, 27, 28, 40, 41, 45
Owens v. Okure, 158

Paradise, United States v., 233
Parden v. Terminal Ry. of Alabama State Docks Dept., 239, 240, 241, 247, 256
Parratt v. Taylor, 63, 67, 69, 70, 71, 72, 73, 74, 75, 76, 77, 78, 79, 80, 81, 82, 83, 84, 86, 87, 88, 89, 90, 92, 93
Patsy v. Board of Regents of State of Fla., 44, 166, 172
Patterson v. McLean Credit Union, 109 S.Ct. 2363, pp. *96*, 135, 136
Patterson v. McLean Credit Union, 805 F.2d 1143, pp. 119, 120, 125, 144
Paul v. Davis, 58, 82, 86, 91, 91
Pembaur v. City of Cincinnati, 8, 14, 15, 16, 17, 18, 19, 21, 23, 27, 28, 33, 125
Pennhurst State School & Hosp. v. Halderman, 104 S.Ct. 900, pp. 249, 258
Pennhurst State School and Hospital v. Halderman, 101 S.Ct. 1531, p. 44
Pennsylvania v. Delaware Valley Citizens' Council for Clean Air, 107 S.Ct. 3078, pp. 184, 185, 186, 187, 188, 189, 190, 191, 192, 193, 195
Pennsylvania v. Delaware Valley Citizens' Council for Clean Air, 106 S.Ct. 3088, pp. 187, 188, 190
Pennsylvania v. Union Gas Co., 2, 4, 210, 241, *242*, 258
Philadelphia, City of v. New Jersey, 246
Plessy v. Ferguson, 109
Poindexter v. Greenhow, 49
Polk County v. Dodson, 33
Port Authority Trans-Hudson Corp. v. Feeney, 239
Portland Feminist Women's Health Center v. Advocates For Life, Inc., 149
Preiser v. Rodriguez, 140, 175, 176, 181
Prentis v. Atlantic Coast Line Co., 199
Price Waterhouse v. Hopkins, 107
Providence, City of, United States v., 235

Quern v. Jordan, 2, 5, 43, 44, 46, 48, 53, 239, 240

Revere, City of v. Massachusetts General Hosp., 33
Rhodes v. Stewart, 182, 203
Rice v. Santa Fe Elevator Corporation, 44
Riverside, City of v. Rivera, 182
Rizzo v. Goode, 35
Robertson v. Wegmann, 171
Roe v. Abortion Abolition Soc., 149
Roe v. Operation Rescue, 150
Roe v. Wade, 151
Runyon v. McCrary, 93, 97, 99, 100, 101, 103, 104, 105, 109, 110, 111, 114, 117, 118, 119, 120, 121, 135

Samuels v. Mackell, 179, 180
San Antonio Independent School Dist. v. Rodriguez, 217
Scott v. Young, 114
Screws v. United States, 84
Shillitani v. United States, 229, 232
Siegert v. Gilley, 58
Skadegaard v. Farrell, 150
Spallone v. United States, 216, 219, *226*, 237
Springfield, Mass., City of v. Kibbe, 32
State of (see name of state)
Stathos v. Bowden, 147
Steagald v. United States, 8
St. Louis, City of v. Praprotnik, *8*, *12*, *29*, *32*, *40*, 125, 134, 135
Stone v. Powell, 178
Supreme Court of Virginia v. Consumers Union of United States, Inc., 230, 236
Suter v. Artist M., 93
Swann v. Charlotte-Mecklenburg Bd. of Ed., 221, 229, 233

Takahashi v. Fish and Game Commission, 126, 138
Tennessee v. Garner, 34
Tenney v. Brandhove, 230, 231, 236
Testa v. Katt, 51
Texas Dept. of Community Affairs v. Burdine, 106, 107
Texas & P. Ry. Co. v. Rigsby, 137
Texas State Teachers Ass'n v. Garland Independent School Dist., 183
Tillman v. Wheaton-Haven Recreation Ass'n, Inc., 114
Touche Ross & Co. v. Redington, 143
Town of (see name of town)
Trainor v. Hernandez, 198, 200

United Broth. of Carpenters and Joiners of America, Local 610, AFL-CIO v. Scott, 149, 152

TABLE OF CASES

United States v. ____(see opposing party)

Vasquez v. Hillery, 98, 109
Venegas v. Mitchell, 182, 189
Verlinden B.V. v. Central Bank of Nigeria, 245
Village of (see name of village)
Volk v. Coler, 149, 153
Von Hoffman v. City of Quincy, 211, 216, 217

Washington v. Davis, 84
Welch v. Texas Dept. of Highways and Public Transp., 2, 98, 137, 239, 240, 250, 251, 252, 253, 256
West Virginia University Hospitals, Inc. v. Casey, 183
Whitcomb v. Chavis, 229

Whitley v. Albers, 203
Wilder v. Virginia Hosp. Ass'n, 93
Will v. Michigan Dept. of State Police, 2, 4, 5, 42, 54, 55, 56, 58, 128, 239
Wilson v. Garcia, 158, 164, 165, 169, 170, 171, 174
Wilson v. Omaha Indian Tribe, 43
Wilson v. Seiter, 203, 204
Wright v. City of Roanoke Redevelopment and Housing Authority, 93
Wyatt v. Security Inn Food & Beverage, Inc., 109

Yonkers, City of, United States v., 229
Young, Ex parte, 2, 47, 249, 252
Younger v. Harris, 175, 176, 177, 179, 180, 197, 198, 199, 200, 201

Zinermon v. Burch, 62, 90

TABLE OF SECONDARY AUTHORITIES

References are to Pages

Achtenberg, Immunity under 42 U.S.C. § 1983: Interpretive Approach and the Search for the Legislative Will, 86 Nw.L.Rev. 497 (1992)—p. 3.

Althouse, The Misguided Search for State Interest in Abstention Cases: Observations on the Occasion of *Pennzoil v. Texaco*, 63 N.Y.U.L.Rev. 1051 (1988)—p. 201.

Amar, *Marbury*, Section 13, and the Original Jurisdiction of the Supreme Court, 56 U.Chi.L.Rev. 443 (1989)—p. 238.

Amar, Of Sovereignty and Federalism, 96 Yale L.J. 1425 (1987)—p. 248.

Amar and Widawsky, Child Abuse as Slavery: A Thirteenth Amendment Response to *DeShaney*, 105 Harv.L.Rev. 1359 (1992)—p. 62.

Anderson, Implementation of Consent Decrees in Structural Reform Litigation, 1986 U.Ill.L.Rev. 725—p. 202.

Anderson, Release and Resumption of Jurisdiction Over Consent Decrees in Structural Reform Litigation, 42 U.Miami L.Rev. 401 (1987)—p. 202.

Baker, "Our Federalism" in *Pennzoil Co. v. Texaco, Inc.* or How the *Younger* Doctrine Keeps Getting Older Not Better, 9 Review of Litigation 303 (1990)—p. 197.

Bandes, *Monell, Parratt, Daniels*, and *Davidson*: Distinguishing a Custom or Policy from a Random, Unauthorized Act, 72 Iowa L.Rev. 101 (1986)—pp. 41, 93.

Beerman, Administrative Failure and Local Democracy: The Politics of *DeShaney*, 1990 Duke L.J. 1078 (1990)—p. 62.

Beermann, Government Official Torts and the Takings Clause: Federalism and State Sovereign Immunity, 68 Boston U.L.Rev. 277 (1988)—p. 92.

BeVier, What Privacy is Not, 12 Harv.J.L. & Pub.Pol'y 99 (1989)—p. 151.

Blum, *Monell, DeShaney*, and *Zinermon*: Official Policy, Affirmative Duty, Established State Procedure and Local Government Liability under Section 1983, 24 Creighton L.Rev. 1 (1990)—p. 62.

Blum, Section 1981 Revisited: Looking Beyond *Runyon* and *Patterson*, 32 Howard L.J. 1 (1989)—p. 121.

Brand, The Second Front in the Fight for Civil Rights: The Supreme Court, Congress, and Statutory Fees, 69 Tex.L.Rev. 291 (1990)—p. 184.

Brown, Accountability in Government and Section 1983, 25 U.Mich.J.L.Ref. 53 (1991)—p. 41.

Brown, Correlating Municipal Liability and Official Immunity Under Section 1983, 1989 U.Ill.L.Rev. 625 (1989)—p. 41.

Brown, De-Federalizing Common Law Torts: Empathy for *Parratt, Huston*, and *Daniels*, 28 B.C.L.Rev. 813 (1987)—p. 92.

Brown, Has the Supreme Court Confessed Error on the Eleventh Amendment? Revisionist Scholarship and State Immunity, 68 U.N.C.L.Rev. 867 (1990)—p. 258.

Brown, Municipal Liability under § 1983 and the Ambiguities of Burger Court Federalism: A Comment on City of *Oklahoma City v. Tuttle* and *Pembaur v. City of Cincinnati*—the "Official Policy" Cases, 27 B.C.L.Rev. 883 (1986)—p. 41.

Burnham, Separating Constitutional and Common-Law Torts: A Critique and a Proposed Constitutional Theory of Duty, 73 Minn.L.Rev. 515 (1989)—p. 92.

Burnham, Taming the Eleventh Amendment Without Overruling *Hans v. Louisiana*, 40 Case Western Res.L.Rev. 931 (1989-90)—p. 238.

Burnham and Fayz, The State as a "Non-Person" Under Section 1983: Some Comments on *Will* and Suggestions for the Future, 70 Ore.L.Rev. 1 (1991)—p. 54.

Burton, Racial Discrimination in Contract Performance: *Patterson* and a State Law Alternative, 25 Harv.C.R.-C.L.L.R. 431 (1990)—p. 121.

TABLE OF SECONDARY AUTHORITIES

Cardozo, The Nature of the Judicial Process 149 (1921)—pp. 99, 117.

Cogan, Section 1985(3)'s Restructuring of Equality: An Essay on Texts, History, Progress and Cynicism, 39 Rutgers L.Rev. 515 (1987)—p. 144.

Collins, "Economic Rights," Implied Constitutional Actions, and the Scope of Section 1983, 77 Georgetown L.J. 1493 (1989)—p. 1.

Collins, The Right to Avoid Trial: Justifying Federal Court Intervention into Ongoing State Court Proceedings, 66 N.C.L.Rev. 49 (1987)—p. 197.

Comment, Section 1991 and Discriminatory Discharge: A Contextual Analysis, 64 Temple L.Rev. 173 (1991)—p. 121.

Davies, In Search of the "Paradigmatic Wrong"?: Selecting a Limitations Period for Section 1983, 36 Kan.L.Rev. 133 (1987)—p. 158.

Dawson, The Federalist, No. 81, p. 657 (1876) (Hamilton)—p. 245.

Devitt & Blackmar, Federal Jury Practice & Instructions § 103.23 (1987)—p. 149.

Easley, The Supreme Court and the 11th Amendment: Mourning the Last Opportunity to Synthesize Conflicting Precedents, 64 Denver U.L.Rev. 485 (1988)—p. 238.

Eaton and Wells, Government Inaction as a Constitutional Tort: *DeShaney* and its Aftermath, 66 Wash.L.Rev. 107 (1991)—p. 62.

Eisenberg and Schwab, The Importance of Section 1981, 73 Cornell L.Rev. 596 (1988)—pp. 114, 121.

Eisenberg and Schwab, The Reality of Constitutional Tort Litigation, 72 Corn.L.Rev. 641 (1987)—p. 1.

Fallon, The Ideologies of Federal Courts Law, 74 Va.L.Rev. 1141 (1988)—pp. 197, 238.

Fallon and Meltzer, New Law, Non-Retroactivity and Constitutional Remedies, 104 Harv.L.Rev. 1731 (1991)—p. 3.

Fisher, Caging *Lyons*: The Availability of Injunctive Relief in Section 1983 Actions, 18 Loyola U.Chi.L.J. 1085 (1987)—p. 202.

Fletcher, A Historical Interpretation of the 11th Amendment: A Narrow Construction of an Affirmative Grant of Jurisdiction Rather than a Prohibition Against Jurisdiction, 35 Stan.L.Rev. 1033 (1983)—p. 248.

Fletcher, The Diversity Explanation of the Eleventh Amendment: A Reply to Critics, 56 U.Chi.L.Rev. 1261 (1989)—p. 238.

Fletcher, The Structure of Standing, 98 Yale L.J. 221 (1988)—p. 202.

Friedman, A Revisionist Theory of Abstention, 88 Mich.L.Rev. 530 (1989)—p. 197.

Friedman, *Parratt v. Taylor*: Opening and Closing the Door on Section 1983, 9 Hast. Con.L.Q. 545 (1982)—p. 92.

Friedman, When Rights Encounter Reality: Enforcing Federal Remedies, 65 So.Cal.L.Rev. 735 (1992)—p. 237.

Garcia, The Scope of Police Immunity from Civil Suit under Title 42, Section 1983 and *Bivens*: A Realistic Appraisal, 11 Whittier L.Rev. 511 (1989)—p. 3.

Gerard, A Restrained Perspective on Activism, 64 Chi-Kent L.Rev. 605 (1988)—p. 202.

Gerhardt, The *Monell* Legacy: Balancing Federalism Concerns and Municipal Accountability under § 1983, 62 S.Cal.L.Rev. 539—p. 40.

Gibbons, The 11th Amendment and State Sovereign Immunity: A Reinterpretation, 83 Colum.L.Rev. 1889 (1983)—p. 248.

Gildin, Immunizing Intentional Violations of Constitutional Rights through Judicial Legislation: The Extension of *Harlow v. Fitzgerald* to Section 1983 Actions, 38 Emory L.J. 369 (1989)—p. 4.

Gildin, The Standard of Culpability in Section 1983 and *Bivens* Actions: The Prima Facie Case, Qualified Immunity and the Constitution, 11 Hofstra L.Rev. 557 (1983)—p. 84.

Goldstein, *Blyew*: Variations on a Jurisdictional Theme, 41 Stan.L.Rev. 469 (1989)—p. 121.

Herman, Beyond Parity: Section 1983 and the State Courts, 54 Brooklyn L.Rev. 1057 (1989)—p. 1.

Heyman, The First Duty of Government: Protection, Liberty and the Fourteenth Amendment, 41 Duke L.J. 507 (1991)—p. 62.

Hirshman, Foreward: Kicking Over the Traces of Self-Government, 64 Chi-Kent L.Rev. 435 (1988)—p. 202.

Jackson, One Hundred Years of Folly: the Eleventh Amendment and the 1988 Term, 64 So.Cal.L.Rev. 51 (1990)—p. 258.

Jackson, The Supreme Court, the Eleventh Amendment, and State Sovereign Immunity, 98 Yale L.J. 1 (1988)—pp. 238, 248.

TABLE OF SECONDARY AUTHORITIES

Jarvis and Jarvis, The Continuing Problems of Statutes of Limitations in Section 1983 Cases, Is the Answer Out at Sea?, 22 John Marshall L.Rev. 285 (1988)—p. 158.

Jeffries, Compensation for Constitutional Torts: Reflections on the Significance of Fault, 88 Mich.L.Rev. 82 (1989)—pp. 4, 41.

Jeffries, Damages for Constitutional Violations: The Relation of Risk to Injury in Constitutional Torts, 75 Va.L.Rev. 46 (1989)—pp. 4, 42.

Jones, Battered Spouses' Section 1983 Damage Actions Against the Unresponsive Police after *DeShaney*, 93 W.Va.L.Rev. 251 (1990–91)—p. 62.

Kaczorowski, The Enforcement Provisions of the Civil Rights Act of 1866: A Legislative History in Light of *Runyon v. McCrary*, 98 Yale L.J. 565 (1989)—p. 121.

Kaufman and Schwartz, Civil Rights in Transition: Sections 1981 and 1982 Cover Discrimination on the Basis of Ancestry and Ethnicity, 4 Touro L.Rev. 183 (1988)—p. 96.

Kennedy, Reconstruction and the Politics of Scholarship, 98 Yale L.J. 521 (1989)—p. 121.

Kinports, Habeas Corpus, Qualified Immunity, and Crystal Balls: Predicting the Course of Constitutional Law, 33 Ariz.L.Rev. 115 (1991)—p. 3.

Kinports, Qualified Immunity in Section 1983 Cases: The Unanswered Questions, 23 Ga.L.Rev. 597 (1898)—p. 3.

Kirkpatrick, Defining a Constitutional Tort Under Section 1983: The State-of-Mind-Requirement, 46 U.Cinn.L.Rev. 45 (1977)—p. 84.

Kreimer, Releases, Redress, and Police Misconduct: Reflections on Agreements to Waive Civil Rights Actions in Exchange for Dismissal of Criminal Charges, 136 Pa.L.Rev. 851 (1988)—p. 181.

Kritchevsky, The Availability of a Federal Remedy Under 42 U.S.C. § 1983 for Prosecution Under an Unconstitutional State Statute: The Sixth Circuit Struggles in *Richardson v. City of South Euclid*, 22 U.Tol.L.Rev. 303 (1991)—pp. 58, 92.

Kritchevsky, Making Sense of State of Mind: Determining Responsibility in Section 1983 Municipal Liability Litigation, 60 G.W.L.Rev. 417 (1992)—p. 41.

Lee, Sovereign Immunity and the 11th Amendment: The Uses of History, 18 Urb.Law 519 (1986)—p. 248.

Levinson, Due Process Challenges to Governmental Actions: The Meaning of *Parratt* and *Hudson*, 18 Urb.Law. 189 (1986)—p. 92.

Lewis, Jr. and Blumoff, Reshaping Section 1983's Asymmetry, 140 U.Pa.L.Rev. 755 (1992)—p. 42.

Logan, Judicial Federalism in the Court of History, 66 Ore.L.Rev. 453 (1987)—p. 197.

Love, Presumed General Compensatory Damages in Constitutional Tort Litigation: A Corrective Justice Perspective, 49 W. & L.L.Rev. 67 (1992)—p. 4.

Macurdy, Classical Nostalgia: Racism, Contract Ideology, and Formalist Legal Reasoning in *Patterson v. McLean Credit Union*, 18 N.Y.U.Rev. of Law & Social Change 987 (1990–91)—p. 121.

Marcos, Wanted: A Federal Standard for Evaluating the Adequate State Forum, 50 Maryland L.Rev. 131 (1991)—p. 197.

Marshall, Fighting the Words of the Eleventh Amendment, 102 Harv.L.Rev. 1342 (1989)—pp. 238, 248.

Marshall, The Diversity Theory of the Eleventh Amendment: A Critical Evaluation, 102 Harv.L.Rev. 1372 (1989)—p. 238.

Massey, Marshall, Marshall and Fletcher, Exchange on the Eleventh Amendment, 57 U.Chi.L.Rev. 117 (1990)—p. 238.

Massey, State Sovereignty and the Tenth and Eleventh Amendments, 56 U.Chi. L.Rev. 61 (1989)—p. 238.

Matasar, Personal Immunities under Section 1983: The Limits of the Court's Historical Analysis, 40 Ark.L.Rev. 741 (1987)—p. 2.

Mead, Evolution of the "Species of Tort Liability" Created by 42 U.S.C. § 1983: Can Constitutional Tort be Saved From Extinction?, 55 Fordham L.Rev. 1 (1986)—p. 92.

Mead, 42 U.S.C. § 1983 Municipal Liability: The *Monell* Sketch Becomes a Distorted Picture, 65 N.C.L.Rev. 518 (1987)—p. 41.

Meltzer, Deterring Constitutional Violations by Law Enforcement Officials: Plaintiffs and Defendants as Private Attorneys General, 88 Colum.L.Rev. 247 (1988)—p. 202.

Monaghan, Federal Statutory Review under Section 1983 and the APA, 91 Colum.L.Rev. 233 (1991)—p. 94.

TABLE OF SECONDARY AUTHORITIES

Monaghan, State Law Wrongs, State Law Remedies, and the 14th Amendment, 86 Colum.L.Rev. 979 (1986)—p. 92.

Nahmod, Constitutional Damages and Corrective Justice: A Different View, 76 Va. L.Rev. 997 (1990)—pp. 4, 42.

Neuman, Law Review Articles that Backfire, 21 J.L. Reform 697 (1988)—p. 92.

Nichol, Federalism, State Courts, and Section 1983, 73 Va.L.Rev. 959 (1987)—p. 197.

Note, Superfund and California's Implementation: Potential Conflict, 19 C.W.L.R. 373 (1983)—p. 246.

Oliver, Municipal Liability for Police Misconduct under 42 U.S.C. § 1983 after *City of Oklahoma City v. Tuttle*, 64 Wash.U.L.Q. 151 (1986)—p. 41.

Oren, Immunity and Accountability in Civil Rights Litigation: Who Should Pay?, 50 U.Pitt.L.Rev. 935 (1989)—p. 3.

Oren, The State's Failure to Protect Children and Substantive Due Process: *DeShaney* in Context, 68 N.C.L.Rev. 659 (1990)—p. 62.

Redlich, The Ninth Amendment as a Constitutional Prison, 12 Harv.J.L. & Pub.Pol'y 23 (1989)—p. 151.

Rossell, Applied Social Science Research: What Does It Say About the Effectiveness of School Desegregation Plans?, 12 J.Legal Studies 69 (1983)—p. 222.

Rotunda, *Runyon v. McCrary* and the Mosaic of State Action, 67 Wash.U.L.Q. 47 (1989)—p. 121.

Rowe, The Supreme Court on Attorney Fee Awards, 1985 and 1986 Terms: Economics, Ethics, and Ex Ante Analysis, 1 Geo.J.Legal Ethics 621 (1988)—p. 184.

Rudovsky, The Qualified Immunity Doctrine in the Supreme Court: Judicial Activism and the Restriction of Constitutional Rights, 138 U.Pa.L.Rev. 23 (1989)—p. 3.

Schwab and Eisenberg, Explaining Constitutional Tort Litigation: The Influence of the Attorney Fees Statute and the Government as Defendant, 73 Corn.L.Rev. 719 (1988)—p. 184.

Schwartz, The Postdeprivation Remedy Doctrine of *Parratt v. Taylor* and Its Application to Cases of Land Use Regulation, 21 Ga.L.Rev. 601 (1987)—p. 92.

Schwartz, The *Preiser* Puzzle: Continued Frustrating Conflict Between the Civil Rights and Habeas Corpus Remedies for State Prisoners, 37 De Paul L.Rev. 85 (1988)—p. 176.

Schwartz and Kaufman, Addendum: Civil Rights In Jeopardy, 4 Touro L.Rev. 245 (1988)—p. 121.

Seventh Circuit Symposium: The Federal Courts and the Community, 64 Chi-Kent L.Rev. 435 (1988)—p. 202.

Shane, Rights, Remedies and Restraint, 64 Chi-Kent L.Rev. 531 (1988)—p. 202.

Shapiro, Choosing the Appropriate State Statute of Limitations for Section 1983 Claims After *Wilson v. Garcia*: A Theory Applied to Maryland Law, 16 U.Balt.L.Rev. 242 (1987)—pp. 158, 170.

Shapiro, Keeping Civil Rights Actions Against State Officials in Federal Court: Avoiding the Reach of *Parratt v. Taylor* and *Hudson v. Palmer*, 3 Law & Inequality 161 (1985)—p. 92.

Shapiro, Wrong Turns: The 11th Amendment and the *Pennhurst* Case, 98 Harv.L.Rev. 61 (1984)—p. 248.

Sherry, The Eleventh Amendment and Stare Decisis: Overruling *Hans v. Louisiana*, 57 U.Chi.L.Rev. 1260 (1990)—p. 238.

Shreve, Letting Go of the Eleventh Amendment, 64 Indiana L.J. 601 (1989)—p. 238.

Shreve, Symmetries of Access in Civil Rights Litigation: Politics, Pragmatism, and Will, 66 Ind.L.J. 1 (1990)—p. 54.

Silver, Unloading the Lodestar: Toward a New Fee Award Procedure, 70 Tex.L.Rev. 865 (1992)—p. 184.

Smolla, The Displacement of Federal Due Process Claims by State Tort Remedies: *Parratt v. Taylor* and *Logan v. Zimmerman Brush Co.*, 1982 U.Ill.L.Rev. 831—p. 92.

Snyder, The Final Authority Analysis: A Unified Approach to Municipal Liability under § 1983, 1986 Wis.L.Rev. 633—p. 40.

Solimine, Enforcement and Interpretation of Settlements of Federal Civil Rights Actions, 19 Rutgers L.J. 295 (1988)—p. 181.

Steinglass, Pendent Jurisdiction and Civil Rights Litigation, 7 Civil Rights Litigation and Attorney Fees Annual Handbook 31 (1991)—p. 158.

Steinglass, Section 1983 Litigation in State Courts (1989)—p. 1.

Strauss, Legality, Activism, and the Patronage Case, 64 Chi-Kent L.Rev. 585 (1988)—p. 202.

Stravitz, *Younger* Abstention Reaches a Civil Maturity: *Pennzoil Co. v. Texaco*,

TABLE OF SECONDARY AUTHORITIES

Inc., 57 Fordham L.Rev. 997 (1989)—p. 200.

Sullivan, Historical Reconstruction, Reconstruction History, and the Proper Scope of Section 1981, 98 Yale L.J. 541 (1989)—p. 121.

Symposium: *Patterson v. McClean*, 87 Mich.L.Rev. 1 (1988)—p. 121.

Tarlock, Remedying the Irremediable: The Lessons of *Gatreaux*, 64 Chi-Kent L.Rev. 573 (1988)—p. 202.

Tribe, American Constitutional Law § 3–27, p. 190 n. 3 (2d ed. 1988)—p. 47.

Tribe, Intergovernmental Immunities in Litigation, Taxation, and Regulation: Separation of Powers Issues in Controversies About Federalism, 89 Harv.L.Rev. 682 (1976)—p. 248.

Urbonya, Establishing a Deprivation of a Constitutional Right to Personal Security Under Section 1983: The Use of Unjustified Force by State Officials in Violation of the Fourth, Eighth, and Fourteenth Amendments, 51 Albany L.Rev. 171 (1987)—p. 92.

Urbonya, Problematic Standards of Reasonableness: Qualified Immunity in Section 1983 Actions for a Police Officer's Use of Excessive Force, 62 Temple L.Rev. 61 (1989)—p. 3.

Vairo, Making *Younger* Civil: The Consequences of Federal Court Deference to State Court Proceedings—A Response to Professor Stravitz, 58 Forham L.Rev. 173 (1989)—p. 200.

Weinberg, The *Monroe* Mystery Solved: Beyond the "Unhappy History" Theory of Civil Rights Litigation, 1991 B.Y.U.L.Rev. 737 (1991)—p. 1.

Welling and Jones, Prison Reform Issues for the Eighties: Modification and Dissolution of Injunctions in the Federal Courts, 20 Conn.L.Rev. 865 (1988)—p. 205.

Wells, Is Disparity a Problem?, 22 Ga.L.Rev. 283 (1988)—p. 197.

Wells, The Impact of Substantive Interests on the Law of Federal Courts, 30 Wm. & Mary L.Rev. 499 (1989)—p. 258.

Wells and Easton, Substantive Due Process and the Scope of Constitutional Torts, 18 Ga.L.Rev. 201 (1984)—p. 91.

Whitman, Goverment Responsibility for Constitutional Torts, 85 Mich.L.Rev. 225 (1986)—pp. 27, 40, 93.

Winborne, Civil Actions Against State Government, Its Divisions, Agencies, and Officers 559–569 (1982)—p. 161.

Yackle, Reform and Regret: The Story of Federal Judicial Involvement in the Alabama Prison System (1989)—p. 205.

1992 Supplement

to

CIVIL RIGHTS ACTIONS:

SECTION 1983 AND
RELATED STATUTES

*

Chapter I

42 U.S.C. § 1983

Page 13, add to footnote e:

For other narrowing constructions that helped disable § 1983 throughout much of its history, see Michael G. Collins, "Economic Rights," Implied Constitutional Actions, and the Scope of Section 1983, 77 Georgetown L.J. 1493, 1499–1506 (1989). Finally, for an interesting effort to solve the "mystery" of *Monroe*—that is, why § 1983 had been so unimportant before that decision—see Louise Weinberg, The *Monroe* Mystery Solved: Beyond the "Unhappy History" Theory of Civil Rights Litigation, 1991 B.Y.U.L.Rev. 737 (1991). Weinberg relates the holding of *Monroe* to contemporary developments in constitutional law.

Page 16, Add at the end of Note 3:

Whatever the perceived advantages of the choice to litigate in federal court, it is clear that § 1983 actions may also be brought in state court. And while most § 1983 actions are brought in federal court, resort to state court is increasingly common. A thorough analysis of this development, including possible tactical advantages in the choice of a state court and specific issues that may arise there, may be found in Steven H. Steinglass, Section 1983 Litigation in State Courts (1989). See also Susan Herman, Beyond Parity: Section 1983 and the State Courts, 54 Brooklyn L.Rev. 1057 (1989).

It is the normal result, absent congressional direction to the contrary, that state courts are *permitted* to hear federal claims. Thus, it is not surprising that the Supreme Court has recognized the authority of state courts to hear § 1983 cases.[g] It is a different question whether state courts are *required* to hear § 1983 claims even though, for reasons of local policy, they would prefer not to do so. This question was resolved in Howlett v. Rose, 496 U.S. 356 (1990), where the Court held that state courts *must* hear § 1983 claims brought in a court otherwise competent to hear that type of claim.[h]

[g] For an example, see footnote 1 in *Maine v. Thiboutot,* Casebook page 164.

[h] The state courts may refuse to hear a § 1983 case if, under local law, they have a "valid excuse." A "valid excuse" must be a neutral procedural policy (the standard example is forum non conveniens) that is applied to all cases (not just federal ones) heard in the court in question and that is not otherwise inconsistent with any governing federal policy.

Page 16, add a footnote at the end of the next to last paragraph of Note 4:

[i] For the results of one of the few empirical studies of § 1983 litigation, see Theodore Eisenberg and Stewart Schwab, The Reality of Constitutional Tort Litigation, 72 Corn.L.Rev. 641 (1987).

Page 18, substitute for footnote a:

[a] The remaining Justices have explicitly rejected the diversity interpretation. In addition to *Welch,* see Pennsylvania v. Union Gas Company, 491 U.S. 1 (1989).

Page 20, substitute for the first full paragraph and change footnote k to *l*:

One other major development should be noted. The Court held in Fitzpatrick v. Bitzer, 427 U.S. 445 (1976), that Congress could override state sovereign immunity in legislation enacted under the enforcement clause (§ 5) of the 14th amendment.[i] Thus, Congress may authorize exactly what the 11th amendment has been interpreted to prohibit—suits that require a state to pay money damages. But as subsequent cases have emphasized, Congress must express its intention to permit such suits "in unmistakable statutory language."[j] Any ambiguity in Congressional intent is resolved in favor of state immunity. Importantly for present purposes, the Court held in Quern v. Jordan, 440 U.S. 332 (1979), that § 1983 is *not* a sufficiently clear expression by Congress of an intention to override the 11th amendment.[k] Thus suits against state officials under § 1983 must comply with the 11th amendment.

[i] Subsequently, it held in Pennsylvania v. Union Gas, 491 U.S. 1 (1989), that Congress possessed the same power under the commerce clause.

[j] See Dellmuth v. Muth, 491 U.S. 223 (1989); Hoffman v. Connecticut Department of Income Maintenance, 492 U.S. 96 (1989); Pennsylvania v. Union Gas Company, 491 U.S. 1 (1989); Welch v. Texas Department of Highways and Public Transportation, 483 U.S. 468 (1987); Atascadero State Hospital v. Scanlon, 473 U.S. 234 (1985).

[k] The effect of *Quern* was to preclude suits for damages against states in *federal* court. It rejected the argument that Congress had abrogated the 11th amendment immunity in § 1983. But since the 11th amendment acts only as a limitation on the jurisdiction of the *federal* courts, it was still debatable (at least theoretically) whether damage actions could be brought against states under § 1983 in *state* court. This question was addressed in Will v. Michigan Department of State Police, 491 U.S. 58 (1989), which held that a state is not a "person" under § 1983 and thus does not come within § 1983 irrespective of any 11th amendment immunity. The result is that suits for damages against the state—or a state official if the money is to be paid from the state treasury—are unavailable in either state or federal court. *Will* does not preclude suits for an *injunction* against state officials under § 1983. It thus preserves the fiction of *Ex parte Young.*

Page 28, add a footnote after the first sentence of Note 2:

[a] For criticism of the Court's reliance on history, see Richard A. Matasar, Personal Immunities under Section 1983: The Limits of the Court's Historical Analysis, 40 Ark.L.Rev. 741 (1987).

Page 28, add a footnote after the citation to *Atcherson* in the second paragraph of Note 3:

[b] The emphasis on function performed, rather than office held, was reconfirmed in Forrester v. White, 484 U.S. 219 (1988). The Supreme Court unanimously held that a state judge was not entitled to absolute immunity for the allegedly unconstitutional discharge of a court employee. That act was deemed administrative in nature and thus outside the scope of absolute judicial immunity.

Page 28, add at the end of the last full paragraph:

The scope of prosecutorial immunity was clarified in Burns v. Reed, ___ U.S. ___ (1991). Cathy Burns was charged with shooting her two sons while under the influence of a multiple personality, but the charges were dropped after the trial court suppressed incriminating statements obtained under hypnosis. She then sued the prosecutor, claiming that he had violated her constitutional rights in (at least) two distinct respects. First, he approved the request by police officers to use hypnosis. Second, in a probable cause hearing to obtain a search warrant, he elicited testimony of Burns's "confession" without mentioning the use of hypnosis. The Supreme Court held that absolute immunity extended only to the second claim, which was "intimately associated with the judicial phase of the criminal process" under *Imbler v. Pachtman*. For the first claim, involving faulty legal advice to the police, the prosecutor enjoyed only qualified immunity. The Court made clear that advising police is part of the prosecutor's investigative and administrative responsibilities, which, as *Imbler* suggested, warrants only qualified immunity from civil liability.

Page 32, add at the end of Note 5:

David Achtenberg, Immunity under 42 U.S.C. § 1983: Interpretive Approach and the Search for the Legislative Will, 86 Nw.L.Rev. 497 (1992) (analyzing interpretive approaches to the immunity issue and arguing that the values of the enacting Congress require primacy for protection of individual rights).

Page 36, add a footnote at the end of Note 6:

c For an attempt to balance these evils in a careful plan for implementing *Harlow*, see Kit Kinports, Qualified Immunity in Section 1983 Cases: The Unanswered Questions, 23 Ga.L.Rev. 597 (1989). For extensive criticism of *Harlow* and *Anderson*, see Laura Oren, Immunity and Accountability in Civil Rights Litigation: Who Should Pay?, 50 U.Pitt.L.Rev. 935 (1989), and David Rudovsky, The Qualified Immunity Doctrine in the Supreme Court: Judicial Activism and the Restriction of Constitutional Rights, 138 U.Pa.L.Rev. 23 (1989).

Finally, two recent articles examine qualified immunity in the broader context of "new law"—that is, the various circumstances in which the fact that constitutional decisions are new or unclear or unpredictable may have legal consequences. See Richard Fallon and Daniel Meltzer, New Law, Non-Retroactivity, and Constitutional Remedies, 104 Harv.L.Rev. 1731 (1991), and Kit Kinports, Habeas Corpus, Qualified Immunity, and Crystal Balls: Predicting the Course of Constitutional Law, 33 Ariz.L.Rev. 115 (1991).

Page 39, add a footnote at the end of Note 7:

c For analysis of qualified immunity in an interesting context, see Kathryn Urbonya, Problematic Standards of Reasonableness: Qualified Immunity in Section 1983 Actions for a Police Officer's Use of Excessive Force, 62 Temple L.Rev. 61 (1989). Urbonya notes that the fourth amendment standard for use of excessive force duplicates the *Harlow v. Fitzgerald* standard of objective reasonableness. Therefore, she concludes, in this "unique" fourth amendment context, qualified immunity is "an unnecessary defense." See also Alfredo Garcia, The Scope of Police Immunity from Civil Suit under Title 42, Section 1983 and *Bivens*: A Realistic Appraisal, 11 Whittier L.Rev. 511 (1989).

Page 41, add a footnote at the end of Note 9:

e For an argument that state and federal officials should not be treated the same, see Gary S. Gildin, Immunizing Intentional Violations of Constitutional Rights through Judicial Legislation: The Extension of *Harlow v. Fitzgerald* to Section 1983 Actions, 38 Emory L.J. 369 (1989). Gildin claims that *Harlow v. Fitzgerald* extended the qualified immunity of federal officials beyond the common-law standard that purportedly governs § 1983 cases. Therefore, he concludes, the widespread assumption that *Harlow* applies in § 1983 actions (see *Anderson v. Creighton*) contradicts the Congressional intent to incorporate common-law immunities in § 1983 actions.

Page 43, add a footnote at the end of Note 2:

a For the surprising argument that the limitation of recovery imposed by the law of qualified immunity is actually consistent with the goal of compensation, see Jeffries, Compensation for Constitutional Torts: Reflections on the Significance of Fault, 88 Mich.L.Rev. 82 (1989). This article views "compensation" through the lens of Aristotelian corrective justice. In this conception, the requirement of fault imposed by the defense of qualified immunity is an essential feature of an appropriate compensatory regime. Of course, no such justification can be made for absolute immunity, which, on any view, curtails appropriate compensation.

For criticism of this analysis, see Sheldon Nahmod, Constitutional Damages and Corrective Justice: A Different View, 76 Va.L.Rev. 997 (1990).

Page 51, add a footnote at the end of Note 6:

b A different sort of problem with damage awards under § 1983 is raised in Jeffries, Damages for Constitutional Violations: The Relation of Risk to Injury in Constitutional Torts, 75 Va.L.Rev. 46 (1989). The article suggests the application in § 1983 actions of the conventional tort doctrine that compensatory damages should be limited to injuries within the risks that made the actor's conduct tortious. An analogous rule in constitutional torts would limit damages liability for constitutional violations to the sorts of harms that the constitutional prohibition was meant to prevent. This sort of approach might be more generous in the area of dignitary harms but would be more restrictive with respect to compensation for constitutionally irrelevant injuries.

For criticism of this analysis, see Sheldon Nahmod, Constitutional Damages and Corrective Justice: A Different View, 76 Va.L.Rev. 997 (1990). For an argument in support of *Stachura*-type damages where necessary to "correct injustice," see Jean C. Love, Presumed General Compensatory Damages in Constitutional Tort Litigation: A Corrective Justice Perspective, 49 W.&L.L.Rev. 67 (1992).

Page 80, add a new Note: *

1a. State as "Person" under § 1983. Before *Monell*, the Court assumed that *Monroe*'s conclusion that a municipality was not a "person" under § 1983 also applied to states. When *Monell* undercut that premise, the question arose whether states might also be held directly liable under § 1983.

The question is complicated by the 11th amendment, which has been read to allow actions for money damages against states only where Congress has made a clear statement of its intent to impose such liability. See Pennsylvania v. Union Gas Company, 491 U.S. 1 (1989)

---

* This Note is provided as an alternative for those who do not wish to teach *Will* as a main case. A more extensive version of the decision appears at page 42 of this Supplement, infra.

(main case at page 242 of this Supplement, infra); Atascadero State Hospital v. Scanlon, 473 U.S. 234 (1985) (Casebook, page 736); Fitzpatrick v. Bitzer, 427 U.S. 445 (1976) (main case at page 729 of the Casebook). Justice Brennan suggested that § 1983 might meet this test, see Hutto v. Finney, 437 U.S. 678, 700 (1978) (Brennan, J., concurring), but a majority of his colleagues disagreed. In Quern v. Jordan, 440 U.S. 332 (1979), the Court ruled that § 1983 did not abrogate 11th amendment immunity.

Quern settled the issue for federal courts, but the question remained whether states might be sued directly in state court, where the 11th amendment does not apply. See Maine v. Thiboutot, 448 U.S. 1, 9 n. 7 (1980). The Supreme Court finally answered that question in Will v. Michigan Department of State Police, 491 U.S. 58 (1989), which held that "person" in § 1983 does not include states or state officials acting in their official capacities. Writing for the Court, Justice White argued that the intent to make states directly liable had not been shown with the clarity required to alter the "usual constitutional balance" between the states and the national government. He found nothing in the history or purpose of § 1983 clearly evidencing such intent. The Dictionary Act's definition of "person" as including "bodies politic and corporate" was not decisive, as there was evidence the 19th-century usage of that phrase included municipal corporations but not states.

Justice Brennan dissented in an opinion joined by Justices Marshall, Blackmun, and Stevens. Brennan thought the Dictionary Act definition of "person" did include states, and he found that meaning confirmed by the legislative history of § 1983. He saw the Court's decision as improperly relying on the 11th amendment, which, although admittedly inapplicable, nevertheless "lurks everywhere in today's decision and, in truth, determines its outcome." In a separate dissent, Justice Stevens emphasized the inconsistency of allowing states to be sued as such for prospective relief but not for compensatory damages.[c]

Page 105, add a new Note 3:

3. *American Trucking Associations, Inc. v. Smith.* American Trucking Associations, Inc. v. Smith, 496 U.S. 167 (1990), was a refund suit filed in state court by Arkansas taxpayers. The basis of the claim was that a highway use tax was unconstitutional. The tax had been enacted in 1983, and the suit was filed in that year. In 1987, the Supreme Court held in American Trucking Associations, Inc. v. Scheiner, 483 U.S. 266 (1987), that similar taxes imposed by Pennsylvania were unconstitutional. *Smith,* which was pending in the Supreme Court when *Scheiner* was decided, was remanded to the Arkansas

---

[c] The Court subsequently concluded, over the dissents of Justices Brennan and Marshall (Justice Kennedy not participating), that neither territories nor their officers are "persons" under § 1983. Ngiraingas v. Sanchez, 495 U.S. 182 (1990).

Supreme Court for reconsideration in light of *Scheiner*. The Arkansas Supreme Court denied relief, holding that *Scheiner* was to be applied prospectively only. The case then came back to the Supreme Court. The judgment was for the most part affirmed,[b] with the Court divided four-one-four.

Justice O'Connor wrote a plurality opinion, joined by Chief Justice Rehnquist, Justice White, and Justice Kennedy. She held that *Scheiner* "established a new principle of law in the area of our dormant commerce clause jurisprudence" and that, based on a three-part inquiry, it should not be applied retroactively. Her analysis derived from Chevron Oil Co. v. Huson, 404 U.S. 97 (1971). The three factors were:

> "First, the decision to be applied nonretroactively must establish a new principle of law, either by overruling clear past precedent on which litigants may have relied, or by deciding an issue of first impression whose resolution was not clearly foreshadowed. Second, . . . we must . . . weigh the merits and demerits in each case by looking to the prior history of the rule in question, its purpose and effect, and whether retrospective operation will further or retard its operation. Finally, we [must] weig[h] the inequity imposed by retroactive application, for where a decision of this Court could produce substantial inequitable results if applied retroactively, there is ample basis in our cases for avoiding the injustice or hardship by a holding of nonretroactivity."

The plurality rejected the argument that deterrence of constitutional violations suggested retroactivity under the second factor. As to the third factor, the facts that "the state promulgated and implemented its tax scheme in reliance" on the old law and that a "refund, if required by state or federal law, could deplete the state treasury, thus threatening the state's current operations and future plans" were among the controlling considerations.

The Trucking Association relied on *Owen* in making its contrary argument. O'Connor responded:

> "Our delineation of the scope of liability under a statute designed to permit suit against government entities and officials provides little guidance for determining the fairest way to apply our own decisions. Indeed, the policy concerns involved are quite distinct. In *Owen*, we discerned that according municipalities a special immunity from liability for violations of constitutional rights would not best serve the goals of § 1983, even if those rights had not been clearly established

---

[b] The Court held that *Scheiner* applied only to taxable events that occurred after its date of decision. The Arkansas Supreme Court was reversed in part for failing to apply *Scheiner* to one subsequent tax year, but its holding that the case did not apply to prior tax years was affirmed.

when the violation occurred. Such a determination merely makes municipalities, like private individuals, responsible for anticipating developments in the law. We noted that such liability would motivate each of the city's elected officials to 'consider whether his decision comports with constitutional mandates and . . . weigh the risk that a violation might result in an award of damages from the public treasury.' This analysis does not apply when a decision clearly breaks with precedent, a type of departure which, by definition, public officials could not anticipate nor have any responsibility to anticipate."

Justice Scalia joined the O'Connor result in a separate opinion that did not address the meaning of *Owen*.[c]

The dissenters, in an opinion by Justice Stevens, would have applied *Scheiner* to all cases still open on direct review at the time it was decided. It dealt with *Owen* in a footnote:

"Our decision in *Owen* is necessarily predicated upon the view that a court should apply the law in effect at the time of decision in considering whether the state has violated the Constitution. Although the plurality is technically correct that *Owen* did not hold that constitutional decisions should always apply 'retroactively,' that case, and the Congress that enacted § 1983, surely did not contemplate that state actors could achieve through the judicially crafted doctrine of retroactivity, the immunity not only from damages but also from liability denied them on the floors of Congress."

Does this colloquy mean that four Justices are prepared to make an exception to *Owen* in cases where a "new" constitutional rule is announced that represents a clear break with the past? If so, how would this be different from affording municipal government a good faith immunity defense?

Page 105, substitute for pages 105–24:

INTRODUCTORY NOTES ON DETERMINING "OFFICIAL POLICY"

1. Introduction. *Monell* limited governmental liability to acts taken pursuant to an official policy or custom. This requirement has proved troublesome. Presumably, the issue is clear where, as in *Monell*, the decision is taken pursuant to a rule or regulation of general applicability. Much more difficult questions arise when governmental liability is sought for a single act or decision by government officials.

---

[c] Justice Scalia thought that "prospective decisionmaking is incompatible with the judicial role," but concurred on the ground that, since he had dissented in *Scheiner*, it would be perverse for him to apply stare decisis to require Arkansas to refund taxes that would upset its settled expectations.

The Supreme Court's most recent pronouncements on when governmental action will be held to result from "official policy" appear below.

The cases fall into two categories. The first concerns when the action of a government agent can properly be attributable to the agency itself. This issue is addressed in the note on *Pembaur* below and in the main case that follows, *City of St. Louis v. Praprotnik*. The second concerns whether, and if so when, government can be held liable for the failure to train its officials. This issue is addressed in *City of Canton v. Harris*, which appears as a main case following *Praprotnik*.

2. *Pembaur v. City of Cincinnati*. Pembaur v. City of Cincinnati, 475 U.S. 469 (1986), arose from an investigation of alleged welfare fraud in Dr. Pembaur's medical clinic. During that investigation, a grand jury issued subpoenas for two of Pembaur's employees, both of whom failed to appear. The prosecutor then obtained warrants ordering the county sheriff to arrest and detain the two employees.

When deputy sheriffs arrived at the clinic to serve the warrants, Pembaur locked the door separating the reception area from the rest of the clinic and refused to let them enter. After consultation with the Cincinnati city police, the deputies called their supervisor to ask for instructions. The supervisor told them to call William Whalen, assistant prosecutor of the county, and to follow his directions. Whalen conferred with his superior and relayed the instruction to "go in and get" the recalcitrant witnesses. When advised of these instructions, the city police officers on the scene obtained an axe and chopped down the door. The deputies then entered and searched for the witnesses. They arrested two individuals who, though they fit the descriptions in the warrants, turned out to be the wrong persons.

Some four years after the incident in question, Steagald v. United States, 451 U.S. 204 (1981), ruled that, absent exigent circumstances, the police cannot enter an individual's home or business without a search warrant, merely because they are seeking to execute an arrest warrant for a third person. *Steagald* was conceded to apply retroactively, and thus became the basis for Pembaur's § 1983 action against all involved. The issue that ultimately came to the Supreme Court was the liability of the county for the actions of its officers.

At trial, the evidence showed no prior instance where the sheriff had been denied access to property in an attempt to arrest a third person. There was also no written policy on the issue. The question of the county's liability therefore turned on its responsibility for the decision of its officials on this particular occasion.

Speaking for the Court, Justice Brennan said:

> "The Deputy Sheriffs who attempted to serve the [arrest warrants] at petitioner's clinic found themselves in a difficult situation. Unsure of the proper course of action to follow, they sought instructions from their supervisors. The instructions

they received were to follow the orders of the County Prosecutor. The prosecutor made a considered decision based on his understanding of the law and commanded the officers forcibly to enter petitioner's clinic. That decision directly caused the violation of petitioner's fourth amendment rights.

"Respondent argues that the County Prosecutor lacked authority to establish municipal policy respecting law enforcement practices because only the County Sheriff may establish policy respecting such practices. Respondent suggests that the County Prosecutor was merely rendering 'legal advice' when he ordered the Deputy Sheriffs to 'go in and get' the witnesses. Consequently, the argument concludes, the action of the individual Deputy Sheriffs in following this advice and forcibly entering petitioner's clinic was not pursuant to a properly established municipal policy.

"We might be inclined to agree with respondent if we thought that the prosecutor had only rendered 'legal advice.' However, the Court of Appeals concluded, based upon its examination of Ohio law, that both the County Sheriff and the County Prosecutor could establish county policy under appropriate circumstances, a conclusion that we do not question here. Ohio Rev.Code Ann. § 309.09 provides that county officers may 'require . . . instructions from [the County Prosecutor] in matters connected with their official duties.' Pursuant to standard office procedure, the Sheriff's office referred this matter to the prosecutor and then followed his instructions. The Sheriff testified that his department followed this practice under appropriate circumstances and that it was 'the proper thing to do' in this case. We decline to accept respondent's invitation to overlook this delegation of authority by disingenuously labeling the prosecutor's clear command mere 'legal advice.' In ordering the Deputy Sheriffs to enter petitioner's clinic the County Prosecutor was acting as the final decisionmaker for the county, and the county may therefore be held liable under § 1983."

There were several separate opinions. Justice White concurred to suggest that liability was proper *only* because the search was not forbidden by any applicable law at the time it was made. If controlling law had plainly prohibited the search, he argued, the local officers could "not be said to have the authority to make contrary policy": "Had the sheriff or prosecutor in this case failed to follow an existing warrant requirement, it would be absurd to say that he was nevertheless executing county policy in authorizing the forceful entry. . . ." Here, however, the sheriff and the prosecutor exercised the discretion vested in them and "chose a course that was not forbidden by any applicable law." This decision therefore became "county policy" and was "no less so" because it later turned out to be unconstitutional.[a]

Justice Powell, joined by Chief Justice Burger and Justice Rehnquist, dissented. He argued that "no official county policy could have been created solely by an off-hand telephone response from a busy county prosecutor":

> "Proper resolution of this case calls for identification of the applicable principles for determining when policy is created. The Court today does not do this, but instead focuses almost exclusively on the status of the decisionmaker. Its reasoning is circular: it contends that policy is what policymakers make, and policymakers are those who have authority to make policy. . . .
>
> "In my view, the question whether official policy—in any normal sense of the term—has been made in a particular case is not answered by explaining who has final authority to make policy. The question here is not '*could* the county prosecutor make policy?' but rather, '*did* he make policy?' By focusing on the authority granted to the official under state law, the Court's test fails to answer the key federal question presented. The Court instead turns the question into one of state law. Under a test that focuses on the authority of the decisionmaker, the Court has only to look to state law for the resolution of this case. Here the Court of Appeals found that 'both the County Sheriff and the County Prosecutor had authority under Ohio law to establish county policy under appropriate circumstances.' Apparently that recitation of authority is all that is needed under the Court's test because no discussion is offered to demonstrate that the Sheriff or the Prosecutor actually used that authority to establish official county policy in this case. . . .
>
> "In my view, proper resolution of the question whether official policy has been formed should focus on two factors: (i) the nature of the decision reached or the action taken, and (ii) the process by which the decision was reached or the action was taken.
>
> "Focusing on the nature of the decision distinguishes between policies and mere ad hoc decisions. Such a focus also reflects the fact that most policies embody a rule of general applicability. That is the tenor of the Court's statement in *Monell* that local government units are liable under § 1983 when the action that is alleged to be unconstitutional 'imple-

---

[a] Justice O'Connor briefly endorsed these views in an opinion concurring in part and concurring in the judgment. Justice Stevens also wrote to reiterate his belief that county liability could be based on respondeat superior.

ments or executes a policy statement, ordinance, regulation, or decision officially adopted and promulgated by the body's officers.' The clear implication is that policy is created when a rule is formed that applies to all similar situations . . ..[6] When a rule of general applicability has been approved, the government has taken a position for which it can be held responsible.

"Another factor indicating that policy has been formed is the process by which the decision at issue was reached. Formal procedures that involve, for example, voting by elected officials, prepared reports, extended deliberation or official records indicate that the resulting decisions taken 'may fairly be said to represent official policy.' Owen v. City of Independence, 445 U.S. 622 (1980), provides an example. . . .

"Applying these factors to the instant case demonstrates that no official policy was formulated. Certainly, no rule of general applicability was adopted. The Court correctly notes that the Sheriff 'testified that the department had no written policy respecting the serving of [arrest warrants] on the property of third persons and that the proper response in any given situation would depend upon the circumstances.' Nor could he recall a specific instance in which entrance had been denied and forcibly gained. The Court's result today rests on the implicit conclusion that the Prosecutor's response—'go in and get them'—altered the prior case-by-case approach of the department and formed a new rule to apply in all similar cases. Nothing about the Prosecutor's response to the inquiry over the phone, nor the circumstances surrounding the response, indicates that such a rule of general applicability was formed.

"Similarly, nothing about the way the decision was reached indicates that official policy was formed. The prosecutor, without time for thoughtful consideration or consultation, simply gave an off-the-cuff answer to a single question. There was no *process* at all. The Court's holding undercuts the basic rationale of *Monell* and unfairly increases the risk of liability on the level of government least able to bear it. I dissent."

---

[6] "The focus on a rule of general applicability does not mean that more than one instance of its application is required. The local government unit may be liable for the first application of a duly constituted unconstitutional policy."

CITY OF ST. LOUIS v. PRAPROTNIK
Supreme Court of the United States, 1988.
485 U.S. 112.

JUSTICE O'CONNOR announced the judgment of the Court and delivered an opinion, in which CHIEF JUSTICE REHNQUIST, JUSTICE WHITE, and JUSTICE SCALIA join.

This case calls upon us to define the proper legal standard for determining when isolated decisions by municipal officials or employees may expose the municipality itself to liability under 42 U.S.C. § 1983.

I

The principal facts are not in dispute. Respondent James H. Praprotnik is an architect who began working for petitioner City of St. Louis in 1968. For several years, respondent consistently received favorable evaluations of his job performance, uncommonly quick promotions, and significant increases in salary. By 1980, he was serving in a management-level city planning position at petitioner's Community Development Agency (CDA).

The Director of CDA, Donald Spaid, had instituted a requirement that the agency's professional employees, including architects, obtain advance approval before taking on private clients. Respondent and other CDA employees objected to the requirement. In April 1980, respondent was suspended for 15 days by CDA's Director of Urban Design, Charles Kindleberger, for having accepted outside employment without prior approval. Respondent appealed to the city's Civil Service Commission, a body charged with reviewing employee grievances. Finding the penalty too harsh, the Commission reversed the suspension, awarded respondent back pay, and directed that he be reprimanded for having failed to secure a clear understanding of the rule.

The Commission's decision was not well received by respondent's supervisors at CDA. Kindleberger later testified that he believed respondent had lied to the Commission, and that Spaid was angry with respondent.

Respondent's next two annual job performance evaluations were markedly less favorable than those in previous years. In discussing one of these evaluations with respondent, Kindleberger apparently mentioned his displeasure with respondent's 1980 appeal to the Civil Service Commission. Respondent appealed both evaluations to the Department of Personnel. In each case, the Department ordered partial relief and was upheld by the city's Director of Personnel or the Civil Service Commission.

In April 1981, a new mayor came into office, and Donald Spaid was replaced as Director of CDA by Frank Hamsher. As a result of budget cuts, a number of layoffs and transfers significantly reduced the size of

CDA and of the planning section in which respondent worked. Respondent, however, was retained.

In the spring of 1982, a second round of layoffs and transfers occurred at CDA. At that time, the city's Heritage and Urban Design Division (Heritage) was seeking approval to hire someone who was qualified in architecture and urban planning. Hamsher arranged with the Director of Heritage, Henry Jackson, for certain functions to be transferred from CDA to Heritage. This arrangement, which made it possible for Heritage to employ a relatively high-level "city planning manager," was approved by Jackson's supervisor, Thomas Nash. Hamsher then transferred respondent to Heritage to fill this position.

Respondent objected to the transfer, and appealed to the Civil Service Commission. The Commission declined to hear the appeal because respondent had not suffered a reduction in his pay or grade. Respondent then filed suit in federal district court, alleging that the transfer was unconstitutional. The city was named as a defendant, along with Kindleberger, Hamsher, Jackson (whom respondent deleted from the list before trial), and Deborah Patterson, who had succeeded Hamsher at CDA.

At Heritage, respondent became embroiled in a series of disputes with Jackson and Jackson's successor, Robert Killen. Respondent was dissatisfied with the work he was assigned, which consisted of unchallenging clerical functions far below the level of responsibilities that he had previously enjoyed. At least one adverse personnel decision was taken against respondent, and he obtained partial relief after appealing that decision.

In December 1983, respondent was laid off from Heritage. The lay off was attributed to a lack of funds, and this apparently meant that respondent's supervisors had concluded that they could create two lower-level positions with the funds that were being used to pay respondent's salary. Respondent then amended the complaint in his lawsuit to include a challenge to the layoff. He also appealed to the Civil Service Commission, but proceedings in that forum were postponed because of the pending lawsuit and have never been completed.

The case went to trial on two theories: (1) that respondent's first amendment rights had been violated through retaliatory actions taken in response to his appeal of his 1980 suspension; and (2) that respondent's layoff from Heritage was carried out for pretextual reasons in violation of due process. The jury returned special verdicts exonerating each of the three individual defendants, but finding the city liable under both theories. Judgment was entered on the verdicts, and the city appealed.

A panel of the Court of appeals for the Eighth Circuit found that the due process claim had been submitted to the jury on an erroneous legal theory and vacated that portion of the judgment. With one judge dissenting, however, the panel affirmed the verdict holding the city liable for violating respondent's first amendment rights. Only the second of these holdings is challenged here.

The Court of Appeals found that the jury had implicitly determined that respondent's layoff from Heritage was brought about by an unconstitutional city policy. Applying a test under which a "policymaker" is one whose employment decisions are "final" in the sense that they are not subjected to de novo review by higher-ranking officials, the Court of Appeals concluded that the city could be held liable for adverse personnel decisions taken by respondent's supervisors. In response to petitioner's contention that the city's personnel policies are actually set by the Civil Service Commission, the Court of Appeals concluded that the scope of review before that body was too "highly circumscribed" to allow it fairly to be said that the Commission, rather than the officials who initiated the actions leading to respondent's injury, were the "final authority" responsible for setting city policy. . . .

We granted certiorari and we now reverse.

II

[Part II of Justice O'Connor's opinion concluded that the legal standard for municipal liability had been properly presented for review.]

III

A

. . . In the years since *Monell* was decided, the Court has considered several cases involving isolated acts by government officials and employees. We have assumed that an unconstitutional governmental policy could be inferred from a single decision taken by the highest officials responsible for setting policy in that area of the government's business. See Owen v. City of Independence, 445 U.S. 622 (1980); Newport v. Fact Concerts, Inc., 453 U.S. 247 (1981). At the other end of the spectrum, we have held that an unjustified shooting by a police officer cannot, without more, be thought to result from official policy. Oklahoma City v. Tuttle, 471 U.S. 808 (1985).

Two terms ago, in Pembaur v. Cincinnati, 475 U.S. 469 (1986), we undertook to define more precisely when a decision on a single occasion may be enough to establish an unconstitutional municipal policy. Although the Court was unable to settle on a general formulation, Justice Brennan's plurality opinion articulated several guiding principles. First, a majority of the Court agreed that municipalities may be held liable under § 1983 only for acts for which the municipality itself is actually responsible, "that is, acts which the municipality has officially sanctioned or ordered." Second, only those municipal officials who have "final policymaking authority" may by their actions subject the government to § 1983 liability. Third, whether a particular official has "final policymaking authority" is a question of *state law*. Fourth, the challenged action must have been taken pursuant to a policy adopted by the official or officials responsible under state law for making policy *in that area* of the city's business.

The Courts of Appeals have already diverged in their interpretation of these principles. Today, we set out again to clarify the issue that we last addressed in *Pembaur*.

B

We begin by reiterating that the identification of policymaking officials is a question of state law. "Authority to make municipal policy may be granted directly by a legislative enactment or may be delegated by an official who possesses such authority, and of course, whether an official had final policymaking authority is a question of state law." *Pembaur v. Cincinnati*, supra, at 483 (plurality opinion).[1] Thus, the identification of policymaking officials is not a question of federal law and it is not a question of fact in the usual sense. The states have extremely wide latitude in determining the form that local government takes, and local preferences have led to a profusion of distinct forms. . . . Without attempting to canvass the numberless factual scenarios that may come to light in litigation, we can be confident that state law (which may include valid local ordinances and regulations) will always direct a court to some official or body that has the responsibility for making law or setting policy in any given area of a local government's responsibility.[2]

---

[1] Unlike Justice Brennan, we would not replace this standard with a new approach in which state law becomes merely "an appropriate starting point" for an "assessment of a municipality's actual power structure." Municipalities cannot be expected to predict how courts or juries will assess their "actual power structures," and this uncertainty could easily lead to results that would be hard in practice to distinguish from the results of a regime governed by the doctrine of respondeat superior. It is one thing to charge a municipality with responsibility for the decisions of officials invested by law, or by a "custom or usage" having the force of law, with policymaking authority. It would be something else, and something inevitably more capricious, to hold a municipality responsible for every decision that is perceived as "final" through the lens of a particular factfinder's evaluation of the city's "actual power structure."

[2] Justice Stevens, who believes that *Monell* incorrectly rejected the doctrine of respondeat superior, suggests a new theory that reflects his perceptions of the congressional purposes underlying § 1983. This theory would apparently ignore state law, and distinguish between "high" officials and "low" officials on the basis of an independent evaluation of the extent to which a particular official's actions have "the potential of controlling governmental decisionmaking," or are "perceived as the actions of the city itself." Whether this evaluation would be conducted by judges or juries, we think the legal test is too imprecise to hold much promise of consistent adjudication or principled analysis. We can see no reason, except perhaps a desire to come as close as possible to respondeat superior without expressly adopting that doctrine, that could justify introducing such unpredictability into a body of law that is already so difficult. . . .

We are not, of course, predicting that state law will always speak with perfect clarity. We have no reason to suppose, however, that federal courts will face greater difficulties here than those that they routinely address in other contexts. We are also aware that there will be cases in which policymaking responsibility is shared among more than one official or body. In the case before us, for example, it appears that the mayor or aldermen are authorized to adopt such ordinances relating to personnel administration as are compatible with the City Charter. See St. Louis City Charter, art. XVIII, § 7(b). The Civil Service Commission, for its part, is required to "prescribe . . . rules for the administration and enforcement of the provisions of this article, and of any ordinance adopted in pursuance thereof, and not inconsistent therewith." § 7(a). Assuming that applicable law does not make the decisions of the Commission reviewable by the mayor and aldermen, or vice versa, one would have to conclude that policy decisions made either by the mayor and aldermen or by the Commission would be attributable to the city itself. In any event, however, a federal court would not be justified in assuming that municipal policymaking authority lies somewhere other than where the applicable law purports to put it. And certainly there can be no justification for giving a jury the discretion to determine which officials are high enough in the government that their actions can be said to represent a decision of the government itself.

As the plurality in *Pembaur* recognized, special difficulties can arise when it is contended that a municipal policymaker has delegated his policymaking authority to another official. If the mere exercise of discretion by an employee could give rise to a constitutional violation, the result would be indistinguishable from respondeat superior liability. If, however, a city's lawful policymakers could insulate the government from liability simply by delegating their policymaking authority to others, § 1983 could not serve its intended purpose. It may not be possible to draw an elegant line that will resolve this conundrum, but certain principles should provide useful guidance.

First, whatever analysis is used to identify municipal policymakers, egregious attempts by local governments to insulate themselves from liability for unconstitutional policies are precluded by a separate doctrine. Relying on the language of § 1983, the Court has long recognized that a plaintiff may be able to prove the existence of a widespread practice that, although not authorized by written law or express municipal policy, is "so permanent and well settled as to constitute a 'custom or usage' with the force of law." Adickes v. S.H. Kress & Co., 398 U.S. 144, 167–68 (1970). That principle, which has not been affected by Monell v. N.Y. City Dept. of Social Services, 436 U.S. 658 (1978), or subsequent cases, ensures that most deliberate municipal evasions of the Constitution will be sharply limited.

Second, as the *Pembaur* plurality recognized, the authority to make municipal policy is necessarily the authority to make *final* policy. When an official's discretionary decisions are constrained by policies not of that official's making, those policies, rather than the subordinate's departures from them, are the act of the municipality. Similarly, when a subordinate's decision is subject to review by the municipality's authorized policymakers, they have retained the authority to measure the official's conduct for conformance with *their* policies. If the authorized policymakers approve a subordinate's decision and the basis for it, their ratification would be chargeable to the municipality because their decision is final.

C

Whatever refinements of these principles may be suggested in the future, we have little difficulty concluding that the Court of Appeals applied an incorrect legal standard in this case. In reaching this conclusion, we do not decide whether the first amendment forbade the city from retaliating against respondent for having taken advantage of the grievance mechanism in 1980. . . .

The city cannot be held liable under § 1983 unless respondent proved the existence of an unconstitutional municipal policy. Respondent does not contend that anyone in city government ever promulgated, or even articulated, such a policy. Nor did he attempt to prove that such retaliation was ever directed against anyone other than himself. Respondeat contends that the record can be read to establish that his supervisors were angered by his 1980 appeal to the Civil Service Commission; that new supervisors in a new administration chose, for reasons passed on through some informal means, to retaliate against respondent two years later by transferring him to another agency; and that this transfer was part of a scheme that led, another year and a half later, to his lay off. Even if one assumes that all this was true, it says nothing about the actions of those whom the law established as the makers of municipal policy in matters of personnel administration. The mayor and aldermen enacted no ordinance designed to retaliate against respondent or against similarly situated employees. On the contrary, the city established an independent Civil Service Commission and empowered it to review and correct improper personnel actions. Respondent does not deny that his repeated appeals from adverse personnel decisions repeatedly brought him at least partial relief, and the Civil Service Commission never so much as hinted that retaliatory transfers or lay offs were permissible. Respondent points to no evidence indicating that the Commission delegated to anyone its final authority to interpret and enforce the following policy set out in article XVIII of the city's Charter, § 2(a):

"Merit and fitness. All appointments and promotions to positions in the service of the city and all measures for the control and regulation of employment in such positions, and separation therefrom, shall be on the sole basis of merit and fitness. . . ."

The Court of Appeals concluded that "appointing authorities," like Hamsher and Killen were authorized to establish employment policy for the city with respect to transfers and layoffs. To the contrary, the City Charter expressly states that the Civil Service Commission has the power and the duty:

"To consider and determine any matter involved in the administration and enforcement of this [Civil Service] article and the rules and ordinances adopted in accordance therewith that may be referred to it for decision by the director [of personnel], or on appeal by any appointing authority, employe, or taxpayer of the city, from any act of the director of any appointing authority. The decision of the commission in all such matters shall be final, subject, however, to any right of action under law of the state or of the United States."

This case therefore resembles the hypothetical example in *Pembaur:* "[I]f [city] employment policy was set by the [mayor and aldermen and by the Civil Service Commission], only [those] bod[ies'] decisions would provide a basis for [city] liability. This would be true even if the [mayor and aldermen and the Commission] left the [appointing authorities] discretion to hire and fire employees and [they] exercised that discretion in an unconstitutional manner. . . ." A majority of the Court of Appeals panel determined that the Civil Service Commission's review of individual employment actions gave too much deference to the decisions of appointing authorities like Hamsher and Killen. Simply going along with discretionary decisions made by one's subordinates, however, is not a delegation to them of the authority to make policy. It is equally consistent with a presumption that the subordinates are faithfully attempting to comply with the policies that are supposed to guide them. It would be a different matter if a particular decision by a subordinate was cast in the form of a policy statement and expressly approved by the supervising policymaker. It would also be a different matter if a series of decisions by a subordinate official manifested a "custom or usage" of which the supervisor must have been aware. In both those cases, the supervisor could realistically be deemed to have adopted a policy that happened to have been formulated or initiated by a lower-ranking official. But the mere failure to investigate the basis of a subordinate's discretionary decisions does not amount to a delegation of policymaking authority, especially where (as here) the wrongfulness of the subordinate's decision arises from a retaliatory motive or other unstated rationale. In such circumstances, the purposes of § 1983 would not be served by treating a subordinate employee's decision as if it were a reflection of municipal policy.

Justice Brennan's opinion, concurring in the judgment, finds implications in our discussion that we do not think necessary or correct. We nowhere say or imply, for example, that "a municipal charter's precatory admonition against discrimination or any other employment practice not based on merit and fitness effectively insulates the municipality from any liability based on acts inconsistent with that policy." Rather, we would respect the decisions, embodied in state and local law, that allocate policymaking authority among particular individuals and bodies. Refusals to carry out stated policies could obviously help to show that a municipality's actual policies were different from the ones that had been announced. If such a showing were made, we would be confronted with a different case than the one we decide today.

Nor do we believe that we have left a "gaping" hole in § 1983 that needs to be filled with the vague concept of "de facto final policymaking authority." Except perhaps as a step towards overruling *Monell* and adopting the doctrine of respondeat superior, ad hoc searches for officials possessing such "de facto" authority would serve primarily to foster needless unpredictability in the application of § 1983.

IV

[T]he decision of the Court of Appeals is reversed, and the case is remanded for further proceedings consistent with this opinion.

It is so ordered.

JUSTICE KENNEDY took no part in the consideration or decision of this case.

JUSTICE BRENNAN, with whom JUSTICE MARSHALL and JUSTICE BLACKMUN join, concurring.

[T]his case at bottom presents a relatively straightforward question: whether respondent's supervisor at the Community Development Agency, Frank Hamsher, possessed the authority to establish final employment policy for the city of St. Louis such that the city can be held liable under 42 U.S.C. § 1983 for Hamsher's allegedly unlawful decision to transfer respondent to a dead-end job. Applying the test set out two terms ago by the plurality in Pembaur v. Cincinnati, 475 U.S. 469 (1986), I conclude that Hamsher did not possess such authority and I therefore concur in the Court's judgment reversing the decision below. I write separately, however, because I believe that the commendable desire of today's plurality to "define more precisely when a decision on a single occasion may be enough" to subject a municipality to § 1983 liability has led it to embrace a theory of municipal liability that is both unduly narrow and unrealistic, and one that ultimately would permit municipalities to insulate themselves from liability for the acts of all but a small minority of actual city policymakers.

I

. . . The District Court instructed the jury that generally a city is not liable under § 1983 for the acts of its employees, but that it may be held to answer for constitutional wrongs "committed by an official high enough in the government so that his or her actions can be said to represent a government decision." . . . The Court of Appeals for the Eighth Circuit [affirmed, reasoning] that the city could be held accountable for an improperly motivated transfer and layoff if it had delegated to the responsible officials, either directly or indirectly, the authority to act on behalf of the city, and if the decisions made within the scope of this delegated authority were essentially final. Applying this test, the court noted that under the City Charter, "appointing authorities," or department heads, such as Hamsher could undertake transfers and layoffs subject only to the approval of the Director of Personnel, who undertook no substantive review of such decisions and simply conditioned his approval on formal compliance with city procedures. Moreover, because the Civil Service Commission engaged in highly circumscribed and deferential review of layoffs and, at least so far as this case reveals, no review whatever of lateral transfers, the court concluded that an appointing authority's transfer and layoff decisions were final.

Having found that Hamsher was a final policymaker whose acts could subject petitioner to § 1983 liability, the court determined that the jury had ample evidence from which it could find that Hamsher transferred respondent in retaliation for the latter's exercise of first amendment rights, and that the transfer in turn precipitated respondent's layoff. . . .

II

. . . Municipalities, of course, conduct much of the business of governing through human agents. Where those agents act in accordance with formal policies, or pursuant to informal practices "so permanent and well settled as to constitute a 'custom or usage' with the force of law," Adickes v. S.H. Kress & Co., 398 U.S. 144, 167–68 (1970), we naturally ascribe their acts to the municipalities themselves and hold the latter responsible for any resulting constitutional deprivations. Monell v. N.Y. City Dept. of Social Services, 436 U.S. 658 (1978), which involved a challenge to a city-wide policy requiring all pregnant employees to take unpaid leave after their fifth month of pregnancy, was just such a case. Nor have we ever doubted that a single decision of a city's properly constituted legislative body is a municipal act capable of subjecting the city to liability. See, e.g., Newport v. Fact Concerts, Inc., 453 U.S. 247 (1981) (city council canceled concert permit for content-based reasons); Owen v. City of Independence, 445 U.S. 622 (1980) (city council passed resolution firing police chief without any pretermination hearing). In these cases we neither required, nor as the plurality suggests, assumed that these decisions reflected generally applicable "policies" as that term is commonly understood, because it was perfectly obvious that the actions of the municipalities' policymaking organs, whether isolated or not, were properly charged to the municipalities themselves. And, in *Pembaur* we recognized that "the power to establish policy is no more the exclusive province of the legislature at the local level than at the state or national level," and that the isolated decision of an executive municipal policymaker, therefore, could likewise give rise to municipal liability under § 1983.

In concluding that Frank Hamsher was a policymaker, the Court of Appeals relied on the fact that the city had delegated to him "the authority, either directly or indirectly, to act on [its] behalf," and that his actions within the scope of this delegated authority were effectively final. In *Pembaur,* however, we made clear that a municipality is not liable merely because the official who inflicted the constitutional injury had the final authority to *act* on its behalf; rather, as four of us explained, the official in question must possess "final authority to establish municipal policy with respect to the [challenged] action." Thus, we noted, "[t]he fact that a particular official—even a policymaking official—has discretion in the exercise of particular functions does not, without more, give rise to municipal liability based on an exercise of that discretion." [J]ust as in *Owen* and *Fact Concerts* we deemed it fair to hold municipalities liable for the isolated unconstitutional acts of their legislative bodies, regardless of whether those acts were meant to establish generally applicable "policies," so too in *Pembaur* four of us concluded that it is equally appropriate to hold municipalities accountable for the isolated constitutional injury inflicted by an executive final municipal policymaker, even though the decision giving rise to the injury is not intended to govern future situations. In either case, as long as the contested decision is made in an area over which the official or legislative body *could* establish a final policy capable of governing future municipal conduct, it is both fair and consistent with the purposes of § 1983 to treat the decision as that of the municipality itself, and to hold it liable for the resulting constitutional deprivation.

In my view, *Pembaur* controls this case. As an "appointing authority," Hamsher was empowered under the City Charter to initiate lateral transfers such as the one challenged here, subject to the approval of both the Director of Personnel and the appointing authority of the transferee agency. The Charter, however, nowhere confers upon agency heads any authority to establish city *policy,* final or otherwise, with respect to such transfers. Thus, for example, Hamsher was not authorized to promulgate binding guidelines or criteria governing how or when lateral transfers were to be accomplished. Nor does the record reveal that he in fact sought to exercise any such authority in these matters. There is no indication, for example, that Hamsher ever purported to institute or announce a practice of general applicability concerning transfers. Instead, the evidence discloses but one transfer decision—the one involving respondent—which Hamsher ostensibly undertook pursuant to a city-wide program of fiscal restraint and budgetary reductions. At most, then the record demonstrates that Hamsher had the authority to determine how best to *effectuate* a policy announced by his superiors, rather than the power to *establish* that policy. . . . Hamsher had discretionary authority to transfer CDA employees laterally; that he may have used this authority to punish respondent for the exercise of his first amendment rights does not, without more, render the city liable for respondent's resulting constitutional injury.[4] . . . Because the court identified only one unlawfully motivated municipal employee involved in respondent's transfer and layoff, and because that employee did not possess final policymaking authority with respect to the contested decision,[5] the city may not be held accountable for any constitutional wrong respondent may have suffered.

III

These determinations, it seems to me, are sufficient to dispose of this case, and I therefore think it unnecessary to decide, as the plurality does, who the actual policymakers in St. Louis are. I question more than the mere necessity of these determinations, however, for I believe that in the course of passing on issues not before us, the plurality announces legal principles that are inconsistent with our earlier cases and unduly restrict the reach of § 1983 in cases involving municipalities.

---

[4] While the Court of Appeals erred to the extent it equated the authority to act on behalf of a city with the power to establish municipal policy, in my view the lower court quite correctly concluded that the CSC's highly circumscribed and deferential review of Hamsher's decisions in no way rendered those decisions less than final. [T]he facts of this case reveal that CSC believed it lacked the authority to review lateral transfers. Accordingly, had Frank Hamsher actually possessed policymaking authority with respect to such decisions, I would have little difficulty concluding that such authority was final.

[5] I am unable to agree with Justice Stevens that the record provides sufficient evidence of complicity on the part of other municipal policymakers such that we may sustain the jury's verdict against petitioner on a conspiracy theory neither espoused nor addressed by the court below. Justice Stevens' dissent relies to a large extent on respondent's controversial public testimony about the Serra sculpture, and the unwelcome reception that testimony drew in the mayor's office. Whatever else may be said about the strength of this evidence, however, the dissent's reliance on it is flawed in one crucial respect: the jury instructions concerning respondent's first amendment claim refer exclusively to the exercise of his appellate rights before the CSC and make no mention whatever of his public testimony. Under these circumstances, the jury was simply not at liberty to impose liability against petitioner based on the allegedly retaliatory actions of the mayor and his close associates [and] we may not sustain its verdict on the basis of such evidence.

The plurality begins its assessment of St. Louis' power structure by asserting that the identification of policymaking officials is a question of state law, by which it means that the question is neither one of federal law nor of fact, at least "not in the usual sense." Instead, the plurality explains, courts are to identify municipal policymakers by referring exclusively to applicable state statutory law. Not surprisingly, the plurality cites no authority for this startling proposition, nor could it, for we have never suggested that municipal liability should be determined in so formulaic and unrealistic a fashion. In any case in which the policymaking authority of a municipal tortfeasor is in doubt, state law will naturally be the appropriate starting point, but ultimately the factfinder must determine where such policymaking authority actually resides, and not simply "where the applicable law purports to put it." . . . Thus, although I agree with the plurality that juries should not be given open-ended "*discretion* to determine which officials are high enough in the government that their actions can be said to represent a decision of the government itself," (emphasis added), juries can and must find the predicate facts necessary to a determination of whether a given official possesses final policymaking authority. While the jury instructions in this case were regrettably vague, the plurality's solution tosses the baby out with the bath water. The identification of municipal policymakers is an essentially factual determination "in the usual sense," and is therefore rightly entrusted to a properly instructed jury.

Nor does the "custom or usage" doctrine adequately compensate for the inherent inflexibility of a rule that leaves the identification of policymakers exclusively to state statutory law. That doctrine, under which municipalities and states can be held liable for unconstitutional practices so well settled and permanent that they have the force of law has little if any bearing on the question whether a city has delegated de facto final policymaking authority to a given official. A city practice of delegating final policymaking authority to a subordinate or mid-level official would not be unconstitutional in and of itself, and an isolated unconstitutional act by an official entrusted with such authority would obviously not amount to a municipal "custom or usage." Under *Pembaur*, of course, such an isolated act *should* give rise to municipal liability. Yet a case such as this would fall through the gaping hole the plurality's construction leaves in § 1983, because state statutory law would not identify the municipal actor as a policymaking official, and a single constitutional deprivation, by definition, is not a well settled and permanent municipal practice carrying the force of law.

For these same reasons, I cannot subscribe to the plurality's narrow and overly rigid view of when a municipal official's policymaking authority is "final." Attempting to place a gloss on *Pembaur's* finality requirement, the plurality suggests that whenever the decisions of an official are subject to some form of review—however limited—that official's decisions are nonfinal. Under the plurality's theory, therefore, even where an official wields policymaking authority with respect to a challenged decision, the city would not be liable for that official's policy decision unless *reviewing* officials affirmatively approved both the "decision and the basis for it." Reviewing officials, however, may as a matter of practice never invoke their plenary oversight authority, or their review powers may be highly circumscribed. Under such circumstances, the subordinate's decision is in effect the final municipal pronouncement on the subject. Certainly a § 1983 plaintiff is entitled to place such considerations before the jury, for the law is concerned not with the niceties of legislative draftsmanship but with the realities of municipal decisionmaking, and any assessment of a municipality's actual power structure is necessarily a factual and practical one.[7]

Accordingly, I cannot endorse the plurality's determination, based on nothing more than its own review of the city charter, that the mayor, the aldermen, and the CSC are the only policymakers for the city of St. Louis. While these officials may well have policymaking authority, that hardly ends the matter; the question before us is whether the officials responsible for respondent's allegedly unlawful transfer were final policymakers. As I have previously indicated, I do not believe that CDA Director Frank Hamsher possessed any policymaking authority with respect to lateral transfers and thus I do not believe that his allegedly improper decision to transfer respondent could, without more, give rise to municipal liability. Although the plurality reaches the same result, it does so by reasoning that because others could have reviewed the decisions of Hamsher and Killen, the latter officials simply could not have been final policymakers.

This analysis, however, turns a blind eye to reality, for it ignores not only the lower court's determination, nowhere disputed, that CSC review was highly circumscribed and deferential, but that in this very case the Commission *refused* to judge the propriety of Hamsher's transfer decision because a lateral transfer was not an "adverse" employment action falling within its jurisdiction. Nor does the plurali-

---

[7] The plurality also asserts that "[w]hen an official's discretionary decisions are constrained by policies not of that official's making, those policies, rather than the subordinate's departures from them, are the act of the municipality." While I have no quarrel with such a proposition in the abstract, I cannot accept the plurality's apparent view that a municipal charter's precatory admonition against discrimination or any other employment practice not based on merit and fitness effectively insulates the municipality from any liability based on acts inconsistent with that policy. Again, the relevant inquiry is whether the policy in question is actually and effectively enforced through the city's review mechanisms. Thus in this case, a policy prohibiting lateral transfers for unconstitutional or discriminatory reasons would not shield the city from liability if an official possessing final policymaking authority over such transfers acted in violation of the prohibition, because the CSC would lack jurisdiction to review the decision and thus could not enforce the policy. Where as here, however, the official merely possesses discretionary authority over transfers, the city policy is irrelevant, because the official's actions cannot subject the city to liability in any event.

ty account for the fact that Hamsher's predecessor, Donald Spaid, promulgated what the city readily acknowledges was a binding policy regarding secondary employment;[8] although the CSC ultimately modified the sanctions respondent suffered as a result of his apparent failure to comply with that policy, the record is devoid of any suggestion that the Commission reviewed the substance or validity of the policy itself. Under the plurality's analysis, therefore, even the hollowest promise of review is sufficient to divest all city officials save the mayor and governing legislative body of final policymaking authority. . . . Because the plurality's mechanical "finality" test is fundamentally at odds with the pragmatic and factual inquiry contemplated by *Monell,* I cannot join what I perceive to be its unwarranted abandonment of the traditional factfinding process in § 1983 actions involving municipalities.

Finally, I think it necessary to emphasize that despite certain language in the plurality opinion suggesting otherwise, the Court today need not and therefore does not decide that a city can only be held liable under § 1983 where the plaintiff "prove[s] the existence of an unconstitutional municipal policy." . . . That question is certainly not presented by this case, and nothing we say today forecloses its future consideration. . . .

JUSTICE STEVENS, dissenting.

If this case involved nothing more than a personal vendetta between a municipal employee and his superiors, it would be quite wrong to impose liability on the City of St. Louis. In fact, however, the jury found that top officials in the city administration relying on pretextual grounds, had taken a series of retaliatory actions against respondent because he had testified truthfully on two occasions, one relating to personnel policy and the other involving a public controversy of importance to the mayor and the members of his cabinet. No matter how narrowly the Court may define the standards for imposing liability upon municipalities in § 1983 litigation, the judgment entered by the District Court in this case should be affirmed.

In order to explain why I believe that affirmance is required by this Court's precedents,[1] it is necessary to begin with a more complete

---

[8] Although the plurality is careful in its discussion of the facts to label Director Spaid's directive a "requirement" rather than a "policy," the city itself draws no such fine semantic distinctions. Rather, it states plainly that Spaid "promulgated a 'secondary employment' *policy* that sought to control outside employment by CDA architects," and that "[respondent] resented the policy . . . ."

[1] This would, of course, be an easy case if the Court disavowed its dicta in part II of its opinion in Monell v. N.Y. City Dept. of Social Services, 436 U.S. 658, 691–95 (1978). Like many commentators who have confronted the question, I remain convinced that Congress intended the doctrine of respondeat superior to apply in § 1983 litigation. Given the Court's reiteration of the contrary ipse dixit in *Monell* and subsequent opinions, however, I shall join the Court's attempt to draw an intelligible boundary between municipal agents' actions that bind and those that do not. . . .

statement of the disputed factual issues that the jury resolved in respondent's favor. . . .

The City of St. Louis hired respondent as a licensed architect in 1968. During the ensuing decade, he was repeatedly promoted and consistently given "superior" performance ratings. In April of 1980, while serving as the Director of Urban Design in the Community Development Agency (CDA), he was recommended for a two-step salary increase by his immediate superior.

Thereafter, on two occasions he gave public testimony that was critical of official city policy. In 1980 he testified before the Civil Service Commission (CSC) in support of his successful appeal from a 15-day suspension. In that testimony he explained that he had received advance oral approval of his outside employment and voiced his objections to the requirement of prior written approval. The record demonstrates that this testimony offended his immediate superiors at the CDA.

In 1981 respondent testified before the Heritage and Urban Design Commission (HUD) in connection with a proposal to acquire a controversial rusting steel sculpture by Richard Serra. In his testimony he revealed the previously undisclosed fact that an earlier city administration had rejected an offer to acquire the same sculpture, and also explained that the erection of the sculpture would require the removal of structures on which the city had recently expended about $250,000. This testimony offended top officials of the city government, possibly including the mayor, who supported the acquisition of the Serra sculpture, as well as respondent's agency superiors. They made it perfectly clear that they believed that respondent had violated a duty of loyalty to the mayor by expressing his personal opinion about the sculpture. . . .

After this testimony respondent was the recipient of a series of adverse personnel actions that culminated in his transfer from an important management level professional position to a rather menial assignment for which he was "grossly overqualified" and his eventual layoff. [E]vidence in the record amply supports the conclusion that respondent was first transferred and then laid off, not for fiscal and administrative reasons, but in retaliation for his public testimony before the CSC and HUD. It is undisputed that respondent's right to testify in support of his civil service appeal and his right to testify in opposition to the city's acquisition of the Serra sculpture were protected by the first amendment to the federal Constitution. Given the jury's verdict, the case is therefore one in which a municipal employee's federal constitutional rights were violated by officials of the city government. . . .

In Monell v. N.Y. Dept. of Social Services, 436 U.S. 658 (1978), we held that municipal corporations are "persons" within the meaning of

42 U.S.C. § 1983. Since a corporation is incapable of doing anything except through the agency of human beings, that holding necessarily gave rise to the question of what human activity undertaken by agents of the corporation may create municipal liability in § 1983 litigation.[19]

[In *Monell* and subsequent cases] the Court has permitted a municipality to be held liable for the unconstitutional actions of its agents when those agents: enforced a rule of general applicability, *Monell;* were of sufficiently high stature and acted through a formal process, Owen v. City of Independence, 445 U.S. 622 (1980); or were authorized to establish policy in the particular area of city government in which the tort was committed, Pembaur v. Cincinnati, 475 U.S. 469 (1986). Under these precedents, the City of St. Louis should be held liable in this case.

Both *Pembaur* and the plurality and concurring opinions today acknowledge that a high official who has ultimate control over a certain area of city government can bind the city through his unconstitutional actions even though those actions are not in the form of formal rules or regulations. Although the Court has explained its holdings by reference to the nonstatutory term "policy," it plainly has not embraced the standard understanding of that word as covering a rule of general applicability. Instead it has used that term to include isolated acts not intended to be binding over a class of situations. But when one remembers that the real question in cases such as this is not "what constitutes city policy?" but rather "when should a city be liable for the acts of its agents?", the inclusion of single acts by high officials makes sense, for those acts bind a municipality in a way that the misdeeds of low officials do not.

Every act of a high official constitutes a kind of "statement" about how similar decisions will be carried out; the assumption is that the same decision would have been made, and would again be made, across a class of cases. Lower officials do not control others in the same way. Since their actions do not dictate the responses of various subordinates, those actions lack the potential of controlling governmental decisionmaking; they are not perceived as the actions of the city itself. If a county police officer had broken down Dr. Pembaur's door on the officer's own initiative, this would have been seen as the action of an overanxious officer, and would not have sent a message to other officers

---

[19] The "theme" of *Monell*—"that some basis for government liability other than vicarious liability for the acts of individuals must be found"—has proved to be a "difficult" one largely because "there is no obvious way to distinguish the acts of a municipality from the acts of the individuals whom it employs." Whitman, Government Responsibility for Constitutional Torts, 85 Mich.L.Rev. 225, 236 (1986). In other words, every time a municipality is held liable in tort, even in a case like *Monell,* actions of its human agents are necessarily involved. Accordingly, our task is not to draw a line between the actions of the city and the actions of its employees, but rather to develop a principle for determining *which* human acts should bind a municipality.

that similar actions would be countenanced. . . . Here, the mayor, those working for him, and the agency heads are high-ranking officials; accordingly, we must assume that their actions have city-wide ramifications, both through their similar response to a like class of situations, and through the response of subordinates who follow their lead.

Just as the actions of high-ranking and low-ranking municipal employees differ in nature, so do constitutional torts differ. An illegal search, *Pembaur,* or seizure, Oklahoma City v. Tuttle, 471 U.S. 808 (1985), is quite different from a firing without due process, *Owen;* the retaliatory personnel action involved in today's case is in still another category. One thing that the torts in *Pembaur, Tuttle,* and *Owen* had in common is that they occurred "in the open"; in each of those cases, the ultimate judgment of unconstitutionality was based on whether undisputed events (the breaking-in in *Pembaur,* the shooting in *Tuttle,* the firing in *Owen*) comported with accepted constitutional norms. But the typical retaliatory personnel action claim pits one story against another; although everyone admits that the transfer and discharge of respondent occurred, there is sharp, and ultimately central, dispute over the reasons—the motivation—behind the actions. *The very nature of the tort is to avoid a formal process. Owen's* relevance should thus be clear. For if the Court is willing to recognize the existence of municipal policy in a nonrule case as long as high enough officials engaged in a formal enough process, it should not deny the existence of such a policy merely because those same officials act "underground," as it were. It would be a truly remarkable doctrine for this Court to recognize municipal liability in an employee discharge case when high officials are foolish enough to act through a "formal process," but not when similarly high officials attempt to avoid liability by acting on the pretext of budgetary concerns, which is what the jury found based on the evidence presented at trial.

Thus, holding St. Louis liable in this case is supported by both *Pembaur* and *Owen.* We hold a municipality liable for the decisions of its high officials in large part because those decisions, by definition, would be applied across a class of cases. Just as we assume in *Pembaur* that the county prosecutor (or his subordinate) would issue the same break-down-the-door order in similar cases, and just as we assume in *Owen* that the city council (or those following its lead) would fire an employee without notice of reasons or opportunity to be heard in similar cases, so too must we assume that whistleblowers like respondent would be dealt with in similar retaliatory fashion if they offend the mayor, his staff, and relevant agency heads, or if they offend those lower-ranking officials who follow the example of their superiors. Furthermore, just as we hold a municipality liable for discharging an employee without due process when its city council acts formally—for a due process violation is precisely the *type* of constitutional tort that a city council might commit when it acts formally—so too must we hold a municipality liable for discharging an employee in retaliation against his public speech when similarly high officials act informally—for a first amendment retaliation tort is precisely the *type* of constitutional tort that high officials might commit when they act in concert and informally.

Whatever difficulties the Court may have with binding municipalities on the basis of the unconstitutional conduct of individuals, it should have no such difficulties binding a city when many of its high officials—including officials directly under the mayor, agency heads, and possibly the mayor himself—cooperate to retaliate against a whistleblower for the exercise of his first amendment rights.

I would affirm the judgment of the Court of Appeals.

NOTE ON *PRAPROTNIK*

The opinions in *Praprotnik* suggest three different ways of distinguishing between those acts for which the municipality will be liable and those for which it will not. Justice O'Connor emphasizes state law as the crucial inquiry. Does that mean, as Justice Brennan charged, that a municipality could insulate itself from liability by issuing "precatory statements" against unconstitutional employment policies? By providing adequate internal review of personnel decisions? How will a court distinguish between self-protective window dressing and genuine attempts to set one's own house in order by adopting appropriate employment policies?

Justice Brennan would distinguish between final authority to act on behalf of the municipality and final authority to make official policy with respect to that act. Is this distinction clear? Does it aim at something important, or is it mere characterization?

Justice Stevens' suggests that municipalities should be liable for the acts of high-ranking officials but not for those of low-ranking officials. Why? Does the rank of the official necessarily correlate with the official status of that person's actions? Why should the decisive factor be the position held by the *person* who acted unlawfully rather than the relation between the government and the action itself?

Which of these approaches seems the best way of addressing the official policy requirement? Is there some better way of going about it?

CITY OF CANTON v. HARRIS
Supreme Court of the United States, 1989.
489 U.S. 378.

JUSTICE WHITE delivered the opinion of the Court.

In this case, we are asked to determine if a municipality can ever be liable under 42 U.S.C. § 1983 for constitutional violations resulting from its failure to train municipal employees. We hold that, under certain circumstances, such liability is permitted by the statute.

I

In April 1978, respondent Geraldine Harris was arrested by officers of the Canton Police Department. Harris was brought to the police station in a patrol wagon.

When she arrived at the station, Harris was found sitting on the floor of the wagon. She was asked if she needed medical attention, and responded with an incoherent remark. After she was brought inside the station for processing, Mrs. Harris slumped to the floor on two occasions. Eventually, the police officers left Mrs. Harris lying on the floor to prevent her from falling again. No medical attention was ever summoned for Mrs. Harris. After about an hour, Mrs. Harris was released from custody, and taken by an ambulance (provided by her family) to a nearby hospital. There, Mrs. Harris was diagnosed as suffering from several emotional ailments; she was hospitalized for one week, and received subsequent outpatient treatment for an additional year.

Some time later, Mrs. Harris commenced this action alleging many state law and constitutional claims against the city of Canton and its officials. Among these claims was one seeking to hold the city liable under 42 U.S.C. § 1983 for its violation of Mrs. Harris' right, under the due process clause of the 14th amendment, to receive necessary medical attention while in police custody.

A jury trial was held on Mrs. Harris' claims. Evidence was presented that indicated that, pursuant to a municipal regulation,[2] shift commanders were authorized to determine, in their sole discretion, whether a detainee required medical care. In addition, testimony also suggested that Canton shift commanders were not provided with any special training (beyond first-aid training) to make a determination as to when to summon medical care for an injured detainee.

---

[2] The city regulation in question provides that a police officer assigned to act as "jailer" at the city police station:

"shall, when a prisoner is found to be unconscious or semi-unconscious, or when he or she is unable to explain his or her condition, or who complains of being ill, have such person taken to a hospital for medical treatment, with permission of his supervisor before admitting the person to city jail."

At the close of the evidence, the District Court submitted the case to the jury, which rejected all of Mrs. Harris' claims except one: her § 1983 claim against the city resulting from its failure to provide her with medical treatment while in custody. In rejecting the city's subsequent motion for judgment notwithstanding the verdict, the District Court explained the theory of liability as follows:

> "The evidence construed in a manner most favorable to Mrs. Harris could be found by a jury to demonstrate that the city of Canton had a custom or policy of vesting complete authority with the police supervisor of when medical treatment would be administered to prisoners. Further, the jury could find from the evidence that the vesting of such carte blanche authority with the police supervisor without adequate training to recognize when medical treatment is needed was grossly negligent or so reckless that future police misconduct was almost inevitable or substantially certain to result."

On appeal, the Sixth Circuit affirmed this aspect of the District Court's analysis, holding that "a municipality is liable for failure to train its police force, [where] the plaintiff . . . prove[s] that the municipality acted recklessly, intentionally, or with gross negligence." The Court of Appeals also stated that an additional prerequisite of this theory of liability was that the plaintiff must prove "that the lack of training was so reckless or grossly negligent that deprivations of persons' constitutional rights were substantially certain to result." Thus, the Court of Appeals found that there had been no error in submitting Mrs. Harris' "failure to train" claim to the jury. However, the Court of Appeals reversed the judgment for respondent, and remanded this case for a new trial, because it found that certain aspects of the District Court's jury instructions might have led the jury to believe that it could find against the city on a mere respondeat superior theory. Because the jury's verdict did not state the basis on which it had ruled for Mrs. Harris on her § 1983 claim, a new trial was ordered.

The city petitioned for certiorari, arguing that the Sixth Circuit's holding represented an impermissible broadening of municipal liability under § 1983. We granted the petition.

II

We first address respondent's contention that the writ of certiorari should be dismissed as improvidently granted, because "petitioner failed to preserve for review the principal issues it now argues in this Court." [The Court held that it was proper to proceed to a decision on the merits.]

III

In Monell v. New York City Dept. of Social Services, 436 U.S. 658 (1978), we decided that a municipality can be found liable under § 1983 only where the municipality *itself* causes the constitutional violation at issue. Respondeat superior or vicarious liability will not attach under § 1983. "It is only when the 'execution of the government's policy or custom . . . inflicts the injury' that the municipality may be held liable under § 1983." City of Springfield v. Kibbe, 480 U.S. 257, 267 (1987) (O'Connor, J., dissenting) (quoting *Monell*).

Thus, our first inquiry in any case alleging municipal liability under § 1983 is the question of whether there is a direct causal link between a municipal policy or custom, and the alleged constitutional deprivation. . . .

A

[P]etitioner urges us to adopt the rule that a municipality can be found liable under § 1983 only where "the policy in question [is] itself unconstitutional." Whether such a rule is a valid construction of § 1983 is a question the Court has left unresolved. See, e.g., City of St. Louis v. Praprotnik, 485 U.S. 112, 147 (1988) (Brennan, J., concurring in judgment). Under such an approach, the outcome here would be rather clear: we would have to reverse and remand the case with instructions that judgment be entered for petitioner.[5] There can be little doubt that on its face the city's policy regarding medical treatment for detainees is constitutional. The policy states that the City Jailer "shall . . . have [a person needing medical care] taken to a hospital for medical treatment, with permission of his supervisor. . . ." It is difficult to see what constitutional guarantees are violated by such a policy.

Nor, without more, would a city automatically be liable under § 1983 if one of its employees happened to apply the policy in an unconstitutional manner, for liability would then rest on respondeat superior. The claim in this case, however, is that if a concededly valid policy is unconstitutionally applied by a municipal employee, the city is liable if the employee has not been adequately trained and the constitu-

---

[5] In this Court, in addition to suggesting that the city's failure to train its officers amounted to a "policy" that resulted in the denial of medical care to detainees, respondent also contended the city had a "custom" of denying medical care to those detainees suffering from emotional or mental ailments. As respondent described it in her brief, and at argument, this claim of an unconstitutional "custom" appears to be little more than a restatement of her "failure-to-train as policy" claim. However, to the extent that this claim poses a distinct basis for the city's liability under § 1983, we decline to determine whether respondent's contention that such a "custom" existed is an alternate grounds for affirmance. The "custom" claim was not passed on by the Court of Appeals—nor does it appear to have been presented to that court as a distinct ground for its decision. Thus, we will not consider it here.

tional wrong has been caused by that failure to train. For reasons explained below, we conclude . . . that there are limited circumstances in which an allegation of a "failure to train" can be the basis for liability under § 1983. Thus, we reject petitioner's contention that only unconstitutional policies are actionable under the statute.

B

Though we agree with the court below that a city can be liable under § 1983 for inadequate training of its employees, we cannot agree that the District Court's jury instructions on this issue were proper, for we conclude that the Court of Appeals provided an overly broad rule for when a municipality can be held liable under the "failure to train" theory. . . . We hold . . . that the inadequacy of police training may serve as the basis for § 1983 liability only where the failure to train amounts to deliberate indifference to the rights of persons with whom the police come into contact.[8] This rule is most consistent with our admonition in *Monell* and Polk County v. Dodson, 454 U.S. 312, 326 (1981), that a municipality can be liable under § 1983 only where its policies are the "moving force [behind] the constitutional violation." Only where a municipality's failure to train its employees in a relevant respect evidences a "deliberate indifference" to the rights of its inhabitants can such a shortcoming be properly thought of as a city "policy or custom" that is actionable under § 1983. As Justice Brennan's opinion in Pembaur v. Cincinnati, 475 U.S. 469, 483–84 (1986) (plurality) put it: "[M]unicipal liability under § 1983 attaches where—and only where—a deliberate choice to follow a course of action is made from among various alternatives" by city policy makers. Only where a failure to train reflects a "deliberate" or "conscious" choice by a municipality—a "policy" as defined by our prior cases—can a city be liable for such a failure under § 1983.

Monell's rule that a city is not liable under § 1983 unless a municipal policy causes a constitutional deprivation will not be satis-

---

[8] The "deliberate indifference" standard we adopt for § 1983 "failure to train" claims does not turn upon the degree of fault (if any) that a plaintiff must show to make out an underlying claim of a constitutional violation. For example, this Court has never determined what degree of culpability must be shown before the particular constitutional deprivation asserted in this case—a denial of the due process right to medical care while in detention—is established. Indeed, in Revere v. Massachusetts General Hospital, 463 U.S. 239, 243–45 (1983), we reserved decision on the question of whether something less than [the] eighth amendment's "deliberate indifference" test may be applicable in claims by detainees asserting violations of their due process right to medical care while in custody.

We need not resolve here the question left open in *Revere* for two reasons. First, petitioner has conceded that, as the case comes to us, we must assume that respondent's constitutional right to receive medical care was denied by city employees—whatever the nature of that right might be. Second, the proper standard for determining when a municipality will be liable under § 1983 for constitutional wrongs does not turn on any underlying culpability test that determines when such wrongs have occurred.

fied by merely alleging that the existing training program for a class of employees, such as police officers, represents a policy for which the city is responsible.[9] That much may be true. The issue in a case like this one, however, is whether that training program is adequate; and if it is not, the question becomes whether such inadequate training can justifiably be said to represent "city policy." It may seem contrary to common sense to assert that a municipality will actually have a policy of not taking reasonable steps to train its employees. But it may happen that in light of the duties assigned to specific officers or employees the need for more or different training is so obvious, and the inadequacy so likely to result in the violation of constitutional rights, that the policymakers of the city can reasonably be said to have been deliberately indifferent to the need.[10] In that event, the failure to provide proper training may fairly be said to represent a policy for which the city is responsible, and for which the city may be held liable if it actually causes injury.[11]

In resolving the issue of a city's liability, the focus must be on adequacy of the training program in relation to the tasks the particular officers must perform. That a particular officer may be unsatisfactorily trained will not alone suffice to fasten liability on the city, for the officer's shortcomings may have resulted from factors other than a faulty training program. It may be, for example, that an otherwise sound program has occasionally been negligently administered. Neither will it suffice to prove that an injury or accident could have been avoided if an officer had had better or more training, sufficient to equip him to avoid the particular injury-causing conduct. Such a claim could be made about almost any encounter resulting in injury, yet not condemn the adequacy of the program to enable officers to respond

[9] The plurality opinion in Oklahoma City v. Tuttle, 471 U.S. 808 (1985), explained why this must be so:

"Obviously, if one retreats far enough from a constitutional violation some municipal 'policy' can be identified behind almost any . . . harm inflicted by a municipal official; for example, [a police officer] would never have killed Tuttle if Oklahoma City did not have a 'policy' of establishing a police force. But *Monell* must be taken to require proof of a city policy different in kind from this latter example before a claim can be sent to a jury on the theory that a particular violation was 'caused' by the municipal 'policy.' "

[10] For example, city policy makers know to a moral certainty that their police officers will be required to arrest fleeing felons. The city has armed its officers with firearms, in part to allow them to accomplish this task. Thus, the need to train officers in the constitutional limitations on the use of deadly force, see Tennessee v. Garner, 471 U.S. 1 (1985), can be said to be "so obvious," that failure to do so could properly be characterized as "deliberate indifference" to constitutional rights.

It could also be that the police, in exercising their discretion, so often violate constitutional rights that the need for further training must have been plainly obvious to the city policy makers, who, nevertheless, are "deliberately indifferent" to the need.

[11] The record indicates that city did train its officers and that its training included first-aid instruction. Petitioner argues that it could not have been obvious to the city that such training was insufficient to administer the written policy, which was itself constitutional. This is a question to be resolved on remand.

properly to the usual and recurring situations with which they must deal. And plainly, adequately trained officers occasionally make mistakes; the fact that they do says little about the training program or the legal basis for holding the city liable.

Moreover, for liability to attach in this circumstance the identified deficiency in a city's training program must be closely related to the ultimate injury. Thus in the case at hand, respondent must still prove that the deficiency in training actually caused the police officers' indifference to her medical needs. Would the injury have been avoided had the employee been trained under a program that was not deficient in the identified respect? Predicting how a hypothetically well trained officer would have acted under the circumstances may not be an easy task for the factfinder, particularly since matters of judgment may be involved, and since officers who are well trained are not free from error and perhaps might react very much like the untrained officer in similar circumstances. But judge and jury, doing their respective jobs, will be adequate to the task.

To adopt lesser standards of fault and causation would open municipalities to unprecedented liability under § 1983. In virtually every instance where a person has had his or her constitutional rights violated by a city employee, a § 1983 plaintiff will be able to point to something the city "could have done" to prevent the unfortunate incident. Thus, permitting cases against cities for their "failure to train" employees to go forward under § 1983 on a lesser standard of fault would result in de facto respondeat superior liability on municipalities—a result we rejected in *Monell.* It would also engage the federal courts in an endless exercise of second-guessing municipal employee-training programs. This is an exercise we believe the federal courts are ill-suited to undertake, as well as one that would implicate serious questions of federalism. Cf. Rizzo v. Goode, 423 U.S. 362, 378–80 (1976).

Consequently, while claims such as respondent's—alleging that the city's failure to provide training to municipal employees resulted in the constitutional deprivation she suffered—are cognizable under § 1983, they can only yield liability against a municipality where that city's failure to train reflects deliberate indifference to the constitutional rights of its inhabitants.

IV

The final question here is whether this case should be remanded for a new trial, or whether, as petitioner suggests, we should conclude that there are no possible grounds on which respondent can prevail. It is true that the evidence in the record now does not meet the standard of § 1983 liability we have set forth above. But, the standard of proof the District Court ultimately imposed on respondent (which was consistent with Sixth Circuit precedent) was a lesser one than the one we adopt today. Whether respondent should have an opportunity to prove her case under the "deliberate indifference" rule we have adopted is a matter for the Court of Appeals to deal with on remand.

V

Consequently, for the reasons given above, we vacate the judgment of the Court of Appeals and remand this case for further proceedings consistent with this opinion.

It is so ordered.

JUSTICE BRENNAN, concurring.

The Court's opinion, which I join, makes clear that the Court of Appeals is free to remand this case for a new trial.

JUSTICE O'CONNOR, with whom JUSTICE SCALIA and JUSTICE KENNEDY join, concurring in part and dissenting in part.

I join parts I, II, and all of part III of the Court's opinion except footnote 11. I thus agree that where municipal policymakers are confronted with an obvious need to train city personnel to avoid the violation of constitutional rights and they are deliberately indifferent to that need, the lack of necessary training may be appropriately considered a city "policy" subjecting the city itself to liability under our decision in Monell v. New York City Dept. of Social Services, 436 U.S. 658 (1978). As the Court observes, "[o]nly where a failure to train reflects a 'deliberate' or 'conscious' choice by a municipality—a 'policy' as defined by our prior cases—can a city be liable for such a failure under § 1983." I further agree that a § 1983 plaintiff pressing a "failure to train" claim must prove that the lack of training was the "cause" of the constitutional injury at issue and that this entails more than simply showing "but for" causation. Lesser requirements of fault and causation in this context would "open municipalities to unprecedented liability under § 1983," and would pose serious federalism concerns.

My single point of disagreement with the majority is thus a small one. Because I believe, as the majority strongly hints, that respondent has not and could not satisfy the fault and causation requirements we adopt today, I think it unnecessary to remand this case to the Court of Appeals for further proceedings. This case comes to us after a full trial during which respondent vigorously pursued numerous theories of municipal liability including an allegation that the city had a "custom" of not providing medical care to detainees suffering from emotional illnesses. Respondent thus had every opportunity and incentive to adduce the type of proof necessary to satisfy the deliberate indifference standard we adopt today. Rather than remand in this context, I would apply the deliberate indifference standard to the facts of this case.

After undertaking that analysis below, I conclude that there is no evidence in the record indicating that the city of Canton has been deliberately indifferent to the constitutional rights of pretrial detainees.

I

. . . Where, as here, a claim of municipal liability is predicated upon a failure to act, the requisite degree of fault must be shown by proof of a background of events and circumstances which establish that the "policy of inaction" is the functional equivalent of a decision by the city itself to violate the Constitution. Without some form of notice to the city, and the opportunity to conform to constitutional dictates both what it does and what it chooses not to do, the failure to train theory of liability could completely engulf *Monell,* imposing liability without regard to fault. Moreover, absent a requirement that the lack of training at issue bears a very close causal connection to the violation of constitutional rights, the failure to train theory of municipal liability could impose "prophylactic" duties on municipal governments only remotely connected to underlying constitutional requirements themselves. [Section] 1983 is not a "federal good government act" for municipalities. Rather it creates a federal cause of action against persons, including municipalities, who deprive citizens of the United States of their constitutional rights.

Sensitive to these concerns, the Court's opinion correctly requires a high degree of fault on the part of city officials before an omission that is not in itself unconstitutional can support liability as a municipal policy under *Monell.* As the Court indicates, "it may happen that . . . the need for more or different training is so obvious, and the inadequacy so likely to result in the violation of constitutional rights, that the policymakers of the city can reasonably be said to have been deliberately indifferent to the need." Where a § 1983 plaintiff can establish that the facts available to city policymakers put them on actual or constructive notice that the particular omission is substantially certain to result in the violation of the constitutional rights of their citizens, the dictates of *Monell* are satisfied. Only then can it be said that the municipality has made " 'a deliberate choice to follow a course of action . . . from among various alternatives.' "

In my view, it could be shown that the need for training was obvious in one of two ways. First, a municipality could fail to train its employees concerning a clear constitutional duty implicated in recurrent situations that a particular employee is certain to face. As the majority notes, the constitutional limitations established by the Court on the use of deadly force by police officers present one such situation. The constitutional duty of the individual officer is clear, and it is equally clear that failure to inform city personnel of that duty will create an extremely high risk that constitutional violations will ensue.

The claim in this case—that police officers were inadequately trained in diagnosing the symptoms of emotional illness—falls far short of the kind of "obvious" need for training that would support a finding of deliberate indifference to constitutional rights on the part of the city. As the Court's opinion observes, this Court has not yet addressed the precise nature of the obligations that the due process clause places upon the police to seek medical care for pretrial detainees who have been *physically* injured while being apprehended by the police. There are thus no clear constitutional guideposts for municipalities in this area, and the diagnosis of mental illness is not one of the "usual and recurring situations with which [the police] must deal." The lack of training at issue here is not the kind of omission that can be characterized, in and of itself, as a "deliberate indifference" to constitutional rights.

Second, I think municipal liability for failure to train may be proper where it can be shown that policymakers were aware of, and acquiesced in, a pattern of constitutional violations involving the exercise of police discretion. In such cases, the need for training may not be obvious from the outset, but a pattern of constitutional violations could put the municipality on notice that its officers confront the particular situation on a regular basis, and that they often react in a manner contrary to constitutional requirements. . . .

The Court's opinion recognizes this requirement, but declines to evaluate the evidence presented in this case in light of the new legal standard. From the outset of this litigation, respondent has pressed a claim that the city of Canton had a custom of denying medical care to pretrial detainees with emotional disorders. Indeed, up to and including oral argument before this Court, counsel for respondent continued to assert that respondent was attempting to hinge municipal liability upon "both a custom of denying medical care to a certain class of prisoners, and a failure to train police that led to this particular violation." At the time respondent filed her complaint in 1980, it was clear that proof of the existence of a custom entailed a showing of "practices . . . so permanent and well settled as to constitute a 'custom or usage' with the force of law." Adickes v. S.H. Kress & Co., 398 U.S. 144, 168 (1970).

Whatever the prevailing standard at the time concerning liability for failure to train, respondent thus had every incentive to adduce proof at trial of a pattern of violations to support her claim that the city had an unwritten custom of denying medical care to emotionally ill detainees. In fact, respondent presented no testimony from any witness indicating that there had been past incidents of "deliberate indifference" to the medical needs of emotionally disturbed detainees or that any other circumstance had put the city on actual or constructive notice of a need for additional training in this regard. At trial, David Maser, who was Chief of Police of the city of Canton from 1971 to 1980, testified without contradiction that during his tenure he received no complaints that detainees in the Canton jails were not being accorded proper medical treatment. Former Officer Cherry, who had served as a jailer for the Canton Police Department, indicated that he had never had to seek medical treatment for persons who were emotionally upset at the prospect of arrest, because they usually calmed down when a member of the department spoke with them or one of their family members arrived. There is quite simply nothing in this record to indicate that the city of Canton had any reason to suspect that failing to provide this kind of training would lead to injuries of any kind, let alone violations of the due process clause. . . .

Allowing an inadequate training claim such as this one to go to the jury based upon a single incident would only invite jury nullification of *Monell.* "To infer the existence of a city policy from the isolated misconduct of a single, low-level officer, and then to hold the city liable on the basis of that policy, would amount to permitting precisely the theory of strict respondeat superior liability rejected in *Monell.*" Oklahoma City v. Tuttle, 471 U.S. 808, 831 (1985) (Brennan, J., concurring). As the authors of the Ku Klux Klan Act themselves realized, the resources of local government are not inexhaustible. The grave step of shifting of those resources to particular areas where constitutional violations are likely to result through the deterrent power of § 1983 should certainly not be taken on the basis of an isolated incident. If § 1983 and the Constitution require the city of Canton to provide detailed medical and psychological training to its police officers, or to station paramedics at its jails, other city services will necessarily suffer, including those with far more direct implications for the protection of constitutional rights. Because respondent's evidence falls far short of establishing the high degree of fault on the part of the city required by our decision today, and because there is no indication that respondent could produce any new proof in this regard, I would reverse the judgment of the Court of Appeals and order entry of judgment for the city.

NOTES ON "OFFICIAL POLICY" AND FAILURE TO TRAIN

1. **Questions and Comments on *Harris*.** The *Harris* Court appears to be unanimous about the *standards* that should govern municipal liability for failure to train, though the Justices disagree about application of those standards to the facts of the case. Both opinions embrace the oxymoron "deliberate indifference" as the gov-

erning concept. Is the central feature of this inquiry subjective or objective? That is, is the inquiry one that seeks to determine what municipal policymakers were actually thinking about the constitutional rights at stake or what they *should have* thought based on external indicators? If the latter what kinds of external indicators seem sufficient?

Recall that *Owen v. City of Independence* held, over the dissents of Justices Powell (replaced by Kennedy), Burger (replaced by Scalia), Stewart (replaced by O'Connor), and Rehnquist, that municipal government enjoys no qualified immunity from § 1983 liability and, in Justice Powell's words, "may be liable in damages for violating a constitutional right that was unknown when the events . . . occurred." To what extent do *Harris* and *Praprotnik* constitute the revenge of the *Owen* dissenters? Do the current standards for determining municipal liability differ from the standards that would apply if municipal government were entitled to a qualified immunity defense?

2. Bibliography. The Court's decisions on the conditions for imposing governmental liability under § 1983 have spawned substantial comment. A comprehensive attempt to implement *Monell*'s "policy or custom" requirement is made in Barbara Rook Snyder, The Final Authority Analysis: A Unified Approach to Municipal Liability under § 1983, 1986 Wis.L.Rev. 633. Snyder argues that municipalities should be held liable for the acts of an official or employee vested with "final authority" over the matter in question. She explicates this analysis over a wide range of circumstances and concludes that its adoption would bring consistency and predictability to municipal liability under § 1983.

See also the recent and comprehensive analysis in Michael J. Gerhardt, The *Monell* Legacy: Balancing Federalism Concerns and Municipal Accountability under § 1983, 62 S.Cal.L.Rev. 539 (1989). Gerhardt sees *Monell* and the cases that follow as striking a balance between a nationalist concern to achieve municipal accountability and a federalist concern to limit the impact of § 1983 liability. Gerhardt defines and differentiates "policy" and "custom" and proposes resolution of various disputed issues. He also makes an anticipatory analysis of *Canton* and carefully explicates the prior "failure to train" cases. Broadly speaking, Gerhardt's positions are generally consistent with the views of Justice Brennan. For detailed criticism of *Praprotnik*, see id. at 575–81.

For a different perspective, see Christina Whitman, Government Responsibility for Constitutional Torts, 85 Mich.L.Rev. 225 (1986). Whitman sees an essential problem in the application of traditional tort concepts to the sphere of government wrongs. In her view, the Supreme Court has focused too closely on individual attitude and responsibility as determinants of governmental liability. This leads to the post-

Monell search for individual decisionmakers with sufficient authority to "speak for" the municipality. Neglected are questions about "how institutions can, as institutions, cause injuries." A focus on institutional structures, rather than individual responsibility, could "expand our sensitivity to previously disregarded harms." "Our struggle with the consequences of racism and sexism has made us aware that injuries do not flow solely from the acts of evil or careless persons." They may also be the "consequence of social structures and expectations." Thus, "a law that addresses only the isolated behavior of individuals, whether private or official, sees only some of the ways in which power can be abused. . . ."

For further analysis of this important issue, see Susan Bandes, *Monell, Parratt, Daniels,* and *Davidson:* Distinguishing a Custom or Policy from a Random, Unauthorized Act, 72 Iowa L.Rev. 101 (1986); George D. Brown, Municipal Liability under § 1983 and the Ambiguities of Burger Court Federalism: A Comment on *City of Oklahoma City v. Tuttle* and *Pembaur v. City of Cincinnati*—the "Official Policy" Cases, 27 B.C.L.Rev. 883 (1986), which analyzes this line of cases in light of the continuing tension between nationalist and federalist tendencies on the Supreme Court; Mark R. Brown, Correlating Municipal Liability and Official Immunity Under Section 1983, 1989 U.Ill.L.Rev. 625 (1989), which argues that governmental liability and the official immunity of individual officers should be inversely correlated so as to eliminate any gap in accountability for constitutional violations; Susanah M. Mead, 42 U.S.C. § 1983 Municipal Liability: The *Monell* Sketch Becomes a Distorted Picture, 65 N.C.L.Rev. 518 (1987), which urges reconsideration of the *Monell* Court's rejection of respondeat superior; and Solomon Oliver, Municipal Liability for Police Misconduct under 42 U.S.C. § 1983 after *City of Oklahoma City v. Tuttle,* 64 Wash.U.L.Q. 151 (1986), a pre-*Harris* article which considers the important questions left open by *Tuttle* on the failure-to-train issue.

See also Mark R. Brown, Accountability in Government and Section 1983, 25 U.Mich.J.L.Ref. 53 (1991) (arguing that high-ranking government officials should be liable for failure to control subordinates, even if they do not personally engage in wrongdoing); Barbara Kritchevsky, Making Sense of State of Mind: Determining Responsibility in Section 1983 Municipal Liability Litigation, 60 G.W.L.Rev. 417 (1992) (arguing that municipal liability should depend on the state of mind of municipal policymakers, not on that of the sometimes blameless municipal employees who directly cause the injury).

Page 126, add a footnote after the title to Note 2:

[a] The ideas sketched out in this note are expanded and significantly revised in Jeffries, Compensation for Constitutional Torts: Reflections on the Significance of Fault, 88 Mich.L.Rev. 82 (1989). The article argues that a requirement of fault is not inimical to the goal of compensation, but is in fact an essential feature of a normatively sound compensatory regime. On this view, *Owen* was wrongly decided—

at least on the non-instrumental grounds suggested by the term "compensation." Deterrence is not considered.

Other questions broached in this Note—specifically, the illustrative problems drawn from the fourth and first amendments—are discussed in Jeffries, Damages for Constitutional Violations: The Relation of Risk to Injury in Constitutional Torts, 75 Va.L.Rev. 1461 (1989).

For criticism of both articles, see Sheldon Nahmod, Constitutional Damages and Corrective Justice: A Different View, 76 Va.L.Rev. 997 (1990). For further criticism of these views and a thoughtful argument for modified respondeat superior liability for government entities, see Harold S. Lewis, Jr. and Theodore Y. Blumoff, Reshaping Section 1983's Asymmetry, 140 U.Pa.L.Rev. 755 (1992).

Page 128, place the existing materials on governmental liability under the heading "SUBSECTION A: MUNICIPAL LIABILITY". Then add the following: *

SUBSECTION B: STATE LIABILITY

WILL v. MICHIGAN DEPARTMENT OF STATE POLICE
Supreme Court of the United States, 1989.
491 U.S. 58.

JUSTICE WHITE delivered the opinion of the Court.

This case presents the question whether a state, or an official of the state while acting in his or her official capacity, is a "person" within the meaning of 42 U.S.C. § 1983.

Petitioner Ray Will filed suit in Michigan Circuit Court alleging various violations of the United States and Michigan Constitutions as grounds for a claim under § 1983. He alleged that he had been denied a promotion to a data systems analyst position with the Department of State Police for an improper reason, that is, because his brother had been a student activist and the subject of a "red squad" file maintained by respondent. Named as defendants were the Department of State Police and the Director of State Police in his official capacity, also a respondent here.

The Circuit Court . . . concluded that petitioner had established a violation of the United States Constitution. . . . The judge also ruled that respondents were persons for purposes of § 1983. [The Michigan Supreme Court, however, determined] that the state itself is not a person under § 1983 [and] that a state official acting in his or her official capacity also is not such a person. . . .

Prior to Monell v. New York City Dept. of Social Services, 436 U.S. 658 (1978), the question whether a state is a person within the meaning of § 1983 had been answered by this Court in the negative. In Monroe

---

* This addition is provided as an alternative for those who wish to teach *Will* as a main case. Note treatment is given to the case at page 4 of this Supplement, supra.

v. Pape, 365 U.S. 167, 187–91 (1961), the Court had held that a municipality was not a person under § 1983. '[T]hat being the case," we reasoned, § 1983 "could not have been intended to include states as parties defendant." Fitzpatrick v. Bitzer, 427 U.S. 445, 452 (1976).

But in *Monell*, the Court overruled *Monroe*, holding that a municipality was a person under § 1983. Since then, various members of the Court have debated whether a state is a person within the meaning of § 1983, but this Court has never expressly dealt with that issue.[4]

Some courts, including the Michigan Supreme Court here, have construed our decision in Quern v. Jordan, 440 U.S. 332 (1979), as holding by implication that a state is not a person under § 1983. *Quern* held that § 1983 does not override a state's 11th amendment immunity. . . ..

Petitioner filed the present § 1983 action in Michigan state court, which places the question whether a state is a person under § 1983 squarely before us since the 11th amendment does not apply in state courts. For the reasons that follow, we reaffirm today what we had concluded prior to *Monell* and what some have considered implicit in *Quern:* that a state is not a person within the meaning of § 1983.

We observe initially that if a state is a "person" within the meaning of § 1983, the section is to be read as saying that "every person, including a State, who, under color of any statute, ordinance, regulation, custom or usage, of any State or Territory or the District of Columbia, subjects. . . ." This would be a decidedly awkward way of expressing an intent to subject the states to liability. At the very least, reading the statute in this way is not so clearly indicated that it provides reason to depart from the often-expressed understanding that " 'in common usage, the term 'person' does not include the sovereign, [and] statutes employing the [word] are ordinarily construed to exclude it.' " Wilson v. Omaha Indian Tribe, 442 U.S. 653, 667 (1979).

This approach is particularly applicable where it is claimed that Congress has subjected the states to liability to which they had not been subjected before. In *Wilson v. Omaha Indian Tribe,* supra, we followed this rule in construing the phrase "white person" contained in 25 U.S.C. § 194 as not including the "sovereign states of the Union." This

---

[4] Petitioner cites a number of cases from this Court that he asserts have "assumed" that a state is a person. Those cases include ones in which a state has been sued by name under § 1983, see, e.g., Maine v. Thiboutot, 448 U.S. 1 (1980). . . . But the Court did not address the meaning of person in any of those cases, and in none of the cases was resolution of that issue necessary to the decision. Petitioner's argument evidently rests on the proposition that whether a state is a person under § 1983 is "jurisdictional" and "thus could have been raised by the Court on its own motion" in those cases. Even assuming that petitioner's premise and characterization of the cases is correct, "this Court has never considered itself bound [by prior sub silentio holdings] when a subsequent case finally brings the jurisdictional issue before us." Hagans v. Levine, 415 U.S. 528, 535 n. 5 (1974).

common usage of the term "person" provides a strong indication that person as used in § 1983 likewise does not include a state.

The language of § 1983 also falls far short of satisfying the ordinary rule of statutory construction that if Congress intends to alter the "usual constitutional balance between the states and the federal government," it must make its intention to do so "unmistakably clear in the language of the statute." Atascadero State Hospital v. Scanlon, 473 U.S. 234, 242 (1985). *Atascadero* was an 11th amendment case, but a similar approach is applied in other contexts. Congress should make its intention "clear and manifest" if it intends to pre-empt the historic powers of the states, Rice v. Santa Fe Elevator Corp., 331 U.S. 218, 230 (1947), or if it intends to impose a condition on the grant of federal moneys, Pennhurst State School and Hospital v. Halderman, 451 U.S. 1, 16 (1981). "In traditionally sensitive areas, such as legislation affecting the federal balance, the requirement of clear statement assures that the legislature has in fact faced, and intended to bring into issue, the critical matters involved in the judicial decision." United States v. Bass, 404 U.S. 336, 349 (1971).

Our conclusion that a state is not a person within the meaning of § 1983 is reinforced by Congress' purpose in enacting the statute. Congress enacted § 1 of the Civil Rights Act of 1871, the precursor to § 1983, shortly after the end of the Civil War "in response to the widespread deprivations of civil rights in the southern states and the inability or unwillingness of authorities in those states to protect those rights or punish wrongdoers." Felder v. Casey, 487 U.S. 131, 147 (1988). Although Congress did not establish federal courts as the exclusive forum to remedy these deprivations, it is plain that "Congress assigned to the federal courts a paramount role" in this endeavor, Patsy v. Board of Regents of Florida, 457 U.S. 496, 503 (1982).

Section 1983 provides a federal forum to remedy many deprivations of civil liberties, but it does not provide a federal forum for litigants who seek a remedy against a state for alleged deprivations of civil liberties. The 11th amendment bars such suits unless the state has waived its immunity or unless Congress has exercised its undoubted power under § 5 of the 14th amendment to override that immunity. That Congress, in passing § 1983, had no intention to disturb the states' 11th amendment immunity and so to alter the federal-state balance in that respect was made clear in our decision in *Quern*. Given that a principal purpose behind the enactment of § 1983 was to provide a federal forum for civil rights claims, and that Congress did not provide such a federal forum for civil rights claims against states, we cannot accept petitioner's argument that Congress intended nevertheless to create a cause of action against states to be brought in state courts, which are precisely the courts Congress sought to allow civil rights claimants to avoid through § 1983.

This does not mean, as petitioner suggests, that we think that the scope of the 11th amendment and the scope of § 1983 are not separate issues. Certainly they are. But in deciphering congressional intent as to the scope of § 1983, the scope of the 11th amendment is a consideration, and we decline to adopt a reading of § 1983 that disregards it.

Our conclusion is further supported by our holdings that in enacting § 1983, Congress did not intend to override well established immunities or defenses under the common law. "One important assumption underlying the Court's decisions in this area is that members of the 42nd Congress were familiar with common law principles, including defenses previously recognized in ordinary tort litigation, and that they likely intended these common law principles to obtain, absent specific provisions to the contrary." Newport v. Fact Concerts, Inc., 453 U.S. 247, 258 (1981). . . . The doctrine of sovereign immunity was a familiar doctrine at common law. . . . We cannot conclude that § 1983 was intended to disregard the well established immunity of a state from being sued without its consent.[7]

The legislative history of § 1983 does not suggest a different conclusion. Petitioner contends that the congressional debates on § 1 of the 1871 Act indicate that § 1983 was intended to extend to the full reach of the 14th amendment and thereby to provide a remedy " 'against all forms of official violation of federally protected rights.' " He refers us to various parts of the vigorous debates accompanying the passage of § 1983 and revealing that it was the failure of the states to take appropriate action that was undoubtedly the motivating force behind § 1983. The inference must be drawn, it is urged, that Congress must have intended to subject the states themselves to liability. But the intent of Congress to provide a remedy for unconstitutional state action does not without more include the sovereign states among those persons against whom § 1983 actions would lie. Construing § 1983 as a remedy for "official violation of federally protected rights" does no more than confirm that the section is directed against state action—action "under color of" state law. It does not suggest that the state itself was a person that Congress intended to be subject to liability.

Although there were sharp and heated debates, the discussion of § 1 of the bill, which contained the present § 1983, was not extended. And although in other respects the impact on state sovereignty was much taked about, no one suggested that § 1 would subject the states themselves to a damages suit under federal law. There was

---

[7] Our recognition in Monell v. New York City Dept. of Social Services, 436 U.S. 658 (1978), that a municipality is a person under § 1983, is fully consistent with this reasoning. In Owen v. City of Independence, 445 U.S. 622 (1980), we noted that by the time of the enactment of § 1983, municipalities no longer retained the sovereign immunity they had previously shared with the states. . . .

complaint that § 1 would subject state officers to damages liability, but no suggestion that it would also expose the states themselves. We find nothing substantial in the legislative history that leads us to believe that Congress intended the word "person" in § 1983 included the states of the Union. And surely nothing in the debates rises to the clearly expressed legislative intent necessary to permit that construction.

Likewise, the "Dictionary Act," [8] on which we relied in *Monell*, does not counsel a contrary conclusion here. As we noted in *Quern*, that act, while adopted prior to § 1 of the Civil Rights Act of 1871, was adopted after § 2 of the Civil Rights Act of 1866, from which § 1 of the 1871 Act was derived. Moreover, we disagree with Justice Brennan that at the time the Dictionary Act was passed "the phrase 'bodies politic and corporate' was understood to include the states." Rather, an examination of authorities of the era suggests that the phrase was used to mean corporations, both private and public (municipal), and not to include the states.[9]

Finally, *Monell* itself is not to the contrary. True, prior to *Monell*, the Court had reasoned that if municipalities were not persons then surely states also were not. And *Monell* overruled *Monroe*, undercutting that logic. But it does not follow that if municipalities are persons then so are states. States are protected by the 11th amendment while municipalities are not, and we consequently limited our holding in *Monell* "to local government units which are not considered part of the state for 11th amendment purposes." Conversely, our holding here does not cast any doubt on *Monell*, and applies only to states or governmental entities that are considered "arms of the state" for 11th amendment purposes. See, e.g., Mt. Healthy City School District Board of Education v. Doyle, 429 U.S. 274, 280 (1977).

Petitioner asserts, alternatively, that state officials should be considered "persons" under § 1983 even though acting in their official capacities. In this case, petitioner named as defendant not only the Michigan Department of State Police but also the Director of State Police in his official capacity.

Obviously, state officials literally are persons. But a suit against a state official in his or her official capacity is not a suit against the official but rather is a suit against the official's office. As such, it is no different from a suit against the state itself. We see no reason to adopt a different rule in the present context, particularly when such a rule

---

[8] The Dictionary Act provided that:

"in all acts herafter passed . . . the word 'person' may extend and be applied to bodies politic and corporate . . . unless the context shows that such words were intended to be used in a more limited sense." Act of Feb. 25, 1871, § 2.

[9] [Justice White's extensive references to contemporary dictionaries are omitted. He concluded that Justice Brennan's citation of contrary authorities "at best suggest that the phrase is ambiguous, which still renders the Dictionary Act incapable of supplying the necessary clear intent."]

would allow petitioner to circumvent congressional intent by a mere pleading device.[10]

We hold that neither a state or its officials acting in their official capacities are "persons" under § 1983. The judgment of the Michigan Supreme Court is affirmed.

JUSTICE BRENNAN, with whom JUSTICE MARSHALL, JUSTICE BLACKMUN, and JUSTICE STEVENS join, dissenting.

Because this case was brought in state court, the Court concedes, the 11th amendment is inapplicable here. Like the guest who wouldn't leave, however, the 11th amendment lurks everywhere in today's decision and, in truth, determines its outcome.

I

Section 1 of the Civil Rights Act of 1871, 42 U.S.C. § 1983, renders certain "persons" liable for deprivations of constitutional rights. The question presented is whether the word "persons" in this statute includes the states and state officials acting in their official capacities.

One might expect that this statutory question would generate a careful and thorough analysis of the language, legislative history, and general background of § 1983. If this is what one expects, however, one will be disappointed by today's decision. For this case is not decided on the basis of our ordinary method of statutory construction; instead, the Court disposes of it by means of various rules of statutory interpretation that it summons to its aid each time the question looks close. Specifically, the Court invokes the following interpretative principles: the word "persons" is ordinarily construed to exclude the sovereign; congressional intent to affect the federal-state balance must be "clear and manifest"; and intent to abrogate the states 11th amendment immunity must appear in the language of the statute itself. The Court apparently believes that each of these rules obviates the need for close analysis of a statute's language and history. Properly applied, however, only the last of these interpretative principles has this effect, and that principle is not pertinent to the case before us.

The Court invokes, first, the "often expressed understanding" that " 'in common usage, the term "person" does not include the sovereign, [and] statutes employing the [word] are ordinarily construed to exclude it.' " . . . The idea that the word "persons" ordinarily excludes the sovereign can be traced to the "familiar principle that the King is not bound by any act of Parliament unless he be named therein by special

---

[10] Of course a state official in his or her official capacity, when sued for injunctive relief, would be a person under § 1983 because "official-capacity actions for prospective relief are not treated as actions against the state." Kentucky v. Graham, 473 U.S. 159, 167 n. 14 (1985); Ex parte Young, 209 U.S. 123 (1908). This distinction is "commonplace in sovereign immunity doctrine," L. Tribe, American Constitutional Law § 3–27, p. 190 n. 3 (2d ed. 1988), and would not have been foreign to the 19th-century Congress that enacted § 1983. . . .

and particular words." Dollar Savings Bank v. United States, 86 U.S. (19 Wall.) 227, 239 (1874). As this passage suggests, however, this interpretive principle applies only to "the enacting sovereign." United States v. California, 297 U.S. 175, 186 (1936). [Moreover, it] is merely "an aid to consistent construction of statutes of the enacting sovereign when their purpose is in doubt, but it does not require that the aim of a statute fairly to be inferred be disregarded because not explicitly stated." *United States v. California,* supra, at 186. . . .

The second interpretative principle that the Court invokes comes from cases . . . which require a "clear and manifest" expression of congressional intent to change some aspect of federal-state relations. These cases do not, however, permit substitution of an absolutist rule of statutory construction for thorough statutory analysis. Indeed, in each of these decisions the Court undertook a careful and detailed analysis of the statutory language and history under consideration. . . .

The only principle of statutory construction employed by the Court that would justify a perfunctory and inconclusive analysis of a statute's language and history is one that is irrelevant to this case. This is the notion "that if Congress intends to alter 'the usual constitutional balance between the states and the federal government,' it must make its intention to do so 'unmistakably clear in the language of the statute.'" Quoting Atascadero State Hospital v. Scanlon, 473 U.S. 234, 242 (1985). As the Court notes, *Atascadero* was an 11th amendment case; the "constitutional balance" to which *Atascadero* refers is that struck by the 11th amendment as this Court has come to interpret it. Although the Court apparently wishes it were otherwise, the principle of interpretation that *Atascadero* announced is unique to cases involving the 11th amendment.

Where the 11th amendment applies, the Court has devised a clear statement principle more robust than its requirement of clarity in any other situation. . . . Since this case was brought in state court, however, this strict drafting requirement has no application here. The 11th amendment can hardly be "a consideration" in a suit to which it does not apply.

That this Court has generated a uniquely daunting requirement of clarity in 11th amendment cases explains why Quern v. Jordan, 440 U.S. 332 (1979), did not decide the question before us today. Because only the 11th amendment permits use of this clear statement principle, the holding of *Quern v. Jordan* that § 1983 does not abrogate states' 11th amendment immunity tells us nothing about the meaning of the term "persons" in § 1983 as a matter of ordinary statutory construction. *Quern's* conclusion thus does not compel, or even suggest, a particular result today. . . .

In short, the only principle of statutory interpretation that permits the Court to avoid a careful and thorough analysis of § 1983's language and history is the clear statement principle that this Court has come to apply in 11th amendment cases—a principle that is irrelevant to this state court action. In my view, a careful and detailed analysis of § 1983 leads to the conclusion that states are "persons" within the meaning of that statute.

II

. . . Although § 1983 itself does not define the term "person," we are not without a statutory definition of this word. "Any analysis of the meaning of the word 'person' in § 1983 . . . must begin . . . with the Dictionary Act." Monell v. New York Dept. of Social Services, 436 U.S. 658, 719 (1978) (Rehnquist, J., dissenting). Passed just two months before § 1983, and designed to "suppl[y] rules of construction for all legislation," the Dictionary Act provided:

> "That in all acts hereafter passed . . . the word 'person' may extend and be applied to bodies politic and corporate . . . unless the context shows that such words were intended to be used in a more limited sense. . . ."

In *Monell*, we held this definition to be not merely allowable but mandatory, requiring that the word "person" be construed to include "bodies politic and corporate" unless the statute under consideration "by its terms called for a deviation from this practice." Thus, we concluded, where nothing in the "context" of a particular statute "call[s] for a restricted interpretation of the word 'person,' the language of that [statute] should prima facie be construed to include 'bodies politic' among the entities that could be sued."

Both before and after the time when the Dictionary Act and § 1983 were passed, the phrase "bodies politic and corporate" was understood to include the states. [Citations omitted.]

The reason why states are "bodies politic and corporate" is simple: just as a corporation is an entity that can act only through its agents, "[t]he state is a political corporate body, can act only through agents, and can command only by laws." Poindexter v. Greenhow, 114 U.S. 270, 288 (1885). As a "body politic and corporate," a state falls squarely within the Dictionary Act's definition of a "persons."

While it is certainly true that the phrase "bodies politic and corporate" referred to private and public corporations, this fact does not draw into question the conclusion that this phrase also applied to the states. Phrases may, of course, have multiple referents. Indeed, each and every dictionary cited by the Court accords a broader realm—one that comfortably, and in most cases explicitly, includes the sovereign— to this phrase than the Court gives it today. [Citations omitted.]

. . . The relevance of the fact that § 2 of the Civil Rights Act of 1866—the model for § 1 of the 1871 Act—was passed before the

Dictionary Act . . . eludes me. Congress chose to use the word "persons" in the 1871 Act even after it had passed the Dictionary Act, presumptively including "bodies politic and corporate" within the category of "persons." Its decision to do so—and its failure to indicate in the 1871 Act that the Dictionary Act's presumption was not to apply—demonstrate the Congress did indeed intend "persons" to include bodies politic and corporate. . . .

Thus, the question before us is whether the presumption that the word "persons" in § 1 of the Civil Rights Act of 1871 included bodies politic and corporate—and hence the states—is overcome by anything in the statute's language and history. Certainly nothing in the statutory language overrides this presumption. The statute is explicitly directed at action taken "under color of" state law, and thus supports rather than refutes the idea that the "persons" mentioned in the statute include the states. . . .

[The Court] asserts that reading "states" where the statute mentions "persons" would be "decidedly awkward." The Court does not describe the awkwardness that it perceives, but I take it that its objection is that the under-color-of-law requirement would be redundant if states were included in the state because states necessarily act under color of state law. But § 1983 extends as well to natural persons, who do not necessarily so act; in order to ensure that *they* would be liable only when they did so, the statute needed the under-color-of-law requirement. . . . Taking the example closest to this case, we might have observed in *Monell* that § 1983 was clumsily written if it included municipalities, since these, too, may act only under color of state authority. Nevertheless, we held there that the statute does apply to municipalities. . . .

The legislative history and background of the statute confirm that the presumption created by the Dictionary Act was not overridden in § 1 of the 1871 Act, and that, even without such a presumption, it is plain that "persons" in the 1871 Act must include the states. I discussed in detail the legislative history of this statute in my opinion concurring in the judgment in *Quern v. Jordan,* supra, at 358–65, and I shall not cover that ground again here. Suffice it to say that, in my view, the legislative history of this provision, though spare, demonstrates that Congress recognized and accepted the fact that the statute was directed at the states themselves. One need not believe that the statute satisfies this Court's heightened clear statement principle, reserved for 11th amendment cases, in order to conclude that the language and legislative history of § 1983 show that the word "persons" must include the states. . . .

III

To describe the breadth of the Court's holding is to demonstrate its unwisdom. If states are not "persons" within the meaning of § 1983, then they may not be sued under that statute regardless of whether they have consented to suit. Even if, in other words, a state formally and explicitly consented to suits against it in federal or state court, no § 1983 plaintiff could proceed against it because states are not within the statute's category of possible defendants.

This is indeed an exceptional holding. Not only does it depart from our suggestion in Alabama v. Pugh, 438 U.S. 781, 781 (1978), that a state could be a defendant under § 1983 if it consented to suit, but it also renders ineffective the choices some states have made to permit such suits against them. See, e.g., Della Grotta v. Rhode Island, 781 F.2d 343 (1st Cir. 1986). I do not understand what purpose is served, what principle of federalism or comity is promoted, by refusing to give force to a state's explicit consent to suit.

The Court appears to be driven to this peculiar result in part by its view that "in enacting § 1983, Congress did not intend to override well established immunities or defenses under the common law." But the question whether states are "persons" under § 1983 is separate and distinct from the question whether they may assert a defense of common law sovereign immunity. In our prior decisions involving common law immunities, we have not held that the existence of an immunity defense excluded the relevant state actor from the category of "persons" liable under § 1983, and it is a mistake to do so today. Such an approach entrenches the effect of common law immunity even where the immunity itself has been waived.

For my part, I would reverse the judgment below and remand for resolution of the question whether Michigan would assert common law sovereign immunity in defense to this suit and, if so, whether that assertion of immunity would preclude the suit.

Given the suggestion in the court below that Michigan enjoys no common law immunity for violations of its own constitution, there is certainly a possibility that that court would hold that the state also lacks immunity against § 1983 suits for violations of the federal Constitution. Moreover, even if that court decided that the state's waiver of immunity did not apply to § 1983 suits, there is a substantial question whether Michigan could so discriminate between virtually identical causes of action only on the ground that one was a state suit and the other a federal one. Cf. Testa v. Katt, 330 U.S. 386 (1947). Finally, even if both of these questions were resolved in favor of an immunity defense, there would remain the question whether it would be reasonable to attribute to Congress an intent to allow states to decide for themselves whether to take cognizance of § 1983 suits brought against them.

Because the court below disposed of the case on the ground that states were not "persons" within the meaning of § 1983, it did not pass upon these difficult and important questions. I therefore would remand this case to the state court to resolve these questions in the first instance.

JUSTICE STEVENS, dissenting.

Legal doctrines often flourish long after their raison d'etre has perished. The doctrine of sovereign immunity rests on the fictional premise that the "King can do no wrong." Even though the plot to assassinate James I in 1605, the execution of Charles I in 1649, and the Colonists' reaction to George III's stamp tax made rather clear the fictional character of the doctrine's underpinnings, British subjects found a gracious means of compelling the King to obey the law rather than simply repudiating the doctrine itself. They held his advisors and agents responsible.

In our administration of § 1983, we have also relied on fictions to protect the illusion that a sovereign state, absent consent, may not be held accountable for its delicts in federal court. Under a settled course of decision, in contexts ranging from school desegregation to the provision of public assistance benefits to the administration of prison systems and other state facilities, we have held the states liable under § 1983 for their constitutional violations through the artifice of naming a public officer as a nominal party. Once one strips away the 11th amendment overlay applied to actions in federal court, it is apparent that the Court in those cases has treated the state as the real party in interest both for the purposes of granting prospective and ancillary relief and of denying retroactive relief. When suit is brought in state court, where the 11th amendment is inapplicable, it follows that the state can be named directly as a party under § 1983.

An official capacity suit is the typical way in which we have held states responsible for their duties under federal law. Such a suit, we have explained, "'generally represent[s] only another way of pleading an action against an entity of which an officer is an agent.'" Kentucky v. Graham, 473 U.S. 159, 165 (1985) (quoting Monell v. New York City Dept. of Social Services, 436 U.S. 658, 690 n. 55 (1978)). In the peculiar 11th amendment analysis we have applied to such cases, we have recognized that an official capacity action is in reality always against the state and balanced interests to determine whether a particular type of relief is available. The Court has held that when a suit seeks equitable relief or money damages from a state officer for injuries suffered in the past, the interests in compensation and deterrence are insufficiently weighty to override the state's sovereign immunity. See Edelman v. Jordan, 415 U.S. 651, 668 (1974). On the other hand, although prospective relief awarded against a state officer also "implicate[s] 11th amendment concerns" the interests in "ending a continuing violation of state law" outweigh the interests in state sovereignty and justify an award under § 1983 of an injunction that operates against the state's officers or even directly against the state itself. See, e.g., Quern v. Jordan, 440 U.S. 332, 337 (1979); Milliken v. Bradley, 433 U.S. 267, 289 (1977).

In *Milliken v. Bradley*, for example, a unanimous Court upheld a federal court order requiring the state of Michigan to pay $5,800,000 to fund educational components in a desegregation decree. . . . Our treatment of states as "persons" under § 1983 is also exemplified by our decisions holding that ancillary relief, such as attorneys fees, may be awarded directly against the state. [See] Hutto v. Finney, 437 U.S. 678 (1978). . . .

The Civil Rights Act of 1871 was "intended to provide a remedy, to be broadly construed, against all forms of official violation of federally protected rights." *Monell*, supra, at 700–01. Our holdings that a § 1983 action can be brought against state officials in their official capacity for constitutional violations properly recognize and are faithful to that profound mandate. If prospective relief can be awarded against state officials under § 1983 and the state is the real party in interest in such suits, the state must be a "person" which can be held liable under § 1983. No other conclusion is available. Eleventh amendment principles may limit the state's capacity to be sued as such in federal court. But since those principles are not applicable to suits in state court, see Nevada v. Hall, 440 U.S. 410 (1979), there is no need to resort to the fiction of an official capacity suit and the state may and should be named directly as a defendant in a § 1983 action.

The Court concludes, however, that "a state official in his or her official capacity, when sued for injunctive relief, would be a person under § 1983," ante n. 10, while that same party sued in the same official capacity is not a person when the plaintiff seeks monetary relief. . . .

The Court having constructed an edifice for the purposes of the 11th amendment on the theory that the state is always the real party in interest in a § 1983 official capacity action against a state officer, I would think the majority would be impelled to conclude that the state is a "person" under § 1983. As Justice Brennan has demonstrated, there is also a compelling textual argument that states are parties under § 1983. In addition, the Court's construction draws an illogical distinction between wrongs committed by county or municipal officials on the one hand, and those committed by state officials on the other. Finally, there is no necessity to import into this question of statutory construction doctrine created to protect the fiction that one sovereign cannot be sued in the courts of another sovereign. Aside from all of these reasons, the Court's holding that a state is not a party under § 1983 departs from a long line of judicial authority based on exactly that premise.

I respectfully dissent.

NOTES ON *WILL v. MICHIGAN DEPARTMENT OF STATE POLICE*

1. **Questions and Comments.** Justice Brennan's rationale leads, as he recognizes, to the issue whether a state could assert an immunity grounded in *state* law to a § 1983 damages suit filed in state court. Would it have provided better support for the majority result if the Court had held states and state officials acting in their official capacity to be "persons" under § 1983, but then had left to state law whether an immunity defense could be raised to a damages action? Would such an approach make better sense of the injunction cases? How else can the Court's footnote 10 be reconciled with the reasoning of *Will*? Is it enough that the damages-injunction distinction is "commonplace in sovereign immunity doctrine"?

For an analysis using *Will* as the basis for explicating legal pragmatism, see Gene R. Shreve, Symmetries of Access in Civil Rights Litigation: Politics, Pragmatism, and *Will*, 66 Ind.L.J. 1 (1990). For an article by the professor who argued *Will* lamenting the result in that case, see William Burnham and Michael C. Fayz, The State as a "Non-Person" Under Section 1983: Some Comments on *Will* and Suggestions for the Future, 70 Ore.L.Rev. 1 (1991).

2. **Territories as "Persons":** *Ngiraingas v. Sanchez.* The question in Ngiraingas v. Sanchez, 495 U.S. 182 (1990), was whether the territory of Guam and its officers acting in their official capacities were "persons" within § 1983. For the Court, Justice Blackmun found "no sign" in the legislative history "that Congress was thinking of territories when it enacted the statute over a century ago in 1871." Moreover, when the statute was amended in 1874 to cover actions taken under color of a territorial law, Congress in contemporaneous legislation "pointedly redefined the word 'person' to make it clear that a territory would not be included."

Justice Brennan, joined by Justice Marshall, disagreed.[a] He read the legislative history differently and found Congress' redefinition of the term "person" in 1874 less than clear. Justice Brennan also found the reasoning of *Will* inapplicable because "territories have never possessed the type of immunity thought to be enjoyed by states." He concluded:

[a] Justice Kennedy did not participate. Justice Scalia declined to join that part of Justice Blackmun's opinion that relied on legislative history.

"The Court in *Will* reasoned that Congress would not have abrogated state sovereign immunity, exemplified by the 11th amendment, without a clearer statement of its intent to do so; today, the Court finds that a territory lacking such sovereign immunity, either under the common law or by congressional grace, is not a 'person' either. These conclusions are in tension. To the extent that our decision in *Will* reasoned that states are not 'persons' within the meaning of § 1983 because Congress *presumably* would not have abrogated state sovereign immunity without a clear statement of its intent to do so, the *opposite* presumption should control this case: because Congress has such plenary legal authority over a territory's affairs and because a territory can assert no immunity against the laws of Congress (except insofar as Congress itself grants immunity), we ought to *presume* that territories are 'persons' for purposes of § 1983."

3. State Officials as "Persons" When Acting in Official Capacity: *Hafer v. Melo.* Shortly after her election as Auditor General of Pennsylvania, Hafer discharged Melo and a number of other public employees. The employees sued under § 1983, seeking reinstatement and damages. The District Court dismissed the § 1983 claims because it read *Will* to preclude liability for employment decisions taken in Hafer's official capacity as Auditor General. The Circuit Court reversed, and the Supreme Court granted certiorari in Hafer v. Melo, ___ U.S. ___ (1991), "to address the question whether state officers may be held personally liable for damages under § 1983 based upon actions taken in their official capacities."

Justice O'Connor wrote the opinion for a unanimous Court (Justice Thomas not participating). She began by emphasizing the distinction between "personal capacity" and "official capacity" suits:

"In Kentucky v. Graham, 473 U.S. 159 (1985), the Court sought to eliminate lingering confusion about the distinction between personal- and official-capacity suits. We emphasized that official-capacity suits ' "generally represent only another way of pleading an action against an entity of which an officer is an agent." ' Id., at 165. A suit against a state official in her official capacity therefore should be treated as a suit against the state. Indeed, when an official sued in this capacity in federal court dies or leaves office, her successor automatically assumes her role in the litigation. Because the real party in interest in an official-capacity suit is the governmental entity and not the named official, 'the entity's "policy or custom" must have played a part in the violation of federal law.' *Graham*, supra, at 166. For the same reason, the only immunities available to the defendant in an official-capacity action are those that the governmental entity possesses.

"Personal-capacity suits, on the other hand, seek to impose individual liability upon a government officer for actions taken under color of state law. Thus, '[o]n the merits, to establish personal liability in a § 1983 action, it is enough to show that the official, acting under color of state law, caused the deprivation of a federal right.' Id., at 166. While the plaintiff in a personal-capacity suit need not establish a connection to governmental 'policy or custom,' officials sued in their personal capacities, unlike those sued in their official capacities, may assert personal immunity defenses such as objectively reasonable reliance on existing law." [b]

Justice O'Connor then turned to the defendant's argument based on *Will*:

"*Will* itself makes clear that the distinction between official-capacity suits and personal-capacity suits is more than 'a mere pleading device.' State officers sued for damages in their official capacity are not 'persons' for purposes of the suit because they assume the identity of the government that employs them. By contrast, officers sued in their personal capacity come to court as individuals. A government official in the role of personal-capacity defendant thus fits comfortably within the statutory term 'person.' Cf. [footnote 10 in *Will*] ('[A] state official in his or her official capacity, when sued for injunctive relief, would be a person under § 1983 because "official-capacity actions for prospective relief are not treated as actions against the State" ').

"Hafer seeks to overcome the distinction between official- and personal-capacity suits by arguing that § 1983 liability turns not on the capacity in which state officials are sued, but on the capacity in which they acted when injuring the plaintiff. Under *Will*, she asserts, state officials may not be held liable in their personal capacity for actions they take in their official capacity. Although one Court of Appeals has endorsed this view, we find it both unpersuasive as an interpretation of § 1983 and foreclosed by our prior decisions.

"Through § 1983, Congress sought 'to give a remedy to parties deprived of constitutional rights, privileges and immunities by an official's abuse of his position.' Monroe v. Pape, 365 U.S. 167, 172 (1961). Accordingly, it authorized suits to

---

[b] The Circuit Court characterized the claims as having been filed against the defendant in her "personal capacity." It did so based on inferences from the nature of the proceedings in the District Court. The Supreme Court noted that several circuits "adhere to this practice," while others "impose a more rigid pleading requirement." The Court then said: "Because this issue is not properly before us, we simply reiterate the Third Circuit's view that '[i]t is obviously preferable for the plaintiff to be specific in the first instance to avoid any ambiguity.' "

redress deprivations of civil rights by persons acting 'under color of any [state] statute, ordinance, regulation, custom, or usage.' 42 U.S.C. § 1983. The requirement of action under color of state law means that Hafer may be liable for discharging respondents precisely because of her authority as Auditor General. We cannot accept the novel proposition that this same official authority insulates Hafer from suit."

The defendant, Justice O'Connor noted, sought to limit the scope of her argument by distinguishing between acts "taken outside the official's authority or not essential to the operation of state government" and those "both within the official's authority and necessary to the performance of governmental functions." The defendant characterized her actions as falling within the latter category and argued that acts of this sort should be considered acts of the state and beyond the reach of § 1983.

The Court disagreed. It found the effort to draw such lines inconsistent with the text and intent of § 1983 and with the Court's prior immunity decisions:

> "Her theory would absolutely immunize state officials from personal liability for acts within their authority and necessary to fulfilling governmental responsibilities. Yet our cases do not extend absolute immunity to all officers who engage in necessary official acts. . . . This Court has refused to extend absolute immunity beyond a very limited class of officials, including the President of the United States, legislators carrying out their legislative functions, and judges carrying out their judicial functions, 'whose special functions or constitutional status requires complete protection from suit.' Harlow v. Fitzgerald, 457 U.S. 800, 807 (1982). State executive officials are not entitled to absolute immunity for their official actions. In several instances, moreover, we have concluded that no more than a qualified immunity attaches to administrative employment decisions, even if the same official has absolute immunity when performing other functions. See [, e.g.,] Forrester v. White, 484 U.S. 219 (1988) (dismissal of court employee by state judge). That Hafer may assert personal immunity within the framework of these cases in no way supports her argument here."

The Court accordingly concluded as follows:

> "We hold that state officials, sued in their individual capacities, are 'persons' within the meaning of § 1983. The 11th amendment does not bar such suits,[c] nor are state officers

---

[c] The defendant also argued that "imposing personal liability on officeholders may infringe on state sovereignty by rendering government less effective" and that therefore "the 11th amendment forbids personal-capacity suits against state officials in

absolutely immune from personal liability under § 1983 solely by virtue of the 'official' nature of their acts."

All clear now?

Page 145, add a footnote at the end of Note 2:

ᵃ For commentary on an analogous problem, see Barbara Kritchevsky, The Availability of a Federal Remedy Under 42 U.S.C. § 1983 for Prosecution Under an Unconstitutional State Statute: The Sixth Circuit Struggles in *Richardson v. City of South Euclid,* 22 U.Tol.L.Rev. 303 (1991).

Page 145, add a new Note 2a:

2a. *Siegert v. Gilley. Paul* was followed in Siegert v. Gilley, ___ U.S. ___ (1991). Siegert was a clinical psychologist who resigned from a government hospital to avoid being fired. He then sought employment at a U.S. Army hospital in West Germany, but was turned down because of a bad recommendation from his former supervisor, who described the psychologist as "both inept and unethical, perhaps the least trustworthy individual I have supervised in my 13 years" on the job. Siegert then filed a *Bivens* suit claiming that the supervisor had "maliciously and in bad faith published a defamatory per se statement . . . which [he] knew to be untrue, or with reckless disregard as to whether it was true or not."

The case came to the Supreme Court as a dispute over qualified immunity (see *Harlow v. Fitzgerald,* Casebook page 32), but the Court held that Siegert had not alleged any violation of constitutional rights. Speaking through Chief Justice Rehnquist, the majority cited *Paul* for the proposition that defamation was not a constitutional violation, even if the defendant, as was alleged here, acted with "malice." Justice Marshall, joined by Justices Blackmun and Stevens, argued that *Paul* was inapplicable, because Siegert had not suffered merely injury to reputation, but also loss of eligibility for future government employment. "It is a perverse jurisprudence," Marshall concluded, "that recognizes the loss of a 'legal' right to buy liquor as a significant deprivation but fails to accord equal significance to the foreclosure of opportunities for government employment."

Page 145, add a new Note:

4. *DeShaney v. Winnebago County Dept. of Social Services.* The Court was presented with another controversial determination of federal court." The Court would have none of this either. The argument could not be based on *Will,* and moreover was inconsistent, in the Court's view, with applicable 11th amendment precedent. The Court added: "To be sure, imposing personal liability on state officers may hamper their performance of public duties. But such concerns are properly addressed within the framework of our personal immunity jurisprudence. Insofar as respondents seek damages against Hafer personally, the 11th amendment does not restrict their ability to sue in federal court."

the content of "liberty" in its decision in what has come to be known as the "Poor Joshua" case,[a] DeShaney v. Winnebago County Dept. of Social Services, 489 U.S. 189 (1989). Joshua was four years old when he was beaten so severely by his father that he fell into a coma, required brain surgery, and was left with "brain damage so severe that he is expected to spend the rest of his life confined to an institution for the profoundly retarded." He had been the victim of repeated abuse following the time 26 months earlier when a complaint was first filed on his behalf to the county social service authorities. There were at least three hospitalizations and numerous other suspected injuries during this period and, though some efforts were made to create a more protective home environment, the authorities refused coercive intervention. Joshua and his mother[b] brought a § 1983 action in federal court against the county, its department of social services, and various department officials. The complaint "alleged that respondents had deprived Joshua of his liberty without due process of law, in violation of his rights under the 14th amendment, by failing to intervene to protect him against a risk of violence at his father's hands of which they knew or should have known." The District Court granted summary judgment for the defendants and the Court of Appeals affirmed. The Supreme Court also affirmed.

Though describing the facts as "undeniably tragic," Chief Justice Rehnquist's opinion for the Court held:

> "[N]othing in the language of the due process clause itself requires the state to protect the life, liberty, and property of its citizens against invasion by private actors. The clause is phrased as a limitation on the state's power to act, not as a guarantee of certain minimum levels of safety and security. It forbids the state itself to deprive individuals of life, liberty, or property without 'due process of law,' but its language cannot fairly be extended to impose an affirmative obligation on the state to ensure that those interests do not come to harm through other means. . . . Its purpose was to protect the people from the state, not to ensure that the state protected them from each other. The framers were content to leave the extent of governmental obligation in the latter area to the democratic political processes. . . . As a general matter, then, we conclude that a state's failure to protect an individual against private violence simply does not constitute a violation of the due process clause."[c]

[a] The phrase comes from the last paragraph of Justice Blackmun's dissent, which begins: "Poor Joshua! Victim of repeated attacks by an irresponsible, bullying, cowardly, and intemperate father . . . ."

[b] Joshua's parents were divorced in Wyoming. Custody was awarded to the father, who later moved to Wisconsin, remarried, and was again divorced. The father was tried and convicted of child abuse.

[c] The Chief Justice had previously noted that the claim was "one invoking the substantive rather than the procedural component of the due process clause; petitioners

It was argued that a duty to protect "may arise out of certain 'special relationships' created or assumed by the state with respect to particular individuals." The Court granted as much. Prior cases had held, for example, that such duties arose with respect to persons in prison or involuntarily committed:

> "But these cases afford petitioners no help. Taken together, they stand only for the proposition that when the state takes a person into its custody and holds him there against his will, the Constitution imposes upon it a corresponding duty to assume some responsibility for his safety and general well-being. The rationale for this principle is simple enough: when the state by the affirmative exercise of its power so restrains an individual's liberty that it renders him unable to care for himself, and at the same time fails to provide for his basic human needs—e.g., food, clothing, shelter, medical care, and reasonable safety—it transgresses the substantive limits on state action set by the eighth amendment and the due process clause. The affirmative duty to protect arises not from the state's knowledge of the individual's predicament or from its expressions of intent to help him, but from the limitation which it has imposed on his freedom to act on his own behalf. In the substantive due process analysis, it is the state's affirmative act of restraining the individual's freedom to act on his own behalf—through incarceration, institutionalization, or other similar restraint of personal liberty—which is the 'deprivation of liberty' triggering the protections of the due process clause, not its failure to act to protect his liberty interests against harms inflicted by other means."

The Chief Justice then concluded:

> "Judges and lawyers, like other humans, are moved by natural sympathy in a case like this to find a way for Joshua and his mother to receive adequate compensation for the grievous harm inflicted upon them. But before yielding to that impulse, it is well to remember once again that the harm was inflicted not by the state of Wisconsin, but by Joshua's father. The most that can be said of the state functionaries in this case is that they stood by and did nothing when suspicious circumstances dictated a more active role for them. In defense of them it must also be said that had they moved too soon to take custody of the son away from the father, they would likely have been met with charges of improperly intruding into the parent-child relationship, charges based on the same due pro-

---

do not claim that the state denied Joshua protection without according him appropriate procedural safeguards, but that it was categorically obligated to protect him in these circumstances."

cess clause that forms the basis for the present charge of failure to provide adequate protection.

"The people of Wisconsin may well prefer a system of liability which would place upon the state and its officials the responsibility for failure to act in situations such as the present one. They may create such a system, if they do not have it already, by changing the tort law of the state in accordance with the regular law-making process. But they should not have it thrust upon them by this Court's expansion of the due process clause of the 14th amendment." [d]

Justice Brennan, joined by Justices Marshall and Blackmun, dissented. Justice Brennan stated that he "would focus first on the action that Wisconsin *has* taken with respect to Joshua and children like him, rather than on the actions that the state had failed to take." From this perspective, he extracted from the prison and involuntary commitment cases the principle that "if a state cuts off private sources of aid and then refuses aid itself, it cannot wash its hands of the harm that results from its inaction." Here the state had "cut off private sources of aid" by monopolizing the path of relief open to persons in Joshua's situation:

"In these circumstances, a private citizen, or even a person working in a government agency other than [the Department of Social Services (DSS)], would doubtless feel that her job was done as soon as she had reported her suspicions of child abuse to DSS. Through its child-welfare program, in other words, the state of Wisconsin has relieved ordinary citizens and governmental bodies other than the department of any sense of obligation to do anything more than report their suspicions of child abuse to DSS. If DSS ignores or dismisses these suspicions, no one will step in to fill the gap. Wisconsin's child-protection program thus effectively confined Joshua DeShaney within the walls of Randy DeShaney's violent home until such time as DSS took action to remove him. Conceivably, then, children like Joshua are made worse off by the existence of this program when the persons and entities charged with carrying it out fail to do their jobs.

"It simply belies reality, therefore, to contend that the state 'stood by and did nothing' with respect to Joshua. Through its child-protection program, the state actively inter-

---

[d] Chief Justice Rehnquist added in a footnote:

"Petitioners also argue that the Wisconsin child protection statutes gave Joshua an 'entitlement' to receive protective services in accordance with the terms of the statute, an entitlement which would enjoy due process protection against state deprivation under our decision in Board of Regents v. Roth, 408 U.S. 564 (1972). But this argument is made for the first time in petitioners' brief to this Court: it was not pleaded in the complaint, argued to the Court of Appeals as a ground for reversing the District Court, or raised in the petition for certiorari. We therefore decline to consider it here."

vened in Joshua's life and, by virtue of this intervention, acquired even more certain knowledge that Joshua was in grave danger. These circumstances, in my view, plant this case solidly within the tradition of cases like [those governing prisons and involuntary commitments]."

Justice Brennan added that liability could not be found in cases where the failure to intervene resulted from "the sound exercise of professional judgment," but required a level of "arbitrariness that we have in the past condemned." "Moreover," he continued, "that the due process clause is not violated by merely negligent conduct, see Daniels v. Williams, 474 U.S. 327 (1986), and Davidson v. Cannon, 474 U.S. 344 (1986), means that a social worker who simply makes a mistake of judgment under what are admittedly complex and difficult conditions will not find herself liable in damages under § 1983." [e]

Page 146, substitute for pages 146–64:

ZINERMON v. BURCH
Supreme Court of the United States, 1990.
494 U.S. 113.

JUSTICE BLACKMUN delivered the opinion of the Court.

I

Respondent Darrell Burch brought this suit under 42 U.S.C. § 1983 against the 11 petitioners, who are physicians, administrators, and staff members at Florida State Hospital (FSH) in Chattahoochee, and others. Respondent alleges that petitioners deprived him of his liberty, without due process of law, by admitting him to FSH as a "voluntary" mental patient when he was incompetent to give informed consent to his

---

[e] For critical commentary on *DeShaney*, see Jack M. Beerman, Administrative Failure and Local Democracy: The Politics of *DeShaney*, 1990 Duke L.J. 1078 (1990) (exploring the normative basis for a constitutional obligation on government to protect the weak and helpless); Karen M. Blum, *Monell*, *DeShaney*, and *Zinermon*: Official Policy, Affirmative Duty, Established State Procedure and Local Government Liability under Section 1983, 24 Creighton L.Rev. 1 (1990) (examining the impact of *DeShaney* on substantive due process claims against local governments); Thomas Eaton and Michael Wells, Government Inaction as a Constitutional Tort: *DeShaney* and its Aftermath, 66 Wash.L.Rev. 107 (1991) (arguing that the decision does not categorically bar affirmative obligations on government but invites attention to the state's role in putting the individual at risk); Steven J. Heyman, The First Duty of Government: Protection, Liberty and the Fourteenth Amendment, 41 Duke L.J. 507 (1991) (challenging "the reasoning at the core of *DeShaney*"); James T.R. Jones, Battered Spouses' Section 1983 Damage Actions Against the Unresponsive Police after *DeShaney*, 93 W.Va.L.Rev. 251 (1990–91) (discussing the impact of *DeShaney* on damage suits by abused spouses against the police); Laura Oren, the State's Failure to Protect Children and Substantive Due Process: *DeShaney* in Context, 68 N.C.L.Rev. 659 (1990) (the "context" in which Oren places *DeShaney* is that of family violence and child protection, viewed partly from a feminist perspective). For an effort to reorient thinking about the *DeShaney* problem towards the 13th amendment, see Akhil Amar and Daniel Widawsky, Child Abuse as Slavery: A Thirteenth Amendment Response to *DeShaney*, 105 Harv.L.Rev. 1359 (1992).

admission. Burch contends that in his case petitioners should have afforded him procedural safeguards required by the Constitution before involuntary commitment of a mentally ill person, and that petitioners' failure to do so violated his due process rights.

Petitioners argue that Burch's complaint failed to state a claim under § 1983 because, in their view, it alleged only a random, unauthorized violation of the Florida statutes governing admission of mental patients. Their argument rests on Parratt v. Taylor, 451 U.S. 527 (1981), and Hudson v. Palmer, 468 U.S. 517 (1984), where this Court held that a deprivation of a constitutionally protected property interest caused by a state employee's random, unauthorized conduct does not give rise to a § 1983 procedural due process claim, unless the state fails to provide an adequate postdeprivation remedy. The Court in those two cases reasoned that in a situation where the state cannot predict and guard in advance against a deprivation, a postdeprivation tort remedy is all the process the state can be expected to provide, and is constitutionally sufficient.

[The District Court granted petitioners' motion to dismiss], pointing out that Burch did not contend that Florida's statutory procedure for mental health placement was inadequate to ensure due process, but only that petitioners failed to follow the state procedure. Since the state could not have anticipated or prevented this unauthorized deprivation of Burch's liberty, the District Court reasoned, there was no feasible predeprivation remedy, and, under *Parratt* and *Hudson,* the state's postdeprivation tort remedies provided Burch with all the process that was due him.

On appeal, an 11th Circuit panel affirmed the dismissal [but after a rehearing en banc the Court of Appeals] reversed the District Court, and remanded the case. . . . This Court granted certiorari to resolve the conflict—so evident in the divided views of the judges of the 11th Circuit—that has arisen in the Court of Appeals over the proper scope of the *Parratt* rule.

Because this case concerns the propriety of a [motion to dismiss], the question before us is a narrow one. We decide only whether the *Parratt* rule necessarily means that Burch's complaint fails to allege any deprivation of due process, because he was constitutionally entitled to nothing more than what he received—an opportunity to sue petitioners in tort for his allegedly unlawful confinement. The broader questions of what procedural safeguards the due process clause requires in the context of an admission to a mental hospital, and whether Florida's statutes meet these constitutional requirements, are not presented in this case. Burch did not frame his action as a challenge to the constitutional adequacy of Florida's mental health statutes. Both before the 11th Circuit and in his brief here, he disavowed any challenge to the statutes themselves, and restricted his claim to the contention that petitioners' failure to provide constitutionally adequate safeguards in his case violated his due process rights.[3]

II

A

For purposes of review of a [motion to dismiss], the factual allegations of Burch's complaint are taken as true. Burch's complaint, and the medical records and forms attached to it as exhibits, provide the following factual background:

On December 7, 1981, Burch was found wandering along a Florida highway, appearing to be hurt and disoriented. He was taken to Apalachee Community Mental Health Services (ACMHS) in Tallahassee. ACMHS is a private mental health care facility designated by the state to receive patients suffering from mental illness. Its staff in their evaluation forms stated that, upon his arrival at ACMHS, Burch was hallucinating, confused, psychotic, and believed he was "in heaven." His face and chest were bruised and bloodied, suggesting that he had fallen or had been attacked. Burch was asked to sign forms giving his consent to admission and treatment. He did so. He remained at ACMHS for three days, during which time the facility's staff diagnosed his condition as paranoid schizophrenia and gave him psychotropic medication. On December 10, the staff found that Burch was "in need of longer-term stabilization" and referred him to FSH, a public hospital owned and operated by the state as a mental health treatment facility. Later that day, Burch signed forms requesting admission and authorizing treatment at FSH. He was then taken to FSH by a county sheriff.

Upon his arrival at FSH, Burch signed other forms for voluntary admission and treatment. One form, entitled "Request for Voluntary Admission," recited that the patient requests admission for "observation, diagnosis, care and treatment of [my] mental condition," and that the patient, if admitted, agrees "to accept such treatment as may be prescribed by members of the medical and psychiatric staff in accordance with the provisions of expressed and informed consent." Two of the petitioners, Janet V. Potter and Marjorie R. Parker, signed this

---

[3] Inasmuch as Burch does not claim that he was deprived of due process by an established state procedure, our decision in Logan v. Zimmerman Brush Co., 455 U.S. 422 (1982), is not controlling. In that case, the plaintiff challenged not a state official's error in implementing state law, but "the 'established state procedure' that destroys his entitlement without according him proper procedural safeguards."

Burch apparently concedes that, if Florida's statutes were strictly complied with, no deprivation of liberty without due process would occur. If only those patients who are competent to consent to admission are allowed to sign themselves in as "voluntary" patients, then they would not be deprived of any liberty interest at all. And if all other patients—those who are incompetent and those who are unwilling to consent to admission—are afforded the protections of Florida's involuntary placement procedures, they would be deprived of their liberty only after due process.

form as witnesses. Potter is an accredited records technician; Parker's job title does not appear on the form.

On December 23, Burch signed a form entitled "Authorization for Treatment." This form stated that he authorized "the professional staff of [FSH] to administer treatment, except electroconvulsive treatment"; that he had been informed of "the purpose of treatment; common side effects thereof; alternative treatment modalities; approximate length of care," and of his power to revoke consent to treatment; and that he had read and fully understood the authorization. Petitioner Zinermon, a staff physician at FSH, signed the form as the witness.

On December 10, Doctor Zinermon wrote a "progress note" indicating that Burch was "refusing to cooperate," would not answer questions, "appears distressed and confused," and "related that medication has been helpful." A nursing assessment form dated December 11 stated that Burch was confused and unable to state the reason for his hospitalization and still believed that "[t]his is heaven." Petitioner Zinermon on December 29 made a further report on Burch's condition, stating that, on admission, Burch had been "disoriented, semi-mute, confused and bizarre in appearance and thought . . . not cooperative to the initial interview," and "extremely psychotic, appeared to be paranoid and hallucinating." The doctor's report also stated that Burch remained disoriented, delusional, and psychotic.

Burch remained at FSH until May 7, 1982, five months after his initial admission to ACMHS. During that time, no hearing was held regarding his hospitalization and treatment.

After his release, Burch complained that he had been admitted inappropriately to FSH and did not remember signing a voluntary admission form. His complaint reached the Florida Human Rights Advocacy Committee of the state's Department of Health and Rehabilitation Services. The committee investigated and replied to Burch by letter dated April 4, 1984. The letter stated that Burch in fact had signed a voluntary admission form, but that there was "documentation that you were heavily medicated and disoriented on admission and . . . you were probably not competent to be signing legal documents." The letter also stated that, at a meeting of the committee with FSH staff on August 4, 1983, "hospital administration was made aware that they were very likely asking medicated clients to make decisions at a time when they were not mentally competent."

In February 1985, Burch filed a complaint in the United States District Court for the Northern District of Florida. He alleged, among other things, that ACMHS and the 11 individual petitioners, acting under color of Florida law, and "by and through the authority of their respective positions as employees at FSH . . . as part of their regular and official employment at FSH, took part in admitting plaintiff to FSH as a 'voluntary' patient." Specifically, he alleged:

"Defendants, and each of them, knew or should have known that plaintiff was incapable of voluntary, knowing, understanding and informed consent to admission and treatment at FSH. Nonetheless, defendants, and each of them, seized plaintiff and against plaintiff's will confined and imprisoned him and subjected him to involuntary commitment and treatment for the period from December 10, 1981, to May 7, 1982. For said period of 149 days, plaintiff was without the benefit of counsel and no hearing of any sort was held at which he could have challenged his involuntary admission and treatment at FSH.

". . . Defendants, and each of them, deprived plaintiff of his liberty without due process of law in contravention of the 14th amendment to the United States Constitution. Defendants acted with willful, wanton and reckless disregard of and indifference to plaintiff's Constitutionally guaranteed right to due process of law."

B

Burch's complaint thus alleges that he was admitted and detained at FSH for five months under Florida's statutory provisions for "voluntary" admission. These provisions are part of a comprehensive statutory scheme under which a person may be admitted to a mental hospital in several different ways.

First, Florida provides for short-term emergency admission. If there is reason to believe that a person is mentally ill and likely "to injure himself or others" or is in "need of care or treatment and lacks sufficient capacity to make a responsible application on his own behalf," he may immediately be detained for up to 48 hours. A mental health professional, a law enforcement officer, or a judge may effect an emergency admission. After 48 hours, the patient is to be released unless he "voluntarily gives express and informed consent to evaluation or treatment," or a proceeding for court-ordered evaluation or involuntary placement is initiated.

Second, under a court order a person may be detained at a mental health facility for up to five days for evaluation, if he is likely "to injure himself or others" or if he is in "need of care or treatment which, if not provided, may result in neglect or refusal to care for himself and . . . such neglect or refusal poses a real and present threat of substantial harm to his well-being." Anyone may petition for a court-ordered evaluation of a person alleged to meet these criteria. After five days, the patient is to be released unless he gives "express and informed consent" to admission and treatment, or unless involuntary placement proceedings are initiated.

Third, a person may be detained as an involuntary patient, if he meets the same criteria as for evaluation, and if the facility administrator and two mental health professionals recommend involuntary placement. Before involuntary placement, the patient has a right to notice, a judicial hearing, appointed counsel, access to medical records and personnel, and an independent expert examination. If the court determines that the patient meets the criteria for involuntary placement, it then decides whether the patient is competent to consent to treatment. If not, the court appoints a guardian advocate to make treatment decisions. After six months, the facility must either release the patient, or seek a court order for continued placement by stating the reasons therefor, summarizing the patient's treatment to that point, and submitting a plan for future treatment.

Finally, a person may be admitted as a voluntary patient. Mental hospitals may admit for treatment any adult "making application by express and informed consent," if he is "found to show evidence of mental illness and to be suitable for treatment." "Express and informed consent" is defined as "consent voluntarily given in writing after sufficient explanation and disclosure . . . to enable the person . . . to make a knowing and willful decision without any element of force, fraud, deceit, duress, or other form of constraint or coercion." A voluntary patient may request discharge at any time. If he does, the facility administrator must either release him within three days, or initiate the involuntary placement process. At the time of his admission and each six months thereafter, a voluntary patient and his legal guardian or representatives must be notified in writing of the right to apply for a discharge.

Burch, in apparent compliance with [the Florida statutes], was admitted by signing forms applying for voluntary admission. He alleges, however, that petitioners violated this statute in admitting him as a voluntary patient, because they knew or should have known that he was incapable of making an informed decision as to his admission. He claims that he was entitled to receive the procedural safeguards provided by Florida's involuntary placement procedure, and that petitioners violated his due process rights by failing to initiate this procedure. The question presented is whether these allegations suffice to state a claim under § 1983, in light of *Parratt* and *Hudson*.

III

A

To understand the background against which this question arises, we return to the interpretation of § 1983 articulated in Monroe v. Pape, 365 U.S. 167 (1961). In *Monroe,* this Court rejected the view that § 1983 applies only to violations of constitutional rights that are authorized by state law, and does not reach abuses of state authority that are forbidden by the state's statutes or Constitution, or are torts under the state's common law. It explained that § 1983 was intended not only to "override" discriminatory or otherwise unconstitutional state laws, and to provide a remedy for violations of civil rights "where state law was inadequate," but also to provide a federal remedy "where the state remedy, though adequate in theory, was not available in practice." The Court said:

> "It is no answer that the state has a law which if enforced would give relief. The federal remedy is supplementary to the state remedy, and the latter need not be first sought and refused before the federal one is invoked."

Thus, overlapping state remedies are generally irrelevant to the question of the existence of a cause of action under § 1983. A plaintiff, for example, may bring a § 1983 action for an unlawful search and seizure despite the fact that the search and seizure violated the state's Constitution or statutes, and despite the fact that there are common-law remedies for trespass and conversion. . . .

This general rule applies in a straightforward way to two of the three kinds of § 1983 claims that may be brought against the state under the due process clause of the 14th amendment. First, the clause incorporates many of the specific protections defined in the Bill of Rights. A plaintiff may bring suit under § 1983 for state officials' violation of his rights to, e.g., freedom of speech or freedom from unreasonable searches and seizures. Second, the due process clause contains a substantive component that bars certain arbitrary, wrongful government actions "regardless of the fairness of the procedures used to implement them." Daniels v. Williams, 474 U.S. 327, 331 (1986). As to these two types of claims, the constitutional violation actionable under § 1983 is complete when the wrongful action is taken. A plaintiff, under *Monroe v. Pape,* may invoke § 1983 regardless of any state-tort remedy that might be available to compensate him for the deprivation of these rights.

The due process clause also encompasses a third type of protection, a guarantee of fair procedure. A § 1983 action may be brought for a violation of procedural due process, but here the existence of state remedies is relevant in a special sense. In procedural due process claims, the deprivation by state action of a constitutionally protected interest in "life, liberty, or property" is not in itself unconstitutional; what is unconstitutional is the deprivation of such an interest *without due process of law.* The constitutional violation actionable under § 1983 is not complete when the deprivation occurs; it is not complete unless and until the state fails to provide due process. Therefore, to determine whether a constitutional violation has occurred, it is necessary to ask what process the state provided, and whether it was constitutionally adequate. This inquiry would examine the procedural safeguards built into the statutory or administrative procedure of effecting the deprivation, and any remedies for erroneous deprivations provided by statute or tort law.

In this case, Burch does not claim that his confinement at FSH violated any of the specific guarantees of the Bill of Rights. Burch's complaint could be read to include a substantive due process claim, but that issue was not raised in the petition for certiorari, and we express no view on whether the facts Burch alleges could give rise to such a claim. The claim at issue falls within the third, or procedural, category of § 1983 claims based on the due process clause.

B

Due process, as this Court often has said, is a flexible concept that varies with the particular situation. To determine what procedural protections the Constitution requires in a particular case, we weigh several factors:

> "First, the private interest that will be affected by the official action; second, the risk of an erroneous deprivation of such interest through the procedures used, and the probable value, if any, of additional or substitute procedural safeguards; and finally, the government's interest, including the function involved and the fiscal and administrative burdens that the additional or substitute procedural requirement would entail."
>
> Mathews v. Eldridge, 424 U.S. 319, 335 (1976).

Applying this test, the Court usually has held that the Constitution requires some kind of a hearing *before* the state deprives a person of liberty or property. . . . In some circumstances, however, the Court has held that a statutory provision for a postdeprivation hearing, or a common-law tort remedy for erroneous deprivation, satisfies due process.

This is where the *Parratt* rule comes into play. *Parratt* and *Hudson* represent a special case of the general *Mathews v. Eldridge* analysis, in which postdeprivation tort remedies are all the process that is due, simply because they are the only remedies the state could be expected to provide. In *Parratt,* a state prisoner brought a § 1983 action because prison employees negligently had lost materials he had ordered by mail.[14] The prisoner did not dispute that he had a postdeprivation remedy. Under state law, a tort-claim procedure was available by which he could have recovered the value of the materials. This Court ruled that the tort remedy was all the process the prisoner was due, because any predeprivation procedural safeguards that the state did provide, or could have provided, would not address the risk of

---

[14] Parratt was decided before this Court ruled, in Daniels v. Williams, 474 U.S. 327, 336 (1986), that a negligent act by a state official does not give rise to § 1983 liability.

this kind of deprivation. The very nature of a negligent loss of property made it impossible for the state to predict such deprivations and provide predeprivation process. The Court explained:

> "The justifications which we have found sufficient to uphold takings of property without any predeprivation process are applicable to a situation such as the present one involving a tortious loss of a prisoner's property as a result of a random and unauthorized act by a state employee. In such a case, the loss is not a result of some established state procedure and the state cannot predict precisely when the loss will occur. It is difficult to conceive of how the state could provide a meaningful hearing before the deprivation takes place."

Given these special circumstances, it was clear that the state, by making available a tort remedy that could adequately redress the loss, had given the prisoner the process he was due. Thus, *Parratt* is not an exception to the *Mathews* balancing test, but rather an application of that test to the unusual case in which one of the variables in the *Mathews* equation—the value of predeprivation safeguards—is negligible in preventing the kind of deprivation at issue. Therefore, no matter how significant the private interest at stake and the risk of its erroneous deprivation, the state cannot be required constitutionally to do the impossible by providing predeprivation process.

In *Hudson,* the Court extended this reasoning to an intentional deprivation of property. A prisoner alleged that, during a search of his prison cell, a guard deliberately and maliciously destroyed some of his property, including legal papers. Again, there was a tort remedy by which the prisoner could have been compensated. In *Hudson,* as in *Parratt,* the state official was not acting pursuant to any established state procedure, but, instead, was apparently pursuing a random, unauthorized personal vendetta against the prisoner. The Court pointed out: "The state can no more anticipate and control in advance the random and unauthorized intentional conduct of its employees than it can anticipate similar negligent conduct." Of course, the fact that the guard's conduct was intentional meant that he himself could "foresee" the wrongful deprivation, and could prevent it simply by refraining from his misconduct. Nonetheless, the Court found that an individual state employee's ability to foresee the deprivation is "of no consequence," because the proper inquiry under *Parratt* is "whether the *state* is in a position to provide for predeprivation process" (emphasis added).

C

Petitioners argue that the dismissal [of the complaint] was proper because, as in *Parratt* and *Hudson,* the state could not possibly have provided predeprivation process to prevent the kind of "random, unauthorized" wrongful deprivation of liberty Burch alleges, so the postdeprivation remedies provided by Florida's statutory and common law necessarily are all the process Burch was due.[15]

Before turning to that issue, however, we must address a threshold question raised by Burch. He argues that *Parratt* and *Hudson* cannot apply to his situation, because those cases are limited to deprivations of property, not liberty.

Burch alleges that he was deprived of his liberty interest in avoiding confinement in a mental hospital without either informed consent or the procedural safeguards of the involuntary placement process. Petitioners do not seriously dispute that there is a substantial liberty interest in avoiding confinement in a mental hospital. Burch's confinement at FSH for five months without a hearing or any other procedure to determine either that he validly had consented to admission, or that he met the statutory standard for involuntary placement, clearly infringes on this liberty interest.

Burch argues that postdeprivation tort remedies are *never* constitutionally adequate for a deprivation of liberty, as opposed to property, so the *Parratt* rule cannot apply to this case. We, however, do not find support in precedent for a categorical distinction between a deprivation of liberty and one of property. . . .

It is true that *Parratt* and *Hudson* concerned deprivations of property. It is also true that Burch's interest in avoiding six months' confinement is of an order different from inmate Parratt's interest in mail-order materials valued at $23.50. But the reasoning of *Parratt* and *Hudson* emphasizes the state's inability to provide predeprivation process because of the random and unpredictable nature of the deprivation, not the fact that only property losses were at stake. In situations where the state feasibly can provide a predeprivation hearing before taking property, it generally must do so regardless of the adequacy of a postdeprivation tort remedy to compensate for the taking. Conversely, in situations where a predeprivation hearing is unduly burdensome in proportion to the liberty interest at stake, or where the state is truly unable to anticipate and prevent a random deprivation of a liberty interest, postdeprivation remedies might satisfy due process. Thus, the fact that a deprivation of liberty is involved in this case does not automatically preclude application of the *Parratt* rule.

To determine whether, as petitioners contend, the *Parratt* rule necessarily precludes § 1983 liability in this case, we must ask whether

---

[15] Burch does not dispute that he had remedies under Florida law for unlawful confinement. Florida's mental health statutes provide that a patient confined unlawfully may sue for damages. ("Any person who violates or abuses any rights or privileges of patients" is liable for damages, subject to good-faith immunity but not immunity for negligence). Also, a mental patient detained at a mental health facility, or a person acting on his behalf, may seek a writ of habeas corpus to "question the cause and legality of such detention and request . . . release." Finally, Florida recognizes the common-law tort of false imprisonment.

predeprivation procedural safeguards could address the risk of deprivations of the kind Burch alleges. To do this, we examine the risk involved. The risk is that some persons who come into Florida's mental health facilities will apparently be willing to sign forms authorizing admission and treatment, but will be incompetent to give the "express and informed consent" required for voluntary placement. . . . Indeed, the very nature of mental illness makes it foreseeable that a person needing mental health care will be unable to understand any proffered "explanation and disclosure of the subject matter" of the forms that person is asked to sign, and will be unable "to make a knowing and willful decision" whether to consent to admission. A person who is willing to sign forms but is incapable of making an informed decision is, by the same token, unlikely to benefit from the voluntary patient's statutory right to request discharge. Such a person thus is in danger of being confined indefinitely without benefit of the procedural safeguards of the involuntary placement process, a process specifically designed to protect persons incapable of looking after their own interests.

Persons who are mentally ill and incapable of giving informed consent to admission would not necessarily meet the statutory standard for involuntary placement, which requires either that they are likely to injure themselves or others, or that their neglect or refusal to care for themselves threatens their well-being. The involuntary placement process serves to guard against the confinement of a person who, though mentally ill, is harmless and can live safely outside an institution. Confinement of such a person not only violates Florida law, but also is unconstitutional. O'Connor v. Donaldson, 422 U.S. 563, 575 (1975) (there is no constitutional basis for confining mentally ill persons involuntarily "if they are dangerous to no one and can live safely in freedom"). Thus, it is at least possible that if Burch had had an involuntary placement hearing, he would not have been found to meet the statutory standard for involuntary placement, and would not have been confined at FSH. Moreover, even assuming that Burch would have met the statutory requirements for involuntary placement, he still could have been harmed by being deprived of other protections built into the involuntary placement procedure, such as the appointment of a guardian advocate to make treatment decisions, and periodic judicial review of placement.[19]

The very risks created by the application of the informed-consent requirement to the special context of mental health care are borne out

---

[19] Hence, Burch might be entitled to actual damages, beyond the nominal damages awardable for a procedural due process violation unaccompanied by any actual injury, see Carey v. Piphus, 435 U.S. 247, 266–67 (1978), if he can show either that if the proper procedure had been followed he would have remained at liberty and that he suffered harm by being confined, or that even if he would have been committed anyway under the involuntary placement procedure, the lack of this procedure harmed him in some way.

by the facts alleged in this case. It appears from the exhibits accompanying Burch's complaint that he was simply given admission forms to sign by clerical workers, and, after he signed, was considered a voluntary patient. Burch alleges that petitioners knew or should have known that he was incapable of informed consent. [T]he way in which Burch allegedly was admitted to FSH certainly did not ensure compliance with the statutory standard for voluntary admission.

We now consider whether predeprivation safeguards would have any value in guarding against the kind of deprivation Burch allegedly suffered. Petitioners urge that here, as in *Parratt* and *Hudson,* such procedures could have no value at all, because the state cannot prevent its officials from making random and unauthorized errors in the admission process. We disagree.

The Florida statutes, of course, do not allow incompetent persons to be admitted as "voluntary" patients. But the statutes do not direct any member of the facility staff to determine whether a person is competent to give consent, nor to initiate the involuntary placement procedure for every incompetent patient. A patient who is willing to sign forms but incapable of informed consent certainly cannot be relied on to protest his "voluntary" admission and demand that the involuntary placement procedure be followed. The staff are the only persons in a position to take notice of any misuse of the voluntary admission process, and to ensure that the proper procedure is followed.

Florida chose to delegate to petitioners a broad power to admit patients to FSH, i.e., to effect what, in the absence of informed consent, is a substantial deprivation of liberty. Because petitioners had state authority to deprive persons of liberty, the Constitution imposed on them the state's concomitant duty to see that no deprivation occur without adequate procedural protections.

It may be permissible constitutionally for a state to have a statutory scheme like Florida's, which gives state officials broad power and little guidance in admitting mental patients. But when those officials fail to provide constitutionally required procedural safeguards to a person whom they deprive of liberty, the state officials cannot then escape liability by invoking *Parratt* and *Hudson.* It is immaterial whether the due process violation Burch alleges is best described as arising from petitioners' failure to comply with state procedures for admitting involuntary patients, or from the absence of a specific requirement that petitioners determine whether a patient is competent to consent to voluntary admission. Burch's suit is neither an action challenging the facial adequacy of a state's statutory procedures, nor an action based only on state officials' random and unauthorized violation of state laws. Burch is not simply attempting to blame the state for misconduct by its employees. He seeks to hold state officials accountable for their abuse of their broadly delegated, uncircumscribed power to effect the deprivation at issue.

This case, therefore, is not controlled by *Parratt* and *Hudson*, for three basic reasons:

First, petitioners cannot claim that the deprivation of Burch's liberty was unpredictable. Under Florida's statutory scheme, only a person competent to give informed consent may be admitted as a voluntary patient. There is, however, no specified way of determining, before a patient is asked to sign admission forms, whether he is competent. It is hardly unforeseeable that a person requesting treatment for mental illness might be incapable of informed consent, and that state officials with the power to admit patients might take their apparent willingness to be admitted at face value and not initiate involuntary placement procedures. Any erroneous deprivation will occur, if at all, at a specific, predictable point in the admission process—when a patient is given admission forms to sign.

This situation differs from the state's predicament in *Parratt*. While it could anticipate that prison employees would occasionally lose property through negligence, it certainly "cannot predict precisely when the loss will occur." Likewise, in *Hudson*, the state might be able to predict that guards occasionally will harass or persecute prisoners they dislike, but cannot "know when such deprivations will occur."

Second, we cannot say that predeprivation process was impossible here. Florida already has an established procedure for involuntary placement. The problem is only to ensure that this procedure is afforded to all patients who cannot be admitted voluntarily, both those who are unwilling and those who are unable to give consent.

In *Parratt*, the very nature of the deprivation made deprivation process "impossible." It would do no good for the state to have a rule telling its employees not to lose mail by mistake, and it "borders on the absurd to suggest that a state must provide a hearing to determine whether or not a corrections officer should engage in negligent conduct." *Daniels*, supra, at 342 n. 19 (Stevens, J., concurring in judgments). In *Hudson*, the errant employee himself could anticipate the deprivation since he intended to effect it, but the state still was not in a position to provide predeprivation process, since it could not anticipate or control such random and unauthorized intentional conduct. Again, a rule forbidding a prison guard from maliciously destroying a prisoner's property would not have done any good; it would be absurd to suggest that the state hold a hearing to determine whether a guard should engage in such conduct.

Here, in contrast, there is nothing absurd in suggesting that, had the state limited and guided petitioners' power to admit patients, the deprivation might have been averted. Burch's complaint alleges that petitioners "knew or should have known" that he was incompetent, and nonetheless admitted him as a voluntary patient in "willful, wanton, and reckless disregard" of his constitutional rights. Understood in context, the allegation means only that petitioners disregarded their duty to ensure that the proper procedures were followed, not that they, like the prison guard in *Hudson,* were bent upon effecting the substantive deprivation and would have done so despite any and all predeprivation safeguards. Moreover, it would indeed be strange to allow state officials to escape § 1983 liability for failing to provide constitutionally required procedural protections, by assuming that those procedures would be futile because the same state officials would find a way to subvert them.

Third, petitioners cannot characterize their conduct as "unauthorized" in the sense the term is used in *Parratt* and *Hudson.* The state delegated to them the power and authority to effect the very deprivation complained of here, Burch's confinement in a mental hospital, and also delegated to them the concomitant duty to initiate the procedural safeguards set up by state law to guard against unlawful confinement. In *Parratt* and *Hudson,* the state employees had no similar broad authority to deprive prisoners of their personal property, and no similar duty to initiate (for persons unable to protect their own interests) the procedural safeguards required before deprivations occur. The deprivation here is "unauthorized" only in the sense that it was not an act sanctioned by state law, but, instead, was a "depriv[ation] of constitutional rights . . . by an official's abuse of his position." *Monroe,* supra, at 172.[20]

We conclude that petitioners cannot escape § 1983 liability by characterizing their conduct as a "random, unauthorized" violation of Florida law which the state was not in a position to predict or avert, so that all the process Burch could possibly be due is a postdeprivation damages remedy. Burch, according to the allegations of his complaint, was deprived of a substantial liberty interest without either valid consent or an involuntary placement hearing, by the very state officials charged with the power to deprive mental patients of their liberty and the duty to implement procedural safeguards. Such a deprivation is foreseeable, due to the nature of mental illness, and will occur, if at all, at a predictable point in the admission process. Unlike *Parratt* and *Hudson,* this case does not represent the special instance of the *Mathews* due process analysis where postdeprivation process is all that is due because no predeprivation safeguards would be of use in preventing the kind of deprivation alleged.

[20] Contrary to the dissent's view of *Parratt* and *Hudson,* those cases do not stand for the proposition that in every case where a deprivation is caused by an "unauthorized . . . departure from established practices" state officials can escape § 1983 liability simply because the state provides tort remedies. This reading of *Parratt* and *Hudson* detaches those cases from their proper role as special applications of the settled principles expressed in *Monroe* and *Mathews.*

We express no view on the ultimate merits of Burch's claim; we hold only that his complaint was sufficient to state a claim under § 1983 for violation of his procedural due process rights.

The judgment of the Court of Appeals is affirmed.

It is so ordered.

JUSTICE O'CONNOR, with whom THE CHIEF JUSTICE, JUSTICE SCALIA, and JUSTICE KENNEDY join, dissenting.

Without doubt, respondent Burch alleges a serious deprivation of liberty, yet equally clearly he alleges no violation of the 14th amendment. The Court concludes that an allegation of state actors' wanton, unauthorized departure from a state's established policies and procedures, working a deprivation of liberty, suffices to support a procedural due process claim even though the state provides adequate post-deprivation remedies for that deprivation. The Court's opinion unnecessarily transforms well-established procedural due process doctrine and departs from controlling precedent. I respectfully dissent.

Parratt v. Taylor, 451 U.S. 527 (1981), and Hudson v. Palmer, 468 U.S. 517 (1984), should govern this case. Only by disregarding the gist of Burch's complaint—that state actors' wanton and unauthorized departure from established practice worked the deprivation—and by transforming the allegations into a challenge to the adequacy of Florida's admissions procedures can the Court attempt to distinguish this case from *Parratt* and *Hudson*.

Burch alleges a deprivation occasioned by petitioners' contravention of Florida's established procedures. Florida allows the voluntary admission process to be employed to admit to its mental hospitals only patients who have made "application by express and informed consent for admission," and requires that the elaborate involuntary admission process be used to admit patients requiring treatment and incapable of giving such consent. Burch explicitly disavows any challenge to the adequacy of those established procedural safeguards accompanying Florida's two avenues of admission to mental hospitals. . . .

Parratt and *Hudson* should readily govern procedural due process claims such as respondent's. Taken together, the decisions indicate that for deprivations worked by such random and unauthorized departures from otherwise unimpugned and established state procedures the state provides the process due by making available adequate postdeprivation remedies. In *Parratt,* the Court addressed a deprivation which "occurred as a result of the unauthorized failure of agents of the state to follow established state procedure." The random nature of the state actor's unauthorized departure made it not "practicable for the state to provide a predeprivation hearing," and adequate postdeprivation remedies available through the state's tort system provided the process due under the 14th amendment. *Hudson* applied this reasoning to intentional deprivations by state actors and confirmed the distinction between deprivation pursuant to "an established state procedure" and that pursuant to "random and unauthorized action." In *Hudson,* the Court explained that the *Parratt* doctrine was applicable because "the *state* cannot possibly know in advance of a negligent deprivation of property," and that "[t]he controlling inquiry is solely whether the state is in a position to provide for predeprivation process."

Application of *Parratt* and *Hudson* indicates that respondent has failed to state a claim allowing recovery under 42 U.S.C. § 1983. Petitioners' actions were unauthorized: they are alleged to have wrongly and without license departed from established state practices. Florida officials in a position to establish safeguards commanded that the voluntary admission process be employed only for consenting patients and that the involuntary hearing procedures be used to admit unconsenting patients. Yet it is alleged that petitioners "with willful, wanton and reckless disregard of and indifference to" Burch's rights contravened both commands. As in *Parratt,* the deprivation "occurred as a result of the unauthorized failure of agents of the state to follow established state procedure." The wanton or reckless nature of the failure indicates it to be random. The state could not foresee the particular contravention and was hardly "in a position to provide for predeprivation process," *Hudson,* supra, at 534, to ensure that officials bent upon subverting the state's requirements would in fact follow those procedures. For this wrongful deprivation resulting from an unauthorized departure from established state practice, Florida provides adequate postdeprivation remedies, as two courts below concluded, and which the Court and respondent do not dispute. *Parratt* and *Hudson* thus should govern this case and indicate that respondent has failed to allege a violation of the 14th amendment.

The allegedly wanton nature of the subversion of the state procedures underscores why the state cannot in any relevant sense anticipate and meaningfully guard against the random and unauthorized actions alleged in this case. The Court suggests that the state could foresee "that a person requesting treatment for mental illness might be incapable of informed consent." While foreseeability of that routine difficulty in evaluating prospective patients is relevant in considering the general adequacy of Florida's voluntary admission procedures, *Parratt* and *Hudson* address whether the state can foresee and thus be required to forestall the deliberate or reckless departure from established state practice. Florida may be able to predict that over time some state actors will subvert its clearly implicated requirements. Indeed, that is one reason that the state must implement an adequate remedial scheme. But Florida "cannot predict precisely when the loss will occur," *Parratt,* supra, at 541, and the due process clause does not require the state to do more than establish appropriate remedies for any wrongful departure from its prescribed practices.

The Court attempts to avert the force of *Parratt* and *Hudson* by characterizing petitioners' alleged failures as only the routine but erroneous application of the admissions process. According to the Court, Burch suffered an "erroneous deprivation" and the "risk of deprivations of the kind Burch alleges" is that incompetent "persons who come into Florida's mental health facilities will apparently be willing to sign forms," prompting officials to "mak[e] random and unauthorized errors in the admission process." The Court's characterization omits petitioners' alleged wrongful state of mind and thus the nature and source of the wrongful deprivation.

A claim of negligence will not support a procedural due process claim, see Daniels v. Williams, 474 U.S. 327 (1986), and it is an unresolved issue whether an allegation of gross negligence or recklessness suffices. Ibid., at 334 n. 3. Respondent, if not the Court, avoids these pitfalls. According to Burch, petitioners "knew" him to be incompetent or were presented with such clear evidence of his incompetence that they should be charged with such knowledge. Petitioners also knew that Florida law required them to provide an incompetent prospective patient with elaborate procedural safeguards. Far from alleging inadvertent or negligent disregard of duty, respondent alleges that petitioners "acted with willful, wanton and reckless disregard of and indifference" to his rights by treating him without providing the hearing that Florida requires. That is, petitioners did not bumble or commit "errors" by taking Burch's "apparent willingness to be admitted at face value." Rather, they deliberately or recklessly subverted his rights and contravened state requirements.

The unauthorized and wrongful character of the departure from established state practice makes additional procedures an "impracticable" means of preventing the deprivation. "The underlying rationale of *Parratt* is that when deprivations of property are effected through random and unauthorized conduct of a state employee, predeprivation procedures are simply 'impracticable' since the state cannot know when such deprivations will occur." *Hudson,* supra, at 533. The Court suggests that additional safeguards surrounding the voluntary admission process would have quite possibly reduced the risk of deprivation. This reasoning conflates the value of procedures for preventing error in the repeated and usual case (evaluated according to the test set forth in Mathews v. Eldridge, 424 U.S. 319 (1976)) with the value of additional predeprivation procedures to forestall deprivations by state actors bent upon departing from or indifferent to complying with established practices. Unsurprisingly, the Court is vague regarding how its proffered procedures would prevent the deprivation Burch alleges, and why the safeguards would not form merely one more set of procedural protections that state employees could willfully, recklessly and wantonly subvert. Indeed, Burch alleges that, presented with the clearest evidence of his incompetence, petitioners nonetheless wantonly or recklessly denied him the protections of the state's admission procedures and requirements. The state actor so indifferent to guaranteed protections would be no more prevented from working the deprivation by additional procedural requirements than would the mail handler in *Parratt* or the prison guard in *Hudson*. In those cases, the state could have, and no doubt did, provide a range of predeprivation requirements and safeguards guiding both prison searches and care of packages. . . . In all three cases, the unpredictable, wrongful departure is beyond the state's reasonable control. Additional safeguards designed to secure correct results in the usual case do not practicably forestall state actors who flout the state's command and established practice.

Even indulging the Court's belief that the proffered safeguards would provide "some" benefit, *Parratt* and *Hudson* extend beyond circumstances in which procedural safeguards would have had "negligible" value. In *Parratt* and *Hudson* additional measures would conceivably have had some benefit in preventing the alleged deprivations. A practice of barring individual or unsupervised shakedown searches, a procedure of always pairing or monitoring guards, or a requirement that searches be conducted according to "an established policy" (the proposed measure rejected as unnecessary in *Hudson*) might possibly have helped to prevent the type of deprivation considered in *Hudson*. More sensible staffing practices, better training, or a more rigorous tracking procedure may have averted the deprivation at issue in *Parratt*. In those cases, like this one, the state knew the exact context in which the wrongful deprivation would occur. Yet the possibility of implementing such marginally beneficial measures, in light of the type of alleged deprivation, did not alter the analysis. The state's inability to foresee and to forestall the wrongful departure from established procedures renders additional predeprivation measures "impracticable" and not required by the dictates of due process.

Every command to act imparts the duty to exercise discretion in accord with the command and affords the opportunity to abuse that discretion. The *Mathews* test measures whether the state has sufficiently constrained discretion in the usual case, while the *Parratt* doctrine requires the state to provide a remedy for any wrongful abuse. The Court suggests that this case differs from *Parratt* and *Hudson* because petitioners possessed a sort of delegated power. Yet petitioners no more had the delegated power to depart from the admission procedures and requirements than did the guard in *Hudson* to exceed the limits of his established search and seizure authority, or the prison official in *Parratt* wrongfully to withhold or misdeliver mail. Petitioners' delegated duty to act in accord with Florida's admissions procedures is akin to the mailhandler's duty to follow and implement the procedures surrounding delivery of packages, or the guard's duty to conduct the search properly. In the appropriate circumstances and pursuant to established procedures, the guard in *Hudson* was charged with seizing property pursuant to a search. The official in *Parratt* no doubt possessed some power to withhold certain packages from prisoners. *Parratt* and *Hudson* distinguish sharply between deprivations caused by unauthorized acts and those occasioned by established state procedures. The delegation argument blurs this line and ignores the unauthorized nature of petitioners' alleged departure from established practices.

The suggestion that the state delegated to petitioners insufficiently trammeled discretion conflicts with positions that the Court ostensibly embraces. The issue whether petitioners possessed undue discretion is bound with and more properly analyzed as an aspect of the adequacy of the state's procedural safeguards, yet the Court claims Burch did not present this issue and purports not to decide it. By suggesting that petitioners' acts are attributable to the state, the Court either abandons its position that "Burch does not claim that he was deprived of due process by an established state procedure" or abandons *Parratt* and *Hudson*'s distinction between established procedures and unauthorized departures from those practices. Petitioners were not charged with formulating policy, and the complaint does not allege widespread and common departure from required procedures. Neither do the Court's passing reflections that a hearing is constitutionally required in the usual case of treatment of an incompetent patient advance the argument. That claim either states the conclusion that the state's combined admission procedures are generally inadequate, or repudiates *Parratt* and *Hudson*'s focus upon random and unauthorized acts and upon the state's ability to formulate safeguards. To the extent that a liberty interest exists in the application of the involuntary admission procedures whenever appropriate, it is the random and unauthorized action of state actors that effected the deprivation, one for which Florida also provides adequate postdeprivation process. . . .

The Court's delegation of authority argument, like its claim that "we cannot say that predeprivation process was impossible here," revives an argument explicitly rejected in *Hudson*. In *Hudson,* the Court rebuffed the argument that "because an agent of the state who intends to deprive a person of his property can provide predeprivation process, then as a matter of due process he must do so." By failing to consider whether "the *state* cannot possibly know in advance" of the wrongful contravention and by abandoning "[t]he controlling inquiry . . . whether the state is in a position to provide for predeprivation process," the Court embraces the "fundamental misunderstanding of *Parratt.*" Each of the Court's distinctions abandons an essential element of the *Parratt* and *Hudson* doctrines, and together they disavow those cases' central insights and holdings.

The Court's reliance upon the state's inappropriate delegation of duty also creates enormous line-drawing problems. Today's decision applies to deprivations occasioned by state actors given "little guidance" and "broadly delegated, uncircumscribed power" to initiate required procedures. At some undefined point, the breadth of the delegation of power requires officials to channel the exercise of that power or become liable for its misapplications. When guidance is provided and the power to effect the deprivation circumscribed, no liability arises. And routine exercise of the power must be sufficiently fraught with the danger of "erroneous deprivation." In the absence of this broadly delegated power that carries with it pervasive risk of wrongful deprivation, *Parratt* and *Hudson* still govern. In essence, the Court's rationale applies when state officials are loosely charged with fashioning effective procedures or ensuring that required procedures are not routinely evaded. In a roundabout way, this rationale states the unexceptional conclusion that liability exists when officials' actions amount to the established state practice, a rationale unasserted in this case and, otherwise, appropriately analyzed under the *Mathews* test.

The Court's decision also undermines two of this Court's established and delicately related doctrines, one articulated in *Mathews* and the other articulated in *Parratt*. As the Court acknowledges, the procedural component of the due process clause requires the state to formulate procedural safeguards and adequate postdeprivation process sufficient to satisfy the dictates of fundamental fairness and the due process clause. Until today, the reasoning embodied in *Mathews* largely determined that standard and the measures a state must establish to prevent a deprivation of a protected interest from amounting to a constitutional violation. *Mathews* employed the now familiar three-part test (considering the nature of the private interest, efficacy of additional procedures, and governmental interests) to determine what predeprivation procedural safeguards were required of the state. That test reflects a carefully crafted accommodation of conflicting interests, weighed and evaluated in light of what fundamental fairness requires. *Parratt* drew upon concerns similar to those embodied in the *Mathews* test. For deprivations occasioned by wrongful departures from unchallenged and established state practices, *Parratt* concluded that adequate postdeprivation process meets the requirements of the due process clause because additional predeprivation procedural safeguards would be "impracticable" to forestall these deprivations. The *Mathews* and *Parratt* doctrines work in tandem. State officials able to formulate safeguards must discharge the duty to establish sufficient predeprivation procedures, as well as adequate postdeprivation remedies to provide process in the event of wrongful departures from established state practice. The doctrines together define the procedural measures that fundamental fairness and the Constitution demand of the state.

The Court today discovers an additional realm of required procedural safeguards. Now, all procedure is divided into three parts. In place of the border clearly dividing the duties required by *Mathews* from those required by *Parratt,* the Court marks out a vast terra incognita of unknowable duties and expansive liability of constitutional dimension. The *Mathews* test, we are told, does not determine the state's obligation to provide predeprivation procedural safeguards. Rather, to avoid the constitutional violation a state must have fully circumscribed and guided officials' exercise of power and provided additional safeguards, without regard to their efficacy or the nature of the governmental interests. Even if the validity of the state's procedures is not directly challenged, the burden is apparently on certain state actors to demonstrate that the state sufficiently constrained their powers. Despite the many cases of this Court applying and affirming *Mathews,* it is unclear what now remains of the test. And the *Parratt* doctrine no longer reflects a general interpretation of the due process clause or the complement of the principles contained in *Mathews*. It is, instead, displaced when the state delegates certain types of duties in certain inappropriate ways. This resulting "no-man's land" has no apparent boundaries. We are provided almost no guidance regarding what the due process clause requires, how that requirement is to be deduced, or why fundamental fairness imposes upon the states the obligation to provide additional safeguards of nearly any conceivable value. We are left only with the implication that where doubt exists, liability of constitutional dimension will be found. Without so much as suggesting that our prior cases have warned against such a result, the Court has gone some measure to " 'make of the 14th amendment a font of tort law to be superimposed upon whatever systems may already be administered by the states.' " *Parratt,* supra, at 544 (quoting Paul v. Davis, 424 U.S. 693, 701 (1976)).

The Court's departure from the *Mathews* and *Parratt* doctrines is particularly unjustified because it is unnecessary for resolution of this case. While I believe that Burch's complaint and subsequent argument do not properly place before the Court a traditional challenge to Florida's voluntary admission procedures, the Court, without so declaring, has decided otherwise. Yet, rather than acknowledge this course, the Court crafts its doctrinal innovations.

Understandably reluctant to grapple with Burch's framing of his complaint, the Court less understandably avoids that difficulty of pleading by creating the innovation which so disrupts established law. The Court discovers that "Burch's suit is neither an action challenging the facial adequacy of a state's statutory procedures, nor an action based only on state officials' random and unauthorized violation of state laws." That is, Burch's suit is not one that established law supports, and thus requires today's unwarranted departure.

The Court believes that Florida's statutory scheme contains a particular flaw. That statutory omission involves the determination of competence in the course of the voluntary admission process, and the Court signals that it believes that these suggested additional safeguards would not be greatly burdensome. The Court further believes that Burch's complaint and argument properly raise these issues and that adopting the additional safeguards would provide relevant benefit to one in Burch's position. The traditional *Mathews* test was designed and, until today, has been employed to evaluate and accommodate these concerns. . . . That test holds Florida to the appropriate standard and, given the Court's beliefs set out above, would perhaps have yielded a result favoring respondent. While this approach, if made explicit, would have required a strained reading of respondent's complaint and arguments, that course would have been far preferable to the strained reading of controlling procedural due process law that the Court today adopts. Ordinarily, a complaint must state a legal cause of action, but here it may be said that the Court has stated a novel cause of action to support a complaint.

I respectfully dissent.

ADDITIONAL NOTES ON CONSTITUTIONAL RIGHTS ENFORCEABLE UNDER § 1983

1. *Parratt v. Taylor.* The plaintiff in Parratt v. Taylor, 451 U.S. 527 (1981), was an inmate in a Nebraska prison. He ordered hobby materials by mail for which he paid $23.50 from his prison account. When they arrived, he was not permitted to take possession of them because he was in segregation. The materials were therefore signed for by two employees of the prison hobby center. When Taylor was released from segregation and able to resume his hobby, the packages were nowhere to be found.

Taylor filed a § 1983 action against the warden and the hobby manager of the prison. He sought damages for the lost materials, claiming that, by their negligence, the defendants had deprived him of property without due process of law in violation of the 14th amendment. The District Court granted Taylor's motion for summary judgment and the Circuit Court affirmed. The Supreme Court granted certiorari and reversed.

Justice Rehnquist wrote for the Court. Three points merit special attention:

(i) **Mental Elements of § 1983.** Justice Rehnquist first asked whether § 1983 itself required proof of intentional or reckless wrongdoing or would allow relief based on negligence. His answer was that "[n]othing in the language of § 1983 or its legislative history limits the statute solely to intentional deprivations of constitutional rights." He noted that "§ 1983, unlike its criminal counterpart, 18 U.S.C. § 242, has never been found by this Court to contain a state-of-mind requirement" and quoted from Monroe v. Pape, 365 U.S. 167 (1961):

"In the *Screws* case we dealt with a statute that imposed criminal penalties for acts 'willfully' done. We construed that word in its setting to mean the doing of an act with 'a specific intent to deprive a person of a federal right.' We do not think that gloss should be put on [§ 1983]. The word 'willfully' does not appear in [§ 1983]. Moreover, [§ 1983] provides a civil remedy, while in the *Screws* case we dealt with a criminal law challenged on the grounds of vagueness. [Section 1983] should be read against the background of tort liability that makes a man responsible for the natural consequences of his actions."

This passage suggested "that § 1983 affords a 'civil remedy' for deprivations of federally protected rights caused by persons acting under color of state law without any express requirement of a particular state of mind."

This is not to say, it should be added, that state of mind never matters in a § 1983 case. The actor's culpability may still be relevant in two ways. First, the underlying constitutional violation may require proof of a particular state of mind. A good example is the equal protection guarantee against racial discrimination, which requires proof of a discriminatory purpose.[a] Second, the actor's state of mind may be relevant to the defense of qualified immunity. All *Parratt* decided was that proof of culpability was not part of the § 1983 cause of action itself. The plaintiff in a § 1983 case has no obligation to establish the defendant's state of mind unless required as a part of the underlying constitutional violation.[b]

(ii) Negligent Deprivation of Due Process. Rehnquist concluded that the "initial inquiry" in any § 1983 action required examination of two elements: whether state action could be found; and if so, whether the action complained of "deprived a person of rights, privileges, or immunities secured by the Constitution or laws of the United States." On the facts of *Parratt* there was no question about state action. The case therefore turned on whether the defendants had "deprived" Taylor of a protected right. This raised the question whether negligent behavior by state officials could "deprive" Taylor of property without due process of law. Rehnquist's answer was brief and unelaborated:

"Unquestionably, respondent's claim satisfies three prerequisites of a valid due process claim: the petitioners acted under color of state law; the hobby kit falls within the definition of

[a] See Village of Arlington Heights v. Metropolitan Housing Dev. Corp., 429 U.S. 252 (1977); Washington v. Davis, 426 U.S. 229 (1976).

[b] For early treatment of the "state of mind" required for § 1983 actions, see Gary S. Gildin, The Standard of Culpability in Section 1983 and *Bivens* Actions: The Prima Facie Case, Qualified Immunity and the Constitution, 11 Hofstra L.Rev. 557 (1983); Laird Kirkpatrick, Defining a Constitutional Tort Under Section 1983: The State-of-Mind Requirement, 46 U.Cinn.L. Rev. 45 (1977).

property; and the alleged loss, even though negligently caused, amounted to a deprivation." c

(iii) **The Process Due.** Rehnquist continued:

"Standing alone, however, these three elements do not establish a violation of the 14th amendment. Nothing in that amendment protects against all deprivations of life, liberty, or property by the state. The 14th amendment protects only against deprivations 'without due process of law.' Our inquiry therefore must focus on whether the respondent has suffered a deprivation of property without due process of law. In particular, we must decide whether the tort remedies which the state of Nebraska provides as a means of redress for property deprivations satisfy the requirements of procedural due process."

The question on which the case turned, then, was whether Nebraska's postdeprivation tort remedy satisfied the procedural demands of the 14th amendment. And the answer was that the remedy was sufficient and that Taylor accordingly "has not alleged a violation of the due process clause of the 14th amendment":

"The fundamental requirement of due process is the opportunity to be heard and it is an 'opportunity which must be granted at a meaningful time and in a meaningful manner.' Armstrong v. Manzo, 380 U.S. 545, 552 (1965). However, as many of the above cases recognize, we have rejected the proposition that 'at a meaningful time and in a meaningful manner' *always* requires the state to provide a hearing prior to the initial deprivation of property. This rejection is based in part on the impracticability in some cases of providing any preseizure hearing under a state-authorized procedure, and the assumption that at some time a full and meaningful hearing will be available.

"The justifications which we have found sufficient to uphold takings of property without any predeprivation process are applicable to a situation such as the present one involving a tortious loss of a prisoner's property as a result of a random

---

c This point prompted a dissent by Justice Powell. He argued:

"[T]he question is whether intent is required before there can be a 'deprivation' of life, liberty, or property. . . . I would not hold that . . . a negligent act, causing unintended loss of or injury to property, works a deprivation in the constitutional sense. . . . A 'deprivation' connotes an intentional act denying something to someone, or, at the very least, a deliberate decision not to act to prevent a loss. The most reasonable interpretation of the 14th amendment would limit due process claims to such active deprivations. [S]uch a rule would avoid trivializing the right of action provided in § 1983. That provision was enacted to deter real *abuses* by state officials in the exercise of governmental powers. It would make no sense to open the federal courts to lawsuits where there has been no affirmative abuse of power, merely a negligent deed by one who happens to be acting under color of state law."

and unauthorized act by a state employee. In such a case, the loss is not a result of some established state procedure and the state cannot predict precisely when the loss will occur. It is difficult to conceive of how the state could provide a meaningful hearing before the deprivation takes place. The loss of property, although attributable to the state as action under 'color of law,' is in almost all cases beyond the control of the state. Indeed, in most cases it is not only impracticable, but impossible, to provide a meaningful hearing before the deprivation. That does not mean, of course, that the state can take property without providing a meaningful postdeprivation hearing. The prior cases which have excused the prior-hearing requirement have rested in part on the availability of some meaningful opportunity subsequent to the initial taking for a determination of rights and liabilities."

Justice Rehnquist added these concluding remarks:

"Our decision today is fully consistent with our prior cases. To accept respondent's argument that the conduct of the state officials in this case constituted a violation of the 14th amendment would almost necessarily result in turning every alleged injury which may have been inflicted by a state official acting under 'color of law' into a violation of the 14th amendment cognizable under § 1983. It is hard to perceive any logical stopping place to such a line of reasoning. Presumably, under this rationale any party who is involved in nothing more than an automobile accident with a state official could allege a constitutional violation under § 1983. Such reasoning 'would make of the 14th amendment a font of tort law to be superimposed upon whatever systems may already be administered by the states.' Paul v. Davis, 424 U.S. 693, 701 (1976). We do not think that the drafters of the 14th amendment intended the amendment to play such a role in our society." [d]

2. Hudson v. Palmer: Application of Parratt to Intentional Wrongs. In *Parratt v. Taylor,* Justice Blackmun concurred specially to say that, with respect to intentional misconduct by a government employee, postdeprivation remedies might well be inadequate to satisfy

---

[d] Justices Stewart, White, and Blackmun wrote separately but concurred in the Court's opinion. Justice Powell concurred in the result on the rationale, as noted above, that no "deprivation" of property in the constitutional sense had occurred. Justice Marshall concurred in part and dissented in part. He agreed that "in cases involving claims of *negligent* deprivation of property without due process of law, the availability of an adequate postdeprivation cause of action for damages under state law may preclude a finding of a violation of the 14th amendment." But he thought that "prison officials have an affirmative obligation to inform a prisoner who claims that he is aggrieved by official action about the remedies available under state law" and that "[i]f they fail to do so, then they should not be permitted to rely on the existence of such remedies as adequate alternatives to a § 1983 action for wrongful deprivation of property."

due process. The question whether the *Parratt* analysis should extend to intentional wrongs came before the Court in Hudson v. Palmer, 468 U.S. 517 (1984).

Hudson was an officer at a correctional institution. He conducted a "shakedown" search of inmate Palmer's cell, where he discovered a ripped pillowcase. Disciplinary proceedings were brought against Palmer, who was made to pay for the cost of the pillowcase. Subsequently, Palmer filed a § 1983 action claiming, inter alia, that Hudson himself had ripped the pillowcase—that is, that he had intentionally and without justification destroyed noncontraband personal property during the shakedown. Hudson denied the allegation and won a summary judgment, which in due course was affirmed by the Supreme Court. Indeed, on this issue, the decision was unanimous. Speaking through Chief Justice Burger, the Court said:

> "While *Parratt* is necessarily limited by its facts to negligent deprivations of property, it is evident, as the Court of Appeals recognized, that its reasoning applies as well to intentional deprivations of property. The underlying rationale of *Parratt* is that when deprivations of property are effected through random and unauthorized conduct of a state employee, predeprivation procedures are simply 'impracticable' since the state cannot know when such deprivations will occur. We can discern no logical distinction between negligent and intentional deprivations of property insofar as the 'practicability' of affording pre-deprivation process is concerned. The state can no more anticipate and control in advance the random and unauthorized intentional conduct of its employees than it can anticipate similar negligent conduct. . . .
>
> "Accordingly, we hold that an unauthorized intentional deprivation of property by a state employee does not constitute a violation of the procedural requirements of the due process clause of the 14th amendment if a meaningful postdeprivation remedy for the loss is available. For intentional, as for negligent deprivations of property by state employees, the state's action is not complete until and unless it provides or refuses to provide a suitable postdeprivation remedy."

At the same time the Court was careful to note that the *Parratt* analysis does not apply to deprivations of property caused pursuant to established state procedure. Such an act violates due process regardless of the postdeprivation remedies available. See Logan v. Zimmerman Brush Co., 455 U.S. 422 (1982).

3. *Daniels v. Williams*: *Parratt* Overruled on the Meaning of "Deprivation." *Parratt* and *Hudson* gave rise to an interesting line of speculation about the continued vitality of state sovereign immunity for garden-variety tortious acts by state employees. Traditionally, states have asserted the right to claim sovereign immunity in their own courts when sued for torts committed by their employees. An attempt to evade this restriction by resort to federal court would be precluded by the 11th amendment. As a result, garden-variety torts by government employees traditionally have been subject to compensation by the state only to the extent that the state explicitly waived its right not to be sued in its own courts.

Parratt and *Hudson* suggested a possible way to evade such restrictions. If a state fails to provide an adequate compensatory remedy for the tortious acts of its employees, then—under the rationale of those decisions—such acts become procedural due process violations. The individuals injured thereby can bring suit under § 1983 by characterizing the tort claim as an instance of procedural inadequacy. Of course, the action must be brought against the employee rather than directly against the state, but that may not matter. Once the procedural due process right to adequate state procedures is "clearly established," the defense of qualified immunity presumably would become unavailable to the employee, and the employee would very likely be indemnified by the state for any adverse judgment.

The Court rejected this line of reasoning in Daniels v. Williams, 474 U.S. 327 (1986). Daniels was a prisoner in the Richmond, Va., city jail. He tripped over a pillow allegedly left on a staircase by Williams, a corrections officer. Daniels asserted that the resulting injury was a "deprivation" of his "liberty" interest in freedom from bodily hurt. Since sovereign immunity arguably blocked ordinary tort recovery, Daniels claimed that he had no "adequate" state remedy and therefore that the deprivation of liberty was without due process of law and hence compensable under § 1983.

The Supreme Court disagreed. Speaking through Justice Rehnquist, the Court adopted Justice Powell's suggestion in *Parratt* that "the due process clause is simply not implicated by a *negligent* act of an official causing unintended loss of or injury to life, liberty, or property." *Parratt v. Taylor* was explicitly overruled "to the extent that it states that mere lack of due care by a state official may 'deprive' an individual of life, liberty or property under the 14th amendment." The Court reasoned that the due process clause was "intended to secure the individual from the arbitrary exercise of the powers of government":

> "By requiring the government to follow appropriate procedures when its agents decide to 'deprive any person of life, liberty, or property,' the due process clause promotes fairness in such decisions. And by barring certain government actions regardless of the fairness of the procedures used to implement them, it serves to prevent governmental power from being 'used for purposes of oppression.'

"We think that the actions of prison custodians in leaving a pillow on the prison stairs, or mislaying an inmate's property, are quite remote from the concerns just discussed. Far from an abuse of power, lack of due care suggests no more than a failure to measure up to the conduct of a reasonable person. To hold that injury caused by such conduct is a deprivation within the meaning of the 14th amendment would trivialize the centuries-old principle of due process of law."

Justice Rehnquist did reserve in a footnote, however, the possibility that something in between "negligence" and "intent" would suffice:

"[Daniels] concedes that [Williams] was at most negligent. Accordingly, this case affords us no occasion to consider whether something less than intentional conduct, such as recklessness or 'gross negligence,' is enough to trigger the protections of the due process clause." [e]

4. *Davidson v. Cannon*. The possibility that *Parratt* and *Hudson* could lead to the erosion of the state's sovereign immunity for ordinary torts was narrowed by *Daniels*, but it was not eliminated. It seems clear that intentional torts are compensable under § 1983 if the state does not provide an adequate postdeprivation procedure, and it remains possible that recklessness or some other intermediate form of culpability will suffice.

Division on the Court over these matters arose in a companion case to *Daniels*, Davidson v. Cannon, 474 U.S. 344 (1986). Davidson sued state prison officials for failure to protect him from another inmate. Prior to the assault, the victim had sent a note to prison authorities warning of the possibility, but they neglected to take timely action. The Court, with Justice Rehnquist again writing, rejected his claim on the authority of *Daniels*.

Justice Blackmun, joined by Justice Marshall, dissented. He agreed that mere negligence by government officials *"ordinarily"* would not be actionable under § 1983, but argued that the Court erred "in elevating this sensible rule of thumb to the status of inflexible constitutional dogma." In some cases, Blackmun concluded, governmental negligence was the kind of abuse of power at which the due process clause was aimed. He thought this was such a case:

"It is one thing to hold that a commonplace slip and fall, or the loss of a $23.50 hobby kit, does not rise to the dignified level of a constitutional violation. It is a somewhat different thing to say that negligence that permits anticipated inmate violence resulting in injury, or perhaps leads to the execution of the wrong prisoner, does not implicate the Constitution's guarantee of due process. . . . It seems to me that when a state

---

[e] Justices Marshall, Blackmun, and Stevens concurred in the result.

assumes sole responsibility for one's physical security and then ignores his call for help, the state cannot claim that it did not know a subsequent injury was likely to occur. [O]nce the state has taken away an inmate's means of protecting himself from attack by other inmates, a prison official's negligence in providing protection can amount to a deprivation of the inmate's liberty. . . ."

Justice Blackmun also argued that the record might support a finding of recklessness, which in his view "must be sufficient" to cause a deprivation under the 14th amendment even if negligence is not. In a separate dissenting opinion, Justice Brennan agreed that "merely negligent conduct . . . does not constitute a deprivation of liberty under the due process clause" but asserted that "official conduct which causes personal injury due to recklessness or deliberate indifference, does deprive the victim of liberty within the meaning of the 14th amendment."

Justice Stevens concurred in the judgments in both *Daniels* and *Davidson*. He declined to join in overruling the *Parratt* holding that negligence could constitute a 14th amendment "deprivation" in the "procedural due process" class of cases. For him, the losses in both *Daniels* and *Davidson* were a "deprivation," forcing him to confront directly the question whether the acceptance in state court of a sovereign immunity defense for official torts denied to the injured party the process that was due. He said it did not:

"*Davidson* puts the question whether a state policy of noncompensability for certain types of harm, in which state action may play a role, renders a state procedure constitutionally defective. In my judgment, a state policy that defeats recovery does not, in itself, carry that consequence. Those aspects of a state's tort regime that defeat recovery are not constitutionally invalid, so long as there is no fundamental unfairness in their operation. Thus, defenses such as contributory negligence or statutes of limitations may defeat recovery in particular cases without raising any question about the constitutionality of a state's procedures for disposing of tort litigation. Similarly, in my judgment, the mere fact that a state elects to provide some of its agents with a sovereign immunity defense in certain cases does not justify the conclusion that its remedial system is constitutionally inadequate. There is no reason to believe that the due process clause of the 14th amendment and the legislation enacted pursuant to § 5 of that amendment should be construed to suggest that the doctrine of sovereign immunity renders a state procedure fundamentally unfair."

5. Questions and Comments on *Parratt* and Its Progeny. After some confusion on the matter, *Zinermon* makes it clear that

Parratt does not signal a general return to the position advocated by Justice Frankfurter in *Monroe v. Pape*. As Justice Blackmun says, "for two of the three kinds of § 1983 claims that may be brought . . . under the due process clause of the 14th amendment," the presence or absence of a state remedy is irrelevant. Specifically, for violations of the Bill of Rights or of the "substantive components" of the due process clause, § 1983 provides remedial protection quite irrespective of any "process" provided by the state. It is only the third kind of claim— generalized interferences with liberty or property not covered by these more specific provisions—with which *Parratt* and its progeny are concerned. For these kinds of claims, once a person has been "deprived" of an identifiable "liberty" or "property" interest by state action, § 1983 will provide a remedy if the state has not provided adequate procedural protections.

Notice the points at which this kind of claim can fail. One first must establish a constitutionally protected "liberty" or "property" interest that is entitled to procedural protection. Compare *Paul v. Davis*. Second, one must prove an as yet uncertain level of culpability by the state actors—more than negligence, and perhaps less than intent, though proof of intentional action is plainly sufficient. Third, the claim is lost if a postdeprivation remedy is available in state court, presumably against either the state itself or the officials involved. And fourth, if Justice Stevens has his way on an issue not yet faced by the Court, the claim may yet be lost even if no postdeprivation remedy is provided. For him the denial of recovery by recognition of a state sovereign immunity defense (or presumably a good faith immunity defense provided to state officials) is not necessarily the failure to provide process that is due.

Is this an accurate analysis of the cases? Is there a simpler way to run the railroad?

Consider the perspective advanced by Michael Wells and Thomas Eaton in Substantive Due Process and the Scope of Constitutional Torts, 18 Ga.L.Rev. 201 (1984). They suggest that both *Parratt v. Taylor* and *Paul v. Davis* may have been correctly decided, but on an analysis very different from that of the Supreme Court. Specifically, they argue that these cases should not have been treated as raising procedural due process claims, but rather as raising questions of substantive due process. In their view, all such cases turn on a basic substantive issue: "Within the universe of state actions that harm individuals, which of those actions should the Court proscribe as deprivations of constitutionally protected life, liberty, or property, and which should be left for the states to grant or deny remedies for at their discretion?" The decisive factor in determining the reach of the constitutional tort, they suggest, is not whether the plaintiff was harmed, but rather "whether the defendant's conduct has passed the boundary of acceptable governmental behavior toward individuals." If not, then the individual injured by government conduct should be remitted to whatever remedies may be provided by state law, including, where state sovereign immunity applies, no remedy at all. Is this approach persuasive?

Finally, if *Parratt* and *Hudson* are right in looking to the adequacy of state law remedies to determine whether there has been a violation of federal due process, should the same approach be applied to *Paul v. Davis?* This question has been raised by Rodney Smolla in The Displacement of Federal Due Process Claims by State Tort Remedies: *Parratt v. Taylor* and *Logan v. Zimmerman Brush Co.*, 1982 U.Ill.L.Rev. 831. According to Smolla, "[t]he critics of *Paul v. Davis* have never explained satisfactorily how a § 1983 action is in any substantive law sense an improvement on the law of libel." Under this analysis, the state's provision of an adequate postdeprivation remedy would satisfy due process, and leave the injured plaintiff with no federal claim to pursue. If the state recognized a common law privilege in a libel action on the facts of *Paul*, would that necessarily make the process less than is due?

6. Bibliography. The issues raised in *Parratt* and its progeny have generated a great deal of comment. See Jack Beermann, Government Official Torts and the Takings Clause: Federalism and State Sovereign Immunity, 68 Boston U.L.Rev. 277 (1988); Mark R. Brown, De–Federalizing Common Law Torts: Empathy for *Parratt, Hudson,* and *Daniels,* 28 B.C.L.Rev. 813 (1987); William Burnham, Separating Constitutional and Common–Law Torts: A Critique and a Proposed Constitutional Theory of Duty, 73 Minn.L.Rev. 515 (1989); Leon Friedman, *Parratt v. Taylor:* Opening and Closing the Door on Section 1983, 9 Hast.Con.L.Q. 545 (1982); Barbara Kritchevsky, The Availability of a Federal Remedy Under 42 U.S.C. § 1983 for Prosecution Under an Unconstitutional State Statute: The Sixth Circuit Struggles in *Richardson v. City of South Euclid*, 22 U.Tol.L.Rev. 303 (1991); Rosalie Berger Levinson, Due Process Challenges to Governmental Actions: The Meaning of *Parratt* and *Hudson,* 18 Urb.Law. 189 (1986); Susanah M. Mead, Evolution of the "Species of Tort Liability" Created by 42 U.S.C. § 1983: Can Constitutional Tort be Saved From Extinction?, 55 Fordham L.Rev. 1 (1986); Henry Paul Monaghan, State Law Wrongs, State Law Remedies, and the 14th Amendment, 86 Colum.L.Rev. 979 (1986); Gerald Neuman, Law Review Articles that Backfire, 21 J.L. Reform 697 (1988); Frederic S. Schwartz, The Postdeprivation Remedy Doctrine of *Parratt v. Taylor* and Its Application to Cases of Land Use Regulation, 21 Ga.L.Rev. 601 (1987); Stephen Shapiro, Keeping Civil Rights Actions Against State Officials in Federal Court: Avoiding the Reach of *Parratt v. Taylor* and *Hudson v. Palmer,* 3 Law & Inequality 161 (1985); and Kathryn R. Urbonya, Establishing a Deprivation of a Constitutional Right to Personal Security Under Section 1983: The Use of Unjustified Force by State Officials in Violation of the Fourth, Eighth, and Fourteenth Amendments, 51 Albany L.Rev. 171 (1987).

Two other articles relate the *Parratt* line of cases to the policy-or-custom requirement of *Monell.* See Susan Bandes, *Monell, Parratt, Daniels,* and *Davidson:* Distinguishing a Custom or Policy from a Random, Unauthorized Act, 72 Iowa L.Rev. 101 (1986); Christina Whitman, Government Responsibility for Constitutional Torts, 85 Mich.L. Rev. 225 (1986).

Page 183, add a footnote at the end of Note 5:

[c] For a similar decision on another five-four split, see Wilder v. Virginia Hospital Association, 496 U.S. 498 (1990). The Court held that a provision of the Medicaid Act requiring that states reimburse hospitals according to rates found by the state to be "reasonable and adequate to meet the costs" was enforceable in a private cause of action under § 1983. The majority followed *Wright* and distinguished *Sea Clammers.* Chief Justice Rehnquist and Justices O'Connor, Scalia, and Kennedy dissented.

By contrast, the Court voted seven-two against § 1983 enforcement of the Adoption Assistance and Child Welfare Act of 1980, 42 U.S.C. §§ 620–28, 670–79a. The statute offers federal reimbursement for certain state expenses in the area of adoption and foster care, provided that the state has in force an approved plan, including "reasonable efforts" to prevent removal of children from their homes and to facilitate reunification of families. In Suter v. Artist, ___ U.S. ___ (1992), the Court ruled the statute did not confer on its beneficiaries a private right enforceable under § 1983. The critical fact was the lack of Congressional intent to create a private damages remedy. Only Justices Blackmun and Stevens dissented.

Page 188, delete Note 9 and add three new Notes:

9. *Jett v. Dallas Independent School District*: Relation Between § 1981 and § 1983. Jett v. Dallas Independent School District, 491 U.S. 701 (1989), involved 42 U.S.C. § 1981, which establishes a right "to make and enforce contracts" free from intentional racial discrimination.[d] On its face, § 1981 only creates rights; it is silent as to remedy. Jett, a public school teacher and football coach, claimed that he was reassigned on the basis of race in violation of § 1981. The question before the Court, in part, was the source of a cause of action he might assert against the school district as a public entity. It was clear from prior decisions that suits against *private* parties under § 1981 could be based on a remedy implied from § 1981 itself. But the Court held that § 1983, which was originally enacted five years after § 1981, supplied the cause of action against units of local government for violations of rights established by § 1981.[e]

[d] It was held in Runyon v. McCrary, 427 U.S. 160 (1976), that § 1981 precluded private schools which otherwise held themselves open to the public from discriminating on the basis of race. *Runyon* is a main case in the Casebook at page 213.

[e] By so holding, the Court then was able to apply decisions under § 1983 to the issue before it, specifically whether the doctrine of respondeat superior rendered the school district itself liable for discriminatory acts by school officials. It was clear under the § 1983 precedents that such lia-

94 CIVIL RIGHTS Ch. 1

10. *Golden State Transit Corp. v. Los Angeles*: § 1983 Actions to Enforce Federal Preemption of State Law. Can § 1983 be used to recover damages for state regulation that is unlawful only because it is preempted by federal law? The answer, it seems, is "It depends."

In 1986 the Supreme Court ruled that Los Angeles could not condition renewal of a taxi franchise on settlement of a labor dispute between the cab company and its union. Golden State Transit Corp. v. City of Los Angeles, 475 U.S. 608 (1986). That action, said the Court, interfered with the company's right under the National Labor Relations Act to use economic weapons in collective bargaining. The company then sued for money damages under § 1983. A divided Supreme Court upheld the company's claim, but in terms that did not comprehend all claims based on federal preemption of state law. Golden State Transit Corp. v. City of Los Angeles, 493 U.S. 103 (1989).

Speaking through Justice Stevens, the majority reasoned that the cab company was "the intended beneficiary of a statutory scheme that prevents governmental interference with the collective-bargaining process." Because the NLRA created rights in both labor and management, not only against each other but also against the state, the cab company could enforce those rights by a damages action under § 1983. In other cases, however, a private party might be only an incidental beneficiary of a federal scheme intended to benefit the general public. In that circumstance, damages under § 1983 would not be available, even though the litigant would have the right to enjoin the preempted state regulation.

Justice Kennedy, joined by Chief Justice Rehnquist and Justice O'Connor, dissented. He argued that § 1983 should not be interpreted to authorize money damages "when the only wrong committed by the state or its local entities is misapprehending the precise location of the boundaries between state and federal power." [f]

11. *Dennis v. Higgins*: § 1983 Actions to Enforce Negative Commerce Clause Claims. *Golden State* was applied in another context in Dennis v. Higgins, ___ U.S. ___ (1991). Dennis was the owner of a motor carrier. He filed suit in a Nebraska state court against the Director of the Nebraska Department of Motor Vehicles, arguing that a particular tax on motor carriers violated the negative commerce clause. One of the claims asserted was based on § 1983. The trial court held the tax unconstitutional on the asserted ground, and enjoined its future collection. But the court dismissed the § 1983

bility was not permitted. See Monell v. Department of Social Services, 436 U.S. 658 (1978), which appears as a main case in the Casebook at page 67. *Jett* itself is a main case in this Supplement at page 121, infra.

[f] For analysis of the implications of *Golden State*, see Henry Paul Monaghan, Federal Statutory Review under Section 1983 and the APA, 91 Colum.L.Rev. 233 (1991).

claim. The state Supreme Court affirmed the dismissal of the § 1983 claim on the ground, inter alia, that "the commerce clause does not establish individual rights against government, but instead allocates power between the state and federal governments."

The Supreme Court reversed in an opinion by Justice White. The issue was whether the commerce clause served only the abstract goals of promoting national economic and political unity, or whether it was also designed to benefit individuals. The Court held that the clause "of its own force imposes limitations on state regulation of commerce, and is the source of a right of action in those injured by regulations that exceed such limitations" and that it therefore confers "rights, privileges, or immunities" within the meaning of those words as used in § 1983.

Justice Kennedy, joined by Chief Justice Rehnquist, dissented. He argued that the majority decision "compounds the error of *Golden State.*"

Chapter II

ADDITIONAL RECONSTRUCTION LEGISLATION

Page 231, add to footnote a:

For consideration of the same issues by the same author after the decisions, see Eileen Kaufman and Martin Schwartz, Civil Rights in Transition: Sections 1981 and 1982 Cover Discrimination on the Basis of Ancestry and Ethnicity, 4 Touro L.Rev. 183 (1988).

Page 256, add the following at the end of Section 2:

PATTERSON v. McLEAN CREDIT UNION

Supreme Court of the United States, 1989.
491 U.S. 164.

JUSTICE KENNEDY delivered the opinion of the Court.

In this case, we consider important issues respecting the meaning and coverage of one of our oldest civil rights statutes, 42 U.S.C. § 1981.

I

Petitioner Brenda Patterson, a black woman, was employed by respondent McLean Credit Union as a teller and a file coordinator, commencing in May 1972. In July 1982, she was laid off. After the termination, petitioner commenced this action in District Court. She alleged that respondent, in violation of 42 U.S.C. § 1981, had harassed her, failed to promote her to an intermediate accounting clerk position, and then discharged her, all because of her race. . . .

The District Court determined that a claim for racial harassment is not actionable under § 1981 and declined to submit that part of the case to the jury. The jury did receive and deliberate upon petitioner's § 1981 claims based on alleged discrimination in her discharge and the failure to promote her, and it found for respondent on both claims. . . .

In the Court of Appeals, petitioner raised two matters which are relevant here. First, she challenged the District Court's refusal to submit to the jury her § 1981 claim based on racial harassment. Second, she argued that the District Court erred in instructing the jury that in order to prevail on her § 1981 claim of discriminatory failure to promote, she must show that she was better qualified than the white employee who she alleges was promoted in her stead. The Court of Appeals affirmed. On the racial harassment issue, the court held that while instances of racial harassment "may implicate the terms and conditions of employment under title VII [of the Civil Rights Act of 1964, 42 U.S.C. § 2000e,] and of course may be probative of the discriminatory intent required to be shown in a § 1981 action," racial harassment itself is not cognizable under § 1981 because "racial harassment does not abridge the right to 'make' and 'enforce' contracts." On the jury instruction issue, the court held that once respondent had advanced superior qualification as a legitimate nondiscriminatory reason for its promotion decision, petitioner had the burden of persuasion to show that respondent's justification was a pretext and that she was better qualified than the employee who was chosen for the job.

We granted certiorari to decide whether petitioner's claim of racial harassment in her employment is actionable under § 1981, and whether the jury instruction given by the District Court on petitioner's § 1981 promotion claim was error. After oral argument on these issues, we requested the parties to brief and argue an additional question:

> "Whether or not the interpretation of 42 U.S.C. § 1981 adopted by this Court in Runyon v. McCrary, 427 U.S. 160 (1976), should be reconsidered."

We now decline to overrule our decision in Runyon v. McCrary, 427 U.S. 160 (1976). We hold further that racial harassment relating to the conditions of employment is not actionable under § 1981 because that provision does not apply to conduct which occurs after the formation of a contract and which does not interfere with the right to enforce established contract obligations. Finally, we hold that the District Court erred in instructing the jury regarding petitioner's burden in proving her discriminatory promotion claim.

II

In *Runyon*, the Court considered whether § 1981 prohibits private schools from excluding children who are qualified for admission, solely on the basis of race. We held that § 1981 did prohibit such conduct, noting that it was already well established in prior decisions that § 1981 "prohibits racial discrimination in the making and enforcement of private contracts." The arguments about whether *Runyon* was decided correctly in light of the language and history of the statute were examined and discussed with great care in our decision. It was recognized at the time that a strong case could be made for the view that the statute does not reach private conduct, but that view did not prevail. Some members of this Court believe that *Runyon* was decided incorrectly, and others consider it correct on its own footing, but the question before us is whether it ought now to be overturned. We conclude after reargument that *Runyon* should not be overruled, and we now reaffirm that § 1981 prohibits racial discrimination in the making and enforcement of private contracts.

The Court has said often and with great emphasis that "the doctrine of stare decisis is of fundamental importance to the rule of law." Welch v. Texas Dept. of Highways and Public Transportation, 483 U.S. 468, 494 (1987). Although we have cautioned that "stare decisis is a principle of policy and not a mechanical formula of adherence to the latest decision," Boys Markets, Inc. v. Retail Clerks, 398 U.S. 235, 241 (1970), it is indisputable that stare decisis is a basic self-governing principle within the judicial branch, which is entrusted with the sensitive and difficult task of fashioning and preserving a jurisprudential system that is not based upon "an arbitrary discretion." The Federalist, No. 78, p. 490 (H. Lodge ed. 1888) (A. Hamilton). See also Vasquez v. Hillery, 474 U.S. 254, 265 (1986) (stare decisis ensures that "the law will not merely change erratically" and "permits society to presume that bedrock principles are founded in the law rather than in the proclivities of individuals").

Our precedents are not sacrosanct, for we have overruled prior decisions where the necessity and propriety of doing so has been established. Nonetheless, we have held that "any departure from the doctrine of stare decisis demands special justification." Arizona v. Rumsey, 467 U.S. 203, 212 (1984). We have said also that the burden borne by the party advocating the abandonment of an established precedent is greater where the Court is asked to overrule a point of statutory construction. Considerations of stare decisis have special force in the area of statutory interpretation, for here, unlike in the context of constitutional interpretation, the legislative power is implicated, and Congress remains free to alter what we have done.

We conclude, upon direct consideration of the issue, that no special justification has been shown for overruling *Runyon*. In cases where statutory precedents have been overruled, the primary reason for the Court's shift in position has been the intervening development of the law, through either the growth of judicial doctrine or further action taken by Congress. Where such changes have removed or weakened the conceptual underpinnings from the prior decision or where the later law has rendered the decision irreconcilable with competing legal doctrines or policies, the Court has not hesitated to overrule an earlier decision. Our decision in *Runyon* has not been undermined by subsequent changes or development in the law.

Another traditional justification for overruling a prior case is that a precedent may be a positive detriment to coherence and consistency in the law, either because of inherent confusion created by an unworkable decision or because the decision poses a direct obstacle to the realization of important objectives embodied in other laws. In this regard, we do not find *Runyon* to be unworkable or confusing. Respondent and various amici have urged that *Runyon*'s interpretation of § 1981, as applied to contracts of employment, frustrates the objectives of title VII. The argument is that a substantial overlap in coverage between the two statutes, given the considerable differences in their remedial schemes, undermines Congress' detailed efforts in title VII to resolve disputes about racial discrimination in private employment through conciliation rather than litigation as an initial matter. After examining the point with care, however, we believe that a sound construction of the language of § 1981 yields an interpretation which does not frustrate the congressional objectives in title VII to any significant degree. See part III, infra.

Finally, it has sometimes been said that a precedent becomes more vulnerable as it becomes outdated and after being " 'tested by experience, has been found to be inconsistent with the sense of justice or with the social welfare.' " *Runyon,* supra, at 191 (Stevens, J., concurring), quoting B. Cardozo, The Nature of the Judicial Process 149 (1921). Whatever the effect of this consideration may be in statutory cases, it offers no support for overruling *Runyon.* In recent decades, state and federal legislation has been enacted to prohibit private racial discrimination in many aspects of our society. Whether *Runyon's* interpretation of § 1981 as prohibiting racial discrimination in the making and enforcement of private contracts is right or wrong as an original matter, it is certain that it is not inconsistent with the prevailing sense of justice in this country. To the contrary, *Runyon* is entirely consistent with our society's deep commitment to the eradication of discrimination based on a person's race or the color of his or her skin.[1]

We decline to overrule *Runyon* and acknowledge that its holding remains the governing law in this area.

---

[1] Justice Brennan chides us for ignoring what he considers "two very obvious reasons" for adhering to *Runyon.* First, he argues at length that *Runyon* was correct as an initial matter. As we have said, however, it is unnecessary for us to address this issue because we agree that, whether or not *Runyon* was correct as an initial matter, there is no special justification for departing here from the rule of stare decisis.

Justice Brennan objects also to the fact that our stare decisis analysis places no reliance on the fact that Congress itself has not overturned the interpretation of § 1981 contained in *Runyon,* and in effect has ratified our decision in that case. This is no oversight on our part. As we reaffirm today, considerations of stare decisis have added force in statutory cases because Congress may alter what we have done by amending the statute. In constitutional cases, by contrast, Congress lacks this option, and an incorrect or outdated precedent may be overturned only by our own reconsideration or by constitutional amendment. It does not follow, however, that Congress' failure to overturn a statutory precedent is reason for this Court to adhere to it. It is "impossible to assert with any degree of assurance that congressional failure to act represents" affirmative congressional approval of the Court's statutory interpretation. Johnson v. Transportation Agency, 480 U.S. 616, 671–72 (1987) (Scalia, J., dissenting). Congress may legislate, moreover, only through the passage of a bill which is approved by both Houses and signed by the President. Congressional inaction cannot amend a duly enacted statute. We think also that the materials relied upon by Justice Brennan as "more positive signs of Congress' views," which are the *failure* of an amendment to a *different statute* offered *before* our decision in *Runyon* and the passage of an attorney's fee statute having nothing to do with our holding in *Runyon* demonstrate well the danger of placing undue reliance on the concept of congressional "ratification."

III

Our conclusion that we should adhere to our decision in *Runyon* that § 1981 applies to private conduct is not enough to decide this case. We must decide also whether the conduct of which petitioner complains falls within one of the enumerated rights protected by § 1981.

A

Section 1981 reads as follows:

> "All persons within the jurisdiction of the United States shall have the same right in every State and Territory to make and enforce contracts, to sue, be parties, give evidence, and to the full and equal benefit of all laws and proceedings for the security of persons and property as is enjoyed by white citizens and shall be subject to like punishment, pains, penalties, taxes, licenses, and exactions of every kind, and to no other."

The most obvious feature of the provision is the restriction of its scope to forbidding discrimination in the "mak[ing] and enforce[ment]" of contracts alone. Where an alleged act of discrimination does not involve the impairment of one of these specific rights, § 1981 provides no relief. Section 1981 cannot be construed as a general proscription of racial discrimination in all aspects of contract relations, for it expressly prohibits discrimination only in the making and enforcement of contracts. . . .

By its plain terms, the relevant provision in § 1981 protects two rights: "the same right . . . to make . . . contracts" and "the same right . . . to . . . enforce contracts." The first of these protections extends only to the formation of a contract, but not to problems that may arise later from the conditions of continuing employment. The statute prohibits, when based on race, the refusal to enter into a contract with someone, as well as the offer to make a contract only on discriminatory terms. But the right to make contracts does not extend, as a matter of either logic or semantics, to conduct by the employer after the contract relation has been established, including breach of the terms of the contract or imposition of discriminatory working conditions. Such postformation conduct does not involve the right to make a contract, but rather implicates the performance of established contract obligations and the conditions of continuing employment, matters more naturally governed by state contract law and title VII.

The second of these guarantees, "the same right . . . to . . . enforce contracts . . . as is enjoyed by white citizens," embraces protection of a legal process, and of a right of access to legal process, that will address and resolve contract-law claims without regard to race. In this respect, it prohibits discrimination that infects the legal process in ways that prevent one from enforcing contract rights, by reason of his or her race, and this is so whether this discrimination is attributed to a statute or simply to existing practices. It also covers wholly *private* efforts to impede access to the courts or obstruct nonjudicial methods of adjudicating disputes about the force of binding obligations, as well as discrimination by private entities, such as labor unions, in enforcing the terms of a contract. Following this principle and consistent with our holding in *Runyon* that § 1981 applies to private conduct, we have held that certain private entities such as labor unions, which bear explicit responsibilities to process grievances, press claims, and represent members in disputes over the terms of binding obligations that run from the employer to the employee, are subject to liability under § 1981 for racial discrimination in the enforcement of labor contracts. See Goodman v. Lukens Steel Co., 482 U.S. 656 (1987). The right to enforce contracts does not, however, extend beyond conduct by an employer which impairs an employee's ability to enforce through legal process his or her established contract rights. As Justice White put it with much force in [his] *Runyon* [dissent], one cannot seriously "contend that the grant of the other rights enumerated in § 1981, [that is, other than the right to "make" contracts,] i.e., the rights 'to sue, be parties, give evidence,' and '*enforce* contracts' accomplishes anything other than the removal of *legal* disabilities to sue, be a party, testify or enforce a contract. Indeed, it is impossible to give such language any other meaning."

B

Applying these principles to the case before us, we agree with the Court of Appeals that petitioner's racial harassment claim is not actionable under § 1981. Petitioner has alleged that during her employment with respondent, she was subjected to various forms of racial harassment from her supervisor. As summarized by the Court of Appeals, petitioner testified that

> "[her supervisor] periodically stared at her for several minutes at a time; that he gave her too many tasks, causing her to complain that she was under too much pressure; that among the tasks given her were sweeping and dusting, jobs not given to white employees. On one occasion, she testified, [her supervisor] also criticized her in staff meetings while not similarly criticizing white employees."

Petitioner also alleges that she was passed over for promotion, not offered training for higher level jobs, and denied wage increases, all because of her race.[2]

---

[2] In addition, another of respondent's managers testified that when he recommended a different black person for a position as a data processor, petitioner's supervisor stated that he did not "need any more problems around here," and that he would "search for additional people who are not black."

With the exception perhaps of her claim that respondent refused to promote her to a position as an accountant, see part IV, infra, none of the conduct which petitioner alleges as part of the racial harassment against her involves either a refusal to make a contract with her or the impairment of her ability to enforce her established contract rights. Rather, the conduct which petitioner labels as actionable racial harassment is postformation conduct by the employer relating to the terms and conditions of continuing employment. This is apparent from petitioner's own proposed jury instruction on her § 1981 racial harassment claim:

> "The plaintiff has also brought an action for harassment in employment against the defendant, under the same statute, 42 U.S.C. § 1981. An employer is guilty of racial discrimination in employment where it has either created or condoned a substantially discriminatory *work environment*. An employee has a right to work in an *environment* free from racial prejudice. If the plaintiff has proven by a preponderance of the evidence that she was subjected to racial harassment by her manager while employed at the defendant, or that she was subjected to a *work environment* not free from racial prejudice which was either created or condoned by the defendant, then it would be your duty to find for plaintiff on this issue." (Emphasis added.)

Without passing on the contents of this instruction, it is plain to us that what petitioner is attacking are the conditions of her employment.

This type of conduct, reprehensible though it be if true, is not actionable under § 1981, which covers only conduct at the initial formation of the contract and conduct which impairs the right to enforce contract obligations through legal process. Rather, such conduct is actionable under the more expansive reach of title VII of the Civil Rights Act of 1964. The latter statute makes it unlawful for an employer to "discriminate against any individual with respect to his compensation, terms, conditions, or privileges of employment." 42 U.S.C. § 2000e–2(a)(1). Racial harassment in the course of employment is actionable under title VII's prohibition against discrimination in the "terms, conditions, or privileges of employment." "[T]he [Equal Employment Opportunity Commission (EEOC)] has long recognized that harassment on the basis of race . . . is an unlawful employment practice in violation of § 703 of title VII of the Civil Rights Act." See EEOC Compliance Manual § 615.7 (1982). While this Court has not yet had the opportunity to pass directly upon this interpretation of title VII, the lower federal courts have uniformly upheld this view, and we implicitly have approved it in a recent decision concerning sexual harassment, Meritor Savings Bank v. Vinson, 477 U.S. 57, 65–66 (1986). As we said in that case, "harassment [which is] sufficiently severe or pervasive 'to alter the conditions of [the victim's] employment and create an abusive working environment,'" is actionable under title VII because it "affects a 'term, condition, or privilege' of employment."

Interpreting § 1981 to cover postformation conduct unrelated to an employee's right to enforce her contract, such as incidents relating to the conditions of employment, is not only inconsistent with that statute's limitation to the making and enforcement of contracts, but would also undermine the detailed and well-crafted procedures for conciliation and resolution of title VII claims. In title VII, Congress set up an elaborate administrative procedure, implemented through the EEOC, that is designed to assist in the investigation of claims of racial discrimination in the workplace and to work towards the resolution of these claims through conciliation rather than litigation. Only after these procedures have been exhausted, and the plaintiff has obtained a "right to sue" letter from the EEOC, may she bring a title VII action in court. Section 1981, by contrast, provides no administrative review or opportunity for conciliation.

Where conduct is covered by both § 1981 and title VII, the detailed procedures of title VII are rendered a dead letter, as the plaintiff is free to pursue a claim by bringing suit under § 1981 without resort to those statutory prerequisites. We agree that, after *Runyon*, there is some necessary overlap between title VII and § 1981, and that where the statutes do in fact overlap we are not at liberty "to infer any positive preference for one over the other." Johnson v. Railway Express Agency, Inc., 421 U.S. 454, 461 (1975). We should be reluctant, however, to read an earlier statute broadly where the result is to circumvent the detailed remedial scheme constructed in a later statute. That egregious racial harassment of employees is forbidden by a clearly applicable law (title VII), moreover, should lessen the temptation for this Court to twist the interpretation of another statute (§ 1981) to cover the same conduct. In the particular case before us, we do not know for certain why petitioner chose to pursue only remedies under § 1981, and not under title VII. But in any event, the availability of the latter statute should deter us from a tortuous construction of the former statute to cover this type of claim.

By reading § 1981 not as a general proscription of racial discrimination in all aspects of contract relations, but as limited to the enumerated rights within its express protection, specifically the right to make and enforce contracts, we may preserve the integrity of title VII's procedures without sacrificing any significant coverage of the civil rights laws.[4] Of course, some overlap will remain between the two

---

[4] Unnecessary overlap between title VII and § 1981 would also serve to upset the delicate balance between employee and employer rights struck by title VII in other respects. For instance, a plaintiff in a title VII action is limited to a recovery of backpay, whereas under § 1981 a plaintiff may be entitled to plenary compensatory damages, as well as punitive damages in an appropriate case. Both the employee and employer will be unlikely to agree to a conciliatory resolution of the dispute under title VII if the employer can be found lia-

statutes: specifically, a refusal to enter into an employment contract on the basis of race. Such a claim would be actionable under title VII as a "refus[al] to hire" based on race, 42 U.S.C. § 2000e–2(a), and under § 1981 as an impairment of "the same right . . . to make . . . contracts . . . as . . . white citizens." But this is precisely where it would make sense for Congress to provide for the overlap. At this stage of the employee-employer relation title VII's mediation and conciliation procedures would be of minimal effect, for there is not yet a relation to salvage.

C

The Solicitor General and Justice Brennan offer two alternative interpretations of § 1981. The Solicitor General argues that the language of § 1981, especially the words "the same right," requires us to look outside § 1981 to the terms of particular contracts and to state law for the obligations and covenants to be protected by the federal statute. Under this view, § 1981 has no actual substantive content, but instead mirrors only the specific protections that are afforded under the law of contracts of each state. Under this view, racial harassment in the conditions of employment is actionable when, and only when, it amounts to a breach of contract under state law. We disagree. For one thing, to the extent that it assumes that prohibitions contained in § 1981 incorporate only those protections afforded by the states, this theory is directly inconsistent with *Runyon*, which we today decline to overrule. A more fundamental failing in the Solicitor's argument is that racial harassment amounting to breach of contract, like racial harassment alone, impairs neither the right to make nor the right to enforce a contract. It is plain that the former right is not implicated directly by an employer's breach in the performance of obligations under a contract already formed. Nor is it correct to say that racial harassment amounting to a breach of contract impairs an employee's right to enforce his contract. To the contrary, conduct amounting to a breach of contract under state law is precisely what the language of § 1981 does not cover. That is because, in such a case, provided that plaintiff's access to state court or any other dispute resolution process has not been impaired by either the state or a private actor, the plaintiff is free to enforce the terms of the contract in state court, and cannot possibly assert, by reason of the breach alone, that he has been deprived of the same right to enforce contracts as is enjoyed by white citizens.

In addition, interpreting § 1981 to cover racial harassment amounting to a breach of contract would federalize all state-law claims for breach of contract where racial animus is alleged, since § 1981

ble for much greater amounts under § 1981.

covers all types of contracts, not just employment contracts. Although we must do so when Congress plainly directs, as a rule we should be and are "reluctant to federalize" matters traditionally covered by state common law. By confining § 1981 to the impairment of the specific rights to make and enforce contracts, Congress cannot be said to have intended such a result with respect to breach of contract claims. It would be no small paradox, moreover, that under the interpretation of § 1981 offered by the Solicitor General, the more a state extends its own contract law to protect employees in general and minorities in particular, the greater would be the potential displacement of state law by § 1981. We do not think § 1981 need be read to produce such a peculiar result.

Justice Brennan, for his part, would hold that racial harassment is actionable under § 1981 when "the acts constituting harassment [are] sufficiently severe or pervasive as effectively to belie any claim that the contract was entered into in a racially neutral manner." We do not find this standard an accurate or useful articulation of which contract claims are actionable under § 1981 and which are not. The fact that racial harassment is "severe or pervasive" does not by magic transform a challenge to the conditions of employment, not actionable under § 1981, into a viable challenge to the employer's refusal to make a contract. We agree that racial harassment may be used as evidence that a divergence in the explicit terms of particular contracts is explained by racial animus. Thus, for example, if a potential employee is offered (and accepts) a contract to do a job for less money than others doing like work, evidence of racial harassment in the workplace may show that the employer, at the time of formation, was unwilling to enter into a nondiscriminatory contract. However, and this is the critical point, the question under § 1981 remains whether the employer, *at the time of the formation of the contract*, in fact intentionally refused to enter into a contract with the employee on racially neutral terms. The plaintiff's ability to plead that the racial harassment is "severe or pervasive" should not allow him to bootstrap a challenge to the conditions of employment (actionable, if at all, under title VII) into a claim under § 1981 that the employer refused to offer the petitioner the "same right to . . . make" a contract. We think it clear that the conduct challenged by petitioner relates not to her employer's refusal to enter into a contract with her, but rather to the conditions of her employment.[6]

---

[6] In his separate opinion, Justice Stevens construes the phrase "the same right . . . to make . . . contracts" with ingenuity to cover various postformation conduct by the employer. But our task here is not to construe § 1981 to punish all acts of discrimination in contracting in a like fashion, but rather merely to give a fair reading to scope of the statutory terms used by Congress. We adhere today to our decision in *Runyon* that § 1981 reaches private conduct, but do not believe that holding compels us to read the statutory terms "make" and "enforce" beyond their plain and common sense meaning. We believe that the lower courts will have little difficulty applying the straightforward principles that we announce today.

106 CIVIL RIGHTS Ch. 2

IV

Petitioner's claim that respondent violated § 1981 by failing to promote her, because of race, to a position as an intermediate accounting clerk is a different matter. As a preliminary point, we note that the Court of Appeals distinguished between petitioner's claims of racial harassment and discriminatory promotion, stating that although the former did not give rise to a discrete § 1981 claim, "[c]laims of racially discriminatory . . . promotion go to the very existence and nature of the employment contract and thus fall easily within § 1981's protection." We think that somewhat overstates the case. Consistent with what we have said in part III, supra, the question whether a promotion claim is actionable under § 1981 depends upon whether the nature of the change in position was such that it involved the opportunity to enter into a new contract with the employer. If so, then the employer's refusal to enter the new contract is actionable under § 1981. In making this determination, a lower court should give a fair and natural reading to the statutory phrase "the same right . . . to make . . . contracts," and should not strain in an undue manner the language of § 1981. Only where the promotion rises to the level of an opportunity for a new and distinct relation between the employee and the employer is such a claim actionable under § 1981. Because respondent has not argued at any stage that petitioner's promotion claim is not cognizable under § 1981, we need not address the issue further here.

This brings us to the question of the District Court's jury instructions on petitioner's promotion claim. We think the District Court erred when it instructed the jury that petitioner had to prove that she was better qualified than the white employee who allegedly received the promotion. In order to prevail under § 1981, a plaintiff must prove purposeful discrimination. General Building Contractors Assn., Inc. v. Pennsylvania, 458 U.S. 375, 391 (1982). We have developed, in analogous areas of civil rights law, a carefully designed framework of proof to determine, in the context of disparate treatment, the ultimate issue of whether the defendant intentionally discriminated against the plaintiff. See Texas Dept. of Community Affairs v. Burdine, 450 U.S. 248 (1981); McDonnell Douglas Corp. v. Green, 411 U.S. 792 (1973). We agree with the Court of Appeals that this scheme of proof, structured as a "sensible, orderly way to evaluate the evidence in light of common experience as it bears on the critical question of discrimination," Furnco Construction Corp. v. Waters, 438 U.S. 567, 577 (1978), should apply to claims of racial discrimination under § 1981.

Although the Court of Appeals recognized that the *McDonnell Douglas/Burdine* scheme of proof should apply in § 1981 cases such as this one, it erred in describing petitioner's burden. Under our well-established framework, the plaintiff has the initial burden of proving, by the preponderance of the evidence, a prima facie case of discrimination. The burden is not onerous. Here, petitioner need only prove by a preponderance of the evidence that she applied for and was qualified for an available position, that she was rejected, and that after she was rejected respondent either continued to seek applicants for the position, or as is alleged here, filled the position with a white employee.

Once the plaintiff establishes a prima facie case, an inference of discrimination arises. In order to rebut this inference, the employer must present evidence that the plaintiff was rejected, or the other applicant was chosen, for a legitimate nondiscriminatory reason. Here, respondent presented evidence that it gave the job to the white applicant because she was better qualified for the position, and therefore rebutted any presumption of discrimination that petitioner may have established. At this point, as our prior cases make clear, petitioner retains the final burden of persuading the jury of intentional discrimination.[a]

Although petitioner retains the ultimate burden of persuasion, our cases make clear that she must also have the opportunity to demonstrate that respondent's proffered reasons for its decision were not its true reasons. In doing so, petitioner is not limited to presenting evidence of a certain type. This is where the District Court erred. The evidence which petitioner can present in an attempt to establish that respondent's stated reasons are pretextual may take a variety of forms. Indeed, she might seek to demonstrate that respondent's claim to have promoted a better-qualified applicant was pretextual by showing that she was in fact better qualified than the person chosen for the position. The District Court erred, however, in instructing the jury that in order to succeed petitioner was *required* to make such a showing. There are certainly other ways in which petitioner could seek to prove that respondent's reasons were pretextual. Thus, for example, petitioner could seek to persuade the jury that respondent had not offered the true reason for its promotion decision by presenting evidence of respondent's past treatment of petitioner, including the instances of the racial harassment which she alleges and respondent's failure to train her for an accounting position. While we do not intend to say this evidence necessarily would be sufficient to carry the day, it cannot be denied that it is one of the various ways in which petitioner might seek to prove intentional discrimination on the part of respondent. She may

---

[a] For an elaborate and sharply divided consideration of the burden of proof requirements in a related context, see Price Waterhouse v. Hopkins, 490 U.S. 228 (1989). Six Justices agreed substantially with the following statement:

"[W]hen a plaintiff in a title VII case proves that her gender played a motivating part in an employment decision, the defendant may avoid a finding of liability only by proving by a preponderance of the evidence that it would have made the same decision even if it had not taken the plaintiff's gender into account." There was division on the Court whether this requirement was an elaboration or a modification of the *McDonnell Douglas/Burdine* rules.—[Footnote by eds.]

not be forced to pursue any particular means of demonstrating that respondent's stated reasons are pretextual. It was, therefore, error for the District Court to instruct the jury that petitioner could carry her burden of persuasion only by showing that she was in fact better qualified than the white applicant who got the job.

V

The law now reflects society's consensus that discrimination based on the color of one's skin is a profound wrong of tragic dimension. Neither our words nor our decisions should be interpreted as signaling one inch of retreat from Congress' policy to forbid discrimination in the private, as well as the public, sphere. Nevertheless, in the area of private discrimination, to which the ordinance of the Constitution does not directly extend, our role is limited to interpreting what Congress may do and has done. The statute before us, which is only one part of Congress' extensive civil rights legislation, does not cover the acts of harassment alleged here.

In sum, we affirm the Court of Appeals' dismissal of petitioner's racial harassment claim as not actionable under § 1981. The Court of Appeals erred, however, in holding that petitioner could succeed in her discriminatory promotion claim under § 1981 only by proving that she was better qualified for the position of intermediate accounting clerk than the white employee who in fact was promoted. The judgment of the Court of Appeals is therefore vacated insofar as it relates to petitioner's discriminatory promotion claim, and the case is remanded for further proceedings consistent with this opinion.

It is so ordered.

JUSTICE BRENNAN, with whom JUSTICE MARSHALL and JUSTICE BLACKMUN join, and with whom JUSTICE STEVENS joins as to parts II–B, II–C, and III, concurring in the judgment in part and dissenting in part.

What the Court declines to snatch away with one hand, it takes with the other. Though the Court today reaffirms § 1981's applicability to private conduct, it simultaneously gives this landmark civil rights statute a needlessly cramped interpretation. The Court has to strain hard to justify this choice to confine § 1981 within the narrowest possible scope, selecting the most pinched reading of the phrase "same right to make a contract," ignoring powerful historical evidence about the Reconstruction Congress' concerns, and bolstering its parsimonious rendering by reference to a statute enacted nearly a century after § 1981, and plainly not intended to affect its reach. When it comes to deciding whether a civil rights statute should be construed to further our nation's commitment to the eradication of racial discrimination, the Court adopts a formalistic method of interpretation antithetical to Congress' vision of a society in which contractual opportunities are equal. I dissent from the Court's holding that § 1981 does not encompass Patterson's racial harassment claim.

I

Thirteen years ago, in deciding *Runyon v. McCrary*, this Court treated as already "well established" the proposition that "§ 1 of the Civil Rights Act of 1866, 42 U.S.C. § 1981, prohibits racial discrimination in the making and enforcement of private contracts," as well as state-mandated inequalities, drawn along racial lines, in individuals' ability to make and enforce contracts. Since deciding *Runyon*, we have upon a number of occasions treated as settled law its interpretation of § 1981 as extending to private discrimination. . . .

The Court's reaffirmation of this long and consistent line of precedents establishing that § 1981 encompasses private discrimination is based upon its belated decision to adhere to the principle of stare decisis—a decision that could readily and would better have been made before the Court decided to put *Runyon* and its progeny into question by ordering reargument in this case. While there is an exception to stare decisis for precedents that have proved "outdated, . . . unworkable, or otherwise legitimately vulnerable to serious reconsideration," Vasquez v. Hillery, 474 U.S. 254, 266 (1986), it has never been arguable that *Runyon* falls within it. Rather, *Runyon* is entirely consonant with our society's deep commitment to eradication of discrimination based on a person's race or the color of her skin. That commitment is not bounded by legal concepts such as "state action," but is the product of a national consensus that racial discrimination is incompatible with our best conception of our communal life, and with each individual's rightful expectation that her full participation in the community will not be contingent upon her race. In the past, this Court has overruled decisions antagonistic to our nation's commitment to the ideal of a society in which a person's opportunities do not depend on her race, e.g., Brown v. Board of Education, 347 U.S. 483 (1954) (overruling Plessy v. Ferguson, 163 U.S. 537 (1896)), and I find it disturbing that the Court has in this case chosen to reconsider, without any request from the parties, a statutory construction so in harmony with that ideal.

Having decided, however, to reconsider *Runyon*, and now to reaffirm it by appeal to stare decisis, the Court glosses over what are in my view two very obvious reasons for refusing to overrule this interpretation of § 1981: that *Runyon* was correctly decided, and that in any event Congress has ratified our construction of the statute.

A

A survey of our cases demonstrates that the Court's interpretation of § 1981 has been based upon a full and considered review of the statute's language and legislative history, assisted by careful briefing, upon which no doubt has been cast by any new information or arguments advanced in the briefs filed in this case. [Justice Brennan's discussion of the prior cases and the legislative history has been omitted.]

B

Even were there doubts as to the correctness of *Runyon*, Congress has in effect ratified our interpretation of § 1981, a fact to which the Court pays no attention. We have justified our practice of according special weight to statutory precedents by reference to Congress' ability to correct our interpretations when we have erred. To be sure, the absence of legislative correction is by no means in all cases determinative, for where our prior interpretation of a statute was plainly a mistake, we are reluctant to "'place on the shoulders of Congress the burden of the Court's own error.'" Monell v. New York City Dept. of Social Services, 436 U.S. 658, 695 (1978). Where our prior interpretation of congressional intent was plausible, however—which is the very least that can be said for our construction of § 1981 in *Runyon*—we have often taken Congress' subsequent inaction as probative to varying degrees, depending upon the circumstances, of its acquiescence. Given the frequency with which Congress has in recent years acted to overturn this Court's mistaken interpretations of civil rights statutes,[9] its failure to enact legislation to overturn *Runyon* appears at least to some extent indicative of a congressional belief that *Runyon* was correctly decided. It might likewise be considered significant that no other legislative developments have occurred that cast doubt on our interpretation of § 1981.

There is no cause, though, to consider the precise weight to attach to the fact that Congress has not overturned or otherwise undermined *Runyon*. For in this case we have more positive signs of Congress' views. Congress has considered and rejected an amendment that would have rendered § 1981 unavailable in most cases as a remedy for private employment discrimination, which is evidence of congressional acquiescence that is "something other than mere congressional silence and passivity." Flood v. Kuhn, 407 U.S. 258, 283 (1972). In addition, Congress has built upon our interpretation of § 1981 in enacting a statute that provides for the recovery of attorney's fees in § 1981 actions.[a] . . .

---

[9] See, e.g., Civil Rights Attorney's Fees Awards Act of 1976, 42 U.S.C. § 1988 (overturning Alyeska Pipeline Service Co. v. Wilderness Society, 421 U.S. 240 (1975)). [Justice Brennan cited other examples from the Pregnancy Discrimination Act, the Voting Rights Act Amendments of 1982, the Handicapped Children's Protection Act of 1986, and the Civil Rights Restoration Act of 1987.]

[a] In the remainder of this part of his opinion, Justice Brennan discussed in detail the proposed amendment to title VII described in footnote 11 of *Runyon*, Casebook page 217, and the legislative history

II

I turn now to the two issues on which certiorari was originally requested and granted in this case. The first of these is whether a plaintiff may state a cause of action under § 1981 based upon allegations that her employer harassed her because of her race. In my view, she may. The Court reaches a contrary conclusion by conducting an ahistorical analysis that ignores the circumstances and legislative history of § 1981. The Court reasons that title VII or modern state contract law "more naturally gover[n]" harassment actions, nowhere acknowledging the anachronism attendant upon the implications that the Reconstruction Congress would have viewed state law, or a federal civil rights statute passed nearly a century later, as the primary bases for challenging private discrimination.

A

The legislative history of § 1981—to which the Court does not advert—makes clear that we must not take an overly narrow view of what it means to have the "same right . . . to make and enforce contracts" as white citizens. The very same legislative history that supports our interpretation of § 1981 in *Runyon* also demonstrates that the 39th Congress intended, in the employment context, to go beyond protecting the freedmen from refusals to contract for their labor and from discriminatory decision to discharge them. Section 1 of the Civil Rights Act was also designed to protect the freedmen from the imposition of working conditions that evidence an intent on the part of the employer not to contract on non-discriminatory terms. Congress realized that, in the former Confederate states, employers were attempting to "adher[e], as to the *treatment of the laborers,* as much as possible to the traditions of the old system, *even where the relations between employers and laborers had been fixed by contract.*" Report of C. Schurz, S. Exec. Doc. No. 2, 39th Cong., 1st Sess., p. 19 (1865) (emphasis added). These working conditions included the use of the whip as an incentive to work harder—the commonplace result of an entrenched attitude that "[y]ou cannot make the negro work without physical compulsion," id., at 16—and the practice of handing out severe and unequal punishment for perceived transgressions. See id., at 20 ("The habit [of corporal punishment] is so inveterate with a great many persons as to render, on the least provocation, the impulse to whip a negro almost irresistible"). Since such "acts of persecution" against *employed* freedmen, ibid., were one of the 39th Congress' concerns in enacting the Civil Rights Act, it is clear that in granting the freedmen

of the provisions for attorneys fees in 42 U.S.C. § 1988. [Footnote by eds.]

the "same right . . . to make and enforce contracts" as white citizens, Congress meant to encompass post-contractual conduct.

B

The Court holds that § 1981, insofar as it gives an equal right to make a contract, "covers only conduct at the initial formation of the contract." This narrow interpretation is not, as the Court would have us believe, the inevitable result of the statutory grant of an equal right "to make contracts,". On the contrary, the language of § 1981 is quite naturally read as extending to cover postformation conduct that demonstrates that the contract was not really made on equal terms at all. It is indeed clear that the statutory language of § 1981 imposes some limit upon the type of harassment claims that are cognizable under § 1981, for the statute's prohibition is against discrimination in the making and enforcement of contracts; but the Court mistakes the nature of that limit.[12] In my view, harassment is properly actionable under the language of § 1981 mandating that all persons "shall have the same right . . . to make . . . contracts . . . as is enjoyed by white citizens" if it demonstrates that the employer has in fact imposed discriminatory terms and hence has not allowed blacks to make a contract on an equal basis.

The question in a case in which an employee makes a § 1981 claim alleging racial harassment should be whether the acts constituting harassment were sufficiently severe or pervasive as effectively to belie any claim that the contract was entered into in a racially neutral manner. Where a black employee demonstrates that she has worked in conditions substantially different from those enjoyed by similarly situated white employees, and can show the necessary racial animus, a jury may infer that the black employee has not been afforded the same right to make an employment contract as white employees. Obviously, as respondent conceded at oral argument, if an employer offers a black and a white applicant for employment the same written contract, but then tells the black employee that her working conditions will be much worse than those of the white hired for the same job because "there's a lot of harassment going on in this work place and you have to agree to that," it would have to be concluded that the white and black had not enjoyed an equal right to make a contract. I see no relevant distinction between that case and one in which the employer's different contractual expectations are unspoken, but become clear during the course of employment as the black employee is subjected to substantially harsher

---

[12] The Court's overly narrow reading of the language of § 1981 is difficult to square with our interpretation of the equal right protected by § 1982 "to inherit, purchase, lease, sell, hold, and convey real and personal property" not just as covering the rights to acquire and dispose of property, but also the "right . . . to *use* property on an equal basis with white citizens," Memphis v. Greene, 451 U.S. 100, 120 (1981) (emphasis added), and "not to have property interests *impaired* because of . . . race," id., at 122 (emphasis added). . . .

conditions than her white co-workers. In neither case can it be said that whites and blacks have had the same right to make an employment contract.[13] The Court's failure to consider such examples, and to explain the abundance of legislative history that confounds its claim that § 1981 unambiguously decrees the result it favors, underscore just how untenable is the Court's position.[14]

Having reached its decision based upon a supposedly literal reading of § 1981, the Court goes on to suggest that its grudging interpretation of this civil rights statute has the benefit of not undermining title VII. It is unclear how the interpretation of § 1981 to reach pervasive postcontractual harassment could be thought in any way to undermine Congress' intentions as regards title VII. Congress has rejected an amendment to title VII that would have rendered § 1981 unavailable as a remedy for employment discrimination, and has explicitly stated that § 1981 "protects similar rights [to title VII] but involves fewer technical prerequisites to the filing of an action"; that the acts "provide alternative means to redress individual grievances"; and that an employee who is discriminated against "should be accorded every protection that the law has in its purview, and . . . the person should not be forced to seek his remedy in only one place." [b] Evidently, title VII and § 1981 provide independent remedies, and neither statute has a preferred status that is to guide interpretation of the other. The Court, indeed, is forced to concede this fact, admitting that where the statutes overlap "we are not at liberty 'to infer any positive preference for one over the other.'" But the Court then goes on to say that the existence of title VII "should lessen the temptation for this Court to twist the interpretation of [§ 1981] to cover the same conduct." This, of course, brings us back to the question of what § 1981, properly interpreted, means. The Court's lengthy discussion of title VII adds nothing to an understanding of that issue.

---

[13] I observe too that a company's imposition of discriminatory working conditions on black employees will tend to deter other black persons from seeking employment. . . .

[14] In Meritor Savings Bank v. Vinson, 477 U.S. 57 (1986), we addressed the question whether allegations of discriminatory workplace harassment state a claim under § 703 of title VII, 42 U.S.C. § 2000e–2(a)(1), which prohibits discrimination "with respect to [an employee's] compensation, terms, conditions, or privileges of employment." We held that sexual harassment creating a hostile workplace environment may ground an action under title VII. "[N]ot all workplace conduct that may be described as 'harassment' affects a 'term, condition, or privilege' of employment within the meaning of title VII," however. 477 U.S., at 67. "For sexual harassment to be actionable it must be sufficiently severe or pervasive 'to alter the conditions of [the victim's] employment and create an abusive working environment.'" Ibid. Similarly, not all workplace conduct that may be described as racial harassment affects an employee's right to make contracts free of discrimination. But racial harassment of sufficient severity may impinge upon that right, as explained in the text, and should be actionable under § 1981. . . .

[b] The quotations in the text are from the legislative history of title VII and the Attorney's Fees statute, quoted by Justice Brennan in portions of part I–B of his opinion that are omitted here. [Footnote by eds.]

114   CIVIL RIGHTS   Ch. 2

The Court's use of title VII is not only question-begging; it is also misleading. Section 1981 is a statute of general application, extending not just to employment contracts, but to *all* contracts. Thus we have held that it prohibits a private school from applying a racially discriminatory admissions policy, *Runyon,* and a community recreational facility from denying membership based on race, Tillman v. Wheaton–Haven Recreation Assn, 410 U.S. 431 (1973). The lower federal courts have found a broad variety of claims of contractual discrimination cognizable under § 1981. E.g., Wyatt v. Security Inn Food & Beverage, Inc., 819 F.2d 69 (4th Cir.1987) (discriminatory application of hotel bar's policy of ejecting persons who do not order drinks); Hall v. Bio–Medical Application, Inc., 671 F.2d 300 (8th Cir.1982) (medical facility's refusal to treat black person potentially cognizable under § 1981); Hall v. Pennsylvania State Police, 570 F.2d 86 (3d Cir.1978) (bank policy to offer its services on different terms dependent upon race); Cody v. Union Electric, 518 F.2d 978 (8th Cir.1975) (discrimination with regard to the amount of security deposit required to obtain service); Howard Security Services, Inc. v. John Hopkins Hospital, 516 F.Supp. 508 (Md.1981) (racially discriminatory award of contract to supply services); Grier v. Specialized Skills, Inc., 326 F.Supp. 856 (W.D.N.C.1971) (discrimination in admissions to barber school); Scott v. Young, 307 F.Supp. 1005 (E.D. Va.1969) (discrimination in amusement park admissions policy). The Court, however, demonstrates no awareness at all that § 1981 is so much broader in scope than title VII, instead focusing exclusively upon the claim that its cramped construction of § 1981 "preserve[s] the integrity of title VII's procedures" and avoids "[u]nnecessary overlap" that would "upset the delicate balance between employee and employer rights struck by title VII." Rights as between an employer and employee simply are not involved in many § 1981 cases, and the Court's restrictive interpretation of § 1981, minimizing the overlap with title VII, may also have the effect of restricting the availability of § 1981 as a remedy for discrimination in a host of contractual situations to which title VII does not extend.

Even as regards their coverage of employment discrimination, § 1981 and title VII are quite different. As we have previously noted, "the remedies available under title VII and under § 1981, although related, and although directed to most of the same ends, are separate, distinct, and independent." Johnson v. Railway Express Agency, Inc., 421 U.S. 454, 461 (1975). Perhaps most important, § 1981 is not limited in scope to employment discrimination by businesses with 15 or more employees, cf. 42 U.S.C. § 2000e(b), and hence may reach the nearly 15% of the work-force not covered by title VII. See Eisenberg and Schwab, The Importance of Section 1981, 73 Cornell L.Rev. 596, 602 (1988). A § 1981 backpay award may also extend beyond the two-year limit of title VII. *Johnson,* supra, at 460. Moreover, a § 1981 plaintiff is not limited to recovering backpay: she may also obtain damages, including punitive damages in an appropriate case. Ibid. Other differences between the two statutes include the right to a jury trial under § 1981, but not title VII; a different statute of limitations in § 1981 cases, see Goodman v. Lukens Steel Co., 482 U.S. 656 (1987); and the availability under title VII, but not § 1981, of administrative machinery designed to provide assistance in investigation and conciliation, see *Johnson,* supra, at 460.[15] The fact that § 1981 provides a remedy for a type of racism that remains a serious social ill broader than that available under title VII hardly provides a good reason to see it, as the Court seems to, as a disruptive blot on the legal landscape, a provision to be construed as narrowly as possible.

C

Applying the standards set forth above, I believe the evidence in this case brings petitioner's harassment claim firmly within the scope of § 1981. Petitioner testified at trial that during her 10 years at McLean she was subjected to racial slurs; given more work than white employees and assigned the most demeaning tasks; passed over for promotion, not informed of promotion opportunities, and not offered training for higher-level jobs; denied wage increases routinely given other employees; and singled out for scrutiny and criticism.

Robert Stevenson, the General Manager and later President of McLean, interviewed petitioner for a file clerk position in 1972. At that time he warned her that all those with whom she would be working were white women, and that they probably would not like working with a black. In fact, however, petitioner testified that it was Stevenson and her supervisors who subjected her to racial harassment, rather than her co-workers. For example, petitioner testified that Stevenson told her on a number of occasions that "blacks are known to work slower than whites by nature" or, as he put it in one instance, that "some animals [are] faster than other animals." Stevenson also

---

[15] The Court suggests that overlap between § 1981 and title VII interferes with title VII's mediation and conciliation procedures. In *Johnson,* supra, at 461, however, we rejected a suggestion that the need for title VII procedures to continue unimpeded by collateral litigation required that the timely filing of a discrimination charge with the EEOC toll the limitation period for § 1981:

"Conciliation and persuasion through the administrative process . . . often constitute a desirable approach to settlement of disputes based on sensitive and emotional charges of invidious employment discrimination. We recognize, too, that the filing of a lawsuit might tend to deter efforts at conciliation, that a lack of success in the legal action could weaken the [EEOC's] efforts to induce voluntary compliance, and that suit is privately oriented and narrow, rather than broad, in application, as successful conciliation tends to be. *But these are the natural effects of the choice Congress has made available to the claimant by its conferring upon him independent administrative and judicial remedies. The choice is a valuable one. Under some circumstances, the administrative route may be highly preferred over the litigatory; under others, the reverse may be true.*" (Emphasis added.)

repeatedly suggested that a white would be able to do petitioner's job better than she could.[16]

Despite petitioner's stated desire to "move up and advance" at McLean to an accounting or secretarial position, she testified that she was offered no training for a higher-level job during her entire tenure at the credit union. White employees were offered training, including a white employee at the same level as petitioner but with less seniority. That less senior white employee was eventually promoted to an intermediate accounting clerk position. As with every other promotion opportunity that occurred, petitioner was never informed of the opening. During the 10 years petitioner worked for McLean, white persons were repeatedly hired for more senior positions, without any notice of these job openings being posted, and without petitioner ever being informed of, let alone interviewed for, any of these opportunities. Petitioner claimed to have received different treatment as to wage increases as well as promotion opportunities. Thus she testified that she had been denied a promised pay raise after her first six months at McLean, though white employees automatically received pay raises after six months.

Petitioner testified at length about allegedly unequal work assignments given by Stevenson and her other supervisors, and detailed the extent of her work assignments. When petitioner complained about her workload, she was given no help with it. In fact, she was given more work, and was told she always had the option of quitting. Petitioner claimed that she was also given more demeaning tasks than white employees, and was the only clerical worker who was required to dust and to sweep. She was also the only clerical worker whose tasks were not reassigned during a vacation. Whenever white employees went on vacation, their work was reassigned; but petitioner's work was allowed to accumulate for her return.

Petitioner further claimed that Stevenson scrutinized her more closely and criticized her more severely than white employees. Stevenson, she testified, would repeatedly stare at her while she was working, although he would not do this to white employees. Stevenson also made a point of criticizing the work of white employees in private, or discussing their mistakes at staff meetings without attributing the error to a particular individual. But he would chastise petitioner and the only other black employee publicly at staff meetings.

The defense introduced evidence at trial contesting each of these assertions by petitioner. But given the extent and nature of the evidence produced by Patterson, and the importance of credibility

[16] A former manager of data processing for McLean testified that when he recommended a black person for a position as a data processor, Stevenson criticized him, saying that he did not "need any more problems around here," that he would interview the person, but not hire him, and that he would then "search for additional people who are not black."

determinations in assigning weight to that evidence, the jury may well have concluded that petitioner was subjected to such serious and extensive racial harassment as to have been denied the right to make an employment contract on the same basis as white employees of the credit union.[17]

III

I agree . . . that petitioner's promotion discrimination claim must be remanded because of the District Court's erroneous instruction as to petitioner's burden. It seems to me, however, that the Court of Appeals was correct when it said that promotion-discrimination claims are cognizable under § 1981 because they "go to the very existence and nature of the employment contract." The Court's disagreement with this common-sense view, and its statement that "the question whether a promotion claim is actionable under § 1981 depends upon whether the nature of the change in position was such that it involved the opportunity to enter into a new contract with the employer," display nicely how it seeks to eliminate with technicalities the protection § 1981 was intended to afford—to limit protection to the form of the contract entered into, and not to extend it, as Congress intended, to the substance of the contract as it is worked out in practice. Under the Court's view, the employer may deny any number of promotions solely on the basis of race, safe from a § 1981 suit, provided it is careful that promotions do not involve new contracts. It is admittedly difficult to see how a "promotion"—which would seem to imply different duties and employment terms—could be achieved without a new contract, and it may well be as a result that promotion claims will always be cognizable under § 1981. Nevertheless, the same criticisms I have made of the Court's decision regarding harassment claims apply here: proof that an employee was not promoted because she is black—while all around white peers are advanced—shows that the black employee has in substance been denied the opportunity to contract on the equal terms that § 1981 guarantees. . . .

JUSTICE STEVENS, concurring in the judgment in part and dissenting in part.

When I first confronted the task of interpreting § 1981, I was persuaded by Justice Cardozo's admonition that it is wise for the judge to " 'lay one's own course of bricks on the secure foundation of the courses laid by others who had gone before.' " Runyon v. McCrary, 427 U.S. 160, 191 (1976) (concurring opinion) (quoting B. Cardozo, The Nature of the Judicial Process 149 (1921)). The Court had already

---

[17] The proposed jury instruction quoted by the Court is scarcely conclusive as to the nature of Patterson's harassment claim. Indeed, it is precisely harassment so pervasive as to create a discriminatory work environment that will demonstrate that a black plaintiff has been denied an opportunity to contract on equal terms with white employees.

construed the statutory reference to the right "to make and enforce contracts" as a guarantee of equal opportunity, and not merely a guarantee of equal rights. Today the Court declines its own invitation to tear down that foundation and begin to build a different legal structure on its original text. I agree, of course, that *Runyon* should not be overruled. I am also persuaded, however, that the meaning that had already been given to "the same right . . . to make and enforce contracts" that "is enjoyed by white citizens"—the statutory foundation that was preserved in *Runyon*—encompasses an employee's right to protection from racial harassment by her employer.

In *Runyon* we held that § 1981 prohibits a private school from excluding qualified children because they are not white citizens. Just as a qualified nonwhite child has a statutory right to equal access to a private school, so does a nonwhite applicant for employment have a statutory right to enter into a personal service contract with a private employer on the same terms as a white citizen. If an employer should place special obstacles in the path of a black job applicant—perhaps by requiring her to confront an openly biased and hostile interviewer—the interference with the statutory right to make contracts to the same extent "as is enjoyed by white citizens" would be plain.

Similarly, if the white and the black applicants are offered the same terms of employment with just one exception—that the black employee would be required to work in dark, uncomfortable surroundings, whereas the white employee would be given a well-furnished, two-window office—the discrimination would be covered by the statute. In such a case, the Court would find discrimination in the making of the contract because the disparity surfaced before the contract was made. Under the Court's understanding of the statute, the black applicant might recover on one of two theories: She might demonstrate that the employer intended to discourage her from taking the job—which is the equivalent of a "refusal to enter into a contract"—or she might show that the employer actually intended to enter a contract, but "only on discriminatory terms." Under the second of these theories of recovery, however, it is difficult to discern why an employer who makes his intentions known has discriminated in the "making" of a contract, while the employer who conceals his discriminatory intent until after the applicant has accepted the job, only later to reveal that black employees are intentionally harassed and insulted, has not.

It is also difficult to discern why an employer who does not decide to treat black employees less favorably than white employees until after the contract of employment is first conceived is any less guilty of discriminating in the "making" of a contract. A contract is not just a piece of paper. Just as a single word is the skin of a living thought, so is a contract evidence of a vital, ongoing relationship between human beings. An at-will employee, such as petitioner, is not merely performing an existing contract; she is constantly remaking that contract.

Whenever significant new duties are assigned to the employee—whether they better or worsen the relationship—the contract is amended and a new contract is made. Thus, if after the employment relationship is formed, the employer deliberately implements a policy of harassment of black employees, he has imposed a contractual term on them that is not the "same" as the contractual provisions that are "enjoyed" by white citizens." Moreover, whether employed at-will or for a fixed term, employees typically strive to achieve a more rewarding relationship with their employers. By requiring black employees to work in a hostile environment, the employer has denied them the same opportunity for advancement that is available to white citizens. A deliberate policy of harassment of black employees who are competing with white citizens is, I submit, manifest discrimination in the making of contracts in the sense in which that concept was interpreted in *Runyon v. McCrary*. I cannot believe that the decision in that case would have been different if the school had agreed to allow the black students to attend, but subjected them to segregated classes and other racial abuse.

Indeed, in Goodman v. Lukens Steel Co., 482 U.S. 656 (1987), we built further on the foundation laid in *Runyon*. We decided that a union's "toleration and tacit encouragement of racial harassment" violates § 1981. Although the Court now explains that the *Lukens* decision rested on the union's interference with its members' right to enforce their collective bargaining agreement, when I joined that opinion I thought—and I still think—that the holding rested comfortably on the foundation identified in *Runyon*. In fact, in the section of the *Lukens* opinion discussing the substantive claim, the Court did not once use the term "enforce" or otherwise refer to that particular language in the statute.

The Court's repeated emphasis on the literal language of § 1981 might be appropriate if it were building a new foundation, but it is not a satisfactory method of adding to the existing structure. In the name of logic and coherence, the Court today adds a course of bricks dramatically askew from "the secure foundation of the courses laid by others," replacing a sense of rational direction and purpose in the law with an aimless confinement to a narrow construction of what it means to "make" a contract.

For the foregoing reasons, and for those stated in parts II(B) and II(C) of Justice Brennan's opinion, I respectfully dissent from the conclusion reached in part III of the Court's opinion. I also agree with Justice Brennan's discussion of the promotion claim.

NOTES ON *PATTERSON v. McLEAN CREDIT UNION*

1. The Order for Reargument. The Court's decision to order reargument of *Patterson* on whether the interpretation of § 1981 in

Runyon v. McCrary should be reconsidered created more controversy within the Court than the opinions in *Patterson* reveal. Justice Blackmun, joined by Justices Brennan, Marshall, and Stevens, dissented. Justice Stevens (joined by Justices Brennan, Marshall, and Blackmun) wrote a separate dissent. Justice Blackmun criticized the Court for "reach[ing] out" to reconsider *Runyon,* adding: "I am at a loss to understand the motivation of five members of this Court to reconsider an interpretation of a civil rights statute that so clearly reflects our society's earnest commitment to ending racial discrimination. . . ." Justice Stevens added:

> "The Court's order today will, by itself, have a deleterious effect on the faith reposed by racial minorities in the continuing stability of a rule of law that guarantees them the 'same right' as 'white citizens.' To recognize an equality right—a right that 12 years ago we thought 'well established'—and then to declare unceremoniously that perhaps we were wrong and had better reconsider our prior judgment, is to replace what is ideally a sense of guaranteed right with the uneasiness of unsecured privilege. Time alone will tell whether the erosion in faith is unnecessarily precipitous, but in the meantime, some of the harm that will flow from today's order may never be completely undone."

These observations brought a sharp response from the majority:

> "Both of the dissents intimate that the statutory question involved in *Runyon v. McCrary* should not be subject to the same principles of stare decisis as other decisions because it benefited civil rights plaintiffs by expanding liability under the statute. We do not believe that the Court may recognize any such exception to the abiding rule that it treat all litigants equally; that is, that the claim of any litigant for the application of a rule to its case should not be influenced by the Court's view of the worthiness of the litigant in terms of extralegal criteria. We think this is what Congress meant when it required each Justice or judge of the United States to swear to 'administer justice without respect to persons, and do equal right to the poor and to the rich.' 28 U.S.C. § 453."

2. The Decision. The actual decision in *Patterson* brought division on another front. The Court was unanimous, in the end, that *Runyon* should not be overruled, but sharply divided on the meaning to be attributed to § 1981. Is Justice Brennan right that "[w]hat the Court declines to snatch away with one hand, it takes with the other"? Has *Runyon* been sapped of its vitality as a modern limitation on discriminatory behavior?

3. The Overruling. The 1991 Civil Rights Act overruled *Patterson* by adding to § 1981 a provision stating that the phrase "make and enforce contracts" includes "the making, performance, modification, and termination of contracts, and the enjoyment of all benefits, privileges, terms, and conditions of the contractual relationship." This change extends the statutory bar to on-the-job racial harassment, as well as to discrimination in hiring.

4. Bibliography. The prospect that *Runyon* might be overruled led to a number of contributions to the literature on § 1981. For a sample, see Karen Blum, Section 1981 Revisited: Looking Beyond *Runyon* and *Patterson*, 32 Howard L.J. 1 (1989); Theodore Eisenberg and Stewart Schwab, The Importance of Section 1981, 73 Corn.L.Rev. 596 (1988); Ronald Rotunda, *Runyon v. McCrary* and the Mosaic of State Action, 67 Wash. U.L.Q. 47 (1989); Martin Schwartz and Eileen Kaufman, Addendum: Civil Rights In Jeopardy, 4 Touro L.Rev. 245 (1988); Barry Sullivan, Historical Reconstruction, Reconstruction History, and the Proper Scope of Section 1981, 98 Yale L.J. 541 (1989). See also Steven J. Burton, Racial Discrimination in Contract Performance: *Patterson* and a State Law Alternative, 25 Harv.C.R.–C.L.L.R. 431 (1990) (suggesting that a state-law remedy for racial harassment can be found in modern contract law); Robert Kaczorowski, The Enforcement Provisions of the Civil Rights Act of 1866: A Legislative History in Light of *Runyon v. McCrary,* 98 Yale L.J. 565 (1989); Randall Kennedy, Reconstruction and the Politics of Scholarship, 98 Yale L.J. 521 (1989) (review of E. Foner, Reconstruction: America's Unfinished Revolution); Symposium: *Patterson v. McClean,* 87 Mich.L.Rev. 1 (1988) (containing a series of articles focusing on the stare decisis issue). For a fascinating glimpse of the history of Supreme Court treatment of the 1866 Civil Rights Act through the window of a forgotten case, see Robert Goldstein, *Blyew:* Variations on a Jurisdictional Theme, 41 Stan.L.Rev. 469 (1989). For reactions to *Patterson,* see Allan H. Macurdy, Classical Nostalgia: Racism, Contract Ideology, and Formalist Legal Reasoning in *Patterson v. McLean Credit Union,* 18 N.Y.U.Rev. of Law & Social Change 987 (1990–91); Comment, Section 1991 and Discriminatory Discharge: A Contextual Analysis, 64 Temple L.Rev. 173 (1991).

JETT v. DALLAS INDEPENDENT SCHOOL DISTRICT
Supreme Court of the United States, 1989.
491 U.S. 701.

JUSTICE O'CONNOR delivered the opinion of the Court.

The question before us in these cases is whether 42 U.S.C. § 1981 provides an independent federal cause of action for damages against local governmental entities, and whether that cause of action is broader than the damage remedy available under 42 U.S.C. § 1983, such that a municipality may be held liable for its employees' violations of § 1981 under a theory of respondeat superior.

I

Petitioner Norman Jett, a white male, was employed by respondent Dallas Independent School District (DISD) as a teacher, athletic director, and head football coach at South Oak Cliff High School (South Oak) until his reassignment to another DISD school in 1983. Petitioner was hired by the DISD in 1957, was assigned to assistant coaching duties at South Oak in 1962, and was promoted to athletic director and head football coach of South Oak in 1970. During petitioner's lengthy tenure at South Oak, the racial composition of the school changed from predominantly white to predominantly black. In 1975, the DISD assigned Dr. Fredrick Todd, a black, as principal of South Oak. Petitioner and Todd clashed repeatedly over school policies, and in particular over petitioner's handling of the school's football program. These conflicts came to a head following a November 19, 1982, football game between South Oak and the predominantly White Plano High School. Todd objected to petitioner's comparison of the South Oak team with professional teams before the match, and to the fact that petitioner entered the official's locker room after South Oak lost the game and told two black officials that he would never allow black officials to work another South Oak game. Todd also objected to petitioner's statements, reported in a local newspaper, to the effect that the majority of South Oak players could not meet proposed NCAA academic requirements for collegiate athletes.

On March 15, 1983, Todd informed petitioner that he intended to recommend that petitioner be relieved of his duties as athletic director and head football coach at South Oak. On March 17, 1983, Todd sent a letter to John Kincaide, the director of athletics for DISD, recommending that petitioner be removed based on poor leadership and planning skills and petitioner's comportment before and after the Plano game. Petitioner subsequently met with John Santillo, director of personnel for DISD, who suggested that petitioner should transfer schools because any remaining professional relationship with Principal Todd had been shattered. Petitioner then met with Linus Wright, the superintendent of the DISD. At this meeting, petitioner informed Superintendent Wright that he believed that Todd's criticisms of his performance as head coach were unfounded and that in fact Todd was motivated by racial animus and wished to replace petitioner with a black head coach. Superintendent Wright suggested that the difficulties between Todd and petitioner might preclude petitioner from remaining in his coaching position at South Oak, but assured petitioner that another position in the DISD would be secured for him.

On March 25, 1983, Superintendent Wright met with Kincaide, Santillo, Todd and two other DISD officials to determine whether petitioner should remain at South Oak. After the meeting, Superintendent Wright officially affirmed Todd's recommendation to remove petitioner from his duties as coach and athletic director at South Oak. Wright indicated that he felt compelled to follow the recommendation of the school principal. Soon after this meeting, petitioner was informed by Santillo that effective August 4, 1983, he was reassigned as a teacher at the DISD Business Magnet School, a position that did not include any coaching duties. Petitioner's attendance and performance at the Business Magnet School were poor, and on May 5, 1983, Santillo wrote petitioner indicating that he was being placed on "unassigned personnel budget" and being reassigned to a temporary position in the DISD security department. Upon receiving Santillo's letter, petitioner filed this lawsuit in the District Court for Northern District of Texas. The DISD subsequently offered petitioner a position as a teacher and freshman football and track coach at Jefferson High School. Petitioner did not accept this assignment, and on August 19, 1983, he sent his formal letter of resignation to the DISD.

Petitioner brought this action against the DISD and Principal Todd in his personal and official capacities, under 42 U.S.C. §§ 1981 and 1983, alleging due process, first amendment, and equal protection violations. Petitioner's due process claim alleged that he had a constitutionally protected property interest in his coaching position at South Oak, of which he was deprived without due process of law. Petitioner's first amendment claim was based on the allegation that his removal and subsequent transfer were actions taken in retaliation for his statements to the press regarding the sports program at South Oak. His equal protection and § 1981 causes of action were based on the allegation that his removal from the athletic director and head coaching positions at South Oak was motivated by the fact that he was white, and that Principal Todd, and through him the DISD, were responsible for the racially discriminatory diminution in his employment status. Petitioner also claimed that his resignation was in fact the product of racial harassment and retaliation for the exercise of his first amendment rights and thus amounted to a constructive discharge. These claims were tried to a jury, which found for petitioner on all counts. The jury awarded petitioner $650,000 against the DISD, $150,000 against Principal Todd and the DISD jointly and severally, and $50,000 in punitive damages against Todd in his personal capacity.

On motion for judgment notwithstanding the verdict respondents argued that liability against the DISD was improper because there was no showing that petitioner's injuries were sustained pursuant to a policy or custom of the school district. The District Court rejected this argument, finding that the DISD Board of Trustees had delegated final and unreviewable authority to Superintendent Wright to reassign personnel as he saw fit. In any event, the trial court found that petitioner's claim of racial discrimination was cognizable under § 1981 as well as § 1983, and indicated that "liability is permitted on solely a basis of respondeat superior when the claim is one of racial discrimination under § 1981." The District Court set aside the punitive damage award against Principal Todd as unsupported by the evidence, found the damage award against the DISD excessive and ordered a remittitur of $200,000, but otherwise denied respondents' motions for judgment n.o.v. and a new trial and upheld the jury's verdict in all respects. Principal Todd has reached a settlement with petitioner and is no longer a party to this action.

On appeal, the Court of Appeals for the Fifth Circuit reversed in part and remanded. Initially, the court found that petitioner had no constitutionally protected property interest "in the intangible, noneconomic benefits of his assignment as coach." Since petitioner had received both his teacher and coach's salary after his reassignment, the change in duties did not deprive him of any state law entitlement protected by the due process clause. The Court of Appeals also set aside the jury's finding that petitioner was constructively discharged from his teaching position within the DISD. The court found the evidence insufficient to sustain the claim that petitioner's loss of coaching duties and subsequent offer of reassignment to a lesser coaching position were so humiliating or unpleasant that a reasonable employee would have felt compelled to resign. While finding the question "very close," the Court of Appeals concluded that there was sufficient evidence from which a reasonable jury could conclude that Principal Todd's recommendation that petitioner be transferred from his coaching duties at South Oak was motivated by impermissible racial animus. The court noted that Todd had replaced petitioner with a black coach, that there had been racial overtones in the tension between Todd and petitioner before the Plano game, that Todd's explanation of his unsatisfactory rating of petitioner was questionable and was not supported by the testimony of other DISD officials who spoke of petitioner's performance in laudatory terms. The court also affirmed the jury's finding that Todd's recommendation that petitioner be relieved of his coaching duties was motivated in substantial part by petitioner's protected statements to the press concerning the academic standing of athletes at South Oak. These remarks addressed matters of public concern, and Todd admitted that they were a substantial consideration in his decision to recommend that petitioner be relieved of his coaching duties.

The Court of Appeals then turned to the DISD's claim that there was insufficient evidence to support a finding of municipal liability under 42 U.S.C. § 1983. The Court of Appeals found that the District Court's instructions as to the school district's liability were deficient in two respects. First, the District Court's instruction did not make clear that the school district could be held liable for the actions of Principal Todd or Superintendent Wright only if those officials were delegated policymaking authority by the school district or acted pursuant to a well settled custom that represented official policy. Second, even if

Superintendent Wright could be considered a policymaker for purposes of the transfer of school district personnel, the jury made no finding that Superintendent Wright's decision to transfer petitioner was either improperly motivated, or consciously indifferent to the improper motivations of Principal Todd.

The Court of Appeals also rejected the District Court's conclusion that the DISD's liability for Principal Todd's actions could be predicated on a theory of respondeat superior under § 1981. The court noted that in Monell v. New York City Dept. of Social Services, 436 U.S. 658 (1978), this Court held that Congress did not intend municipalities to be subject to vicarious liability for the federal constitutional or statutory violations of their employees. The Court of Appeals reasoned that "[t]o impose such vicarious liability for only certain wrongs based on § 1981 apparently would contravene the congressional intent behind § 1983."
. . .

[W]e granted Norman Jett's petition for certiorari . . . . We also granted the DISD's cross-petition for certiorari . . . to clarify the application of our decisions in St. Louis v. Praprotnik, 485 U.S. 112 (1988) (plurality opinion), and Pembaur v. Cincinnati, 475 U.S. 469 (1986) (plurality opinion), to the school district's potential liability for the discriminatory actions of Principal Todd.

We note that at no stage in the proceedings has the school district raised the contention that the substantive scope of the "right . . . to make . . . contracts" protected by § 1981 does not reach the injury suffered by petitioner here. See Patterson v. McLean Credit Union, 491 U.S. 164 (1989). Instead, the school district has argued that the limitations on municipal liability under § 1983 are applicable to violations of the rights protected by § 1981. Because petitioner has obtained a jury verdict to the effect that Dr. Todd violated his rights under § 1981, and the school district has never contested the judgment below on the ground that § 1981 does not reach petitioner's employment injury, we assume for purposes of these cases, without deciding, that petitioner's rights under § 1981 have been violated by his removal and reassignment.

II

. . . In essence, petitioner argues that in 1866 the 39th Congress intended to create a cause of action for damages against municipal actors and others who violated the rights now enumerated in § 1981. While petitioner concedes that the text of the 1866 Act itself is completely silent on this score, petitioner contends that a civil remedy was nonetheless intended for the violation of the rights contained in § 1 of the 1866 Act. Petitioner argues that Congress wished to adopt the prevailing approach to municipal liability to effectuate this damages remedy, which was respondeat superior. Petitioner concludes that

126   CIVIL RIGHTS   Ch. 2

with this federal damages remedy in place in 1866, it was not the intent of the 42nd Congress, which passed present day § 1983, to narrow the more sweeping remedy against local governments which Congress had created five years earlier. Since "repeals by implication are not favored," petitioner concludes that § 1981 must provide an independent cause of action for racial discrimination against local governmental entities, and that this broader remedy is unaffected by the constraints on municipal liability announced in *Monell*. In the alternative, petitioner argues that even if § 1981 does not create an express cause of action for damages against local governmental entities, 42 U.S.C. § 1988 invites this Court to craft a remedy by looking to common law principles, which again point to a rule of respondeat superior. To examine these contentions, we must consider the text and history of both the Civil Rights Act of 1866 and Civil Rights Act of 1871, the precursors of §§ 1981 and 1983 respectively.

The dissent errs in asserting that we have strayed from the question upon which we granted certiorari. Jett's petition for certiorari asks us to decide "[w]hether a public employee who claims job discrimination on the basis of race must show that the discrimination resulted from official 'policy or custom' in order to recover under 42 U.S.C. § 1981." In answering this question, the lower court looked to the relationship between §§ 1981 and 1983, and refused to differentiate "between §§ 1981 and 1983 with respect to municipal respondeat superior liability." In both his petition for certiorari and his brief on the merits in this Court, petitioner Jett took issue with the Court of Appeals' conclusion that the express damages remedy under § 1983 militated against the creation or implication of a broader damages remedy under § 1981. Moreover, petitioner concedes that "private causes of action under §§ 1981 and 1982 do not arise from the express language of those statutes," and asks this Court to "look to state law or to fashion a single federal rule," of municipal damages liability under § 1981. We think it obvious that the question whether a federal damages remedy broader than that provided by § 1983 should be implied from § 1981 is fairly included in the question upon which we granted certiorari.

Equally implausible is the dissent's suggestion that we have somehow unwittingly answered this question in the past. Most of the cases cited by the dissent involved private conduct, and thus quite obviously could not have considered the propriety of judicial implication of a federal damages remedy under § 1981 in the state action context we address here. The only two cases cited by the dissent which involved state actors, Takahashi v. Fish & Game Comm'n, 334 U.S. 410 (1948), and Hurd v. Hodge, 334 U.S. 24 (1948), are completely inapposite. *Takahashi* involved a mandamus action filed in state court, and thus understandably had nothing to say about federal damages remedies against state actors under § 1981. *Hurd* also involved only injunctive relief, and could not have considered the relationship of § 1981 to § 1983, since the latter statute did not apply to the District of Columbia at the time of our decision in that case. District of Columbia v. Carter, 409 U.S. 418 (1973).

A

[At this point, Justice O'Connor undertook a lengthy examination of the legislative history of § 1981 and related civil rights statutes originally proposed in 1865 and ultimately enacted over President Johnson's veto in 1866. She then concluded:]

Several points relevant to our present inquiry emerge from the history surrounding the adoption of the Civil Rights Act of 1866. First, nowhere did the act provide for an express damages remedy for violation of the provisions [that became § 1981.] See Jones v. Alfred H. Mayer Co., 392 U.S. 409, 414, n. 13 (1968) (noting "[t]hat 42 U.S.C. § 1982 is couched in declaratory terms and provides no explicit method of enforcement"). Second, no original federal jurisdiction was created by the 1866 Act which could support a federal damages remedy against state actors. Finally, the penal provision [now 18 U.S.C. § 242], the only provision explicitly directed at state officials, was, in Senator Trumbull's words, designed to punish the "person who, under the color of the law, does the act," not "the community where the custom prevails." Cong.Globe, 39th Cong., 1st Sess., 1758 (1866).

Two events subsequent to the passage of the 1866 Act bear on the relationship between §§ 1981 and 1983. First, on June 13, 1866, just over two months after the passage of the 1866 Act, a joint resolution was passed sending the 14th amendment to the states for ratification. As we have noted in the past, the first section of the 1866 Act, "constituted an initial blueprint of the 14th amendment." General Building Contractors Assn., Inc. v. Pennsylvania, 458 U.S. 375, 389 (1982). Many of the members of the 39th Congress viewed § 1 of the 14th amendment as "constitutionalizing" and expanding the protections of the 1866 Act and viewed what became § 5 of the amendment as laying to rest doubts shared by both sides of the aisle concerning the constitutionality of that measure. See . . . Hurd v. Hodge, 334 U.S. 24, 32 (1948) ("[A]s the legislative debates reveal, one of the primary purposes of many members of Congress in supporting the adoption of the 14th amendment was to incorporate the guaranties of the Civil Rights Act of 1866 in the organic law of the land").

Second, the 41st Congress reenacted the substance of the 1866 Act in a 14th amendment statute, the Enforcement Act of 1870. Section 16 of the 1870 Act was modeled after § 1 of the 1866 Act. Section 17 reenacted with some modification the criminal provisions of § 2 of the earlier civil rights law, and § 18 of the 1870 Act provided that the entire 1866 [Act] was reenacted. We have thus recognized that present day 42 U.S.C. § 1981 is both a 13th and a 14th amendment statute. *General Building Contractors,* supra, at 383–86.

B

What is now § 1983 was enacted as § 1 of "An Act to Enforce the Provisions of the Fourteenth Amendment to the Constitution of the United States and For other Purposes," Act of April 20, 1871. The immediate impetus for the bill was evidence of widespread acts of violence perpetrated against the freedmen and loyal white citizens by groups such as the Ku Klux Klan. On March 23, 1871, President Grant sent a message to Congress indicating that the Klan's reign of terror in the Southern states had "render[ed] life and property insecure," and that "the power to correct these evils [was] beyond the control of state authorities." Cong.Globe, 42nd Cong., 1st Sess., 244 (1871). A special joint committee consisting of 10 distinguished Republicans, five from each House of Congress, was formed in response to President Grant's call for legislation, and drafted the bill that became what is now known as the Ku Klux Klan Act of 1871. As enacted, sections 2 through 6 of the bill specifically addressed the problem of the private acts of violence perpetrated by groups like the Klan.

Unlike the rest of the bill, § 1 is not specifically addressed to the activities of the Klan. As passed by the 42nd Congress, § 1 provided . . . :

> "That any person who, under color of any law, statute, ordinance, regulation, custom, or usage of any State, shall subject, or cause to be subjected, any person within the jurisdiction of the United States to the deprivation of any rights, privileges, or immunities secured by the Constitution of the United States, shall, any such law, statute, ordinance, regulation, custom, or usage of the State to the contrary notwithstanding, be liable to the party injured in any action at law, suit in equity, or other proper proceeding for redress; such proceeding to be prosecuted in the several district or circuit courts of the United States, with and subject to the same rights of appeal, review upon error, and other remedies provided in like cases in such courts . . ."

Three points are immediately clear from the face of the act itself. First, unlike any portion of the 1866 Act, this statute explicitly ordained that any "person" acting under color of state law or custom who was responsible for a deprivation of constitutional rights would "be liable to the party injured in any action at law." Thus, "the 1871 Act was designed to expose state and local officials to a new form of liability." Newport v. Fact Concerts, Inc., 453 U.S. 247, 259 (1981). Second, the 1871 Act explicitly provided original federal jurisdiction for prosecution of these civil actions against state actors. See Will v.

Michigan Dept. of State Police, 491 U.S. 58, ___ (1989) ("[A] principle purpose behind the enactment of § 1983 was to provide a federal forum for civil rights claims"); accord, Mitchum v. Foster, 407 U.S. 225, 239 (1972). Third, the first section of the 1871 Act was explicitly modeled on § 2 of the 1866 Act, and was seen by both opponents and proponents as amending and enhancing the protections of the 1866 Act by providing a new civil remedy for its enforcement against state actors. See Chapman v. Houston Welfare Rights Org., 441 U.S. 600, 610–11, n. 25 (1979) ("Section 1 of the [1871] Act generated the least concern; it merely added civil remedies to the criminal penalties imposed by the 1866 Civil Rights Act").

Even a cursory glance at the House and Senate debates on the 1871 Act makes these three points clear. In introducing the bill to the House, Representative Shellabarger, who served on the joint committee which drafted the bill, stated:

> "The model for it will be found in the second section of the act of April 9, 1866, known as the 'civil rights act.' That section provides a criminal proceeding in identically the same case as this one provides a civil remedy for, except that the deprivation under color of state law must, under the civil rights act, have been on account of race, color or former slavery." Cong. Globe, 42 Cong., 1st Sess., App. 68 (1871).

Representative Shellabarger added that § 1 provided a civil remedy "on the same state of facts" as § 2 of the Civil Rights Act of 1866. Obviously Representative Shellabarger's introduction of § 1 of the bill to his colleagues would have been altogether different if he had been of the view that the 39th Congress, of which he had been a member, had *already* created a *broader* federal damages remedy against state actors in 1866. The view that § 1 of the 1871 Act was an amendment of or supplement to the 1866 Act designed to create new civil remedy against state actors was echoed throughout the debates in the House.

Both proponents and opponents in the House viewed § 1 as working an *expansion* of federal jurisdiction. Supporters continually referred to the failure of the state courts to enforce federal law designed for the protection of the freedman, and saw § 1 as remedying this situation by interposing the federal courts between the state and citizens of the United States. See id., at 376 (Rep. Lowe) ("The case has arisen . . . when the federal government must resort to its own agencies to carry its own authority into execution. Hence this bill throws open the doors of the United States courts to those whose rights under the Constitution are denied or impaired"). Opponents recognized the expansion of original jurisdiction and railed against it on policy and constitutional grounds. See id., at 429 (Rep. McHenry) ("The first section of the bill . . . vests in the federal courts jurisdiction to determine the individual rights of citizens of the same state; a jurisdiction which of right belongs only to the state tribunals").

The Senate debates on § 1 of the 1871 Act are of a similar tenor. . . . Senators addressed § 1 of the act as creating a new civil remedy and expanding federal jurisdiction to accommodate it in terms incompatible with the supposition that the 1866 Act had already created such a cause of action against state actors. . . .

The final aspect of the history behind the adoption of present day § 1983 relevant to the question before us is the rejection by the 42nd Congress of the Sherman amendment, which specifically proposed the imposition of a form of vicarious liability on municipal governments. This history was thoroughly canvassed in the Court's opinion in *Monell,* and only its broadest outlines need be traced here. [Justice O'Connor's treatment of this history is omitted.]

The strong adverse reaction to the Sherman amendment, and continued references to its complete novelty in the law of the United States, make it difficult to entertain petitioner's contention that the 1866 Act had already created a form of vicarious liability against municipal governments. Equally important is the basis for opposition. As we noted in *Monell,* a large number of those who objected to the principle of vicarious liability embodied in the Sherman amendment were of the view that Congress did not have the power to assign the duty to enforce federal law to state instrumentalities by making them liable for the constitutional violations of others. [Prior] decisions of this Court lent direct support to the constitutional arguments of the opponents. . . . In *Monell,* we concluded that it was this constitutional objection which was the driving force behind the eventual rejection of the Sherman amendment.

Although the debate surrounding the constitutional [objection] occurred in the context of the Sherman amendment and not § 1 of the 1871 Act, in *Monell* we found it quite inconceivable that the same legislators who opposed vicarious liability on constitutional grounds in the Sherman amendment debates would have silently adopted the same principle in § 1. Because the "creation of a federal law of respondeat superior would have raised all the constitutional problems associated with the obligation to keep the peace" embodied in the Sherman amendment, we held that the existence of the constitutional background "compell[ed] the conclusion that Congress did not intend municipalities to be held liable [under § 1] unless action pursuant to official municipal policy of some nature caused a constitutional tort." *Monell,* supra, at 691.

[The decisions leading to the constitutional concerns that led to the defeat of the Sherman amendment] were on the books when the 39th Congress enacted § 1 of the 1866 Act. Supporters of the 1866 Act were clearly aware of [them], and cited [them] for the proposition that the federal government could use its *own* instrumentalities to effectuate its laws. There was, however, no suggestion in the debates surrounding the 1866 Act that the statute violated [the constitutional principle] that federal duties could not be imposed on state instrumentalities by rendering them vicariously liable for the violations of others. Just as it affected our interpretation of § 1 of the 1871 Act in *Monell,* we think the complete silence on this score in the face of a constitutional background known to those who enacted the 1866 Act militates against imputing to Congress an intent to silently impose vicarious liability on municipalities under the earlier statute.

As originally enacted, the text of § 1983 referred only to the deprivation "of any rights, privileges, or immunities secured by the Constitution of the United States." In 1874, Congress enacted the Revised Statutes of the United States. The words "and laws" were added to the remedial provision of § 1 of the 1871 Act. . . .

There is no commentary or other information surrounding the addition of the phrase "and laws" to the remedial provisions of present day § 1983. . . .

We have noted in the past that the addition of the phrase "and laws" to the text of what is now § 1983, although not without its ambiguities as to intended scope, was *at least* intended to make clear that the guarantees contained in § 1 of the 1866 Act and § 16 of the Enforcement Act of 1870, were to be enforced against state actors through the express remedy for damages contained in § 1983. See *Chapman,* supra, at 617 (§ 1 of the 1871 Act "served only to ensure that an individual had a cause of action for violations of the Constitution, which in the 14th amendment embodied and extended to all individuals as against state action the substantive protections afforded by § 1 of the 1866 Act"). See also Maine v. Thiboutot, 448 U.S. 1, 7 (1980) ("There is no express explanation offered for the insertion of the phrase 'and laws.' On the one hand, a principal purpose of the added language was to ensure that federal legislation providing specifically for equality of rights would be brought within the ambit of the civil action authorized by that statute").

III

We think the history of the 1866 Act and the 1871 Act recounted above indicates that Congress intended that the explicit remedial provisions of § 1983 be controlling in the context of damages actions brought against state actors alleging violation of the rights declared in § 1981. That we have read § 1 of the 1866 Act to reach private action and have implied a damages remedy to effectuate the declaration of rights contained in that provision does not authorize us to do so in the context of the "state action" portion of § 1981, where Congress has established its own remedial scheme. In the context of the application of § 1981 and § 1982 to private actors, we "had little choice but to hold that aggrieved individuals could enforce this prohibition, *for there existed no other remedy to address such violations of the statute.*" Cannon v. University of Chicago, 441 U.S. 677, 728 (1979) (White, J., dissenting) (emphasis added). That is manifestly not the case here, and whatever the limits of the judicial power to imply or create remedies, it has long been the law that such power should not be exercised in the face of an express decision by Congress concerning the scope of remedies available under a particular statute. See National Railroad Passenger Corp. v. National Assn. of Railroad Passengers, 414 U.S. 453, 458 (1974) ("A frequently stated principle of statutory construction is that when legislation expressly provides a particular remedy or remedies, courts should not expand the coverage of the statute to subsume other remedies).

Petitioner cites 42 U.S.C. § 1988, and argues that provision "compels adoption of a respondeat superior standard." That section, as amended, provides in pertinent part:

> "The jurisdiction in civil . . . matters conferred on the district courts by the provisions of this [chapter and title 18], for the protection of all persons in the United States in their civil rights, and for their vindication, shall be exercised and enforced in conformity with the laws of the United States, so far as such laws are suitable to carry the same into effect; but in all cases where they are not adapted by the object, or are deficient in the provisions necessary to furnish suitable remedies and punish offenses against law, the common law, as modified and changed by the constitution and the statutes of the State wherein the court having jurisdiction of such civil or criminal cause is held, so far as the same is not inconsistent with the Constitution and laws of the United States, shall be extended to and govern the said courts in the trial and disposition of the cause. . . ."

Far from supporting petitioner's call for the creation or implication of a damages remedy broader than that provided by § 1983, we think the plain language of § 1988 supports the result we reach here. As we noted in Moor v. County of Alameda, 411 U.S. 693, 706 (1973), in rejecting an argument similar to petitioner's contention here, "[§ 1988] expressly limits the authority granted federal courts to look to the common law, as modified by state law, to instances in which that law 'is not inconsistent with the Constitution and laws of the United States.'" As we indicated in *Moor,* "Congress did not intend, *as a matter of federal law,* to impose vicarious liability on municipalities for violations of federal civil rights by their employees." Section 1983 provides an explicit remedy in damages which, with its limitations on municipal liability, Congress thought "suitable to carry . . . into effect" the rights guaranteed by § 1981 as against state actors. Thus, if anything,

§ 1988 points us in the direction of the express federal damages remedy for enforcement of the rights contained in § 1981, not state common law principles.

Our conclusion that the express cause of action for damages created by § 1983 constitutes the exclusive federal remedy for violation of the rights guaranteed in § 1981 by state governmental units finds support in our decision in Brown v. GSA, 425 U.S. 820 (1976). In *Brown,* we dealt with the interaction of § 1981 and the provisions of § 717 of title VII, 42 U.S.C. § 2000e–16, which proscribe discrimination in federal employment and establish an administrative and judicial enforcement scheme. The petitioner in *Brown* had been passed over for federal promotion on two occasions, and after the second occasion he filed a complaint with his agency alleging that he was denied promotion because of his race. The agency's Director of Civil Rights concluded after investigation that race had not entered into the promotional process, and informed Brown by letter of his right under § 717(c) to bring an action in federal district court within 30 days of the agency's final decision. Forty-two days later Brown filed suit in federal court, alleging violations of both title VII and § 1981. The lower courts dismissed Brown's complaint as untimely under § 717(c), and this Court affirmed, holding that § 717 of title VII constituted the exclusive remedy for allegations of racial discrimination in federal employment.

The Court began its analysis by noting that "Congress simply failed explicitly to describe § 717's position in the constellation of antidiscrimination law." We noted that in 1972, when Congress extended the strictures of title VII to federal employment, the availability of an implied damages remedy under § 1981 for employment discrimination was not yet clear. The Court found that this perception on the part of Congress, "seems to indicate that the congressional intent in 1972 was to create an exclusive, pre-emptive administrative and judicial scheme for the redress of federal employment discrimination." The Court bolstered its holding by invoking the general principle that "a precisely drawn, detailed statute pre-empts more general remedies."

In *Brown,* as here, while Congress has not definitively spoken as to the relationship of § 1981 and § 1983, there is very strong evidence that the 42nd Congress which enacted the precursor of § 1983 thought that it was enacting the first, and at that time the only, federal damages remedy for the violation of federal constitutional and statutory rights by state governmental actors. The historical evidence surrounding the revision of 1874 further indicates that Congress thought that the declaration of rights in § 1981 would be enforced against state actors through the remedial provisions of § 1983. That remedial scheme embodies certain limitations on the liability of local governmental entities based on federalism concerns which had very real constitutional under-pinnings for the Reconstruction Congresses. As petitioner here would have it, the careful balance drawn by the 42nd Congress between local autonomy and fiscal integrity and the vindication of federal rights could be completely upset by an artifice of pleading.

Since our decision in *Monell,* the Courts of Appeals have unanimously rejected the contention, analogous to petitioner's argument here, that the doctrine of respondeat superior is available against a municipal entity under a *Bivens* -type action implied directly from the 14th amendment. Given our repeated recognition that the 14th amendment was intended in large part to embody and expand the protections of the 1866 Act as against state actors, we believe that the logic of these decisions applies with equal force to petitioner's invitation to this Court to create a damages remedy broader than § 1983 from the declaration of rights now found in § 1981. We hold that the express "action at law" provided by § 1983 for the "deprivation of any rights, privileges, or immunities secured by the Constitution and laws," provides the exclusive federal damages remedy for the violation of the rights guaranteed by § 1981 when the claim is pressed against a state actor. Thus to prevail on his claim for damages against the school district, petitioner must show that the violation of his "right to make contracts" protected by § 1981 was caused by a custom or policy within the meaning of *Monell* and subsequent cases.

IV

. . . Last term in St. Louis v. Praprotnik, 485 U.S. 112 (1988), (plurality opinion), we attempted a clarification of tools a federal court should employ in determining where policymaking authority lies for purposes of § 1983. In *Praprotnik,* the plurality reaffirmed the teachings of our prior cases to the effect that "whether a particular official has 'final policymaking authority' is a question of *state law.*" As with other questions of state law relevant to the application of federal law, the identification of those officials whose decisions represent the official policy of the local governmental unit is itself a legal question to be resolved by the trial judge *before* the case is submitted to the jury. Reviewing the relevant legal materials, including state and local positive law, as well as "'custom or usage' having the force of law," *Praprotnik,* supra, at 124, n. 1, the trial judge must identify those officials or governmental bodies who speak with final policymaking authority for the local governmental actor concerning the action alleged to have caused the particular constitutional or statutory violation at issue. Once those officials who have the power to make official policy on a particular issue have been identified, it is for the jury to determine whether *their* decisions have caused the deprivation of rights at issue by policies which affirmatively command that it occur or by acquiescence in a longstanding practice or custom which constitutes the "standard operating procedure" of the local governmental entity.

. . . Pursuant to its cross-petition . . ., the school district urges us to review Texas law and determine that neither Principal Todd nor Superintendent Wright possessed the authority to make final policy decisions concerning the transfer of school district personnel. Petitioner Jett seems to concede that Principal Todd did not have policymaking authority as to employee transfers, but argues that Superintendent Wright had been delegated authority to make school district policy concerning employee transfers and that his decisions in this area were final and unreviewable.

We decline to resolve this issue on the record before us. We think the Court of Appeals, whose expertise in interpreting Texas law is greater than our own, is in a better position to determine whether Superintendent Wright possessed final policymaking authority in the area of employee transfers, and if so whether a new trial is required to determine the responsibility of the school district for the actions of Principal Todd in light of this determination. We thus affirm the judgment of the Court of Appeals to the extent it holds that the school district may not be held liable for its employees' violation of the rights enumerated in § 1981 under a theory of respondeat superior. We remand the case to the Court of Appeals for it to determine where final policymaking authority as to employee transfers lay in light of the principles enunciated by the plurality opinion in *Praprotnik* outlined above.

It is so ordered.

JUSTICE SCALIA, concurring in part and concurring in the judgment.

I join parts I and IV of the Court's opinion, and part III except insofar as it relies upon legislative history. To hold that the more general provisions of 42 U.S.C. § 1981 establish a mode of liability for a particular category of offense by municipalities that is excluded from the closely related statute (42 U.S.C. § 1983) which deals more specifically with that precise category of offense would violate the rudimentary principles of construction that the specific governs the general and that, where text permits, statutes dealing with similar subjects should be interpreted harmoniously.

JUSTICE BRENNAN, with whom JUSTICE MARSHALL, JUSTICE BLACKMUN, and JUSTICE STEVENS join, dissenting.

To anyone familiar with this last term's debate over whether Runyon v. McCrary, 427 U.S. 160 (1976), should be overruled, see Patterson v. McLean Credit Union, 491 U.S. 164 (1989), today's decision can be nothing short of astonishing. After being led to believe that the hard question under 42 U.S.C. § 1981—the question that prompted this Court, on its own initiative, to set *Patterson* for reargument—was whether the statute created a cause of action relating to *private* conduct, today we are told that the hard question is, in fact, whether it creates such an action on the basis of *governmental* conduct. Strange indeed, simultaneously to question whether § 1981 creates a cause of action on the basis of private conduct (*Patterson*) and whether it creates one for governmental conduct (this case)—and hence to raise the possibility that this landmark civil-rights statute affords no civil redress at all.

In granting certiorari in this case we did not, as the Court would have it, agree to review the question whether one may bring a suit for damages under § 1981 itself on the basis of governmental conduct. The Court hints that petitioner Jett offered this issue for our consideration, ("In essence, petitioner argues that in 1866 the 39th Congress intended to create a cause of action for damages against municipal actors and others who violated the rights now enumerated in § 1981"), when in fact, it was *respondent* who raised this issue, and who did so for the first time in its brief on the merits in this Court. In six years of proceedings in the lower courts, . . . respondent never once suggested that Jett's only remedy was furnished by § 1983. Petitioner was able to respond to this argument only in his reply brief in this Court. While it is true that we often affirm a judgment on a ground not relied upon by the court below, we ordinarily do so only when that ground at least was raised below.

It is not only unfair to decide the case on this basis; it is unwise. The question is important; to resolve it on the basis of largely one-sided briefing, without the benefit of the views of the courts below, is rash. It is also unnecessary. The Court appears to decide today (though its precise holding is less than pellucid) that liability for violations by the government of § 1981 may not be predicated on a theory of respondeat superior. The answer to that question would dispose of Jett's contentions. In choosing to decide, as well, whether § 1983 furnishes the exclusive remedy for violations of § 1981 by the government, the Court makes many mistakes that might have been avoided by a less impetuous course.

Because I would conclude that § 1981 itself affords a cause of action in damages on the basis of governmental conduct violating its terms, and because I would conclude that such an action may be predicated on a theory of respondeat superior, I dissent.

I

. . . The question is whether [§ 1981] permits a cause of action in damages against those who violate its terms.

The Court approaches this issue as though it were new to us, recounting in lengthy and methodical detail the introduction, debate, passage, veto, and enactment of the 1866 Act. The story should by now be familiar to anyone with even a passing acquaintance with this statute. This is so because we have reviewed this history in the course of deciding—and reaffirming the answer to—the very question that the

Court deems so novel today. An essential aspect of the holding in each of [our prior § 1981] cases was the principle that a person injured by a violation of § 1 of the 1866 Act (now 42 U.S.C. §§ 1981 and 1982) may bring an action for damages under that statute against the person who violated it.

We have had good reason for concluding that § 1981 itself affords a cause of action against those who violate its terms. The statute does not explicitly furnish a cause of action for the conduct it prohibits, but this fact was of relatively little moment at the time the law was passed. During the period when § 1 of the 1866 Act was enacted, and for over 100 years thereafter, the federal courts routinely concluded that a statute setting forth substantive rights without specifying remedy contained an implied cause of action for damages incurred in violation of the statute's terms. The classic statement of this principle comes from Texas & Pacific R. Co. v. Rigsby, 241 U.S. 33, 39–40 (1916), in which we observed: "A disregard of the command of the statute is a wrongful act, and where it results in damage to one of the class for whose especial benefit the statute was enacted, the right to recover the damages from the party in default is implied, according to a doctrine of the common law." This case fits comfortably within *Rigsby*'s framework. It is of small consequence, therefore, that the 39th Congress established no explicit damages remedy in § 1 of the 1866 Act.[2]

Indeed, the debates on § 1 demonstrate that the legislators' worry was not that their actions would do too much, but that they would do too little. In introducing the bill that became the 1866 Act, Senator Trumbull explained that the statute was necessary because "[t]here is very little importance in the general declaration of abstract truths and principles [contained in the 13th amendment] unless they can be carried into effect, *unless the persons who are to be affected by them have some means of availing themselves of their benefits*." Cong. Globe,

---

[2] During the 1970s, we modified our approach to determining whether a statute contains an implied cause of action, announcing [a] four-part test [in Cort v. Ash, 422 U.S. 66 (1975).] It would make no sense, however, to apply a test first enunciated in 1975 to a statute enacted in 1866. An inquiry into Congress' actual intent must take account of the interpretive principles in place at the time. See Cannon v. University of Chicago, 441 U.S. 677, 698–99 (1979); Merrill Lynch, Pierce, Fenner & Smith v. Curran, 456 U.S. 353, 375–78 (1982). See also Welch v. Texas Dept. of Highways and Public Transportation, 483 U.S. 468, 496 (1987) (Scalia, J., concurring) (advising against construing a statute on the basis of an interpretive principle announced after the statute was passed.) Thus, I would interpret § 1981 in light of the principle described in *Rigsby*, rather than the one described in *Cort*.

Application even of the test fashioned in *Cort*, however, would lead to the conclusion that Jett may bring a cause of action in damages against respondent under § 1981. Jett belongs to the special class of persons (those who have been discriminated against in the making of contracts) for whom the statute was created; all of the indicators of legislative intent point in the direction of an implied cause of action; such an action is completely consistent with the statute's purposes; and, in view of the fact, that this Civil War-era legislation was in part designed to curtail the authority of the states, it would be unreasonable to conclude that this cause of action is one relegated to state law.

39th Cong., 1st Sess., 474 (1866) (emphasis added). Representative Thayer of Pennsylvania echoed this theme: "When I voted for the amendment to abolish slavery . . . I did not suppose that I was offering . . . a mere paper guarantee. . . . The bill which now engages the attention of the House has for its object to carry out and guaranty the reality of that great measure. It is to give to it practical effect and force. It is to prevent that great measure from remaining a dead letter upon the constitutional page of this country."

In these circumstances, it would be unreasonable to conclude that inferring a private cause of action from § 1981 is incompatible with Congress' intent. Yet in suggesting that § 2 of the 1866 Act demonstrates Congress' intent that criminal penalties serve as the only remedy for violations of § 1, this is exactly the conclusion that the Court apparently would have us draw. Not only, however, is this argument contrary to legislative intent, but we have already squarely rejected it. In Jones v. Alfred H. Mayer Co., 392 U.S. 409 (1968), respondent argued that because § 2 furnished criminal penalties for violations of § 1 occurring "under color of law," § 1 could not be read to provide a civil remedy for violations of the statute by private persons. Dismissing this argument, we explained: "[Section] 1 was meant to prohibit *all* racially motivated deprivations of the rights enumerated in the statute, although only those deprivations perpetrated 'under color of law' were to be criminally punishable under § 2." [3]

The only way that the Court can distinguish *Jones,* and the cases following it, from this case is to argue that our recognition of an implied cause of action against private persons did not include recognition of an action against local governments and government officials. But before today, no one had questioned that a person could sue a government official for damages due to a violation of § 1981. We have, in fact, reviewed two cases brought pursuant to § 1981 against government officials or entities, without giving the vaguest hint that the lawsuits were improperly brought. See Hurd v. Hodge, 334 U.S. 24 (1948); Takahashi v. Fish and Game Comm'n, 334 U.S. 410 (1948). Indeed, in *Jones,* the dissenters relied on *Hurd v. Hodge* in arguing that § 1981 applied *only* to governmental conduct. The lower courts have heeded well the message from our cases: they unanimously agree that suit may be brought directly under § 1981 against government officials who violate the statute's terms.

Perhaps recognizing how odd it would be to argue that one may infer from § 1 of the 1866 Act a cause of action against private persons, but not one against government officials, the Court appears to claim

---

[3] . . . The Court's assertion that the 1866 Act created no original federal jurisdiction for civil actions based on the statute is similarly unavailing. [T]he Court's argument confuses the question of which courts (state or federal) will enforce a cause of action with whether a cause of action exists.

that the 1871 Act erased whatever action against government officials previously existed under the 1866 Act. The Court explains:

> "That we have read § 1 of the 1866 Act to reach private action and have implied a damages remedy to effectuate the declaration of rights contained in that provision does not authorize us to do so in the context of the 'state action' portion of § 1981, where Congress has established its own remedial scheme. In the context of the application of § 1981 and § 1982 to private actors, we 'had little choice but to hold that aggrieved individuals could enforce this prohibition, *for there existed no other remedy to address such violations of the statute.*' That is manifestly not the case here, and whatever the limits of the judicial power to imply or create remedies, it has long been the law that such power should not be exercised in the face of an express decision by Congress concerning the scope of remedies available under a particular statute."

This argument became available only after § 1983 was passed, and thus suggests that § 1983 changed the cause of action implicitly afforded by § 1981. However, not only do we generally disfavor repeals by implication, but we should be particularly hostile to them when the allegedly repealing statute specifically rules them out. In this regard, § 7 of the 1871 Act is highly significant; it provided "[t]hat nothing herein contained shall be construed to supersede or repeal any former act or law except so far as the same may be repugnant thereto." [4]

The Court's argument fails for other reasons as well. Its essential point appears to be that, in § 1983, "Congress has established its own

---

[4] Several amici argue that we need not conclude that § 1983 impliedly repealed the cause of action furnished by § 1981 in order to decide that § 1983 provides the sole remedy for violations of § 1981. Their theory is that an implied cause of action did not exist when the 1871 Act was passed, and that therefore one may argue that the 1871 Act furnished the only remedy for the 1866 Act without arguing that the later statute in any way repealed the earlier one. To support their premise, they observe, first, that it was not until the 1960s that courts recognized a private cause of action under § 1 of the 1866 Act. In doing so, they ignore our earlier cases approving actions brought directly under § 1981. See Hurd v. Hodge, 334 U.S. 24 (1948). In any event, the relevance of the date on which we expressly recognized that one could bring a suit for damages directly under § 1 escapes me; that we did so in the 1960s does not suggest that we would not have done so had we faced the question in the 1860s.

Amici assert, in addition, that "[i]n recognizing an implied cause of action" under § 1981, we "rested in part on congressional actions [establishing federal jurisdiction] that post-date the creation in 1871 of an explicit civil cause of action for violations of § 1981." [But] even if the 1866 Act did not confer [federal jurisdiction over actions to recover damages for violations of the statute], the jurisdictional question is separate from the question whether a cause of action may be inferred from the statute. Indeed, amici appear to recognize as much when they argue that although § 1 did not establish federal jurisdiction to hear civil actions based on the statute, Congress "left the task of civil enforcement to the state courts." I cannot imagine what "civil enforcement" amici have in mind, unless it is the civil remedy that Jett seeks.

remedial scheme" for the "'state action' portion of § 1981."[5] For this argument, the Court may not rely, as it attempts to do, on the principle that "'when legislation expressly provides a particular remedy or remedies, courts should not expand the coverage of the statute to subsume other remedies.'" That principle limits the inference of a remedy for the violation of a statute only when *that same statute* already sets forth specific remedies. It cannot be used to support the argument that the provision of particular remedies in § 1983 tells us whether we should infer a damages remedy for violations of § 1981.

The suggestion, moreover, that today's holding "finds support in" Brown v. GSA, 425 U.S. 820 (1976), is audacious. Section 1983—which, for example, specifies no exhaustion requirement, no damages limitation, no defenses, and no statute of limitations—can hardly be compared with § 717 of the Civil Rights of 1964, at issue in *Brown,* with its many detailed requirements and remedies. Indeed, in Preiser v. Rodriguez, 411 U.S. 475, 489 (1973), we emphasized the "general" nature of § 1983 in refusing to allow former prisoners to challenge a prison's withholding of good-time credits under § 1983 rather than under the federal habeas corpus statute, 28 U.S.C. § 2254. We never before have suggested that § 1983's remedial scheme is so thorough that it preempts the remedies that might otherwise be available under other statutes; indeed, all of our intimations have been to the contrary.

According to the Court, to allow an action complaining of government conduct to be brought directly under § 1981 would circumvent our holding in Monell v. New York City Dept. of Social Services, 436 U.S. 658 (1978), that liability under § 1983 may not be based on a theory of respondeat superior. Not only am I unconvinced that we should narrow a statute as important as § 1981 on the basis of something so vague and inconclusive as "federalism concerns which had very real constitutional underpinnings for the Reconstruction Congress," but I am also unable to understand how *Monell*'s limitation on § 1983 liability begins to tell us whether the same restriction exists under § 1981, enacted five years earlier than § 1983 and covering a far narrower range of conduct. It is difficult to comprehend, in any case, why the Court is worried that construing § 1981 to create a cause of action based on governmental conduct would render local governments vicariously liable for the delicts of their employees, since it elsewhere goes to great lengths to suggest that liability under § 1981 may not be vicarious.

The Court's primary reason for distinguishing between private and governmental conduct under § 1981 appears to be its impression that, because private conduct is not actionable under § 1983, we "had little choice" but to hold that private individuals who violated § 1981 could

---

[5] The one bright spot in today's decision is its reaffirmation of our holding in Maine v. Thiboutot, 448 U.S. 1 (1980).

be sued directly under § 1981. This claim, however, suggests that whether a cause of action in damages exists under § 1981 depends on the scope of § 1983. In deciding whether a particular statute includes an implied cause of action, however, we have not in the past suggested that the answer will turn on the reach of a different statute. . . .

The Court's approach not only departs from our prior analysis of implied causes of action, but also attributes an intent to the 39th Congress that fluctuates depending on the state of the law with regard to § 1983. On the Court's theory, if this case had arisen during the period between our decisions in Monroe v. Pape, 365 U.S. 167 (1961), and *Monell,* when we believed that local governments were not "persons" within the meaning of § 1983, we would apparently have been required to decide that a cause of action could be brought against local governments and their official directly under § 1981. The Court, in fact, confirms this conclusion in distinguishing *Hurd v. Hodge* solely on the ground that we decided it at a time when § 1983 did not apply to the District of Columbia. In other words, on the Court's view, a change in the scope of § 1983 alters the reach of § 1981. I cannot endorse such a bizarre conception of congressional intent.

II

I thus would hold that Jett properly brought his suit against respondent directly under § 1981. It remains to consider whether that statute permits recovery against a local government body on a theory of respondeat superior.

Because § 1981 does not explicitly create a cause of action in damages, we would look in vain for an express statement that the statute contemplates liability based on the doctrine of respondeat superior. In *Monell,* however, our background assumption appears to have been that unless a statute subjecting institutions (such as municipalities) to liability evidences an intent not to impose liability on them based on respondeat superior, such liability will be assumed. The absolute language of § 1981 therefore is significant: "All persons within the jurisdiction of the United States shall have the same right in every State and Territory to make and enforce contracts . . . as is enjoyed by white citizens." Certainly nothing in this wording refutes the argument that vicarious liability may be imposed under this law.

Section 1983, in contrast, forbids a person to "subjec[t], or caus[e] to be subjected" another person to a deprivation of the rights protected by the statute. It is telling that § 1981 does not contain this explicit language of causation. In holding in *Monell* that liability under § 1983 may not be predicated on a theory of respondeat superior, we emphasized that § 1983 "plainly imposes liability on a government that, under color of some official policy, 'causes' an employee to violate another's constitutional rights. . . . Indeed, the fact that Congress did specifically provide that *A*'s tort became *B*'s liability if *B* 'caused' *A* to subject another to a tort suggests that Congress did not intend § 1983 liability to attach where such a causation was absent." The absence of this language in § 1 of the 1866 Act, now § 1981, argues against the claim that liability under this statute may not be vicarious.

While it acknowledged that § 1 of the 1866 Act did not contain the "subjects, or causes to be subjected" language of § 1983, the Court of Appeals nevertheless emphasized that § 2 of the 1866 Act did contain this language. There is not the least inconsistency, however, in arguing that the *criminal* penalties under the 1866 Act may not be imposed on the basis of respondeat superior, but that the civil penalties may be. Indeed, it is no surprise that the history surrounding the enactment of § 2 . . . indicates that Congress envisioned criminal penalties only for those who by their own conduct violated the statute, since vicarious criminal liability would be extraordinary. The same cannot be said of vicarious civil liability.

Nor does anything in the history of § 1981 cast doubt on the argument that liability under the statute may be vicarious. The Court of Appeals placed heavy reliance on Congress' rejection of the Sherman amendment, which would have imposed a dramatic form of vicarious liability on municipalities, five years after passing the 1866 Act. That the Court appears to accept this argument is curious, given our frequent reminder that " 'the views of a subsequent Congress form a hazardous basis for inferring the intent of an earlier one.' " Consumer Product Safety Comm'n v. GTE Sylvania, Inc., 447 U.S. 102, 117 (1980). I do not understand how Congress' rejection of an amendment imposing a very new kind of vicarious liability on municipalities can tell us what a different and earlier Congress intended with respect to conventional vicarious liability.

According to the Court, the history of the Sherman amendment is relevant to the interpretation of § 1981 because it reveals Congress' impression that it had no authority to subject municipalities to the kind of liability encompassed by the amendment. The Court fails to recognize, however, that the circumstances in which municipalities would be vicariously liable under the Sherman amendment are very different from those in which they would be liable under § 1981. [Had the Sherman amendment been enacted, it] would have forced municipalities to ensure that private citizens did not violate the rights of others. . . . To hold a local government body liable for the discriminatory cancellation of a contract entered into by that local body itself, however, is a very different matter. Even assuming that the 39th Congress had the same constitutional concerns as the 42nd, therefore, those concerns cast no doubt on Congress' authority to hold local government bodies vicariously liable under § 1 of the 1866 Act in circumstances such as those present here.

I thus would conclude that liability under § 1981 may be predicated on a theory of respondeat superior.

III

No one doubts that § 1983 was an unprecedented federal statute. The question is not whether § 1983 wrought a change in the law, but whether it did so in such a way as to withdraw a remedy that § 1 of the 1866 Act had implicitly afforded. Unlike the Court, I would conclude that it did not.

[Justice Stevens' separate dissent is omitted.]

NOTES ON *JETT v. DALLAS INDEPENDENT SCHOOL DISTRICT*

1. Background. The decision in *Jett* implicates at least three lines of prior decisions. The first concerns when it is appropriate for the Court to recognize a private damages action for violations of the Constitution. The leading case is Bivens v. Six Unknown Named Agents of Federal Bureau of Narcotics, 403 U.S. 388 (1971), where the Court held that damages could be sought from federal law enforcement officials for violation of the fourth amendment. The decisions since *Bivens* have varied, but the Court has not doubted its *power* to grant such relief. Instead, the cases have turned on whether the Court has been able to find, in the language of *Bivens,* "special factors counselling hesitation in the absence of affirmative action by Congress" or an alternative remedy which Congress explicitly declared to be a substitute for judicially implied relief.

The second line of cases involves the implication of a private damages action from a federal statute which does not explicitly authorize such relief. The cases in this context have gone through three stages: (i) the suggestion of J.I. Case v. Borak, 377 U.S. 426 (1964), that private remedies would be freely available; (ii) the adoption in Cort v. Ash, 422 U.S. 66 (1975), of a complex four-part inquiry to determine when a private remedy should be implied; and (iii) the holding in Touche Ross & Co. v. Reddington, 442 U.S. 560 (1979), that such remedies would not be recognized unless "Congress intended to create the private right of action asserted."

The third line of cases concerns the meaning of the words "and laws" in 42 U.S.C. § 1983. The Court indicated in Maine v. Thiboutot, 448 U.S. 1 (1980), that § 1983 supplied a private cause of action for damages against any state official who violated rights created by any federal statute.[a] Subsequent cases have cast doubt on the breadth of

[a] *Maine v. Thiboutot* appears as a main case at page 164 of the Casebook.

this proposition, but it still remains clear that *some* federal statutes are enforceable against state officials through damage actions based on § 1983. The important question is the starting point for analysis: whether a § 1983 remedy is available *unless* Congress appears to have directed otherwise, or whether it is available only *if* Congress appears to have so intended.

2. Questions and Comments. The Court holds in *Jett* that a remedy cannot be implied from § 1981 against a unit of local government whose officials deny the substantive rights it creates. Instead, § 1981 is to be regarded in this context as the origin of rights that are enforceable only through the cause of action created by § 1983. The plaintiff can recover against a unit of local government, therefore, only if the conditions established under § 1983 can be satisfied. In cases where *private* actors are sued under § 1981, by contrast, the remedy appears to be implied from § 1981 itself. Section 1983 would in any event be irrelevant because of its explicit limitation to actions taken under color of state law.

Which line of cases summarized above is most relevant to the Court's decision? Is the Court's holding consistent with analogous precedents? Would it have been better (and more consistent with cases against *private* actors) for the Court to have reached its result by recognizing that a *cause of action* can be implied from § 1981, but that § 1981, like § 1983, does not embrace the doctrine of respondeat superior in cases of governmental liability? Would this rationale have been more consistent with the prior § 1981 precedents? Why did the Court reject it?

Also, recall that the Court does not address the question whether, after *Patterson v. McLean Credit Union,* Jett's complaint states a violation of rights protected by § 1981. Does it? If the issue had been properly preserved by the defendants, how would the Court have ruled?

Page 290, change the word "three" to "four" in the third line of Note 2 and add the following citation at the end of the first paragraph:

Neil H. Cogan, Section 1985(3)'s Restructuring of Equality: An Essay on Texts, History, Progress, and Cynicism, 39 Rutgers L.Rev. 515 (1987).

Page 291, add after the first full paragraph:

Cogan argues that the Court has misconstrued the original vision underlying § 1985(3). Specifically, he contends that "the Congress attempted to restructure equality among the people of the United States by prohibiting not only the states, but all persons, private as well as official, from depriving any other person of the 'equal protection of the laws' or of 'equal privileges and immunities.'" The intent, he argues, was to "prohibit private discrimination by or against the same classes as to which state discrimination was prohibited." Moreover, Congress sought in § 1985(3) to protect privileges and immunities "more widely against private action than against state action . . . , whether or not belonging to citizens of the United States and whether or not federal in origin." He particularly decries the Court's "reluctance to enforce universal equality in the fundamental rights of citizenship."

Page 291, add before the Notes on §§ 241 and 242:

NATIONAL ORGANIZATION FOR WOMEN v. OPERATION RESCUE

United States Court of Appeals, Fourth Circuit, 1990.
914 F.2d 582.

Before CHAPMAN and WILKINSON, CIRCUIT JUDGES, and ANDERSON, UNITED STATES DISTRICT JUDGE for the District of South Carolina, sitting by designation.

PER CURIAM:

This is an appeal of a permanent injunction entered against six individuals and Operation Rescue, an unincorporated association whose members oppose abortion and its legalization. The District Court enjoined them, inter alia, from "trespassing on, blockading, impeding or obstructing access to or egress from" the premises of plaintiffs, facilities that provide abortions or abortion counseling. The court held that defendants' blockading of abortion facilities infringed the right to travel of women seeking to obtain abortions at clinics in the Washington metropolitan area, in violation of 42 U.S.C. § 1985(3), and certain of their rights under state law. Operation Rescue and the six individual defendants appeal. NOW cross-appeals, along with nine abortion facilities and four other organizational plaintiffs. We reject both appeals and affirm the judgment of the district court.

I.

Plaintiffs are nine clinics in the Washington metropolitan area and Northern Virginia that provide various abortion-related services, and five organizations that seek to preserve a woman's right to obtain an abortion. Defendant Operation Rescue is an organization whose purpose is to prevent abortions and to oppose their legalization. One of the ways Operation Rescue seeks to effectuate these goals is to stage "rescue" demonstrations at abortion facilities. At these demonstrations, the participants "intentionally trespass on the clinic's premises for the purpose of blockading the clinic's entrances and exits, thereby effectively closing the clinic" and "'rescu[ing]' . . . fetuses scheduled for abortion." Nat'l Org. For Women (NOW) v. Operation Rescue, 726 F.Supp. 1483, 1487 (E.D.Va.1989) [decision below]. The individual defendants are persons who oppose abortion and its legalization, and who seek to advance their views in part by "planning, organizing and participating in 'rescue' demonstrations under the banner and auspices of Operation Rescue." Id., at 1488.

On November 8, 1989, plaintiffs filed a motion for a temporary restraining order in United States District Court for the Eastern District of Virginia, seeking to enjoin defendants from, among other things, physically impeding access to certain facilities that offer abortion and related services. The impetus for this action was defendants' alleged plans for meetings, rallies, and "rescue" demonstrations on November 10–12 and 18–20, 1989 in the Washington metropolitan area. No rescue activities took place in Northern Virginia during that period. However, clinics in Maryland and the District of Columbia were closed due to demonstrations on those dates.

The District Court granted plaintiffs' motion for a temporary restraining order after an expedited hearing on November 8–9, 1989. The trial of the action on the merits and the hearing on the application for a preliminary injunction were consolidated and scheduled to be heard on November 16, 1989. After a two day trial in which plaintiffs presented testimony from nine witnesses and defendants elected to present no evidence, the District Court granted the request for a permanent injunction. The court enjoined defendants from "trespassing on, blockading, impeding or obstructing access to or egress from the [listed] premises." The court refused on first amendment grounds to extend the injunction to enjoin rescue activities that tend to "intimidate, harass or disturb patients or potential patients."

The District Court concluded that defendants' activities operated to deny to women seeking abortions and abortion-related services the right to travel interstate in search of medical services in violation of 42 U.S.C. § 1985(3). The court noted that the elements of a cause of action under § 1985(3) are: "(i) conspiracy; (ii) for the purpose of depriving, either directly or indirectly, any person or class of persons of the equal protection of the laws, or of equal privileges and immunities under the laws; (iii) an act in furtherance of the conspiracy; (iv) whereby a person is either injured in his person or property or deprived of any right or privilege of a citizen of the United States." The court held that defendants had violated § 1985(3) by entering into a conspiracy to deprive women, whom it found to be a protected class within the meaning of § 1985(3), of their constitutional right to travel. It reasoned, citing Doe v. Bolton, 410 U.S. 179 (1973), that the rescue demonstrations interfere with the right to travel because substantial numbers of women seeking the services of clinics in the Washington metropolitan area travel interstate to obtain these services.

The court further found that permanent injunctive relief was appropriate because: (i) there was no adequate remedy at law; (ii) the balance of equities favored plaintiffs; and (iii) the public interest was

Ch. 2 *1992 SUPPLEMENT* 147

served by granting the injunction. The court found that women seeking abortions and counseling were likely to suffer irreparable physical and emotional harm as a result of defendants' blockading of abortion facilities. The court noted, for example, that some women require insertion of a pre-abortion laminaria to achieve cervical dilation. Women prevented from entering the clinics for timely removal of this device may risk bleeding, infection, or other possible serious complications, or may be forced to seek services elsewhere. Similarly, the court referenced testimony to the effect that preventing access to abortion clinics could cause clients to experience stress, anxiety, and mental harm. The court concluded that since plaintiffs' actions were lawful, although morally objectionable to defendants, the balance of equities weighed in favor of guaranteeing the public protection of the constitutional right to travel.

Operation Rescue now appeals, and the National Organization for Women cross-appeals the district court's refusal to extend the scope of the injunction.

II.

We have reviewed the record and the reasoning of the District Court in granting the injunction. We affirm the judgment because the District Court found that the activities of appellants in furtherance of their beliefs had crossed the line from persuasion into coercion and operated to deny the exercise of rights protected by law. The legal premises under which the District Court operated are also consistent with the law of the circuits. The court's holding that gender-based animus satisfies the "purpose" element of § 1985(3) has been forecast by this circuit in Buschi v. Kirven, 775 F.2d 1240, 1257 (4th Cir.1985) (animus against classes defined by "race, national origin and sex" meet requirement of class-based animus within meaning of § 1985(3)). At least six circuits have so held. See New York Nat'l Org. for Women (NOW) v. Terry, 886 F.2d 1339, 1359 (2d Cir.1989); Volk v. Coler, 845 F.2d 1422, 1434 (7th Cir.1988); Stathos v. Bowden, 728 F.2d 15, 20 (1st Cir.1984); Novotny v. Great Am. Fed. Savings & Loan Ass'n, 584 F.2d 1235, 1244 (3d Cir.1978), vacated on other grounds, 442 U.S. 366 (1979); Life Ins. Co. of N. Am. v. Reichardt, 591 F.2d 499, 505 (9th Cir.1979); Conroy v. Conroy, 575 F.2d 175, 177 (8th Cir.1978). But cf. Mississippi Women's Medical Clinic v. McMillan, 866 F.2d 788, 794 (5th Cir.1989). The Second Circuit has held under similar facts that blocking access to medical services provided by abortion facilities which serve an interstate clientele violates the constitutional right to travel. See *New York NOW,* 886 F.2d, at 1360–61.

Moreover, we review the entry, scope, and duration of an injunction under an abuse of discretion standard. We find that the District Court operated in conformity with other circuits on the relevant questions of law, and we are unable to conclude that the court abused its discretion in entering an injunction of this scope and duration against the respective parties. Specifically, we reject the argument of Operation Rescue that there was insufficient evidence to grant relief against defendants Bray, McMonagle and Gannett. We also reject NOW's contention that the District Court abused its discretion in limiting the injunction to Northern Virginia and in declining to extend the injunction indefinitely. In addition, we affirm the District Court's refusal to broaden the scope of the injunction to include activities that tend to "intimidate, harass or disturb patients or potential patients" because to do so would risk enjoining activities clearly protected by the first amendment. In addition to the actions enjoined by the District Court, the members of Operation Rescue also sought, through verbal means, to persuade women not to seek the services of abortion clinics and to "impress upon members of society" the moral rightness and intensity of their opposition to abortion. The District Court was within its discretion in declining to extend the injunction in a manner that would interfere with such expressive activity. In view of our disposition of the federal question raised by appellants we also decline to disturb the District Court's refusal to dismiss the state law claims, and we uphold as well its award of costs and attorneys fees. The District Court did not, and we do not, reach the question of whether § 1985(3) can encompass violations of a right to privacy.

Accordingly, the judgment of the District Court is affirmed in all respects for the reasons stated in its opinion.

Affirmed.

NOTES ON THE "OPERATION RESCUE" CASES

1. The Supreme Court's Disposition of the Fourth Circuit Decision. On February 25, 1991, the Supreme Court granted certiorari in the case reproduced above. Eight Justices heard oral argument on October 16, 1991 (before the confirmation of Justice Thomas). On June 8, 1992, the Court restored the case to the calendar for reargument during the fall of 1992.

2. The District Court Decision. The District Court decision in the Fourth Circuit's *NOW* case is reported as National Organization for Women (NOW) v. Operation Rescue, 726 F.Supp. 1483, 1487 (E.D.Va. 1989). The plaintiffs had asserted five causes of action, two of which were based on § 1985(3) and three of which were based on pendent state law claims. The court's findings of fact and conclusions of law with respect to the right to travel aspects of the § 1985(3) claims were as follows:

"31. A cause of action under 42 U.S.C. § 1985(3) has four essential elements: (i) a conspiracy; (ii) for the purpose of depriving, either directly or indirectly, any person or class of persons of the equal protection of the laws, or of equal privileges and immunities under the laws; (iii) an act in furtherance of the conspiracy; (iv) whereby a person is either injured in his person or property or deprived of any right or privilege of a citizen of the United States. Griffin v. Breckenridge, 403 U.S. 88, 102–03 (1971) (as explained in United Bhd. of Carpenters & Joiners v. Scott, 463 U.S. 825, 828–29 (1983)).

"32. 'A conspiracy is a combination of two or more persons, by concerted action to accomplish some unlawful purpose, or to accomplish some lawful purpose by unlawful means.' 3 E. Devitt & C. Blackmar, Federal Jury Practice & Instructions § 103.23 (1987); see also Model Penal Code § 5.03 (Proposed Official Draft 1962). Ample record evidence reflects the existence of a conspiracy among defendants. Specifically, it reflects that the individual defendants combined with each other and with defendant Operation Rescue to plan, organize, coordinate and carry out 'rescue' demonstrations that involved unlawful means, including violation of trespass and nuisance laws and § 1985(3).

"33. The Fourth Circuit has characterized the statute's 'purpose' element as requiring that the conspiracy be 'motivated by a specific class-based, invidiously discriminatory animus.' Buschi v. Kirven, 775 F.2d 1240, 1257 (4th Cir.1985).

"34. Contrary to defendants' argument, gender-based animus satisfies the 'purpose' element of § 1985(3). To meet the requirement of 'class-based discriminatory animus,' the class must possess 'discrete, insular and immutable characteristics comparable to those characterizing classes such as race, national origin and sex.' Buschi, 775 F.2d at 1257 (emphasis added) (denying § 1985(3) protection to a class designated as 'whistleblowers'). Plaintiffs' members and patients constitute a subset of a gender-based class meeting these requirements. There is, to be sure, a lack of uniformity among courts on this issue. See, e.g., Roe v. Abortion Abolition Soc'y, 811 F.2d 931 (5th Cir.1987) (holding that patients, doctors, and abortion clinics and their staffs do not form a protected class under § 1985(3)); National Abortion Fed. v. Operation Rescue, 721 F.Supp. 1168 (C.D.Ca.1989) (same). But, the majority of courts have concluded that a gender-based animus satisfies the conspiracy requirement of § 1985(3). See Volk v. Coler, 845 F.2d 1422, 1434 (7th Cir.1988) ('§ 1985(3) extends . . . to conspiracies to discriminate against persons based on sex.'); Portland Feminist Women's Health Center v. Advocates for Life, Inc.,

712 F.Supp. 165, 169 (D.Or.1988) (§ 1985(3) covers women seeking abortions); Roe v. Operation Rescue, 710 F.Supp. 577, 581 (E.D.Pa.1989) (same); New York State Nat'l Organization for Women v. Terry, 704 F.Supp. 1247 (S.D.N.Y.1989) (same); Hunt v. Weatherbee, 626 F.Supp. 1097 (D.Mass.1986) (sex discrimination covered by § 1985(3)); Skadegaard v. Farrell, 578 F.Supp. 1209 (D.N.J.1984) (same). Thus, this court concludes that a conspiracy to deprive women seeking abortions of their rights guaranteed by law is actionable under § 1985(3).

"35. Defendants engaged in this conspiracy for the purpose, either directly or indirectly, of depriving women seeking abortions and related medical and counselling services, of the right to travel. The right to travel includes the right to unobstructed interstate travel to obtain an abortion and other medical services. Doe v. Bolton, 410 U.S. 179 (1973) (in-state residence requirement as prerequisite to abortion services violates right to travel). Testimony at trial establishes that clinics in Northern Virginia provide medical services to plaintiffs' members and patients who travel from out of state. Defendants' activities interfere with these person's right to unimpeded interstate travel by blocking their access to abortion clinics. And, the court is not persuaded that clinic closings affect only intrastate travel, from the street to the doors of the clinics. Were the court to hold otherwise, interference with the right to travel could occur only at state borders. This conspiracy, therefore, effectively deprives organizational plaintiffs' non-Virginia members of their right to interstate travel.

"36. Since the right to interstate travel is protected from purely private as well as governmental interference, plaintiffs need not show state action to make out a claim under § 1985(3). Griffin v. Breckenridge, 403 U.S. 88, 105–06 (1971); New York State Nat'l Org. for Women v. Terry, 886 F.2d 1339, 1360 (2d Cir.1989).

"37. The record demonstrates that the overt act requirement of the § 1985(3) conspiracy is met here. Defendants' history of obstructionist activity, continued 'rescue' training sessions, and recent violations of temporary restraining orders preventing 'rescue' behavior plainly satisfy the statute's overt act requirement.

"38. While the clinics are closed, patients are unable to receive medical treatment. Medical emergencies could arise in connection with abortions that would require immediate medical attention. Thus, clinic closings pose a serious threat of harm to women who are undergoing, or have undergone, abortions. Thus, defendants' continued threat to plaintiffs' exercise of their federally guaranteed right to travel satisfies the § 1985(3) injury element. Defendants' conduct clearly evidences an intent to continue this conduct.

"39. Plaintiffs have, therefore, clearly established all of the elements of a violation of § 1985(3) and as such, are entitled to relief."

The court's comments on the "right to privacy" claim were as follows:

"40. Plaintiffs also seek relief on the ground that defendants' rescue demonstrations violate § 1985(3) because they infringe on the fundamental right of plaintiffs' members and patients to obtain an abortion. Recognizing the likely absence of state action on these facts,[11] plaintiffs argue, with some lack of clarity, that the putative right to an abortion is of such a fundamental character as to be guaranteed against all interference, not just governmental interference.[12] Such a claim is problematic, both because it is novel and because . . . the law concerning a putative abortion right is in a state of flux. Given this and given that there is another independent basis for relief under § 1985(3), the court concludes that it is unnecessary and imprudent to venture into this thicket. Courts should avoid constitutional questions where other grounds are available and dispositive of the issues presented. Therefore, the court expresses no view as to the merits of plaintiffs' claim premised on a fundamental right to an abortion."

3. The Second Circuit Decision. Both the Court of Appeals and the District Court relied on New York State Nat. Organization for Women (NOW) v. Terry, 886 F.2d 1339 (2d Cir.1989). Relevant portions

---

[11] "Where the claimed abortion right is a penumbral privacy right emanating from the first amendment, state action must be shown to support a claim under § 1985(3). . . . There is some authority, however, that the state action requirement is satisfied when 'rescuers' refuse to notify the police of their next 'rescue' target, thereby rendering police officials incapable of securing equal access to medical treatment for women who choose abortion. New York State Nat'l Org. for Women, 704 F.Supp., at 1260; see also Great Am. Fed. Sav. & Loan Ass'n v. Novotny, 442 U.S. 366, 384 (1979) ('[i]f private persons take conspiratorial action that prevents or hinders the constituted authorities of any state from giving or securing equal treatment, the private persons would cause those authorities to violate the 14th amendment'). But plaintiffs did not argue this point and for the reasons noted in the text, infra, the court need not reach the merits of this doubtful argument."

[12] "Though plaintiffs did not specify the source of such a fundamental privacy right, they may have meant the ninth amendment, for it was referred to in Justice Goldberg's concurring opinion in Griswold v. Connecticut, 381 U.S. 479, 85 S.Ct. 1678, 14 L.Ed.2d 510 (1965) and mentioned by Justice Blackmun in Roe v. Wade, 410 U.S. 113, 93 S.Ct. 705, 35 L.Ed.2d 147 (1973). Some commentators, too, have advocated that amendment as the source of an unenumerated right to privacy. See Redlich, The Ninth Amendment as a Constitutional Prison, 12 Harv.J.L. & Pub. Pol'y 23 (1989). But at least one commentator has sharply criticized the whole notion of grounding any right to an abortion in a fundamental constitutional privacy right. See BeVier, What Privacy is Not, 12 Harv.J.L. & Pub.Pol'y 99 (1989)."

of that decision are reproduced below. The District Court had granted the plaintiffs' motion for summary judgment. The court first addressed the general nature of § 1985(3) claims:

> "To prevail on a § 1985(3) claim, a plaintiff must prove that defendants (1) engaged in a conspiracy; (2) for the purpose of depriving, either directly or indirectly, any person or class of persons the equal protection of the laws, or the equal privileges and immunities under the laws; (3) acted in furtherance of the conspiracy; and (4) deprived such person or class of persons the exercise of any right or privilege of a citizen of the United States. See Griffin v. Breckenridge, 403 U.S. 88, 102–03 (1971).
>
> "It is well-settled that § 1985(3) provides a cause of action for private conspiracies. When the asserted constitutional deprivation is based upon a right guaranteed against government interference—for example, rights secured by the 14th amendment—plaintiffs must demonstrate some 'state involvement.'
>
> "Despite its applicability to purely private conspiracies, § 1985(3) is limited in two interrelated ways. First, the Supreme Court has emphasized that § 1985(3) may not be construed as a 'general federal tort law.' Griffin, 403 U.S., at 101–02. Rather, a plaintiff must demonstrate 'some racial, or perhaps otherwise class-based, invidiously discriminatory animus behind the conspirators' action.' Id., at 102. Second, not all classes of persons fall within the protective ambit of § 1985(3). The Supreme Court has specifically left open the question of whether this statute was aimed against any other class-based animus than that directed against blacks and their supporters at the time of its enactment. Legislative history, the Supreme Court acknowledged, supported the view that § 1985(3) went beyond racially motivated conspiracies, but it held that animus based generally upon the economic views or commercial interests of a class were beyond the statute's scope. United Bhd. of Carpenters & Joiners v. Scott, 463 U.S. 825, 837–39 (1983). Thus, the threshold issue is whether § 1985(3) encompasses conspiracies motivated by an animus against a class of women seeking medical and abortion-related services."

The court then addressed the question whether women were a "protected class" under the statute:

> "The broad language of § 1985(3) does not exclude women from its protections. It speaks instead of 'persons' and 'class[es] of persons,' and seeks to secure to them the 'equal protection of the laws' and the 'equal privileges and immunities under the laws.' Moreover, the act forbids conspiracies that deprive such persons of 'any right or privilege of a *citizen*

of the United States.' § 1985(3) (emphasis added). Admittedly, the 42nd Congress' principal concern was to protect newly emancipated blacks, and those who championed them, against conspiracies. But the act's supporters in Congress repeatedly stressed the theme of preventing 'deprivations which shall attack the equality of rights of American citizens.' See *Griffin,* 403 U.S. at 100.

"In reviewing history, we should not forget that women in 1871 were not accorded the full rights of citizenship. [But d]istinctions based upon immutable characteristics such as sex have long been considered invidiously discriminatory. See, e.g., Frontiero v. Richardson, 411 U.S. 677, 687 (1973) (Congress concluded that classifications based on sex are inherently invidious). By its very language § 1985(3) is necessarily tied to evolving notions of equality and citizenship. As conspiracies directed against women are inherently invidious, and repugnant to the notion of equality of rights for all citizens, they are therefore encompassed under the act.

"Moreover, this Circuit as well as other Circuits have held that § 1985(3) encompasses women as a class, or classes based on political associations, or those based on ethnicity, none of which groups were specifically contemplated by the 42nd Congress. See Volk v. Coler, 845 F.2d 1422, 1434 (7th Cir.1988) ("§ 1985(3) extends . . . to conspiracies to discriminate against persons based on sex, religion, ethnicity or political loyalty."); Conklin v. Lovely, 834 F.2d 543, 549 (6th Cir.1987) (political views); McLean v. International Harvester Co., 817 F.2d 1214, 1218–19 (5th Cir.1987) (section protects classes characterized by 'some inherited or immutable characteristic' or by 'political beliefs or associations'); Hobson v. Wilson, 737 F.2d 1, 21 (D.C.Cir.1984) (political affiliations with racial overtones); Keating v. Carey, 706 F.2d 377, 386–88 (2d Cir.1983) (political affiliation); Life Ins. Co. of North America v. Reichardt, 591 F.2d 499, 505 (9th Cir.1979) (women purchasers of disability insurance); Novotny v. Great American Federal Savings & Loan Ass'n, 584 F.2d 1235, 1241–43 (3d Cir.1978) (en banc) (women), vacated on other grounds, 442 U.S. 366 (1979); Conroy v. Conroy, 575 F.2d 175, 177 (8th Cir.1978) (sex and ethnicity).

"We have previously stated that '[a] narrow interpretation of the statute as protecting only blacks and other analogously oppressed minorities is untenable in light of the history of the Act.' *Keating,* 706 F.2d, at 387. It is likewise untenable to believe that Congress would provide a statutory remedy against private conspiracies, the purpose of which is to deny rights common to every citizen, and exclude women as a class from the shelter of its protection. We therefore hold that women may constitute a class for purposes of § 1985(3)."

At this point the court examined the defendants' activities under § 1985(3):

"The record plainly indicates that defendants engaged in a conspiracy to prevent women from obtaining access to medical facilities. Operation Rescue literature encourages participants to gather in front of clinics and blackade them. Defendants agreed with other individuals to engage in unlawful activity, including violations of both state law and women's constitutional rights. Moreover, defendants facilitated the conspiracy by providing transportation and accommodations to participants. This type of concerted action ultimately involves a conspiracy to engage in unlawful activity.

"Defendants urge that plaintiffs have demonstrated no class-based animus. They contend that 'the concept of animus is one of ill-will.' Yet animus merely describes a person's basic attitude or intention, and because defendants' conspiracy is focused entirely on women seeking abortions, their activities reveal an attitude or animus based on gender. Defendants' argument that their actions are directed against an activity, or only a 'subgroup' of women rather than women in general, is insufficient to escape the scope of § 1985(3). In most cases of invidious discrimination, violations of constitutional rights occur only in response to the attempts of certain members of a class to do something that the perpetrators found objectionable, such as travelling interstate with the perceived purpose of promoting civil rights. See, e.g., *Griffin,* 403 U.S., at 90. It is sophistry for defendants to claim a lack of class-based animus because their actions are directed only against those members of a class who choose to exercise particular rights, but not against class members whose actions do not offend them. The denial of ill-will towards the women they target and the claim that defendants' actions will benefit these women amount to an argument that 'we are doing this for your own good'; a contention that usually shields one's actual motive.

"Defendants cannot seriously urge that they do not intentionally infringe on the right of women to seek access to the clinics. That was one of the major objectives of the demonstrations of May 2, May 3, May 5, May 6 and October 29, 1988 all of which were purposefully aimed to deny the right of women as a class to gain access to clinics. And, to a significant degree, they succeeded. The record is replete with incidents supporting this conclusion and the District Court's findings in this regard cannot be said to be clearly erroneous. Consequently, it is apparent that defendants acted within the scope of § 1985(3) by (1) engaging in a conspiracy; (2) against a cognizable class of persons, with invidious class-based animus; and (3) committed the requisite overt acts in furtherance of the conspiracy.

"The remaining question is whether this conspiracy deprived plaintiffs and the women on whose behalf this claim was asserted of any constitutional right. Plaintiffs allege that these rights were violated in two ways: first, that the conspiracy intended to and did infringe upon women's constitutionally guaranteed right to travel; and, second, that the conspiracy intended to and did infringe upon women's right to obtain abortions.

(1) Right to Travel

"The right to interstate travel is guaranteed by the Constitution. Deprivations of that right are actionable under § 1985(3) with no need to show any state action or involvement. In Doe v. Bolton, 410 U.S. 179 (1973), the Supreme Court held that a residency requirement in a state statute regulating abortion violated the right of interstate travel. The High Court specifically held that the right to travel 'protects persons who enter [a state] seeking the medical services that are available there.'

"As noted, women referred by out-of-state clinics often travel to New York City seeking its superior medical services. Patients residing in other states, the District of Columbia, and Canada, sometimes must undergo a two-day procedure for second trimester abortions. Moreover, defendants' own literature expresses their understanding that clinics in New York City and its environs are preferred targets of demonstrations because of the range of abortion-related services offered there. Jeannine Michael, a counselor at the Eastern Women's Center testified that '[U]nexpected closure of [a clinic] would be particularly acute for our out-of-state clients, whose travel, work, childcare and financial problems would be greater because they would be more difficult to resolve when some distance from home.' Further, the threat of future demonstrations with the consequent closing of clinics may expose women seeking the more medically serious and lengthy second trimester procedures to harm.

"Such encumbrances constitute an infringement upon these women's right to travel. Thus, plaintiffs are entitled to summary judgment on their § 1985(3) claim due to the deprivation of the individual right of a citizen to unhindered interstate travel to seek medical services.

(2) Right to Obtain an Abortion

"With respect to the right to obtain an abortion, the District Court granted plaintiff's motion for summary judgment on this claim as well. It ruled that because the right to privacy stems from the 14th amendment's prohibition on state or governmental interference, plaintiffs were required to demonstrate 'state involvement.' The District Court reasoned that defendants' failure to notify police officials prior to their demonstrations and, on one occasion, their actual agreement with Dobbs Ferry, New York police that no demonstrators would be arrested, sufficiently showed state involvement for purposes of § 1985(3). Whether or not one agrees with this reasoning, having already found the interference with a right to travel an independent constitutional ground upon which to affirm the District Court's § 1985(3) holding, it is unnecessary for us to rule on this constitutional claim."

4. Comments and Questions. Notice that the real issue at stake here is whether cases involving blockading of abortion clinics will be heard in federal or state court. It seems clear that individuals who block access to abortion facilities could be charged with various state crimes (e.g., trespass) or that a variety of tort actions could be filed by injured parties in state court.

Even given that § 1985(3) applies to sex-based discrimination, do the actions of the abortion protesters discriminate against women or a subclass of women? Or do they target anyone who participates in an abortion? Consider the reasoning in Mississippi Women's Medical Clinic v. McMillan, 866 F.2d 788, 794 (5th Cir.1989). The court concluded that abortion protesters had not acted with an invidious discriminatory animus because "the protestors (who are made up of both men and women) confront and try to persuade to their point of view all groups—men, women of all ages, doctors, nurses, staff, the female security guards, etc. . . . [T]he animus of the protestors is to dissuade *anyone* who contributes to the incidence of abortions." Similarly, in an amicus brief filed in *Bray,* the United States argued that anti-abortion demonstrations are not a form of gender-based discrimination because they are aimed at a *practice* rather than a type of person. Are these arguments persuasive?

Consider also the use of the right to travel in these cases. If the right to travel is offended here, could it also be asserted against private action that prevents access to *any* services generally available to the public? Recall that neither the Fourth Circuit in *Bray* nor the Second Circuit in *NOW v. Terry* expressed the underlying constitutional right as the right to travel to obtain *abortion* services. Both courts declined to decide whether the actions of the protesters deprived women of a fundamental right to abortion. What principle, then, limits the right to travel? Is it necessary that there be a limit? Is there any choice here but to decide whether the abortion protesters are interfering with the exercise of a fundamental constitutional right to an abortion?

Chapter III

ADMINISTRATION OF THE CIVIL RIGHTS ACTS: INTERSECTIONS OF STATE AND FEDERAL LAW

Page 315, add to the end of Note 7:

A correlative problem is the extent to which state claims that have a factual relationship to a federal civil rights action can be brought in federal court (and might be regarded as precluded in subsequent state-court litigation if they are not). Congress has recently broadened the jurisdiction of federal courts to hear such claims in 28 U.S.C. § 1367, which brings ancillary jurisdiction and both pendent claim and pendant party jurisdiction under the single heading of "supplemental jurisdiction." For an analysis of the applicability of this statute to claims under § 1983 and other federal civil rights statutes, see Steven H. Steinglass, Pendent Jurisdiction and Civil Rights Litigation, 7 Civil Rights Litigation and Attorney Fees Annual Handbook 31 (1991).

Page 338, add to footnote b:

An application of *Wilson v. Garcia* is examined in Stephen J. Shapiro, Choosing the Appropriate State Statute of Limitations for Section 1983 Claims After *Wilson v. Garcia*: A Theory Applied to Maryland Law, 16 U.Balt.L.Rev. 242 (1987). For more general description and analysis of the various approaches that emerged after *Wilson*, see Julie A. Davies, In Search of the "Paradigmatic Wrong"?: Selecting a Limitations Period for Section 1983, 36 Kan.L.Rev. 133 (1987). For an argument that *Wilson* should be abandoned in favor of a laches doctrine, see Robert Jarvis and Judith Anne Jarvis, The Continuing Problem of Statutes of Limitations in Section 1983 Cases: Is the Answer Out at Sea?, 22 John Marshall L.Rev. 285 (1988).

Page 338, add a new Note:

1a. *Owens v. Okure*: Choice Between Personal Injury Statutes. *Wilson* holds that the state statute of limitations for tort suits "for the recovery of damages for personal injuries" is the best choice for § 1983 actions. What happens if the state has several statutes of limitation for "personal injury" actions?

This situation arose in Owens v. Okure, 488 U.S. 235 (1989). New York had a one-year statute of limitations for intentional torts and a three-year residual statute for personal injury claims not otherwise covered by a specific provision. The plaintiff's action was filed 22 months after the alleged unlawful arrest that provided the basis for his complaint. The District Court denied a motion to dismiss, but certified the question for interlocutory appeal. The Circuit Court and the Supreme Court affirmed. For a unanimous Court, Justice Marshall noted that "[e]very state has multiple intentional tort limitations provisions, carving up the universe of intentional torts into different configurations." By contrast, "every state has one general or residual statute of limitations governing personal injury actions [which are] easily identifiable by language or application." Because "our task today is to provide courts with a rule for determining the appropriate personal injury limitations statute that can be applied with ease and predictability in all 50 states, [w]e . . . hold that where state law provides multiple statutes of limitations for personal injury actions, courts considering § 1983 claims should borrow the general or residual statute for personal injury actions."

Page 360, add a footnote at the end of Note 2:

a. The Court held in McCarthy v. Madigan, ___ U.S. ___ (1992), that a federal prisoner seeking damages under Bivens v. Six Unknown Named Agents of Federal Bureau of Narcotics, 403 U.S. 388 (1971), did not have to exhaust an internal grievance procedure established by the Federal Bureau of Prisons. The Court held the particular grievance procedures unsuited to the claim and did not foreclose a different result under a more carefully tailored regime. The procedures before the Court were inadequate because they "impose[d] short, successive filing deadlines that create a high risk of forfeiture of a claim for failure to comply" and because "the administrative 'remedy' does not authorize an award of monetary damages—the only relief requested by McCarthy in this action." Chief Justice Rehnquist, joined by Justices Scalia and Thomas, agreed with the second rationale only.

Page 364, add at the end of Section 4:

FELDER v. CASEY
Supreme Court of the United States, 1988.
487 U.S. 131.

JUSTICE BRENNAN delivered the opinion of the Court.

A Wisconsin statute provides that before suit may be brought in state court against a state or local governmental entity or officer, the plaintiff must notify the governmental defendant of the circumstances giving rise to the claim, the amount of the claim, and his or her intent to hold the named defendant liable. The statute further requires that, in order to afford the defendant an opportunity to consider the requested relief, the claimant must refrain from filing suit for 120 days after providing such notice. Failure to comply with these requirements constitutes grounds for dismissal of the action. In the present case, the Supreme Court of Wisconsin held that this notice-of-claim statute applies to federal civil rights actions brought in state court under 42 U.S.C. § 1983. Because we conclude that these requirements are preempted as inconsistent with federal law, we reverse.

I

On July 4, 1981, Milwaukee police officers stopped petitioner Bobby Felder for questioning while searching his neighborhood for an armed suspect. The interrogation proved to be hostile and apparently loud, attracting the attention of petitioner's family and neighbors, who succeeded in convincing the police that petitioner was not the man they sought. According to police reports, the officers then directed petitioner to return home, but he continued to argue and allegedly pushed one of them, thereby precipitating his arrest for disorderly conduct. Petitioner alleges that in the course of this arrest the officers beat him about the head and face with batons, dragged him across the ground, and threw him, partially unconscious, into the back of a paddy wagon face first, all in full view of his family and neighbors. Shortly afterwards, in response to complaints from these neighbors, a local city alderman and members of the Milwaukee Police Department arrived on the scene and began interviewing witnesses to the arrest. Three days later, the local alderman wrote directly to the chief of police requesting a full investigation into the incident. Petitioner, who is black, alleges that various members of the police department responded to this request by conspiring to cover up the misconduct of the arresting officers, all of whom are white. The department took no disciplinary action against any of the officers, and the city attorney subsequently dropped the disorderly conduct charge against petitioner.

Nine months after the incident, petitioner filed this action in the Milwaukee County Circuit Court against the city of Milwaukee and certain of its police officers, alleging that the beating and arrest were unprovoked and racially motivated, and violated his rights under the fourth and 14th amendments to the United States Constitution. He sought redress under 42 U.S.C. § 1983, as well as attorneys fees pursuant to § 1988. The officers moved to dismiss the suit based on petitioner's failure to comply with the state's notice-of-claim statute. That statute provides that no action may be brought or maintained against any state governmental subdivision, agency, or officer unless the claimant either provides written notice of the claim within 120 days of the alleged injury, or demonstrates that the relevant subdivision, agency, or officer had actual notice of the claim and was not prejudiced by the lack of written notice. Wis.Stat. § 893.80(1)a) (1983 and Supp. 1987).[2] The statute further provides that the party seeking redress

[2] Section 893.80 provides in relevant part:

"(1) Except as provided in sub. (1m), no action may be brought or maintained against any . . . governmental subdivision or agency thereof nor against any officer, official, agent or employee of the . . . subdivision or agency for acts done in their official capacity or in the course of their agency or employment upon a claim or cause of action unless:

"(a) Within 120 days after the happening of the event giving rise to the claim, written notice of the circumstances of the claim signed by the party, agent or attorney is served on the . . . governmental subdivision or agency and on the officer, official, agent or employee. . . . Failure to give the requisite notice shall not bar action on the claim if the . . . governmental subdivision or agency had actual notice of the claim and the claimant shows to the satisfaction of the court that the delay or failure to give the requisite notice has not been prejudicial to the defendant . . . subdivision or agency or to the defendant officer, official, agent or employee; and

"(b) A claim containing the address of the claimant and an itemized state-must also submit an itemized statement of the relief sought to the governmental subdivision or agency, which then has 120 days to grant or disallow the requested relief. Finally, claimants must bring suit within six months of receiving notice that their claim has been disallowed.

The trial court . . . denied the motion . . . . The Wisconsin Supreme Court . . . reversed. [T]he court reasoned that while Congress may establish the procedural framework under which claims are heard in federal courts, states retain the authority under the Constitution to prescribe the rules and procedures that govern actions in their own tribunals. Accordingly, a party who chooses to vindicate a congressionally created right in state court must abide by the state's procedures. Requiring compliance with the notice-of-claim statute, the court determined, does not frustrate the remedial and deterrent purposes of the federal civil rights laws because the statute neither limits the amount a plaintiff may recover for violation of his or her civil rights, nor precludes the possibility of such recovery altogether. Rather, the court reasoned, the notice requirement advances the state's legitimate interests in protecting against stale or fraudulent claims, facilitating prompt settlement of valid claims, and identifying and correcting inappropriate conduct by governmental employees and officials. Turning to the question of compliance in this case, the court concluded that the complaints lodged with the local police by petitioner's neighbors and the letter submitted to the police chief by the local alderman failed to satisfy the statute's actual notice standard, because these communications neither recited the facts giving rise to the alleged injuries nor revealed petitioner's intent to hold the defendants responsible for those injuries.

We granted certiorari and now reverse.

II

No one disputes the general and unassailable proposition relied upon by the Wisconsin Supreme Court below that states may establish the rules of procedure governing litigation in their own courts. By the

ment of the relief sought is presented to the appropriate clerk or person who performs the duties of a clerk or secretary for the defendant . . . subdivision or agency and the claim is disallowed. Failure of the appropriate body to disallow within 120 days after presentation is a disallowance. Notice of disallowance shall be served on the claimant by registered or certified mail and the receipt therefor, signed by the claimant, or the returned registered letter, shall be proof of service. No action on a claim against any defendant . . . subdivision or agency nor against any defendant officer, official, agent or employee may be brought after 6 months from the date of service of the notice, and the notice shall contain a statement to that effect."

Many states have adopted similar provisions. See generally Civil Actions Against State Government, Its Divisions, Agencies, and Officers 559–69 (W. Winborne ed. 1982).

same token, however, where state courts entertain a federally created cause of action, the "federal right cannot be defeated by the forms of local practice." Brown v. Western Ry of Alabama, 338 U.S. 294, 296 (1949). The question before us today, therefore, is essentially one of pre-emption: is the application of the state's notice-of-claim provision to § 1983 actions brought in state courts consistent with the goals of the federal civil rights laws[?] . . . Because the notice-of-claim statute at issue here conflicts both in its purpose and effects with the remedial objectives of § 1983, and because its enforcement in such actions will frequently and predictably produce different outcomes in § 1983 litigation based solely on whether the claim is asserted in state or federal court, we conclude that the state law is pre-empted when the § 1983 action is brought in a state court.

A

. . . Although we have never passed on the question, the lower federal courts have all, with but one exception, concluded that notice-of-claim provisions are inapplicable to § 1983 actions brought in federal court. These courts have reasoned that, unlike the lack of statutes of limitations in the federal civil rights laws, the absence of any notice-of-claim provision is not a deficiency requiring the importation of such statutes into the federal civil rights scheme. Because statutes of limitation are among the universally familiar aspects of litigation considered indispensable to any scheme of justice, it is entirely reasonable to assume that Congress did not intend to create a right enforceable in perpetuity. Notice-of-claim provisions, by contrast, are neither universally familiar nor in any sense indispensable prerequisites to litigation, and there is thus no reason to suppose that Congress intended federal courts to apply such rules, which "significantly inhibit the ability to bring federal actions."

While we fully agree with this near unanimous consensus of the federal courts, that judgment is not dispositive here, where the question is not one of adoption but of pre-emption. Nevertheless, this determination that notice-of-claim statutes are inapplicable to federal-court § 1983 litigation informs our analysis in two crucial respects. First, it demonstrates that the application of the notice requirement burdens the exercise of the federal right by forcing civil rights victims who seek redress in state courts to comply with a requirement that is entirely absent from civil rights litigation in federal courts. This burden, as we explain below, is inconsistent in both design and effect with the compensatory aims of the federal civil rights laws. Second, it reveals that the enforcement of such statutes in § 1983 actions brought in state court will frequently and predictably produce different outcomes in federal civil rights litigation based solely on whether that litigation takes place in state or federal court. States may not apply such an outcome-determinative law when entertaining substantive federal rights in their courts.

B

[T]he central purpose of the Reconstruction-Era laws is to provide compensatory relief to those deprived of their federal rights by state actors. Section 1983 accomplishes this goal by creating a form of liability that, by its very nature, runs only against a specific class of defendants: government bodies and their officials. Wisconsin's notice-of-claim statute undermines this "uniquely federal remedy" in several interrelated ways. First, it conditions the right of recovery that Congress has authorized, and does so for a reason manifestly inconsistent with the purposes of the federal statute: to minimize governmental liability. Nor is this condition a neutral and uniformly applicable rule of procedure; rather, it is a substantive burden imposed only upon those who seek redress for injuries resulting from the use or misuse of governmental authority. Second, the notice provision discriminates against the federal right. While the state affords the victim of an intentional tort two years to recognize the compensable nature of his or her injury, the civil rights victim is given only four months to appreciate that he or she has been deprived of [federal constitutional or] statutory rights. Finally, the notice provision operates, in part, as an exhaustion requirement, in that it forces claimants to seek satisfaction in the first instance from the governmental defendant. We think it plain that Congress never intended that those injured by governmental wrongdoers could be required, as a condition of recovery, to submit their claims to the government responsible for their injuries.

(1)

[Notice of claim statutes] "are enacted primarily for the benefit of governmental defendants" and enable those defendants to "investigate early, prepare a stronger case, and perhaps reach an early settlement." Moreover, where the defendant is unable to obtain a satisfactory settlement, the Wisconsin statute forces claimants to bring suit within a relatively short period after the local governing body disallows the claim, in order to "assure prompt initiation of litigation." To be sure, the notice requirement serves the additional purpose of notifying the proper public officials of dangerous physical conditions or inappropriate and unlawful governmental conduct, which allows for prompt corrective measures. This interest, however, is clearly not the predominant objective of the statute. Indeed, the Wisconsin Supreme Court has emphasized that the requisite notice must spell out both the amount of damages the claimant seeks and his or her intent to hold the governing body responsible for those damages precisely because these requirements further the state's interest in minimizing liability and the expenses associated with it.

In sum, as respondents explain, the state has chosen to expose its subdivisions to large liability and defense costs, and, in light of that choice, has made the concomitant decision to impose conditions that "assis[t] municipalities in controlling those costs." The decision to subject state subdivisions to liability for violations of federal rights, however, was a choice that Congress, not the Wisconsin legislature, made, and it is a decision that the state has no authority to override. Thus, however understandable or laudable the state's interest in controlling liability expenses might otherwise be, it is patently incompatible with the compensatory goals of the federal legislation, as are the means the state has chosen to effectuate it.

This incompatibility is revealed by the design of the notice-of-claim statute itself, which operates as a condition precedent to recovery in all actions brought in state court against governmental entities or officers. "Congress," we have previously noted, "surely did not intend to assign to state courts and legislatures a conclusive role in the formative function of defining and characterizing the essential elements of a federal cause of action." Wilson v. Garcia, 471 U.S. 261, 269 (1985). Yet that is precisely the consequence of what Wisconsin has done here: although a party bringing suit against a local governmental unit need not allege compliance with the notice statute as part of his or her complaint, the statute confers on governmental defendants an affirmative defense that obligates the plaintiff to demonstrate compliance with the notice requirement before he or she may recover at all, a showing altogether unnecessary when such an action is brought in federal court. States, however, may no more condition the federal right to recover for violations of civil rights than bar that right altogether, particularly where those conditions grow out of a waiver of immunity which, however necessary to the assertion of state-created rights against local governments, is entirely irrelevant insofar as the assertion of the federal right is concerned, and where the purpose and effect of those conditions, when applied in § 1983 actions, is to control the expense associated with the very litigation Congress has authorized.

This burdening of a federal right, moreover, is not the natural or permissible consequence of an otherwise neutral, uniformly applicable state rule. Although it is true that the notice-of-claim statute does not discriminate between state and federal causes of action against local governments, the fact remains that the law's protection extends only to governmental defendants and thus conditions the right to bring suit against the very persons and entities Congress intended to subject to liability. We therefore cannot accept the suggestion [in an amicus brief] that this requirement is simply part of "the vast body of procedural rules, rooted in policies unrelated to the definition of any particular substantive cause of action, that forms no essential part of 'the cause of action' as applied to any given plaintiff." On the contrary, the notice-of-claim provision is imposed only upon a specific class of plaintiffs—those who sue governmental defendants—and, as we have seen, is firmly rooted in policies very much related to, and to a large extent directly contrary to, the substantive cause of action provided those plaintiffs. This defendant-specific focus of the notice requirement serves to distinguish it, rather starkly, from rules uniformly applicable to all suits, such as rules governing service of process or substitution of parties, which respondents cite as examples of procedural requirements that penalize noncompliance through dismissal. That state courts will hear the entire § 1983 cause of action once a plaintiff complies with the notice-of-claim statute, therefore, in no way alters the fact that the statute discriminates against the precise type of claim Congress has created.

(2)

While respondents and amici suggest that prompt investigation of claims inures to the benefit of claimants and local governments alike, by providing both with an accurate factual picture of the incident, such statutes "are enacted primarily for the benefit of governmental defendants" and are intended to afford such defendants an opportunity to prepare a stronger case. Sound notions of public administration may support the prompt notice requirement, but those policies necessarily clash with the remedial purposes of the federal civil rights laws. In *Wilson v. Garcia*, supra, we held that, for purposes of choosing a limitations period for § 1983 actions, federal courts must apply the state statute of limitations governing personal injury claims because it is highly unlikely that states would ever fix the limitations period applicable to such claims in a manner that would discriminate against the federal right. Here, the notice-of-claim provision most emphatically does discriminate in a manner detrimental to the federal right: only those persons who wish to sue governmental defendants are required to provide notice within such an abbreviated time period. Many civil rights victims, however, will fail to appreciate the compensable nature of their injuries within the four-month window provided by the notice-of-claim provision, and will thus be barred from asserting their federal right to recovery in state court unless they can show that the defendant had actual notice of the injury, the circumstances giving rise to it, and the claimant's intent to hold the defendant responsible—a showing which, as the facts of this vividly demonstrate, is not easily made in Wisconsin.

(3)

Finally, the notice provision imposes an exhaustion requirement on persons who choose to assert their federal right in state courts, inasmuch as the § 1983 plaintiff must provide the requisite notice of injury within 120 days of the civil rights violation, then wait an additional 120 days while the governmental defendant investigates the claim and attempts to settle it. In Patsy v. Board of Regents of Florida, 457 U.S. 496 (1982), we held that plaintiffs need not exhaust state administrative remedies before instituting § 1983 suits in federal court. The Wisconsin Supreme Court, however, deemed that decision inapplicable to this state-court suit on the theory that states retain the authority to prescribe the rules and procedures governing suits in their courts. As we have just explained, however, that authority does not extend so far as to permit states to place conditions on the vindication of a federal right. Moreover, as we noted in *Patsy,* Congress enacted § 1983 in response to the widespread deprivations of civil rights in the southern states and the inability or unwillingness of authorities in those states to protect those rights or punish wrongdoers. Although it is true that the principal remedy Congress chose to provide injured persons was immediate access to *federal* courts, it did not leave the protection of such rights exclusively in the hands of the federal judiciary, and instead conferred concurrent jurisdiction on state courts as well. Given the evil at which the federal civil rights legislation was aimed, there is simply no reason to suppose that Congress meant "to provide these individuals immediate access to the federal courts notwithstanding any provision of state law to the contrary," *Patsy,* supra, at 504, yet contemplated that those who sought to vindicate their federal rights in state courts could be required to seek redress in the first instance from the very state officials whose hostility to those rights precipitated their injuries.

Respondents nevertheless argue that any exhaustion requirement imposed by the notice-of-claim statute is essentially de minimis because the statutory settlement period entails none of the additional expense or undue delay typically associated with administrative remedies, and indeed does not alter a claimant's right to seek full compensation through suit. This argument fails for two reasons. First, it ignores our prior assessment of "the dominant characteristic of civil rights actions: *they belong in court.*" Burnett v. Grattan, 468 U.S. 42, 50 (1984) (emphasis added). "These causes of action," we have explained, "exist independent of any other legal or administrative relief that may be available as a matter of federal or state law. They are judicially enforceable *in the first instance.*" Ibid. (emphasis added). The dominant characteristic of a § 1983 action, of course, does not vary depending upon whether it is litigated in state or federal court, and states therefore may not adulterate or dilute the predominant feature of the federal right by imposing mandatory settlement periods, no matter how reasonable the administrative waiting period or the interests it is designed to serve may appear.

Second, our decision in *Patsy* rested not only on the legislative history of § 1983 itself, but also on the fact that in the Civil Rights of

Institutionalized Persons Act of 1980, 42 U.S.C. § 1997e, Congress established an exhaustion requirement for a specific class of § 1983 actions—those brought by adult prisoners challenging the conditions of their confinement—and that in so doing, Congress expressly recognized that it was working a change in the law. Accordingly, we refused to engraft an exhaustion requirement onto another type of § 1983 action where Congress had not provided for one, not only because the judicial imposition of such a requirement would be inconsistent with Congress' recognition that § 1983 plaintiffs normally need not exhaust administrative remedies, but also because decisions concerning both the desirability and the scope and design of any exhaustion requirement turn on a host of policy considerations which "do not invariably point in one direction," and which, for that very reason, are best left to "Congress' superior institutional competence." "[P]olicy considerations alone," we concluded, "cannot justify judicially imposed exhaustion unless exhaustion is consistent with congressional intent." While the exhaustion required by Wisconsin's notice-of-claim statute does not involve lengthy or expensive administrative proceedings, it forces injured persons to seek satisfaction from those alleged to have caused the injury in the first place. Such a dispute resolution system may have much to commend it, but that is a judgment the current Congress must make, for we think it plain that the Congress which enacted § 1983 over 100 years ago would have rejected as utterly inconsistent with the remedial purposes of its broad statute the notion that a state could require civil rights victims to seek compensation from offending state officials before they could assert a federal action in state court.

Finally, to the extent the exhaustion requirement is designed to sift out "specious claims" from the stream of complaints that can inundate local governments in the absence of immunity, we have rejected such a policy as inconsistent with the aims of the federal legislation. In *Burnett,* supra, at 54–55, state officials urged the adoption of a six-month limitations period in a § 1983 action in order that they might enjoy "some reasonable protection from the seemingly endless stream of unfounded, and often stale, lawsuits brought against them." Such a contention, we noted, "reflects in part a judgment that factors such as minimizing the diversion of state officials' attention from their duties outweigh the interest in providing [claimants] ready access to a forum to resolve valid claims." As we explained there, and reaffirm today, "[t]hat policy is manifestly inconsistent with the central objective of the Reconstruction-Era civil rights statutes."

C

Respondents and their supporting amici urge that we approve the application of the notice-of-claim statute to § 1983 actions brought in state court as a matter of equitable federalism. They note that " '[t]he general rule, bottomed deeply in belief in the importance of state control of state judicial procedure, is that federal law takes the state courts as it finds them.'" Litigants who chose to bring their civil rights actions in state courts presumably do so in order to obtain the benefit of certain procedural advantages in those courts, or to draw their juries from urban populations. Having availed themselves of these benefits, civil rights litigants must comply as well with those state rules they find less to their liking.

However equitable this bitter-with-the-sweet argument may appear in the abstract, it has no place under our supremacy clause analysis. Federal law takes state courts as it finds them only insofar as those courts employ rules that do not "impose unnecessary burdens upon rights of recovery authorized by federal laws." *Brown v. Western Ry. of Alabama,* supra, at 298–299. States may make the litigation of federal rights as congenial as they see fit—not as a quid pro quo for compliance with other, incongenial rules, but because such congeniality does not stand as an obstacle to the accomplishment of Congress' goals. As we have seen, enforcement of the notice-of-claim statute in § 1983 actions brought in state court so interferes with and frustrates the substantive right Congress created that, under the supremacy clause, it must yield to the federal interest. This interference, however, is not the only consequence of the statute that renders its application in § 1983 cases invalid. In a state that demands compliance with such a statute before a § 1983 action may be brought or maintained in its courts, the outcome of federal civil rights litigation will frequently and predictably depend on whether it is brought in state or federal court. Thus, the very notions of federalism upon which respondents rely dictate that the state's outcome determinative law must give way when a party asserts a federal right in state court.

Under Erie R. Co. v. Tompkins, 304 U.S. 64 (1938), when a federal court exercises diversity or pendent jurisdiction over state-law claims, "the outcome of the litigation in the federal court should be substantially the same, so far as legal rules determine the outcome of a litigation, as it would be if tried in a state court." Guaranty Trust Co. v. York, 326 U.S. 99, 109 (1945). Accordingly, federal courts entertaining state-law claims against Wisconsin municipalities are obligated to apply the notice-of-claim provision. Just as federal courts are constitutionally obligated to apply state law to state claims, see *Erie,* supra, at 78–79, so too the supremacy clause imposes on state courts a constitutional duty "to proceed in such manner that all the substantial rights of the parties under controlling federal law [are] protected."

Civil rights victims often do not appreciate the constitutional nature of their injuries and thus will fail to file a notice of injury or claim within the requisite time period, which in Wisconsin is a mere four months. Unless such claimants can prove that the governmental defendant had actual notice of the claim, which, as we have already noted, is by no means a simple task in Wisconsin, and unless they also file an itemized claim for damages, they must bring their § 1983 suits in federal court or not at all. Wisconsin, however, may not alter the outcome of federal claims it chooses to entertain in its courts by demanding compliance with outcome-determinative rules that are inapplicable when such claims are brought in federal court, for " '[w]hatever spring[s] the state may set for those who are endeavoring to assert rights that the state confers, the assertion of federal rights, when plainly and reasonably made, is not to be defeated under the name of local practice.' " *Brown v. Western Ry. of Alabama,* supra at 299. The state notice-of-claim statute is more than a mere rule of procedure: as we discussed above, the statute is a substantive condition on the right to sue governmental officials and entities, and the federal courts have therefore correctly recognized that the notice statute governs the adjudication of state-law claims in diversity actions. In *Guaranty Trust,* supra, we held that, in order to give effect to a state's statute of limitations, a federal court could not hear a state-law action that a state court would deem time-barred. Conversely, a state court may not decline to hear an otherwise properly presented federal claim because that claim would be barred under a state law requiring timely filing of notice. State courts simply are not free to vindicate the substantive interests underlying a state rule of decision at the expense of the federal right.

Finally, in *Wilson v. Garcia,* we characterized § 1983 suits as claims for personal injuries because such an approach ensured that the same limitations period would govern all § 1983 actions brought in any given state, and thus comported with Congress' desire that the federal civil rights laws be given a uniform application within each state. A law that predictably alters the outcome of § 1983 claims depending solely on whether they are brought in state or federal court within the same state is obviously inconsistent with this federal interest in intrastate uniformity.

III

In enacting § 1983, Congress entitled those deprived of their civil rights to recover full compensation from the governmental officials responsible for those deprivations. A state law that conditions that right of recovery upon compliance with a rule designed to minimize governmental liability, and that directs injured persons to seek redress in the first instance from the very targets of the federal legislation, is inconsistent in both purpose and effect with the remedial objectives of the federal civil rights law. Principles of federalism, as well as the supremacy clause, dictate that such a state law must give way to vindication of the federal right when that right is asserted in state court.

Accordingly, the judgment of the Supreme Court of Wisconsin is reversed, and the case is remanded for further proceedings not inconsistent with this opinion.

It is so ordered.

JUSTICE WHITE, concurring.

It cannot be disputed that, if Congress had included a statute of limitations in 42 U.S.C. § 1983, any state court that entertained a § 1983 suit would have to apply that statute of limitations. . . . Similarly, where the Court has determined that a particular state statute of limitations ought to be borrowed in order to effectuate the congressional intent underlying a federal cause of action that contains no statute of limitations of its own, any state court that entertains the same federal cause of action must apply the same state statute of limitations. We made such a determination in Wilson v. Garcia, 471 U.S. 261 (1985), which held that § 1983 suits must as a matter of federal law be governed by the state statute of limitations applicable to tort suits for the recovery of damages for personal injuries. . . . It has since been assumed that *Wilson v. Garcia* governs the timeliness of § 1983 suits brought in state as well as federal court. [citations omitted]

The Wisconsin Supreme Court likewise assumed that *Wilson v. Garcia* governed which statute of limitations should apply to petitioner's § 1983 claim. The court then effectively truncated the applicable limitations period, however, by dismissing petitioner's § 1983 suit for failure to file a notice of claim within 120 days of the events at issue as required by Wis.Stat. § 893.80.[3] Hence, petitioner was allowed only about four months in which to investigate whether the facts and the law would support any claim against respondents (or retain a lawyer who would do so), and to notify respondents of his claim, rather than the two or three years that he would have been allowed under Wisconsin law had he sought to assert a similar personal-injury claim against a private party. It is also unlikely that any other state would apply a 120-day limitations period—or, indeed, a limitations period of less than one year—to such a personal-injury claim.[4] This reflects a generally accepted belief among state policymakers that individuals who have

---

[3] To be sure, § 893.80 provides that failure to file a notice of claim within the initial 120-day period "shall not bar an action on the claim if the [governmental] subdivision or agency had actual notice of the claim and the claimant shows to the satisfaction of the court that the delay or failure to give the requisite notice has not been prejudicial to the defendant." The facts of this case demonstrate, however, that the "actual notice" requirement is difficult to satisfy. For example, the Wisconsin Supreme Court held that respondents had not received "actual notice" of petitioner's claim even though the local alderman had written directly to the chief of police requesting an investigation of the incident only three days after its occurrence.

[4] See Shapiro, Choosing the Appropriate State Statute of Limitations for Section 1983 Claims After *Wilson v. Garcia:* A Theory Applied to Maryland Law, 16 U.Balt.L.Rev. 242, 245–46 (1987).

suffered injuries to their personal rights cannot fairly be expected to seek redress within so short a period of time.

The application of the Wisconsin notice-of-claim statute to bar petitioner's § 1983 suit—which is "in reality, 'an action for injury to personal rights' "—thus undermines the purposes of *Wilson v. Garcia* to promote "[t]he federal interests in uniformity, certainty, and the minimization of unnecessary litigation," and assure that state procedural rules do not "discriminate against the federal civil rights remedy." I therefore agree that in view of the adverse impact of Wisconsin's notice-of-claim statute on the federal policies articulated in *Wilson v. Garcia*, the supremacy clause proscribes the statute's application to § 1983 suits brought in Wisconsin state courts.

JUSTICE O'CONNOR, with whom CHIEF JUSTICE REHNQUIST joins, dissenting.

"A state statute cannot be considered 'inconsistent' with federal law merely because the statute causes the plaintiff to lose the litigation." Robertson v. Wegmann, 436 U.S. 584, 593 (1978). Disregarding this self-evident principle, the Court today holds that Wisconsin's notice of claim statute is pre-empted by federal law as to actions under 42 U.S.C. § 1983 filed in state court. This holding is not supported by the statute whose pre-emptive force it purports to invoke, or by our precedents. Relying only on its own intuitions about "the goals of the federal civil rights laws," the Court fashions a new theory of pre-emption that unnecessarily and improperly suspends a perfectly valid state statute. . . .

Wisconsin's notice of claim statute, which imposes a limited exhaustion of remedies requirement on those with claims against municipal governments and their officials, serves at least two important purposes apart from providing municipal defendants with a special affirmative defense in litigation. First, the statute helps ensure that public officials will receive prompt notice of wrongful conditions or practices, and thus enables them to take prompt corrective action. Second, it enables officials to investigate claims in a timely fashion, thereby making it easier to ascertain the facts accurately and to settle meritorious claims without litigation. These important aspects of the Wisconsin statute bring benefits to governments and claimants alike, and it should come as no surprise that 37 other states have apparently adopted similar notice of claim requirements. Without some compellingly clear indication that Congress has forbidden the states to apply such statutes in their own courts, there is no reason to conclude that they are "preempted" by federal law. Allusions to such vague concepts as "the compensatory aims of the federal civil rights laws," which are all that the Court actually relies on, do not provide an adequate substitute for the statutory analysis that we customarily require of ourselves before we reach out to find statutory pre-emption of legitimate procedures used by the states in their own courts.

Section 1983, it is worth recalling, creates no substantive law. It merely provides one vehicle by which certain provisions of the Constitution and other federal laws may be judicially enforced. Its purpose, as we have repeatedly said, " 'was to interpose the *federal courts* between the states and the people, as guardians of the people's federal rights . . . .' " Patsy v. Board of Regents of Florida, 457 U.S. 496, 503 (1982) (quoting Mitchum v. Foster, 407 U.S. 225, 242 (1972)) (emphasis added). For that reason, the original version of § 1983 provided that the federal courts would have exclusive jurisdiction of actions arising under it. See Civil Rights Act of 1871, ch. 22, § 1, 17 Stat. 13. This fact is conclusive proof that the "Congress which enacted § 1983 over 100 years ago," could not possibly have meant thereby to alter the operation of state courts in any way or to "pre-empt" them from using procedural statutes like the one at issue today.

State courts may now entertain § 1983 actions if a plaintiff chooses a state court over the federal forum that is always available as a matter of right. See, e.g., Martinez v. California, 444 U.S. 277, 283 and n.7 (1980). Abandoning the rule of exclusive federal jurisdiction over § 1983 actions, and thus restoring the tradition of concurrent jurisdiction, however, "did not leave behind a pre-emptive grin without a statutory cat." Congress has never given the slightest indication that § 1983 was meant to replace state procedural rules with those that apply in the federal courts. The majority does not, because it cannot, cite any evidence to the contrary.

In an effort to remedy this fatal defect in its position, the majority engages in an extended discussion of *Patsy v. Board of Regents of Florida,* supra. *Patsy,* however, actually undermines the majority's conclusion. In that case, the Court concluded that state exhaustion of remedies requirements were not to be applied in § 1983 actions brought in *federal court.* The Court relied on legislative history indicating that § 1983 was meant to provide a federal forum with characteristics *different* from those in the state courts, and it came only to the limited and hesitant conclusion that "it seems fair to infer that the 1871 Congress did not intend that an individual be compelled *in every case* to exhaust state administrative remedies before filing an action under [§ 1983]." [Emphasis added.] Even this limited conclusion, the Court admitted, was "somewhat precarious," which would have made no sense if the Court had been able to rely on the more general proposition—from which the holding in *Patsy* follows a fortiori—that it adopts today.

Patsy also relied on the Civil Rights of Institutionalized Persons Act of 1980, § 7, 42 U.S.C. § 1997e, which ordinarily requires exhaustion of state remedies before an adult prisoner can bring a § 1983 action in federal court. The Court concluded that the "legislative history of § 1997e demonstrates that Congress has taken the approach of carving out specific exceptions to the general rule that *federal courts* cannot require exhaustion under § 1983." [Emphasis added.] This finding lends further support to the proposition that Congress has never concerned itself with the application of exhaustion requirements in *state* courts, and § 1997e conclusively shows that Congress does not believe that such requirements are somehow inherently incompatible with the nature of actions under § 1983.

For similar reasons, Brown v. Western Ry. of Alabama, 338 U.S. 294 (1949), which is repeatedly quoted by the majority, does not control the present case. In *Brown*, which arose under the Federal Employers' Liability Act (FELA), this Court refused to accept a state court's interpretation of allegations in a complaint asserting a federal statutory right. Concluding that the state court's interpretation of the complaint operated to "detract from 'substantive rights' granted by Congress in FELA cases," the Court "simply h[e]ld that under the facts alleged it was error to dismiss the complaint and that [the claimant] should be allowed to try his case." In the case before us today, by contrast, the statute at issue does not diminish or alter any substantive right cognizable under § 1983. As the majority concedes, the Wisconsin courts "will hear the entire § 1983 cause of action once a plaintiff complies with the notice-of-claim statute."

Unable to find support for its position in § 1983 itself, or in its legislative history, the majority suggests that the Wisconsin statute somehow "discriminates against the federal right." The Wisconsin statute, however, applies to all actions against municipal defendants, whether brought under state or federal law. The majority is therefore compelled to adopt a new theory of discrimination, under which the challenged statute is said to "conditio[n] the right to bring suit against the very persons and entities [viz. local governments and officials] Congress intended to subject to liability." This theory, however, is untenable. First, the statute erects no barrier at all to a plaintiff's right to bring a § 1983 suit against anyone. Every plaintiff has the option of proceeding in federal court, and the Wisconsin statute has not the slightest effect on that right. Second, if a plaintiff chooses to proceed in the Wisconsin state courts, those courts stand ready to hear the entire federal cause of action, as the majority concedes. Thus, the Wisconsin statute "discriminates" only against a right that Congress has never created: the right of a plaintiff to have the benefit of selected federal court procedures after the plaintiff has rejected the federal forum and chosen a state forum instead. The majority's "discrimination" theory is just another version of its unsupported conclusion that Congress intended to force the state courts to adopt procedural rules from the federal courts.

The Court also suggests that there is some parallel between this case and cases that are tried in federal court under the doctrine of Erie R. Co. v. Tompkins, 304 U.S. 64 (1938). Quoting the "outcome-determinative" test of Guaranty Trust Co. v. York, 326 U.S. 99, 109 (1945), the Court opines today that state courts hearing federal suits are obliged to mirror federal procedures to the same extent that federal courts are obliged to mirror state procedures in diversity suits. This suggestion seems to be based on a sort of upside-down theory of federalism, which the Court attributes to Congress on the basis of no evidence at all. Nor are the implications of this "reverse-*Erie*" theory quite clear. If the Court means the theory to be taken seriously, it should follow that defendants, as well as plaintiffs, are entitled to the benefit of all federal court procedural rules that are "outcome determinative." If, however, the Court means to create a rule that benefits only plaintiffs, then the discussion of *Erie* principles is simply an unsuccessful effort to find some analogy, no matter how attenuated, to today's unprecedented holding.

"Borrowing" cases under 42 U.S.C. § 1988, which the Court cites several times, have little more to do with today's decision than does *Erie*. Under that statute and those cases, we are sometimes called upon to fill in gaps in federal law by choosing a state procedural rule for application in § 1983 actions brought in federal court. See, e.g., Wilson v. Garcia, 471 U.S. 261 (1985); Burnett v. Grattan, 468 U.S. 42 (1984). The congressionally imposed necessity of *supplementing* federal law with state procedural rules might well caution us against *supplanting* state procedural rules with federal gaps, but it certainly offers no support for what the Court does today.

Finally Justice White's concurrence argues that Wisconsin's notice of claim statute is in the nature of a statute of limitations, and that the principles articulated in *Wilson v. Garcia,* supra, preclude its application to any action under § 1983. Assuming, arguendo, that state courts must apply the same statutes of limitations that federal courts borrow under § 1988, the concurrence is mistaken in treating this notice of claim requirement as a statute of limitations. As the concurrence acknowledges, the 120-day claim period established by the Wisconsin statute does not apply if the local government had actual notice of the claim and has not been prejudiced by the plaintiff's delay. The concurrence suggests that the Wisconsin statute nonetheless is equivalent to a statute of limitations because the present case demonstrates "that the 'actual notice' requirement is difficult to satisfy." I agree that a sufficiently burdensome notice of claim requirement could effectively act as a statute of limitations. The facts of this case, however, will not support such a characterization of the Wisconsin law. The court below said that no "Detailed claim for damages" need be submitted; rather, the injured party need only "recit[e] the facts giving rise to the injury and [indicate] an intent . . . to hold the city responsible for any damages resulting from the injury." It has not been suggested that petitioner tried to comply with this requirement but encountered difficulties in doing so. Indeed, it would have been easier to file the required notice of claim than to file this lawsuit, which petitioner proved himself quite capable of doing. Far from encountering "difficulties" in complying with the notice of claim statute, petitioner never tried.

As I noted at the outset, the majority correctly characterizes the issue before us as one of statutory pre-emption. In order to arrive at the result it has chosen, however, the Court is forced to search for "inconsistencies" between Wisconsin's notice of claim statute and some ill-defined federal policy that Congress has never articulated, implied, or suggested, let alone enacted. Nor is there any difficulty in explaining the absence of congressional attention to the problem that the Court wrongly imagines it is solving. A plaintiff who chooses to bring a § 1983 action in state court necessarily rejects the federal courts that Congress has provided. Virtually the only conceivable reason for doing so is to benefit from procedural advantages available exclusively in state court. Having voted with their feet for state procedural systems, such plaintiffs would hardly be in a position to ask Congress for a new type of forum that combines the advantages that Congress gave them in the federal system with those that Congress did not give them, and which are only available in state courts. Fortunately for these plaintiffs, however, Congress need not be consulted. The concept of statutory pre-emption takes on new meaning today, and it is one from which I respectfully dissent.

Page 380, substitute for Notes 1 and 2:

1. Questions and Comments on the Relation of § 1983 and Habeas Corpus. Federal habeas corpus requires that available state judicial remedies be exhausted before resort to federal court. One consequence of this requirement is that federal habeas is generally unavailable until state criminal proceedings have been concluded. *Younger* is consistent with this aspect of the law of habeas corpus. It too, as a general matter, forecloses federal judicial relief that would pretermit or undermine pending state criminal proceedings.

As *Preiser* illustrates, however, there is a tension between § 1983 and habeas corpus. Where *Younger* is inapplicable, § 1983 does not require exhaustion of state remedies. Thus, after state criminal proceedings have been completed, there would be no reason—considering *Younger* and the law of § 1983 alone—for resort to further state proceedings before seeking an injunction to set aside a prison sentence that resulted from a criminal conviction. But it is the major function of habeas corpus to provide comparable relief. If § 1983 were available in such a case, the habeas exhaustion requirement would become a dead letter. Some boundary line must thus be drawn between the two regimes if both are to retain independent functions. Does *Preiser* draw the right line?[a] Of what relevance is *Younger* to the issues in *Preiser?*

2. Relation of *Younger* and *Preiser* to § 1983 Actions for Damages. *Preiser* contemplates the possibility of simultaneous state and federal litigation where a prisoner seeks relief from the terms and conditions of confinement and also seeks money damages. Is simultaneous litigation also possible where a defendant in a pending state criminal trial seeks damages in federal court for conduct of an official that will be at issue during the criminal trial? Consider the following cases in connection with this question.

3. *Guerro v. Mulhearn*. In Guerro v. Mulhearn, 498 F.2d 1249 (1st Cir.1974), Guerro had been convicted of a state criminal offense. The validity of the conviction was pending on appeal within the state system. He sought damages under § 1983 for alleged misconduct by state officials that was also at issue in the state proceedings. The defendants argued that the federal suit should be stayed or dismissed until the issues had been finally decided by the state courts. The Court of Appeals held:

> "Requests for relief in the form of money damages under § 1983 are not controlled by *Preiser,* but . . . the reasoning and policy of that case, as well as the policy considerations underlying Younger v. Harris, 401 U.S. 37 (1971), require a federal court to stay its hand where disposition of the damages action would involve a ruling implying that a state conviction is or would be illegal. . . .
>
> "Where the federal court, in dealing with the question of damages caused by violation of civil rights, would have to make rulings by virtue of which the validity of a conviction in contemporary state proceedings would be called in question, the potential for federal-state friction is obvious. The federal ruling would embarrass, and could even intrude into, the state proceedings. Questions concerning the effect to be given the federal ruling in the state courts might be difficult ones and could lead to delay, or even derailment of the course of the state action. It is not impossible that circumstances might arise where a federal judgment for damages could be used by a state defendant to obtain his release from, or prevent, his incarceration, thus presuming upon, if not preempting, the province of the Great Writ. . . ."

The court added that the "touchstone for any decision to defer a civil rights damage action which is parallel to state criminal proceedings is

---

[a] For an extensive analysis of the decisional law that has emerged in the 15 years since the *Preiser* decision and some proposed solutions to the open issues, see Martin Schwartz, The *Preiser* Puzzle: Continued Frustrating Conflict Between the Civil Rights and Habeas Corpus Remedies for State Prisoners, 37 De Paul L.Rev. 85 (1988).

whether the federal court will be making rulings whose necessary implication would be to call in question the validity of the state conviction."

4. *Deakins v. Monaghan*. Deakins v. Monaghan, 484 U.S. 193 (1988), involved the propriety of an eight-hour search of business premises during which hundreds of documents were seized. Various proceedings ensued before the state judge who had issued a warrant for the search in his capacity as supervisor of a state grand jury. A suit for damages and attorney's fees was then filed in federal court under § 1983.[b] The District Court dismissed the damages claim in deference to the pending state grand jury proceedings. The Court of Appeals reversed, holding that dismissal was inappropriate but that the District Court should have stayed its hand until the state proceedings concluded. An indictment was then returned (without reliance on the disputed materials) against some of the persons who had filed the federal suit. After the indictment, the state court to which the case was assigned for trial took jurisdiction over the question whether the disputed documents should be returned or whether they would be available for use in the pending criminal trial. The question decided by the Supreme Court was whether the District Court had properly dismissed the damages complaint.

(i) **Justice Blackmun's Opinion.** Justice Blackmun wrote for the Court:

> "Petitioners argue that the *Younger* doctrine—which requires a federal court to abstain where a plaintiff's federal claims could be adjudicated in a pending state judicial proceeding—applies to complaints seeking only monetary relief. Petitioners further argue that it is within the district court's discretion to dismiss rather than stay a federal complaint for damages and fees where abstention is required. We need not decide the extent to which the *Younger* doctrine applies to a federal action seeking only monetary relief, however, because even if the *Younger* doctrine requires abstention here, the District Court had no discretion to dismiss rather than to stay claims for monetary relief that cannot be redressed in the state proceeding.[6]

[b] The plaintiffs also sought injunctive relief, but later withdrew this aspect of their complaint.

[6] "In his concurring opinion in this case, Justice White urges that we reach the question—not considered at any stage below, and not the subject of our grant of certiorari—whether the *Younger* doctrine applies to cases in which only money damages are sought in the federal forum. Apparently, Justice White also finds it appropriate to conclude that *Younger* requires abstention in this particular case, although he does not analyze this question separately. Because all respondents have represented that they will seek a stay of their damages claim on remand, we see no reason to reach issues so awkwardly presented for review."

[Certiorari was granted by the Court to consider whether *Younger* required a federal court to defer to ongoing state grand jury proceedings. This question was mooted by the subsequent indictment of some of

"In reversing the District Court's dismissal of the claims for damages and attorney's fees, the Court of Appeals applied the Third Circuit rule that requires a district court to stay rather than dismiss claims that are not cognizable in the parallel state proceeding. The Third Circuit rule is sound. It allows a parallel state proceeding to go forward without interference from its federal sibling, while enforcing the duty of federal courts 'to assume jurisdiction where jurisdiction properly exists.'[7] This Court repeatedly has stated that the federal courts have a 'virtually unflagging obligation' to exercise their jurisdiction except in those extraordinary circumstances ' "where the order to the parties to repair to the state court would clearly serve an important countervailing interest." ' Colorado River Water Conservation District v. United States, 424 U.S. 800 (1976).

"We are unpersuaded by petitioners' suggestion that this case presents such extraordinary circumstances. [P]etitioners' speculation that the District Court, if allowed to retain jurisdiction, would 'hover' about the state proceeding, ready to lift its stay whenever it concluded that things were proceeding unsatisfactorily, is groundless. Petitioners seem to assume that the District Court would not hold up its end of the comity bargain—an assumption as inappropriate as the converse assumption that the states cannot be trusted to enforce federal rights with adequate diligence. See Stone v. Powell, 428 U.S. 465, 493–94 n. 35 (1976). . . .

"[P]etitioners [also] argue that allowing the District Court to dismiss the complaint will prevent the piecemeal litigation of the dispute between the parties. But the involvement of the federal courts cannot be blamed for the fragmentary nature of the proceedings in this litigation. Because the state criminal proceeding can provide only equitable relief, any action for damages would necessarily be separate. Indeed, the state forum in which petitioners invite respondents to pursue their claims for monetary relief clearly would require the initiation of a separate action. Piecemeal litigation of the issues involved in this case is thus inevitable.

"In sum, none of the circumstances cited by petitioners to justify the District Court's dismissal of respondents' claims for damages and attorney's fees constitutes the kind of extraordi-

---

the respondents and by the representation of the others that they wished to drop their plea for equitable relief.—Addition to footnote by eds.]

[7] "In [prior decisions], the Court of Appeals recognized that unless it retained jurisdiction during the pendency of the state proceeding, a plaintiff could be barred permanently from asserting his claims in the federal forum by the running of the applicable statute of limitations."

nary circumstances that we have held may justify abdication of the 'virtually unflagging obligation . . . to exercise the jurisdiction given' the federal courts. *Colorado River Water Conservation District v. United States,* supra, at 817."

(ii) Justice White's Concurrence. Justice White, joined by Justice O'Connor, concurred. He agreed that dismissal of the damages claim was inappropriate. But he faulted the Court for not adequately explaining "why the federal courts must or may stay, rather than proceed to adjudicate, the federal constitutional claims for damages." "After all," he continued, "the Court's opinion cites the 'virtually unflagging obligation' of the federal courts to adjudicate claims within their jurisdiction absent extraordinary circumstances. . . . Why, then, stay the § 1983 damages claim asserting a violation of federal constitutional rights? Why does not the District Court's 'unflagging obligation' require it to proceed on that claim?"

Justice White's answer to these questions began with the observation that "[t]he Third Circuit rule, which the Court endorses, appears to rest on 'prudential considerations' and not on the view that *Younger* requires that a damages action be stayed when there is a parallel state criminal (or 'quasi-criminal') proceeding underway." He continued:

> "To affirm the Court of Appeals' judgment ordering a stay requires a more substantial basis than 'prudential consideration[s]' and that basis is not difficult to find: it is that *Younger* requires, not only dismissal of the equitable claim in the case, but also that the damages action not go forward. . . .
>
> "The reasons for such an approach are obvious. As the *Younger* decision itself recognized, it has long been the rule that the federal courts should not interfere with or pre-empt the progress of state criminal proceedings. A judgment in the federal damages action may decide several questions at issue in the state criminal proceeding. . . . If the claims the Court remands today were disposed of on the merits by the District Court, this decision would presumably be owed res judicata effect in the forthcoming state criminal trial of respondents. '[T]he potential for federal-state friction is obvious.' Guerro v. Mulhearn, 498 F.2d 1249, 1253 (1st Cir.1974).
>
> "It was for these same reasons that we held that a federal court should not entertain a declaratory judgment action aimed at adjudicating a federal issue involved in a state criminal proceeding. See Samuels v. Mackell, 401 U.S. 66 (1971). As was true in *Samuels,* here, 'the practical effect of the two forms of relief [here, damages and injunction] will be virtually identical, and the basic policy against federal interference with pending state criminal prosecutions will be frustrated as much by a declaratory judgment [or, I believe, a damage

award] as it would be by an injunction.' See id., at 73. Under *Samuels,* for example, if a state criminal prosecution is ongoing, a federal court cannot adjudicate a plaintiff's request for a declaration that evidence being used in that prosecution was seized contrary to the fourth amendment. Yet if *Younger* does not apply to damages claims, that same court in the same circumstances *could* rule the search unconstitutional as long as the federal plaintiff was seeking damages *in addition to* a determination of the unconstitutionality of the seizure—a prerequisite of any damages award. Why the latter action should be considered *less* problematic for purposes of comity or 'Our Federalism' escapes me. If anything, I would have thought just the opposite to be true.

"In light of . . . our decisions in *Younger* and *Samuels,* it is clear that the District Court should not dismiss the damages claims, yet must not proceed to judgment on them either. Consequently, I would couple our remand of this case with a holding that, pursuant to *Younger,* the lower courts *may not* adjudicate respondents' damages claims until the conclusion of the pending state criminal proceedings.[5]"

5. Questions and Comments on *Guerro* and *Deakins*. What did Justice Blackmun mean by stating that the Court was not deciding whether *Younger* applied, but in the next paragraph of his opinion approving the Third Circuit rule requiring a stay of the District Court proceedings? In this connection, consider Justice Brennan's observations for the Court in Moses H. Cone Memorial Hospital v. Mercury Constr. Corp., 460 U.S. 1 (1983), that "a stay is just as much a refusal to exercise jurisdiction as a dismissal." The point of Justice Brennan's remark was the Court's holding in *Moses H. Cone* that neither a stay nor a dismissal of federal proceedings is appropriate unless the case meets the *Colorado River* "extraordinary circumstances" exception to the "unflagging obligation" of district courts to exercise their jurisdiction. In light of *Moses H. Cone,* how can the Court's decision in *Deakins* be justified? On the merits of the *Younger* question, do *Guerro* and Justice White reach the right result?

Consider also the res judicata effect of the state criminal prosecution on the pending federal litigation. Under either the Court's or Justice White's solution, would the determination in the state criminal proceeding that a search and seizure was constitutional require dismissal of the federal action? If the search were held unconstitutional, what issues would remain for determination in the federal court?

---

[5] "While three of the respondents have been indicted, three others have not. Even if *Younger* does not apply to their claims for damages, the District Court would be prudent, under *Colorado River,* supra, to stay the adjudication of these claims—virtually indistinguishable from the substance of the ongoing state criminal proceedings involving the other respondents—as well."

Finally, consider the intersection of *Preiser* with these problems. Suppose a criminal defendant did not raise a federal constitutional issue in the state criminal trial or on direct appeal, but asserted it after conviction in a § 1983 action for damages. If it were possible to use the claim as the basis for a collateral attack on the conviction in the state courts, should federal relief be withheld until the state remedy had been exhausted? If so, would the combination of *Deakins* and *Preiser* mean that a federal damages action must be stayed until *both* the criminal proceedings themselves *and* any available collateral attack have been pursued? If not, why is simultaneous litigation in state and federal court permitted at the stage of collateral attack but not while the criminal proceedings themselves are pending?

Page 431, add a new Note 3:

3. Bibliography. For commentary on *Rumery*, see Seth F. Kreimer, Releases, Redress, and Police Misconduct: Reflections on Agreements to Waive Civil Rights Actions in Exchange for Dismissal of Criminal Charges, 136 U.Pa.L.Rev. 851 (1988); and Michael E. Solimine, Enforcement and Interpretation of Settlements of Federal Civil Rights Actions, 19 Rutgers L.J. 295 (1988). Kreimer emphasizes the unusual facts of *Rumery* (including the role of counsel and the sophistication of the accused) and argues that enforcing release-dismissal agreements in other contexts would have substantial costs. Prominent among them is the threat to prosecutorial integrity that would be posed by "a continuing incentive to modify criminal prosecution decisions in the interests of goals extraneous to the criminal process," such as protecting the police. Kreimer reports interviews with several prosecutors, most of whom disapprove release-dismissal agreements as a matter of policy. He also argues that release-dismissal agreements could undermine the role of § 1983 in deterring official misconduct and vindicating constitutional rights.

Solimine criticizes *Rumery* on choice-of-law grounds. He argues that the validity of the release-dismissal agreement should have been determined under the contract law of New Hampshire. Solimine argues that a federal common law rule is unnecessary since this is not, in his view, an issue requiring a uniform solution.

Chapter IV

ATTORNEY'S FEES

Pages 449–50, replace the last two sentences before "(ii) 'Prevailing Party'" with the following:

Indeed, the only circumstance found to justify denial of fees was the fact that plaintiff litigated pro se. For a long time, the Circuits divided on whether a pro se plaintiff who was also a lawyer was entitled to fees under § 1988. In Kay v. Ehrler, ___ U.S. ___ (1991), the Supreme Court ruled unanimously that he or she was not. The Justices reasoned that the statutory policy of ensuring successful prosecution of meritorious claims would be enhanced by maintaining the incentive for all plaintiffs, including members of the bar, to retain counsel. Otherwise, it is clear that prevailing plaintiffs almost always recover their fees.

Page 451, add at the end of footnote b:

For even stranger facts, see Rhodes v. Stewart, 488 U.S. 1 (1988). Two prisoners brought a § 1983 action to gain access to a magazine. The District Court entered a declaratory judgment in their favor, even though one prisoner had died and the other had been released, and then awarded attorney's fees. The Supreme Court reversed, holding that a judgment moot when entered did not create a "prevailing party" for purposes of attorney's fees. Rather, a judgment would "constitute relief, for purposes of § 1988, if, and only if, it affects the behavior of the defendant toward the plaintiff." Justices Marshall and Blackmun, joined by Brennan, dissented.

Page 451, add a new footnote at the end of the second paragraph of Note 2:

c Cf. Blanchard v. Bergeron, 489 U.S. 87 (1989), where a unanimous Court ruled that plaintiff's agreement to a contingent-fee arrangement does not limit the attorney's fees recoverable under § 1988.

Page 451, add a new Note 2a:

2a. **Survival of the Contingent Fee.** *Riverside* makes plain that statutory attorney's fees are not limited by the model of the contingent fee. It is equally true that a contingent fee is not limited to the statutory award. In Venegas v. Mitchell, 495 U.S. 82 (1990), the client agreed to pay his lawyer a 40 percent contingency. Judgment was entered for over $2,000,000, to which the court added $117,000 in attorney's fees. The client then claimed that the statutory calculation of a reasonable fee barred his lawyer from collecting the much larger fee authorized by the contract. The Supreme Court unanimously disagreed: "[Section] 1983 controls what the losing defendant must pay, not what the prevailing plaintiff must pay his lawyer." Depriving plaintiffs of the option of agreeing to pay more than the statutory fee "if that is necessary to secure counsel of their choice would not further § 1988's general purpose of enabling such plaintiffs in civil rights cases to secure competent counsel."

Page 451, delete Note 3 and substitute the following:

3. **Limited Success.** A variation of the proportionality issue arises where plaintiffs achieve only limited success. To what extent should the recovery of fees be contingent on the scope of success?

Where a successful claim and an unsuccessful claim are essentially unrelated, the result is obvious. The unsuccessful claim is treated as if it had been raised in a separate lawsuit, and no fees can be awarded for that effort. See Hensley v. Eckerhart, 461 U.S. 424, 435 (1983). Where successful and unsuccessful claims arise from the same facts, the problem is more difficult. In such cases, the "most critical factor is the degree of success obtained." Id. at 436. Trial courts apparently are left to their own discretion in determining what fee is reasonable in light of the success obtained.

This approach led to a split in the lower courts as to the threshold level of success needed for an award of fees. The more demanding test required that the plaintiff prevail on the "central issue" in the litigation and achieve the "primary relief sought." In Texas State Teachers Association v. Garland Independent School District, 489 U.S. 782 (1989), the Supreme Court rejected this standard. Instead, the Court adopted the more permissive view that fees should be awarded where plaintiff succeeds on "any significant issue" in the litigation and achieves "some of the benefit" sought in bringing suit. "Purely technical or de minimis" success does not count, but some fee award is appropriate whenever the plaintiff achieves a "material alteration of the legal relationship of the parties." At that point, the degree of overall success goes only to the amount of the award, not to its availability vel non.

Page 452, add a new Note 3a:

3a. **Expert Witnesses.** What about fees for expert witnesses? In West Virginia University Hospitals, Inc., v. Casey, ___ U.S. ___ (1991), a hospital successfully challenged state medicaid reimbursements and was awarded more than $100,000 in fees for expert witnesses. The experts were found to be "essential" to the presentation of the case, but the Supreme Court nevertheless denied recovery. Decisive for the majority was the pre-existing tradition, evident in other federal statutes, of treating fees for expert witnesses as something separate and apart from attorney's fees. The suggestion that the Court should adopt a contrary interpretation to aid the purposes of the attorney's fees act was rejected. "That argument," said Justice Scalia, "profoundly mistakes our role." Read in context, the statute was clear and could not be enlarged by judicial decision. That Congress might well have included experts had they come to mind did not matter, for it was not a judicial responsibility to correct legislative "forgetfulness." Justices Marshall, Blackmun, and Stevens dissented. Marshall accused the majority of using "the implements of literalism to wound, rather than to minister to, congressional intent. . . ."

Page 455, add at the end of Note 6:

Thomas D. Rowe, Jr., The Supreme Court on Attorney Fee Awards, 1985 and 1986 Terms: Economics, Ethics, and Ex Ante Analysis, 1 Geo. J.Legal Ethics 621 (1988) (analyzing the economic reasoning in recent attorney's fee cases and the likely impact of those decisions on future behavior); Stewart Schwab and Theodore Eisenberg, Explaining Constitutional Tort Litigation: The Influence of the Attorney Fees Statutes and the Government as Defendant, 73 Corn.L.Rev. 719 (1988) (assessing the impact of the attorney's fees statute on litigation and success rates); Jeffrey S. Brand, The Second Front in the Fight for Civil Rights: The Supreme Court, Congress, and Statutory Fees, 69 Tex.L.Rev. 291 (1990) (a wide-ranging review of attorney's fees cases concluding that the congressional policies behind the fees acts have been undercut by recent decisions); Charles Silver, Unloading the Lodestar: Toward a New Fee Award Procedure, 70 Tex.L.Rev. 865 (1992) (proposing an alternative to the lodestar as the basis for fee awards).

Page 456, substitute for pages 456–74:

SECTION 1A: RISK ENHANCEMENT

INTRODUCTORY NOTE ON RISK ENHANCEMENT

One of the most controversial issues in the law of attorney's fees is the question of risk enhancement. Is it proper to enhance the lodestar to account for the risk of not prevailing? In other words, may a court multiply the sum of hours reasonably expended times reasonable hourly rate in order to compensate the plaintiff's attorney for having run of risk of recovering no fee award in the event of an adverse judgment? [a]

Most lower courts said yes. As a result, the practice grew up of applying a "multiplier" to enhance the lodestar in risky cases. The issue reached the Supreme Court (for the second time) in Pennsylvania v. Delaware Valley Citizens' Council for Clean Air, 483 U.S. 711 (1987). (An earlier decision reported under the same title was inconclusive on this point.) In *Delaware Valley,* the citizens group prevailed in litigation to force the state of Pennsylvania to comply with provisions of the Clean Air Act. In awarding attorney's fees under that statute, the lower courts doubled the lodestar calculation for certain phases of the

---

[a.] The availability of enhancement for delay in payment, as distinct from risk of non-payment, was affirmed in Missouri v. Jenkins, 491 U.S. 274 (1989).

litigation to compensate for the risks of contingency. The Supreme Court disapproved this result, but on grounds that left the general permissibility of risk enhancement in much doubt.

Justice White spoke for himself, Chief Justice Rehnquist, and Justices Powell and Scalia. Their position was that risk enhancement should never be allowed. They saw risk enhancement as a way of forcing losing defendants to compensate plaintiffs' lawyers for not prevailing in other cases. Justices Blackmun, Brennan, Marshall, and Stevens disagreed. They argued that an upward adjustment in the lodestar was necessary to make fee awards competitive with the private market for legal services, which must take account of the risk of contingency.

The decisive vote was that of Justice O'Connor, who voted to overturn the fee award but wrote separately to explain her view that a premium for contingency should be allowed in some circumstances. It should be based, she said, not on the novelty or complexity of the issues in a particular case but on a general determination of how a relevant market compensates lawyers for the risk of contingency. Just how this determination was to be made was not spelled out.

Delaware Valley provided few clear answers. On the one hand, the decision seemed to put a brake on the practice of using multipliers to enhance fee awards whenever the litigation seemed particularly risky. On the other hand, five Justices accepted risk enhancement in some circumstances. The decisive vote was that of Justice O'Connor, and the lower courts were left to draw what guidance they could from her opinion.

By the time the issue returned to the Supreme Court, the composition of that body had substantially changed. The result was a much clearer, though surely no less controversial, decision.

CITY OF BURLINGTON v. DAGUE
Supreme Court of the United States, 1992.
___ U.S. ___.

JUSTICE SCALIA delivered the opinion of the Court.

This case presents the question whether a court, in determining an award of reasonable attorney's fees under § 7002(e) of the Solid Waste Disposal Act (SWDA), as amended, 42 U.S.C. § 6972(e), or § 505(d) of the Federal Water Pollution Control Act (Clean Water Act (CWA)), as amended, 33 U.S.C. § 1365(d), may enhance the fee award above the "lodestar" amount in order to reflect the fact that the party's attorneys were retained on a contingent-fee basis and thus assumed the risk of receiving no payment at all for their services. Although different fee-shifting statutes are involved, the question is essentially identical to the one we addressed, but did not resolve, in Pennsylvania v. Delaware Valley Citizens' Council for Clean Air, 483 U.S. 711 (1987) (*Delaware Valley II*).

I

Respondent Dague (whom we will refer to in place of all the respondents) owns land in Vermont adjacent to a landfill that was owned and operated by petitioner City of Burlington. Represented by attorneys retained on a contingent-fee basis, he sued Burlington over its operation of the landfill. The District Court ruled, inter alia, that Burlington had violated provisions of the SWDA and the CWA, and ordered Burlington to close the landfill by January 1, 1990. It also determined that Dague was a "substantially prevailing party" entitled to an award of attorney's fees under the acts. 732 F.Supp. 458 (Vt. 1989).

In calculating the attorney's fees award, the District Court first found reasonable the figures advanced by Dague for his attorneys' hourly rates and for the number of hours expended by them, producing a resulting "lodestar" attorney's fee of $198,027.50. . . . Addressing Dague's request for a contingency enhancement, the court . . . declared that Dague's "risk of not prevailing was substantial" and that "absent an opportunity for enhancement, [Dague] would have faced substantial difficulty in obtaining counsel of reasonable skill and competence in this complicated field of law." It concluded that "a 25% enhancement is appropriate, but anything more would be a windfall to the attorneys." It therefore enhanced the lodestar amount by 25%—$49,506.87.

The Court of Appeals affirmed in all respects. Reviewing the various opinions in *Delaware Valley II,* the court concluded that the issue whether and when a contingency enhancement is warranted remained open. . . . 935 F.2d 1343 (2d Cir.1991). We granted certiorari only with respect to the propriety of the contingency enhancement.

II

We first provide some background to the issue before us. Fees for legal services in litigation may be either "certain" or "contingent" (or some hybrid of the two). A fee is certain if it is payable without regard to the outcome of the suit; it is contingent if the obligation to pay depends on a particular result's being obtained. Under the most common contingent-fee contract for litigation, the attorney receives no payment for his services if his client loses. Under this arrangement, the attorney bears a contingent risk of nonpayment that is the inverse of the case's prospects of success: if his client has an 80% chance of winning, the attorney's contingent risk is 20%.

In *Delaware Valley II,* we reversed a judgment that had affirmed enhancement of a fee award to reflect the contingent risk of nonpayment. In the process, we addressed whether the typical federal fee-shifting statute (there, § 304(d) of the Clean Air Act, 42 U.S.C. § 7604(d)) permits an attorney's fees award to be enhanced on account of contingency. In the principal opinion, Justice White, joined on this point by three other Justices, determined that such enhancement is not permitted. Justice O'Connor, in an opinion concurring in part and concurring in the judgment, concluded that no enhancement for contingency is appropriate "unless the applicant can establish that without an adjustment for risk the prevailing party would have faced substantial difficulties in finding counsel in the local or other relevant market" (internal quotations omitted), and that any enhancement "must be based on the difference in market treatment of contingent fee cases *as a class,* rather than on an assessment of the 'riskiness' of any particular case" (emphasis in original). Justice Blackmun's dissenting opinion, joined by three other Justices, concluded that enhancement for contingency is always statutorily required.

We turn again to this same issue.

III

Section 7002(e) of the SWDA and § 505(d) of the CWA authorize a court to "award costs of litigation (including *reasonable attorney . . . fees*)" (emphasis added). This language is similar to that of many other federal fee-shifting statutes, see, e.g., 42 U.S.C. § 1988; our case law construing what is a "reasonable" fee applies uniformly to all of them.

The "lodestar" figure has, as its name suggests, become the guiding light of our fee-shifting jurisprudence. We have established a "strong presumption" that the lodestar represents the "reasonable" fee, Pennsylvania v. Delaware Valley Citizens' Council for Clean Air, 478 U.S. 546, 565 (1986) (*Delaware Valley I*), and have placed upon the fee applicant who seeks more than that the burden of showing that "such an adjustment is *necessary* to the determination of a reasonable fee." Blum v. Stenson, 465 U.S. 886, 898 (1984) (emphasis added). The Court of Appeals held, and Dague argues here, that a "reasonable" fee for attorneys who have been retained on a contingency-fee basis must go beyond the lodestar, to compensate for risk of loss and of consequent nonpayment. Fee-shifting statutes should be construed, he contends, to replicate the economic incentives that operate in the private legal market, where attorneys working on a contingency-fee basis can be expected to charge some premium over their ordinary hourly rates. Petitioner Burlington argues, by contrast, that the lodestar fee may not be enhanced for contingency.

We note at the outset that an enhancement for contingency would likely duplicate in substantial part factors already subsumed in the lodestar. The risk of loss in a particular case (and, therefore, the attorney's contingent risk) is the product of two factors: (1) the legal and factual merits of the claim, and (2) the difficulty of establishing those merits. The second factor, however, is ordinarily reflected in the lodestar—either in the higher number of hours expended to overcome the difficulty, or in the higher hourly rate of the attorney skilled and experienced enough to do so. Taking account of it again through lodestar enhancement amounts to double-counting.

The first factor (relative merits of the claim) is not reflected in the lodestar, but there are good reasons why it should play no part in the calculation of the award. It is, of course, a factor that always exists (no claim has a 100% chance of success), so that computation of the lodestar would never end the court's inquiry in contingent-fee cases. Moreover, the consequences of awarding contingency enhancement to take account of this "merits" factor would be to provide attorneys with the same incentive to bring relatively meritless claims as relatively meritorious ones. Assume, for example, two claims, one with underlying merit of 20%, the other of 80%. Absent any contingency enhancement, a contingent-fee attorney would prefer to take the latter, since he is four times more likely to be paid. But with a contingency enhancement, this preference will disappear: the enhancement for the 20% claim would be a multiplier of 5 (100/20), which is quadruple the 1.25 multiplier (100/80) that would attach to the 80% claim. Thus, enhancement for the contingency risk posed by each case would encourage meritorious claims to be brought, but only at the social cost of indiscriminately encouraging nonmeritorious claims to be brought as well. We think that an unlikely objective of the "reasonable fees" provisions. "These statutes were not designed as a form of economic relief to improve the financial lot of lawyers." *Delaware Valley I,* supra, at 565.

Instead of enhancement based upon the contingency risk posed by each case, Dague urges that we adopt the approach set forth in the *Delaware Valley II* concurrence. We decline to do so, first and foremost because we do not see how it can intelligibly be applied. On the one hand, it would require the party seeking contingency enhancement to "establish that without the adjustment for risk [he] 'would have faced substantial difficulties in finding counsel in the local or other relevant market.'" 483 U.S., at 733. On the other hand, it would forbid enhancement based "on an assessment of the 'riskiness' of any particular case." 483 U.S., at 731; see 483 U.S., at 734 (no enhancement "based on 'legal' risks or risks peculiar to the case"). But since the predominant reason that a contingent-fee claimant has difficulty finding counsel in any legal market where the winner's attorney's fees will be paid by the loser is that attorneys view his case as too risky (i.e., too unlikely to succeed), these two propositions, as a practical matter, collide.

A second difficulty with the approach taken by the concurrence in *Delaware Valley II* is that it would base the contingency enhancement on "the difference in market treatment of contingent fee cases *as a class.*" 483 U.S., at 731 (emphasis in original). To begin with, for a very large proportion of contingency-fee cases—those seeking not monetary damages but injunctive or other equitable relief—there is no "market treatment." Such cases scarcely exist, except to the extent Congress has created an artificial "market" for them by fee-shifting— and looking to that "market" for the meaning of fee-shifting is obviously circular. Our decrees would follow the "market," which in turn is based on our decrees. But even apart from that difficulty, any approach that applies uniform treatment to the entire class of contingent-fee cases, or to any conceivable subject-matter-based subclass, cannot possibly achieve the supposed goal of mirroring market incentives. As discussed above, the contingent risk of a case (and hence the difficulty of getting contingent-fee lawyers to take it) depends principally upon its particular merits. Contingency enhancement calculated on *any* class-wide basis, therefore, guarantees *at best* (leaving aside the double-counting problem described earlier) that those cases within the class that have the class-average chance of success will be compensated according to what the "market" requires to produce the services, and that *all cases* having above-class-average chance of success will be overcompensated.

Looking beyond the *Delaware Valley II* concurrence's approach, we perceive no other basis, fairly derivable from the fee-shifting statutes, by which contingency enhancement, if adopted, could be restricted to fewer than all contingent-fee cases. And we see a number of reasons for concluding that no contingency enhancement whatever is compatible with the fee-shifting statutes at issue. First, just as the statutory language limiting fees to prevailing (or substantially prevailing) parties bars a prevailing plaintiff from recovering fees relating to claims on which he lost, Hensley v. Eckerhart, 461 U.S. 424 (1983), so should it bar a prevailing plaintiff from recovering for the risk of loss. See *Delaware Valley II,* supra, 483 U.S., at 719–20 (principal opinion). An attorney operating on a contingency-fee basis pools the risks presented by his various cases: cases that turn out to be successful pay for the time he gambled on those that did not. To award a contingency enhancement under a fee-shifting statute would in effect pay for the attorney's time (or anticipated time) in cases where his client does not prevail.

Second, both before and since *Delaware Valley II,* "we have generally turned away from the contingent-fee model"—which would make the fee award a percentage of the value of the relief awarded in the primary action—"to the lodestar model." Venegas v. Mitchell, 495 U.S. 82, 87 (1990). We have done so, it must be noted, even though the lodestar model often (perhaps, generally) results in a larger fee award than the contingent-fee model. See, e.g., Report of the Federal Courts Study Committee 104 (Apr. 2, 1990) (lodestar method may "give lawyers incentives to run up hours unnecessarily, which can lead to overcompensation"). For example, in Blanchard v. Bergeron, 489 U.S. 87 (1989), we held that the lodestar governed, even though it produced a fee that substantially exceeded the amount provided in the contingent-fee agreement between plaintiff and his counsel (which was self-evidently an amount adequate to attract the needed legal services). Contingency enhancement is a feature inherent in the contingent-fee model (since attorneys factor in the particular risks of a case in negotiating their fee and in deciding whether to accept the case). To engraft this feature onto the lodestar model would be to concoct a hybrid scheme that resorts to the contingent-fee model to increase a fee award but not to reduce it. Contingency enhancement is therefore not consistent with our general rejection of the contingent-fee model for fee awards, nor is it necessary to the determination of a reasonable fee.

And finally, the interest in ready administrability that has underlain our adoption of the lodestar approach and the related interest in avoiding burdensome satellite litigation (the fee application "should not result in a second major litigation," *Hensley,* supra, at 437), counsel strongly against adoption of contingency enhancement. Contingency enhancement would make the setting of fees more complex and arbitrary, hence more unpredictable, and hence more litigable. It is neither necessary nor even possible for application of the fee-shifting statutes to mimic the intricacies of the fee-paying market in every respect. See *Delaware Valley I,* supra, at 565.

* * *

Adopting the position set forth in Justice White's opinion in *Delaware Valley II,* supra, we hold that enhancement for contingency is not permitted under the fee-shifting statutes at issue. We reverse the Court of Appeals' judgment insofar as it affirmed the 25% enhancement of the lodestar.

It is so ordered.

JUSTICE BLACKMUN, with whom JUSTICE STEVENS joined, dissenting.

In language typical of most federal fee-shifting provisions, the statutes involved in this case authorize courts to award the prevailing party a "reasonable" attorney's fee. Two principles, in my view, require the conclusion that the "enhanced" fee awarded to respondents was reasonable. First, this Court consistently has recognized that a "reasonable" fee is to be a "fully compensatory fee," Hensley v. Eckerhart, 461 U.S. 424, 435 (1983), and is to be "calculated on the basis of rates and practices prevailing in the relevant market." Missouri v. Jenkins, 491 U.S. 274, 286 (1989). Second, it is a fact of the market that an attorney who is paid only when his client prevails will tend to charge a higher fee than one who is paid regardless of outcome, and relevant professional standards long have recognized that this practice is reasonable.

The Court does not deny these principles. It simply refuses to draw the conclusion that follows ineluctably: If a statutory fee consistent with market practices is "reasonable," and if in the private market an attorney who assumes the risk of nonpayment can expect additional compensation, then it follows that a statutory fee may include additional compensation for contingency and still qualify as reasonable. The Court's decision to the contrary violates the principles we have applied consistently in prior cases and will seriously weaken the enforcement of those statutes for which Congress has authorized fee awards—notably, many of our nation's civil rights laws and environmental laws.

I

Congress' purpose in adopting fee-shifting provisions was to strengthen the enforcement of selected federal laws by ensuring that private persons seeking to enforce those laws could retain competent counsel. In particular, federal fee-shifting provisions have been designed to address two related difficulties that otherwise would prevent private persons from obtaining counsel. First, many potential plaintiffs lack sufficient resources to hire attorneys. Second, many of the statutes to which Congress attached fee-shifting provisions typically will generate either no damages or only small recoveries; accordingly, plaintiffs bringing cases under these statutes cannot offer attorneys a share of a recovery sufficient to justify a standard contingent fee arrangement. See Pennsylvania v. Delaware Valley Citizens' Council for Clean Air (*Delaware Valley II*), 483 U.S. 711, 749 (dissenting opinion). The strategy of the fee-shifting provisions is to attract competent counsel to selected federal cases by ensuring that if they prevail, counsel will receive fees commensurable with what they could obtain in other litigation. If federal fee-bearing litigation is less remunerative than private litigation, then the only attorneys who will take such cases will be underemployed lawyers—who likely will be less competent than the successful, busy lawyers who would shun federal fee-bearing litigation—and public interest lawyers who, by any measure, are insufficiently numerous to handle all the cases for which other competent attorneys cannot be found. See *Delaware Valley II,* supra, at 742–43 (dissenting opinion).

In many cases brought under federal statutes that authorize fee-shifting, plaintiffs will be unable to ensure that their attorneys will be compensated for the risk that they might not prevail. This will be true in precisely those situations targeted by the fee-shifting statutes—where plaintiffs lack sufficient funds to hire an attorney on a win-or-lose basis and where potential damage awards are insufficient to justify a standard contingent fee arrangement. In these situations, unless the fee-shifting statutes are construed to compensate attorneys for the risk of nonpayment associated with loss, the expected return from cases brought under federal fee-shifting provisions will be less than could be obtained in otherwise comparable private litigation offering guaranteed, win-or-lose compensation. Prudent counsel, under these conditions, would tend to avoid federal fee-bearing claims in favor of private litigation, even in the very situations for which the attorney's fee statutes were designed. This will be true even if the fee-bearing claim is more likely meritorious than the competing private claim.

In *Delaware Valley II*, five Justices of this Court concluded that for these reasons the broad statutory term "reasonable attorney's fee" must be construed to permit, in some circumstances, compensation above the hourly win-or-lose rate generally borrowed to compute the lodestar fee. Together with the three Justices who joined my dissenting opinion in that case, I would have allowed enhancement where, and to the extent that, the attorney's compensation is contingent upon prevailing and receiving a statutory award. I indicated that if, by contrast, the attorney and client have been able to mitigate the risk of nonpayment—either in full, by agreeing to win-or-lose compensation or to a contingent share of a substantial damage recovery, or in part, by arranging for partial payment—then to that extent enhancement should be unavailable. I made clear that the "risk" for which enhancement might be available is not the particular factual and legal riskiness of an individual case, but the risk of nonpayment associated with contingent cases considered as a class. Congress, I concluded, did not intend to prohibit district courts from considering contingency in calculating a "reasonable" attorney's fee.[4]

Justice O'Connor's concurring opinion agreed that "Congress did not intend to foreclose consideration of contingency in setting a reasonable fee" and that "compensation for contingency must be based on the difference in market treatment of contingent fee cases *as a class,* rather than on an assessment of the 'riskiness' of any particular case" (emphasis in original). As I understand her opinion, Justice O'Connor further agreed that a court considering an enhancement must determine whether and to what extent the attorney's compensation was contingent, as well as whether and to what extent that contingency was, or could have been, mitigated. Her concurrence added, however, an additional inquiry designed to make the market-based approach "not

---

[4]. A number of bills introduced in Congress would have done just this, by prohibiting "bonuses and multipliers" where a suit is against the United States, a state, or a local government. These bills failed to receive congressional approval. See *Delaware Valley II,* supra, at 739, n. 3 (dissenting opinion). Moreover, in some instances Congress explicitly has prohibited enhancements, as in the 1986 amendments to the Education of the Handicapped Act. See 20 U.S.C. § 1415(e)(4)(C) ("[n]o bonus or multiplier may be used in calculating the fees awarded under this subsection"). Congress' express prohibition on enhancement in this statute suggests that it did not understand the standard fee-shifting language used elsewhere to bar enhancement.

merely justifiable in theory but also objective and nonarbitrary in practice." She suggested two additional "constraints on a court's discretion" in determining whether, and how much, enhancement is warranted. First, "district courts and courts of appeals should treat a determination of how a particular market compensates for contingency as controlling future cases involving the same market," and varying rates of enhancement among markets must be justifiable by reference to real differences in those markets. Second, the applicant bears the burden of demonstrating that without an adjustment for risk "the prevailing party would have faced substantial difficulties in finding counsel in the local or other relevant market" (internal quotations omitted).

II

After criticizing at some length an approach it admits respondents and their amici do not advocate and after rejecting the approach of the *Delaware Valley II* concurrence, the Court states that it "see[s] a number of reasons for concluding that no contingency enhancement whatever is compatible with the fee-shifting statutes at issue." I do not find any of these arguments persuasive.

The Court argues, first, that "[a]n attorney operating on a contingency-fee basis pools the risks presented by his various cases" and uses the cases that were successful to subsidize those that were not. "To award a contingency enhancement under a fee-shifting statute," the Court concludes, would "in effect" contravene the prevailing-party limitation, by allowing the attorney to recover fees for cases in which his client does not prevail. What the words "in effect" conceal, however, is the Court's inattention to the language of the statutes: The provisions at issue in this case, like fee-shifting provisions generally, authorize fee awards to prevailing parties, not their attorneys. Respondents simply do not advocate awarding fees to any party who has not prevailed. Moreover, the Court's reliance on the "prevailing party" limitation is somewhat misleading: the Court's real objection to contingency enhancement is that the amount of an enhanced award would be excessive, not that parties receiving enhanced fee awards are not prevailing parties entitled to an award. . . .

Second, the Court suggests that "both before and since *Delaware Valley II,* 'we have generally turned away from the contingent-fee model'—which would make the fee award a percentage of the value of the relief awarded in the primary action—'to the lodestar model.'" This argument simply plays on two meanings of "contingency." Most assuredly, respondents—who received no damages for their fee-bearing claims—do not advocate "mak[ing] the fee award a percentage" of that amount. Rather, they argue that the lodestar figure must be enhanced because their attorneys' compensation was contingent on prevailing, and because their attorneys could not otherwise be compensated for assuming the risk of nonpayment.

Third, the Court suggests that allowing for contingency enhancement "would make the setting of fees more complex and arbitrary" and would likely lead to "burdensome satellite litigation" that this Court has said should be avoided. The present case is an odd one in which to make this point: the issue of enhancement hardly occupied center stage in the fees portion of this litigation, and it became a time-consuming matter only after the Court granted certiorari, limited to this question alone. Moreover, if Justice O'Connor's standard were adopted, the matter of the amount by which fees should be increased would quickly become settled in the various district courts and courts of appeals for the different kinds of federal litigation. And in any event, speculation that enhancement determinations would be "burdensome" does not speak to the issue whether they are required by the fee-shifting statutes.

The final objection to be considered is the Court's contention that any approach that treats contingent-fee cases as a class is doomed to failure. The Court's argument on this score has two parts. First, the Court opines that "for a very large proportion of contingency-fee cases"—cases in which only equitable relief is sought—"there is no 'market treatment,'" except insofar as Congress has created an "artificial" market with the fee-shifting statutes themselves. It is circular, the Court contends, to "loo[k] to *that* 'market' for the meaning of fee-shifting." And even leaving that difficulty aside, the Court continues, the real "risk" to which lawyers respond is the riskiness of particular cases. Because under a class-based contingency enhancement system the same enhancement will be awarded whether the chance of prevailing was 80% or 20%, "*all cases* having above-class-average chance of success will be overcompensated" (emphasis in original).

Both parts of this argument are mistaken. The circularity objection overlooks the fact that even under the Court's unenhanced lodestar approach, the district court must find a relevant private market from which to select a fee. The Court offers no reason why this market disappears only when the inquiry turns to enhancement. The second part of the Court's argument is mistaken so far as it assumes the only relevant incentive to which attorneys respond is the risk of losing particular cases. As explained above, a proper system of contingency enhancement addresses a different kind of incentive: the common incentive of all lawyers to avoid *any* fee-bearing claim in which the plaintiff cannot guarantee the lawyer's compensation if he does not prevail. Because, as the Court observes, "no claim has a 100% chance of success," *any* such case under a pure lodestar system will offer a lower prospective return per hour than one in which the lawyer will be paid at the same lodestar rate, win or lose. Even the *least* meritorious case in which the attorney is guaranteed compensation whether he wins or loses will be economically preferable to the *most* meritorious fee-bearing claim in which the attorney will be paid only if he prevails, so long as the cases require the same amount of time. Yet as noted above, this latter kind of case—in which potential plaintiffs can neither afford to hire attorneys on a straight hourly basis nor offer a percentage of a substantial damage recovery—is exactly the kind of case for which the fee-shifting statutes were designed.

III

Preventing attorneys who bring actions under fee-shifting statutes from receiving fully compensatory fees will harm far more than the legal profession. Congress intended the fee-shifting statutes to serve as an integral enforcement mechanism in a variety of federal statutes—most notably, civil rights and environmental statutes. The amicus briefs filed in this case make clear that we can expect many meritorious actions will not be filed, or, if filed, will be prosecuted by less experienced and able counsel.[6] Today's decision weakens the protections we afford important federal rights.

I dissent.

JUSTICE O'CONNOR, dissenting.

I continue to be of the view that in certain circumstances a "reasonable" attorney's fee should not be computed by the purely retrospective lodestar figure, but also must incorporate a reasonable incentive to an attorney contemplating whether or not to take a case in the first place. See Pennsylvania v. Delaware Valley Citizens' Council for Clean Air, 483 U.S. 711, 731–34 (1987) (*Delaware Valley II*) (O'Connor, J., concurring in part and concurring in judgment). As Justice Blackmun cogently explains, when an attorney must choose between two cases—one with a client who will pay the attorney's fees win or lose and the other who can only promise the statutory compensation if the case is successful—the attorney will choose the fee-paying client, unless the contingency-client can promise an enhancement of sufficient magnitude to justify the extra risk of nonpayment. Thus, a reasonable fee should be one that would "attract competent counsel," and in some markets this must include the assurance of a contingency enhancement if the plaintiff should prevail. I therefore dissent from the Court's holding that a "reasonable" attorney's fee can never include an enhancement for cases taken on contingency.

In my view the promised enhancement should be "based on the difference in market treatment of contingent fee cases as a class, rather than on an assessment of the 'riskiness' of any particular case" (emphasis omitted). As Justice Blackmun has shown, the Court's reasons for

---

[6.] See Brief for the Lawyers' Committee for Civil Rights Under Law et al. as Amicus Curiae, 16–22; Brief for the Alabama Employment Lawyers Association et al. as Amicus Curiae, 12–13.

rejecting a market-based approach do not stand up to scrutiny. Admittedly, the courts called upon to determine the enhancements appropriate for various markets would be required to make economic calculations based on less-than-perfect data. Yet that is also the case, for example, in inverse condemnation and antitrust cases, and the Court has never suggested that the difficulty of the task or possible inexactitude of the result justifies forgoing those calculations altogether. As Justice Blackmun notes, these initial hurdles would be overcome as the enhancements appropriate to various markets became settled in the district courts and courts of appeals.

In this case, the District Court determined that a 25% contingency enhancement was appropriate by reliance on the likelihood of success in the individual case. The Court of Appeals affirmed on the basis of its holding in Friends of the Earth v. Eastman Kodak Co., 834 F.2d 295 (2d Cir.1987), which asks simply whether, without the possibility of a fee enhancement, the prevailing party would not have been able to obtain competent counsel. Although I believe that inquiry is part of the contingency enhancement determination, I also believe that it was error to base the degree of enhancement on case-specific factors. Because I can find no market-specific support for the 25% enhancement figure in the affidavits submitted by respondents in support of the fee request, I would vacate the judgment affirming the fee award and remand for a market-based assessment of a suitable enhancement for contingency.

Chapter V

ABSTENTION IN CIVIL RIGHTS CASES

Page 545, add to footnote h:

On the application of *Younger* to *damages* actions in federal court while a related state criminal proceeding is pending, see pages 176–81 of this Supplement, supra.

Page 547, add to the end of Note 8:

For an extensive analysis of the relation of *Younger* and its progeny to other forms of federal court intervention into ongoing state proceedings, see Michael G. Collins, The Right to Avoid Trial: Justifying Federal Court Intervention into Ongoing State Court Proceedings, 66 N.C.L.Rev. 49 (1987). A detailed analysis of the history surrounding modern jurisdictional statutes is undertaken in David Logan, Judicial Federalism in the Court of History, 66 Ore.L.Rev. 453 (1987). Logan concludes that "the notions of parity and 'Our Federalism' used by the Supreme Court to justify curtailing national judicial power are simply inconsistent with the historical record. As such, they are illegitimate bases for construing the jurisdiction of federal courts when a litigant seeks a federal forum to protect national rights from state infringements." In Is Disparity a Problem?, 22 Ga.L.Rev. 283 (1988), Michael Wells identifies *Younger* as the beginning of a contraction of federal court jurisdiction in constitutional litigation. He attributes the change to a substantive agenda which, although he does not share the values it reflects, he does not regard as illegitimate. See also Barry Friedman, A Revisionist Theory of Abstention, 88 Mich.L.Rev. 530, 588–94 (1989), which uses *Younger* as the touchstone for a rethinking of all forms of federal court abstention; Thomas E. Baker, "Our Federalism" in *Pennzoil Co. v. Texaco, Inc.* or How the *Younger* Doctrine Keeps Getting Older Not Better, 9 Review of Litigation 303 (1990), which explores the concept of federalism as reflected in the various abstention doctrines; and Maria L. Marcos, Wanted: A Federal Standard for Evaluating the Adequate State Forum, 50 Maryland L.Rev. 131 (1991), which criticizes prevailing standards for determining the adequacy of state remedies and finds a better approach in existing doctrines governing Supreme Court review of state court decisions.

Page 555, add a footnote at the end of Note 1:

[a] For analysis of *Mitchum* and a wide-ranging discussion of *Younger* abstention in relation to the history and contemporary uses of § 1983, see Gene R. Nichol, Jr., Federalism, State Courts, and Section 1983, 73 Va.L.Rev. 959 (1987). For analysis of *Younger* and *Mitchum* as part of a wide-ranging examination of conflicting "federalist" and "nationalist" tendencies in federal courts law, see Richard H. Fallon, Jr., The Ideologies of Federal Courts Law, 74 Va.L.Rev. 1141 (1988).

Page 583, substitute for Note 3:

3. *New Orleans Public Service, Inc. v. Council of City of New Orleans.* In New Orleans Public Service, Inc. v. Council of City of New Orleans, 491 U.S. 350 (1989), the Federal Energy Regulatory Commission (FERC) had determined that New Orleans Public Service, Inc. (NOPSI) should pay 17 per cent of the cost of a nuclear power plant. NOPSI sought a rate increase from the Council of the City of New Orleans in order to cover this cost. After protracted proceedings before the Council and the federal courts, the Council disallowed $135 million of the costs. NOPSI filed suit in federal court, seeking declaratory and injunctive relief against the order on the ground that the FERC determination preempted the Council's decision that the costs were unjustified and, in effect, required the Council to allow NOPSI to recoup its nuclear power costs through higher rates. NOPSI also filed a petition to review the Council order in the appropriate state court. In the state suit, NOPSI raised various state law claims and federal due process and takings claims. When the federal District Court in which the preemption claim had been filed abstained in favor of the pending state proceedings, NOPSI amended its state complaint to add the preemption claim and appealed the District Court abstention order. The Fifth Circuit affirmed the abstention, and the Supreme Court granted certiorari. The pending state proceeding was consolidated with two other cases raising the same issues and remained pending at the time of the Supreme Court decision.

Justice Scalia wrote the opinion for the Court. He first determined that *Burford* abstention [a] was inappropriate, primarily because the federal court's preemption inquiry "would not unduly intrude into the processes of state government or undermine the state's ability to maintain desired uniformity." He then turned to *Younger* abstention:

> ". . . NOPSI's challenge must stand or fall upon the answer to the question whether the Louisiana court action is the type of proceeding to which *Younger* applies. Viewed in isolation, it plainly is not. Although our concern for comity and federalism has led us to expand the protection of *Younger* beyond state criminal prosecutions, to civil enforcement proceedings [citing *Huffman* and *Trainor*], and even to civil proceedings involving certain orders that are uniquely in furtherance of the state courts' ability to perform their judicial functions [citing *Juidice*], it has never been suggested that *Younger* requires abstention in deference to a state judicial

---

[a] The reference is to Burford v. Sun Oil Co., 319 U.S. 315 (1943), which held that certain complex state administrative structures should not be interfered with by federal courts, particularly where there was a concentration of state administrative and judicial proceedings into a single process designed to produce uniformity and where the federal claims were not central to the issues involved and could adequately be heard by the state courts.

proceeding reviewing legislative or executive action. Such a broad abstention requirement would make a mockery of the rule that only exceptional circumstances justify a federal court's refusal to decide a case in deference to the states."

The Council argued that the state judicial proceedings were a mere continuation of the Council action, and that *Younger* should apply to the state proceedings as a whole. The Court responded:

> "Respondents' case for abstention still requires, however, that the *Council proceeding* be the sort of proceeding entitled to *Younger* treatment. We think it is not. While we have expanded *Younger* beyond criminal proceedings, and even beyond proceedings in courts, we have never extended it to proceedings that are not 'judicial in nature.' The Council's proceedings in the present case were not judicial in nature."

At this point the Court reaffirmed the holding in Prentis v. Atlantic Coast Line Co., 211 U.S. 210 (1908), that rate making is a legislative process and that federal intervention must await the conclusion of that process.[b] Here, however, the Council's "legislative" process was concluded. The state court proceedings were "judicial" in nature and were not, as they were in *Prentis*, an extension of the Council's legislative function. Therefore, the Court said, "NOPSI's preemption claim was ripe for federal review when the Council's order was entered." The Court then concluded:

> "As a challenge to completed legislative action, NOPSI's suit represents neither the interference with ongoing judicial proceedings against which *Younger* was directed, nor interference with an ongoing legislative process against which our ripeness holding in *Prentis* was directed. It is, insofar as our policies of federal comity are concerned, no different in substance from a facial challenge to an allegedly unconstitutional statute or zoning ordinance—which we would assuredly not require to be brought in state courts. It is true, of course, that the federal court's disposition of such a case may well affect, or for practical purposes pre-empt, a future—or, as in the present circumstances, even a pending—state court action. But there is no doctrine that the availability or even the pendency of state judicial proceedings excludes the federal courts. Viewed,

---

[b] The *Prentis* case held that a federal court should have refused to review a rate order of the Virginia State Corporation Commission because that body was acting in a legislative capacity and review of right was available in the Virginia Supreme Court of Appeals. Because of the powers of revision exercised by that court, such review was regarded as a continuation of the legislative process. It was thus premature for the federal courts to invervene because the legislative process had not yet been completed. The *Prentis* doctrine is the legislative analogy to the doctrine of exhaustion of administrative remedies. In effect, it holds that it is inappropriate for federal courts to interfere with legislation before it has been enacted, that is, before the legislative process has reached its conclusion.

as it should be, as no more than a state court challenge to completed legislative action, the Louisiana suit comes within none of the exceptions that *Younger* and later cases have established."

The Court accordingly reversed the abstention order and directed that the federal proceedings go forward.

Justice Brennan, joined by Justice Marshall, concurred. He reiterated his view that *Younger* "is generally inapplicable to civil proceedings." Chief Justice Rehnquist concurred in the Court's opinion on the *Younger* aspect of the case, but only in the judgment on the *Burford* point. He wished "not [to] foreclose the possibility of *Burford* abstention in a case like this had the state consolidated review of the orders of local ratemaking bodies in a specialized state court with power to hear a federal pre-emption claim." Justice Blackmun concurred only in the judgment. He agreed with "the core of the majority's reasoning" but noted technical objections to the Court's treatment of both *Younger* and *Burford*.

4. Questions and Comments on the Extension of *Younger* to Civil Proceedings. In *Trainor v. Hernandez,* as in *Huffman* and *Juidice,* the Court explicitly declined to "decide whether *Younger* principles apply to all civil litigation." *New Orleans Public Service* seems to put this question to rest. Civil proceedings were pending in state court at the time the federal District Court was asked to abstain (and "before any proceedings of substance on the merits" in the federal court [c]), yet the Supreme Court was unanimous that *Younger* was inapplicable. Has the Supreme Court drawn a sensible line between those civil cases to which *Younger* applies and those to which it does not? Or would it be better, as Justice Brennan has suggested, for *Younger* to be confined to the criminal context? Are there functional differences that justify the Court's line? That justify treating pending criminal prosecutions differently from the kinds of pending civil litigation to which *Younger* now applies? [d]

[At this point, renumber Note 4, Casebook, page 584, as Note 5 and continue.]

Page 585, add to second line from the top of the page:

A broad defense of the application of *Younger* to civil litigation is undertaken in Howard Stravitz, *Younger* Abstention Reaches a Civil Maturity: *Pennzoil Co. v. Texaco, Inc.*, 57 Fordham L.Rev. 997 (1989). For a reply that argues for a consolidation of various abstention doctrines and broader access to federal courts, see Georgene Vairo, Making *Younger* Civil: The Consequences of Federal Court Deference to State Court Proceedings—A Response to Professor Stravitz, 58 Ford-

[c] See *Hicks v. Miranda,* Casebook, page 566.

[d] Here read footnote a, Casebook, page 584.

ham L.Rev. 173 (1989). See also Ann Althouse, The Misguided Search for State Interest in Abstention Cases: Observations on the Occasion of *Pennzoil v. Texaco,* 63 N.Y.U.L.Rev. 1051 (1988), which carefully considers the operation of *Younger* policies in the context of a particular application.

Chapter VI

SELECTED PROBLEMS IN STRUCTURAL REFORM LITIGATION

Page 593, add to the second full paragraph:

See also The Seventh Circuit Symposium: The Federal Courts and the Community, 64 Chi-Kent L. Rev. 435 (1988) (containing a series of articles examining major structural reform cases in Chicago). Linda Hirshman, Foreward: Kicking Over the Traces of Self-Government, 64 Chi-Kent L. Rev. 435 (1988), leads off the Symposium, followed by articles containing detailed descriptions of three major cases written by architects of the litigation. Four commentaries follow: Peter Shane, Rights, Remedies and Restraint, 64 Chi-Kent L. Rev. 531 (1988); Dan Tarlock, Remedying the Irremediable: The Lessons of *Gatreaux*, 64 Chi-Kent L. Rev. 573 (1988); David Strauss, Legality, Activism, and the Patronage Case, 64 Chi-Kent L. Rev. 585 (1988); and Jules Gerard, A Restrained Perspective on Activism, 64 Chi-Kent L. Rev. 605 (1988).

Page 593, add at the end of the third paragraph of Note 3:

See also Lloyd C. Anderson, Implementation of Consent Decrees in Structural Reform Litigation, 1986 U.Ill.L.Rev. 725 (examining techniques of enforcing the complex consent decrees that can result from structural reform litigation); and, by the same author, Release and Resumption of Jurisdiction Over Consent Decrees in Structural Reform Litigation, 42 U.Miami L.Rev. 401 (1987) (discussing judicial retention or release of jurisdiction to enforce consent decrees); and Daniel J. Meltzer, Deterring Constitutional Violations by Law Enforcement Officials: Plaintiffs and Defendants as Private Attorneys General, 88 Colum.L.Rev. 247 (1988) (examining the judicial provision of remedies based on the need to deter future misconduct rather than on redressing the rights of each litigant; and contrasting the Court's willingness to recognize such remedies as defenses to criminal prosecution with its reluctance to allow offensive claims to such remedies in structural reform litigation).

Page 613, add to Note 2:

Fletcher, The Structure of Standing, 98 Yale L.J. 221 (1988).

Page 632, add to footnote a:

See also Linda Fisher, Caging *Lyons:* The Availability of Injunctive Relief in Section 1983 Actions, 18 Loyola U.Chi.L.J. 1085 (1987), concluding that "[c]oncerns about recurrence are more suitably raised during consideration of the merits of an injunctive claim."

Page 685, add a new Note 5a:

5a. Further Restrictions: *Wilson v. Seiter.* The future of prison reform litigation was thrown into doubt by Wilson v. Seiter, ___ U.S. ___ (1991). *Wilson* held that the eighth amendment's state-of-mind requirement, traditionally applied in cases of personal injury claims by prisoners, also applied in cases involving conditions of confinement. The suit alleged that overcrowding, excessive noise, poor ventilation, etc., amounted to cruel and unusual punishment. Speaking through Justice Scalia, the Court said in part:

> "Our holding in *Rhodes* turned on the objective component of an eighth amendment prison claim (was the deprivation sufficiently serious?), and we did not consider the subjective component (did the officials act with a sufficiently culpable state of mind?). That *Rhodes* had not eliminated the subjective component was made clear by our next relevant case, Whitley v. Albers, 475 U.S. 312 (1986). There an inmate shot by a guard during an attempt to quell a prison disturbance contended that he had been subjected to cruel and unusual punishment. We stated:
>
>> '. . . To be cruel and unusual punishment, conduct that does not purport to be punishment at all must involve more than ordinary lack of due care for the prisoner's interest or safety. . . . It is *obduracy and wantonness, not inadvertence or error in good faith,* that characterize the conduct prohibited by the cruel and unusual punishments clause, whether that conduct occurs in connection with establishing conditions of confinement, supplying medical needs, or restoring official control over a tumultous cellblock.'
>
> "These cases mandate inquiry into a prison official's state of mind when it is claimed that the official has inflicted cruel and unusual punishment. . . . If the pain inflicted is not formally meted out *as punishment* by the statute or the sentencing judge, some mental element must be attributed to the inflicting officer before it can qualify."

On the question of what that mental element should be, the Court rejected the lower court's standard of "persistent malicious cruelty" and accepted a lesser showing of "deliberate indifference" to prisoner welfare. The case was then remanded for application of the proper standard.

Justice White, with whom Justices Marshall, Blackmun, and Stevens joined, agreed with the disposition but argued that the state-of-mind requirement should apply only to specific acts or omissions directed at individual prisoners. In their view, "*Rhodes* makes it crystal clear . . . that eighth amendment challenges to conditions of confinement are to be treated like eighth amendment challenges to punishment that is 'formally meted out *as punishment* by the statute or the sentencing judge'—we examine only the objective severity, not the subjective intent of government officials." Additionally, White argued, the majority's approach was not only wrong but obscure:

> "Not only is the majority's intent requirement a departure from precedent, it likely will prove impossible to apply in many cases. Inhumane prison conditions often are the result of cumulative actions and inactions by numerous officials inside and outside a prison, sometimes over a long period of time. In those circumstances, it is far from clear whose intent should be examined, and the majority offers no real guidance on this issue. In truth, intent simply is not very meaningful when considering a challenge to an institution, such as a prison system."

A major question left open by *Wilson* is the possibility of a "cost defense" to changes of cruel and unusual conditions of confinement. The majority declined to consider the issue on the ground that it had not been properly raised. The minority, however, saw it as a crucial problem:

> "The majority's approach . . . leaves open the possibility . . . that prison officials will be able to defeat a § 1983 action challenging inhumane prison conditions simply by showing that the conditions are caused by insufficient funding from the state legislature rather than by any deliberate indifference on the part of the prison officials. In my view, having chosen to use imprisonment as a form of punishment, a state must ensure that the conditions in its prisons comport with the 'contemporary standard of decency' required by the eighth amendment. As the United Statutes argues [as amicus curiae]: '[S]eriously inhumane, pervasive conditions should not be insulated from constitutional challenge because the officials managing the institution have exhibited a conscientious concern for ameliorating its problems, and have made efforts (albeit unsuccessful) to that end.' The ultimate result of today's decision, I fear is that 'serious deprivations of basic human needs,' *Rhodes,* supra, at 347, will go unredressed due to an unnecessary and meaningless search for 'deliberate indifference.' "[j]

[j] For a continuation of the debate within the Court on the substantive standards that measure the scope of a § 1983 cause of action based on the cruel and unusual punishment clause, see Hudson v. McMillian, ___ U.S. ___ (1992). On its facts, *McMillian* involved whether a "significant injury" was required in a case where several guards were found to have physically beaten an inmate. The Court held that it was not. The debate between the majority and the dissent in part concerned the appropriate eighth amendment standard in prison condition cases.

Page 685, add at the end of the first paragraph of Note 6:

For a fascinating history of the Alabama prison litigation, see Larry W. Yackle, Reform and Regret: The Story of Federal Judicial Involvement in the Alabama Prison System (1989).

Page 686, add at the end of Note 6:

Finally, for discussion of the appropriate standards for modifying or dissolving structural injunctions, see Sarah N. Welling and Barbara W. Jones, Prison Reform Issues for the Eighties: Modification and Dissolution of Injunctions in the Federal Courts, 20 Conn.L.Rev. 865 (1988).

Page 686, add a new section:

SECTION 5: ENFORCING STRUCTURAL REFORM DECREES

MISSOURI v. JENKINS
Supreme Court of the United States, 1990.
495 U.S. 33.

JUSTICE WHITE delivered the opinion of the Court.

The United States District Court for the Western District of Missouri imposed an increase in the property taxes levied by the Kansas City, Missouri, School District (KCMSD) to ensure funding for the desegregation of KCMSD's public schools. We granted certiorari to consider the state of Missouri's argument that the District Court lacked the power to raise local property taxes. For the reasons given below, we hold that the District Court abused its discretion in imposing the tax increase. We also hold, however, that the modifications of the District Court's order made by the Court of Appeals do satisfy equitable and constitutional principles governing the District Court's power.

I

In 1977, KCMSD and a group of KCMSD students filed a complaint alleging that the state of Missouri and surrounding school district had operated a segregated public school system in the Kansas City metropolitan area. The District Court realigned KCMSD as a party defendant, and KCMSD filed a cross-claim against the state, seeking indemnification for any liability that might be imposed on KCMSD for intradistrict segregation.[2] After a lengthy trial, the District Court

---

[2] The complaint originally alleged that the defendants had caused interdistrict segregation of the public schools. After KCMSD was realigned as a defendant, a group of students filed an amended complaint that also alleged intradistrict segregation. The District Court certified a

found that KCMSD and the state had operated a segregated school system within the KCMSD.[3]

The District Court thereafter issued an order detailing the remedies necessary to eliminate the vestiges of segregation and the financing necessary to implement those remedies.[4] The District Court originally estimated the cost of the desegregation remedy to be almost $88,000,000 over three years, of which it expected the state to pay $67,592,072 and KCMSD to pay $20,140,472. The court concluded, however, that several provisions of Missouri law would prevent KCMSD from being able to pay its share of the obligation. The Missouri Constitution limits local property taxes to $1.25 per $100 of assessed valuation unless a majority of the voters in the district approve a higher levy, up to $3.25 per $100; the levy may be raised above $3.25 per $100 only if two-thirds of the voters agree. The "Hancock Amendment" requires property tax rates to be rolled back when property is assessed at a higher valuation to ensure that taxes will not be increased solely as a result of assessments. The Hancock Amendment thus prevents KCMSD from obtaining any revenue increase as a result of increases in the assessed valuation of real property. "Proposition C" allocates one cent of every dollar raised by the state sales tax to a schools trust fund and requires school districts to reduce property taxes by an amount equal to 50% of the previous year's sales tax receipts in the district. However, the trust fund is allocated according to a formula that does not compensate KCMSD for the amount lost in property tax revenues, and the effect of Proposition C is to divert nearly half of the sales taxes collected in KCMSD to other parts of the state.

The District Court believed that it had the power to order a tax increase to ensure adequate funding of the desegregation plan, but it hesitated to take this step. It chose instead to enjoin the effect of the Proposition C rollback to allow KCMSD to raise an additional $4,000,000 for the coming fiscal year. The court ordered KCMSD to submit to the voters a proposal for an increase in taxes sufficient to pay for its share of the desegregation remedy in the following years.

plaintiff class of present and future KCMSD students.

[3] The District Court also found that none of the alleged discriminatory actions had resulted in lingering interdistrict effects and so dismissed the suburban school districts and denied interdistrict relief.

[4] KCMSD was ordered to improve the quality of the curriculum and library, reduce teaching load, and implement tutoring, summer school, and child development programs. The cost of these remedies was to be borne equally by the state and KCMSD. The District Court ordered an extensive capital improvement program to rehabilitate the deteriorating physical plant of KCMSD, the cost of which was estimated as at least $37,000,000, of which $27,000,000 was to be contributed by the state. The District Court also required the defendants to encourage voluntary interdistrict transfer of students. No cost was placed on the interdistrict transfer program, but the state was ordered to underwrite the program in full. The District Court further ordered the state to fund fully other portions of the desegregation program intended to reduce class size and improve student achievement.

The Court of Appeals for the Eighth Circuit affirmed the District Court's findings of liability and remedial order in most respects. The Court of Appeals agreed with the state, however, that the District Court had failed to explain adequately why it had imposed most of the cost of the desegregation plan on the state. The Eighth Circuit ordered the District Court to divide the cost equally between the state and KCMSD. We denied certiorari.

Proceedings before the District Court continued during the appeal. In its original remedial order, the District Court had directed KCMSD to prepare a study addressing the usefulness of "magnet schools" to promote desegregation.[6] A year later, the District Court approved KCMSD's proposal to operate six magnet schools during the 1986–1987 school year. The court again faced the problem of funding, for KCMSD's efforts to persuade the voters to approve a tax increase had failed, as had its efforts to seek funds from the Kansas City Council and the state legislature. Again hesitating to impose a tax increase itself, the court continued its injunction against the Proposition C rollback to enable KCMSD to raise an additional $6,500,000.

In November 1986, the District Court endorsed a marked expansion of the magnet school program. It adopted in substance a KCMSD proposal that every high school, every middle school, and half of the elementary schools in KCMSD become magnet schools by the 1991–1992 school year. It also approved the $142,736,025 budget proposed by KCMSD for implementation of the magnet school plan, as well as the expenditure of $52,858,301 for additional capital improvements.

The District Court next considered, as the Court of Appeals had directed, how to shift the cost of desegregation to KCMSD. The District Court concluded that it would be "clearly inequitable" to require the population of KCMSD to pay of the desegregation cost, and that "even with court help it would be very difficult for the KCMSD to fund more than 25% of the costs of the entire remedial plan." The court reasoned that the state should pay for most of the desegregation cost under the principle that "the person who starts the fire has more responsibility for the damages caused than the person who fails to put it out," and that apportionment of damages between the state and KCMSD according to fault was supported by the doctrine of comparative fault in tort, which had been adopted by the Missouri Supreme Court. . . . The District Court then held that the state and KCMSD were 75% and 25% at fault, respectively, and ordered them to share the cost of the desegregation remedy in that proportion. To ensure complete funding of the remedy, the court also held the two tortfeasors jointly and severally liable for the cost of the plan.

[6] "Magnet schools," as generally understood, are public schools of voluntary enrollment designed to promote integration by drawing students away from their neighborhoods and private schools through distinctive curricula and high quality.

Three months later, the District Court adopted a plan requiring $187,450,334 in further capital improvements. By then it was clear that the KCMSD would lack the resources to pay for its 25% share of the desegregation cost. KCMSD requested that the District Court order the state to pay for any amount that KCMSD could not meet. The District Court declined to impose a greater share of the cost on the state, but it accepted that KCMSD had "exhausted all available means of raising additional revenue." [T]he court ordered the KCMSD property tax levy raised from $2.05 to $4.00 per $100 of assessed valuation through the 1991–1992 fiscal year. KCMSD was also directed to issue $150,000,000 in capital improvement bonds. A subsequent order directed that the revenues generated by the property tax increase be used to retire the capital improvement bonds.

The state appealed, challenging the scope of the desegregation remedy, the allocation of the cost between the state and KCMSD, and the tax increase. . . .

Although the Court of Appeals [affirmed the District Court on most points], it agreed with the state that principles of federal/state comity required the District Court to use "minimally obtrusive methods to remedy constitutional violations." The Court of Appeals thus required that in the future, the District Court should not set the property tax rate itself but should authorize KCMSD to submit a levy to the state tax collection authorities and should enjoin the operation of state laws hindering KCMSD from adequately funding the remedy. The Court of Appeals reasoned that permitting the school board to set the levy itself would minimize disruption of state laws and processes and would ensure maximum consideration of the views of state and local officials. . . .

We granted the state's petition, limited to the question of the property tax increase. . . .

II

[Part II concluded that the state's petition for certiorari was timely.]

III

We turn to the tax increase imposed by the District Court. The state urges us to hold that the tax increase violated article III, the 10th amendment, and principles of federal/state comity. We find it unnecessary to reach the difficult constitutional issues, for we agree with the state that the tax increase contravened the principles of comity that must govern the exercise of the District Court's equitable discretion in this area.

It is accepted by all the parties, as it was by the courts below, that the imposition of a tax increase by a federal court was an extraordinary event. In assuming for itself the fundamental and delicate power of taxation the District Court not only intruded on local authority but circumvented it altogether. Before taking such a drastic step the District Court was obliged to assure itself that no permissible alternative would have accomplished the required task. [O]ne of the most important considerations governing the exercise of equitable power is a proper respect for the integrity and function of local government institutions. Especially is this true where, as here, those institutions are ready, willing, and—but for the operation of state law curtailing their powers—able to remedy the deprivation of constitutional rights themselves.

The District Court believed that it had no alternative to imposing a tax increase. But there was an alternative, the very one outlined by the Court of Appeals: it could have authorized or required KCMSD to levy property taxes at a rate adequate to fund the desegregation remedy and could have enjoined the operation of state laws that would have prevented KCMSD from exercising this power. The difference between the two is far more than a matter of form. Authorizing and directing local government institutions to devise and implement remedies not only protects the function of those institutions but, to the extent possible, also places the responsibility for solutions to the problems of segregation upon those who have themselves created the problems. . . .

The District Court therefore abused its discretion in imposing the tax itself. The Court of Appeals should not have allowed the tax increase to stand and should have reversed the District Court in this respect.

IV

We stand on different ground when we review the modifications to the District Court's order made by the Court of Appeals. As explained, the Court of Appeals held that the District Court in the future should authorize KCMSD to submit a levy to the state tax collection authorities adequate to fund its budget and should enjoin the operation of state laws that would limit or reduce the levy below that amount.

The state argues that the funding ordered by the District Court violates principles of equity and comity because the remedial order itself was excessive. As the state puts it, "[t]he only reason that the court below needed to consider an unprecedented tax increase was the equally unprecedented cost of its remedial programs." We think this argument aims at the scope of the remedy rather than the manner in which the remedy is to be funded and thus falls outside our limited grant of certiorari in this case. As we denied certiorari on the first question presented by the state's petition, which did challenge the scope of the remedial order, we must resist the state's effort to argue that point now. We accept, without approving or disapproving, the Court of Appeals' conclusion that the District Court's remedy was proper. . . .

We turn to the constitutional issues. The modifications ordered by the Court of Appeals cannot be assailed as invalid under the 10th amendment. "The Tenth Amendment's reservation of nondelegated powers to the states is not implicated by a federal-court judgment enforcing the express prohibitions of unlawful state conduct enacted by the 14th amendment." Milliken v. Bradley, 433 U.S. 267, 291 (1977). "The 14th amendment . . . was avowedly directed against the power of the states," Pennsylvania v. Union Gas Co., 491 U.S. 1, ___ (1989) (Scalia, J., concurring in part and dissenting in part), and so permits a federal court to disestablish local government institutions that interfere with its commands.

Finally, the state argues that an order to increase taxes cannot be sustained under the judicial power of article III. Whatever the merits of this argument when applied to the District Court's own order increasing taxes, a point we have not reached, a court order directing a local government body to levy its own taxes is plainly a judicial act within the power of a federal court. We held as much in Griffin v. Prince Edward County School Board, 377 U.S. 218 (1964), where we stated that a District Court, faced with a county's attempt to avoid desegregation of the public schools by refusing to operate those schools, could "require the [County] Supervisors to exercise the power that is theirs to levy taxes to raise funds adequate to reopen, operate, and maintain without racial discrimination a public school system. . . ." *Griffin* followed a long and venerable line of cases in which this Court held that federal courts could issue the writ of mandamus to compel local governmental bodies to levy taxes adequate to satisfy their debt obligations.[20]

The state maintains, however, that even under these cases, the federal judicial power can go no further than to require local governments to levy taxes *as authorized under state law*. In other words, the

---

[20] The old cases recognized two exceptions to this rule, neither of which is relevant here. First, it was held that federal courts could not by writ of mandamus compel state officers to release funds in the state treasury sufficient to satisfy state bond obligations. The Court viewed this as attempt to employ the writ of mandamus as a ruse to avoid the 11th amendment bar against exercising federal jurisdiction over the state. This holding has no application to this case, for the 11th amendment does not bar federal courts from imposing on the states the costs of securing prospective compliance with a desegregation order, Milliken v. Bradley, 433 U.S. 267, 290 (1977), and does not afford local school boards like KCMSD immunity from suit. Second, it was held that the writ of mandamus would not lie to compel the collection of taxes when there was no person against whom the writ could operate. This exception also has no application to this case, where there are state and local officials invested with authority to collect and disburse the property tax and where, as matters now stand, the District Court need only prevent those officials from applying state law that would interfere with the willing levy of property taxes by KCMSD.

state argues that federal courts cannot set aside state-imposed limitations on local taxing authority because to do so is to do more than to require the local government "to exercise the power *that is theirs.*" We disagree. This argument was rejected as early as Von Hoffman v. City of Quincy, 71 U.S. (4 Wall.) 535 (1867). There the holder of bonds issued by the city sought a writ of mandamus against the city requiring it to levy taxes sufficient to pay interest coupons then due. The city defended based on a state statute that limited its power of taxation, and the Circuit Court refused to mandamus the city. This Court reversed, observing that the statute relied on by the city was passed after the bonds were issued and holding that because the city had ample authority to levy taxes to pay its bonds when they were issued, the statute impaired the contractual entitlements of the bondholders, contrary to art. I, § 10, cl. 1 of the Constitution, under which a state may not pass any law impairing the obligation of contracts. The statutory limitation, therefore, could be disregarded and the city ordered to levy the necessary taxes to pay its bonds.

It is therefore clear that a local government with taxing authority may be ordered to levy taxes in excess of the limit set by state statute where there is reason based in the Constitution for not observing the statutory limitation. In *Von Hoffman,* the limitation was disregarded because of the contract clause. Here the KCMSD may be ordered to levy taxes despite the statutory limitations on its authority in order to compel the discharge of an obligation imposed on KCMSD by the 14th amendment. To hold otherwise would fail to take account of the obligations of local governments, under the supremacy clause, to fulfill the requirements that the Constitution imposes on them. . . . Even though a particular remedy may not be required in every case to vindicate constitutional guarantees, where (as here) it has been found that a particular remedy is required, the state cannot hinder the process by preventing a local government from implementing that remedy.

Accordingly, the judgment of the Court of Appeals is affirmed insofar as it required the District Court to modify its funding order and reversed insofar as it allowed the tax increase imposed by the District Court to stand. The case is remanded for further proceedings consistent with this opinion.

JUSTICE KENNEDY with whom THE CHIEF JUSTICE, JUSTICE O'CONNOR, and JUSTICE SCALIA join, concurring in part and concurring in the judgment.

[I agree] that the District Court exceeded its authority by attempting to impose a tax. . . . This is consistent with our precedents and with the basic principles defining judicial power.

In my view, however, the Court transgresses these same principles when it goes further, much further, to embrace by broad dictum an expansion of power in the federal judiciary beyond all precedent. Today's casual embrace of taxation imposed by the unelected, life-tenured federal judiciary disregards fundamental precepts for the democratic control of public institutions. . . .

I

Some essential litigation history is necessary for a full understanding of what is at stake here and what will be wrought if the implications of all the Court's statements are followed to the full extent. The District Court's remedial plan was proposed for the most part by the Kansas City, Missouri, School District (KCMSD) itself, which is in name a defendant in the suit. Defendants, and above all defendants that are public entities, act in the highest and best tradition of our legal system when they acknowledge fault and cooperate to suggest remedies. But in the context of this dispute, it is of vital importance to note the KCMSD demonstrated little concern for the fiscal consequences of the remedy that it helped design.

As the District Court acknowledged, the plaintiffs and the KCMSD pursued a "friendly adversary" relationship. Throughout the remedial phase of the litigation, the KCMSD proposed ever more expensive capital improvements with the agreement of the plaintiffs, and the state objected. Some of these improvements involved basic repairs to deteriorating facilities within the school system. The KCMSD, however, devised a broader concept for district-wide improvement, and the District Court improved it. The plan involved a variation of the magnet school concept. Magnet schools, as the majority opinion notes, offer special programs, often used to encourage voluntary movement of students within the district in a pattern that aids desegregation.

Although we have approved desegregation plans involving magnet schools of this conventional definition, see Milliken v. Bradley, 433 U.S. 267, 272 (1977), the District Court found this insufficient. Instead, the court and the KCMSD decided to make a magnet of the district as a whole. The hope was to draw new non-minority students from outside the district. The KCMSD plan adopted by the Court provided that "every senior high school, every middle school, and approximately one-half of the elementary schools in the KCMSD will become magnet schools by the school year 1991–92." The plan was intended to "improve the quality of education of all KCMSD students." The District Court was candid to acknowledge that the "long term goal of this Court's remedial order is to make available to *all* KCMSD students educational opportunities equal to or greater than those presently available in the average Kansas City, Missouri metropolitan suburban school district" (emphasis in original).

It comes as no surprise that the cost of this approach to the remedy far exceeded KCMSD's budget, or for that matter, its authority to tax.

A few examples are illustrative. Programs such as a "performing arts middle school" [and] a "technical magnet high school" that "will offer programs ranging from heating and air conditioning to cosmetology to robotics," were approved. The plan also included a "25 acre farm and 25 acre wildland area" for science study. The court rejected various proposals by the state to make "capital improvement necessary to eliminate health and safety hazards and to provide a good learning environment," because these proposals failed to "consider the criteria of suburban comparability." The District Court stated: "This 'patch and repair' approach proposed by the state would not achieve suburban comparability or the visual attractiveness sought by the court as it would result in floor coverings with unsightly sections of mismatched carpeting and tile, and individual walls possessing different shades of paint." Finding that construction of new schools would result in more "attractive" facilities than renovation of existing ones, the District Court approved new construction at a cost ranging from $61.80 per square foot to $95.70 per square foot as distinct from renovation at $45 per square foot.

By the time of the order at issue here, the District Court's remedies included some "$260 million in capital improvements and a magnet-school plan costing over $200 million." And the remedial orders grew more expensive as shortfalls in revenue became more severe. . . . As the Eighth Circuit judges dissenting from denial of rehearing in banc put it: "The remedies ordered go far beyond anything previously seen in a school desegregation case. The sheer immensity of the programs encompassed by the district court's order—the large number of magnet schools and the quantity of capital renovations and new construction—are concededly without parallel in any other school district in the country."

The judicial taxation approved by the Eighth Circuit is also without parallel. . . .

The premise of the Court's analysis, I submit, is infirm. Any purported distinction between direct imposition of a tax by the federal court and an order commanding the school district to impose the tax is but a convenient formalism where the court's action is predicated on elimination of state law limitations on the school district's taxing authority. As the Court describes it, the local KCMSD possesses plenary taxing powers, which allow it to impose any tax it chooses if not "hinder[ed]" by the Missouri Constitution and state statutes. This puts the conclusion before the premise. Local government bodies in Missouri, as elsewhere, must derive their power from a sovereign, and that sovereign is the state of Missouri. . . .

For this reason, I reject the artificial suggestion that the District Court may by "prevent[ing] officials from applying state law that would interfere with the willing levy of property taxes by KCMSD," cause the KCMSD to exercise power under *state* law. State laws, including taxation provisions legitimate and constitutional in themselves define the power of the KCMSD. Absent a change in state law, no increase in property taxes could take place in the KCMSD without a federal court order. It makes no difference that the KCMSD stands "ready, willing, and . . . able" to impose a tax not authorized by state law. Whatever taxing power the KCMSD may exercise outside the boundaries of state law would derive from the federal court. The Court never confronts the judicial authority to issue an order for this purpose. Absent a change in state law, the tax is imposed by federal authority under a federal decree. The question is whether a district court possesses a power to tax under federal law, either directly or through delegation to the KCMSD.

II

Article III of the Constitution states that "[t]he judicial Power of the United States, shall be vested in one supreme Court, and in such inferior Courts as the Congress may from time to time ordain and establish." The description of the judicial power nowhere includes the word "tax" or anything that resembles it. This reflects the framers' understanding that taxation was not a proper area for judicial involvement. . . .

The nature of the District Court's order here reveals that it is not a proper exercise of the judicial power. The exercise of judicial power involves adjudication of controversies and imposition of burdens on those who are parties before the court. The order at issue here is not of this character. It binds the broad class of all KCMSD taxpayers. It has the purpose and direct effect of extracting money from persons who have had no presence or representation in the suit. For this reason, the District Court's direct order imposing a tax was more than an abuse of discretion, for any attempt to collect the taxes from the citizens would have been a blatant denial of due process.

Taxation by a legislature raises no due process concerns. . . . The citizens who are taxed are given notice and a hearing through their representatives, whose power is a direct manifestation of the citizens' consent. A true exercise of judicial power provides due process of another sort. Where money is extracted from parties by a court's judgment, the adjudication itself provides the notice and opportunity to be heard that due process demands before a citizen may be deprived of property.

The order here provides neither of these protections. When a tax is imposed by a governmental body other than the legislature, even an administrative agency to which the legislature has delegated taxing authority, due process requires notice to the citizens to be taxed and some opportunity to be heard. The citizens whose tax bills would have been doubled under the District Court's direct tax order would not have had these protections. The taxes were imposed by a District Court that was not "representative" in any sense, and the individual citizens of the KCMSD whose property (they learned later) was at stake were neither served with process nor heard in court. The method of taxation endorsed by today's dicta suffers the same flaw, for a district court order that overrides the citizens' state law protection against taxation without referendum approval can in no sense provide representational due process. No one suggests the KCMSD taxpayers are parties.

A judicial taxation order is but an attempt to exercise a power that always has been thought legislative in nature. . . . The list of legislative powers in article I, § 8, cl. 1 begins with the statement that "[t]he *Congress* shall have Power To lay and collect Taxes. . . ." As we have said, "[t]axation is a legislative function, and Congress . . . is the sole organ for levying taxes." National Cable Television Assn, Inc. v. United States, 415 U.S. 336, 340 (1974).

True, today's case is not an instance of one branch of the federal government invading the province of another. It is instead one that brings the weight of federal authority upon a local government and a state. This does not detract, however, from the fundamental point that the judiciary is not free to exercise all federal power; it may exercise only the judicial power. And the important effects of the taxation order discussed here raise additional federalism concerns that counsel against the Court's analysis. . . .

The confinement of taxation to the legislative branches, both in our federal and state governments, was not random. It reflected our ideal that the power of taxation must be under the control of those who are taxed. . . .

The power of taxation is one that the federal judiciary does not possess. [I]t is the legislature that is accountable to [the people] and represents their will. The authority that would levy the tax at issue here shares none of these qualities. Our federal judiciary, by design, is not representative or responsible to the people in a political sense; it is independent. . . .

The operation of tax systems is among the most difficult aspects of public administration. It is not a function the judiciary as an institution is designed to exercise. Unlike legislative bodies, which may hold hearings on how best to raise revenues, all subject to the views of constituents to whom the legislature is accountable, the judiciary must grope ahead with only the assistance of the parties, or perhaps random amici curiae. Those hearings would be without principled direction, for there exists no body of juridical axioms by which to guide or review them. On this questionable basis, the Court today would give authority for decisions that affect the life plans of local citizens, the revenue available for competing public needs, and the health of the local economy. . . .

The Court relies on dicta from Griffin v. School Board of Prince Edward County, 377 U.S. 218 (1964), to support its statements on judicial taxation. In *Griffin,* the Court faced an unrepentant and recalcitrant school board that attempted to provide financial support for white schools while refusing to operate schools for black schoolchildren. We stated that the district court could "require the supervisors to exercise the power *that is theirs* to levy taxes to raise funds adequate to reopen, operate, and maintain without racial discrimination a public school system" (emphasis added). There is no occasion in this case to discuss the implications of *Griffin's* observation, for it has no application here. *Griffin* endorsed the power of a federal court to order the local authority to exercise *existing* authority to tax.

This case does not involve an order to a local government with plenary taxing power to impose a tax, or an order directed at one whose taxing power as been limited by a state law enacted in order to thwart a federal court order. An order of this type would find support in the *Griffin* dicta, and present a closer question than the one before us. Yet that order might implicate as well the "perversion of the normal legislative process" that we have found troubling in other contexts. See Spallone v. United States, 493 U.S. 265 (1990). A legislative vote taken under judicial compulsion blurs lines of accountability by making it appear that a decision was reached by elected representatives when the reality is otherwise. For this reason, it is difficult to see the difference between an order to tax and direct judicial imposition of a tax.

The Court asserts that its understanding of *Griffin* follows from cases in which the Court upheld the use of mandamus to compel local officials to collect taxes that were authorized under state law in order to meet bond obligations. But as discussed above, there was no state authority in this case for the KCMSD to exercise. In this situation, there could be no authority for a judicial order touching on taxation.

The Court cites a single case, Von Hoffman v. City of Quincy, 71 U.S. (4 Wall.) 535 (1867), for the proposition that a federal court may set aside state taxation limits that interfere with the remedy sought by the district court. But the Court does not heed *Von Hoffman's* holding. There a municipality had authorized a tax levy in support of a specific bond obligation, but later limited the taxation authority in a way that impaired the bond obligation. The Court held the subsequent limitation itself unconstitutional, a violation of the contracts clause. Once the limitation was held invalid, the original specific grant of authority remained. There is no allegation here, no could there be, that the neutral tax limitations imposed by the people of Missouri are unconstitutional. The majority appears to concede that the Missouri tax law does not violate a specific provision of the Constitution, stating instead that state laws may be disregarded on the basis of a vague "reason based in the Constitution." But this broad suggestion does not follow from the holding in *Von Hoffman.*

Examination of the "long and venerable line of cases" cited by the Court to endorse judicial taxation reveals the lack of real support for the Court's rationale. One group of these cases holds simply that the common-law writ of mandamus lies to compel a local official to perform a clear duty imposed by state law. [Citations omitted.] These common-law mandamus decisions do not purport to involve the federal Constitution or remedial powers.

A second set of cases, including the *Von Hoffman* case relied upon by the Court, invalidates on contracts clause grounds statutory limitations on taxation power passed subsequent to grants of tax authority in support of bond observations. [Citations omitted.] These cases, like *Von Hoffman,* are inapposite because there is no colorable argument that the provision of the Missouri Constitution limiting property tax assessments itself that violates the federal Constitution.

A third group of cases involving taxation and municipal bonds is more relevant. These cases hold that where there is no state or municipal taxation authority that the federal court may by mandamus command the officials to exercise, the court itself is without authority to order taxation. . . .

At bottom, today's discussion seems motivated by the fear that failure to endorse judicial taxation power might in some extreme circumstance leave a court unable to remedy a constitutional violation. As I discuss below, I do not think this possibility is in reality a significant one. More important, this possibility is nothing more or less than the necessary consequence of *any* limit on judicial power. If, however, judicial discretion is to provide the sole limit on judicial remedies, that discretion must counsel restraint. Ill-considered entry into the volatile field of taxation is a step that may place at risk the legitimacy that justifies judicial independence.

III

. . . Even were I willing to accept the Court's proposition that a federal court might in some extreme case authorize taxation, this case is not the one. [T]he taxation power is sought here on behalf of a remedial order unlike any before seen.

It cannot be contended that interdistrict comparability, which was the ultimate goal of the District Court's orders, is itself a constitutional command. We have long since determined that "unequal expenditures between children who happen to reside in different districts" do not violate the equal protection clause. San Antonio Independent School District v. Rodriguez, 411 U.S. 1, 54–55 (1973). The District Court in this case found, and the Court of Appeals affirmed, that there was no interdistrict constitutional violation that would support interdistrict relief. Instead, the District Court's conclusion that desegregation might be easier if more nonminority students could be attracted into the KCMSD was used as the hook on which to hang numerous policy choices about improving the quality of education in general within the KCMSD. The state's complaint that this suit represents the attempt of a school district that could not obtain public support for increased spending to enlist the District Court to finance its educational policy cannot be dismissed out of hand. . . .

This Court has never approved a remedy of the type adopted by the District Court. There are strong arguments against the validity of such a plan. A remedy that uses the quality of education as a lure to attract nonminority students will place the District Court at the center of controversies over educational philosophy that by tradition are left to this nation's communities. . . . District courts can and must take needed steps to eliminate racial discrimination and ensure the operation of unitary school systems. But it is discrimination, not the ineptitude of educators or the indifference of the public, that is the evil to be remedied. An initial finding of discrimination cannot be used as the basis for a wholesale shift of authority over day-to-day school operations from parents, teachers, and elected officials to an unaccountable district judge whose province is law, not education.

Perhaps it is good educational policy to provide a school district with the items included in the KCMSD capital improvement plan, for example: high schools in which every classroom will have air conditioning, an alarm system, and 15 microcomputers; a 2,000-square-foot planetarium; greenhouses and vivariums; a 25-acre farm with an air-conditioned meeting room for 104 people; a Model United States wired for language translation; broadcast capable radio and television studios with an editing and animation lab; a temperature controlled art gallery; movie editing and screening rooms; a 3,500-square-foot dust-free diesel mechanics room; 1,875-square-foot elementary school animal rooms for use in a Zoo Project; swimming pools; and numerous other facilities. But these items are part of legitimate political debate over educational policy and spending priorities, not the Constitution's command of racial equality. Indeed, it may be that a mere 12-acre petting farm . . . might satisfy constitutional requirements, while preserving scarce public funds for legislative allocation to other public needs, such as paving streets, feeding the poor, building prisons, or housing the homeless. . . .

I am required in light of our limited grant of certiorari to assume that the remedy chosen by the District Court was a permissible exercise of its remedial discretion. But it is misleading to suggest that a failure to fund this particular remedy would leave constitutional rights without a remedy. . . . To suggest that a constitutional violation will go unremedied if a district does not, through capital improvements or other means, turn every school into a magnet school, and the entire district into a magnet district, is to suggest that the remedies approved in our past cases should have been disapproved as insufficient to deal with the violations. . . .

The prudence we have required in other areas touching on federal court intrusion into local government, see, e.g., Spallone v. United States, 493 U.S. 265 (1990), is missing here. Even on the assumption that a federal court might order taxation in an extreme case, the unique nature of the taxing power would demand that this remedy be used as a last resort. In my view, a taxation order should not even be considered . . . unless there has been a finding that without the particular remedy at issue the constitutional violation will go unremedied. . . . There is no indication in the record that the District Court gave any consideration to the possibility that an alternative remedial plan, while less attractive from an educational policy viewpoint, might nonetheless suffice to cure the constitutional violation. . . .

The suggestion that our limited grant of certiorari requires us to decide this case blinkered as to the actual remedy underlying it is ill-founded. A limited grant of certiorari is not a means by which the Court can pose for itself an abstract question. Our jurisdiction is limited to particular cases and controversies. The only question this Court has authority to address is whether a judicial tax was appropriate *in this case.* Moreover, the petition for certiorari in this case included the contention that the District Court should not have considered the power to tax before considering whether its choice of remedy was the only possible way to achieve desegregation as a part of its argument on Question 2, which the Court granted. Far from being an improper invitation to go outside the question presented, attention to the extraordinary remedy here is the Court's duty. . . . If the Court is to take upon itself the power to tax, respect for its own integrity demands that the power be exercised in support of true constitutional principle, not "suburban comparability" and "visual attractiveness."

IV

This case is a stark illustration of the ever-present question whether ends justify means. Few ends are more important than enforcing the guarantee of equal educational opportunity for our nation's children. But rules of taxation that override state political structures not themselves subject to any constitutional infirmity raise serious questions of federal authority, questions compounded by the odd posture of a case in which the Court assumes the validity of a novel conception of desegregation remedies we never before have approved. The historical record of voluntary compliance with the decree of *Brown v. Board of Education* is not a proud chapter in our constitutional history, and the judges of the District Courts and Courts of Appeals have been courageous and skillful in implementing its mandate. But courage and skill must be exercised with due regard for the proper and historic role of the courts.

I do not acknowledge the troubling departures in today's majority opinion as either necessary or appropriate to ensure full compliance with the equal protection clause and its mandate to eliminate the cause and effects of racial discrimination in the schools. Indeed, while this case happens to arise in the compelling context of school desegregation, the principles involved are not limited to that context. There is no obvious limit to today's discussion that would prevent judicial taxation in cases involving prisons, hospitals, or other public institutions, or indeed to pay a large damages award levied against a municipality under 42 U.S.C. § 1983. The assertion of judicial power in one of the most sensitive of policy areas, that involving taxation, begins a process that over time could threaten fundamental alteration of the form of government our Constitution embodies.

James Madison observed: "Justice is the end of government. It is the end of civil society. It ever has been, and ever will be pursued, until it be obtained, or until liberty be lost in the pursuit." The Federalist, No. 51, p. 352 (J. Cooke ed. 1961). In pursuing the demand of justice for racial equality, I fear that the Court today loses sight of other basic political liberties guaranteed by our constitutional system, liberties that can coexist with a proper exercise of judicial remedial powers adequate to correct constitutional violations.

NOTES ON *MISSOURI v. JENKINS*

1. Introduction to Desegregation Strategies. To the uninitiated, the connection between the District Court's order in *Jenkins* and school segregation may seem obscure. On the surface, magnet schools and capital improvements have no obvious link to the racial distribution of students within the KCMSD. Yet these steps—and the raising of taxes to pay for them—were ordered as remedies for the unconstitutional segregation of Kansas City schools by state and local officials. No other basis for judicial authority was asserted. The relation between these remedies and the underlying constitutional violation requires a brief look at the evolving law of school desegregation.

The evil attacked in Brown v. Board of Education, 347 U.S. 483 (1954), was the formal and categorical separation of students by race. This officially enforced educational apartheid was practiced throughout the South and in several border states. Accordingly, early desegregation efforts focused exclusively on that region. Rapid progress was made in some border areas, but not in the South. Fully 10 years after *Brown,* most southern school districts had only token integration, and the vast majority of black children still attended all-black schools. Finally, in 1968, the Supreme Court lost patience. Green v. County School Board, 391 U.S. 430 (1968), required that desegregation be eliminated "root and branch" and that it be done "*now.*" This decision transformed the law of desegregation. No longer was it sufficient, as most lower courts had thought, for the government to stop *requiring* separation by race. Now, the school systems had an *affirmative obligation* to undo the effects of prior segregation. The object was a "unitary" school system, one without racially identifiable schools.

On the facts of *Green,* the affirmative obligation to desegregate was easily discharged. The county had only two schools, one black and one white, with residents of both races distributed more or less randomly throughout the jurisdiction. All that was required was to split the county into two districts and to send all children, both black and white, to the school in their district. This sort of plan was the rural equivalent of neighborhood schools, and it achieved substantial desegregation throughout the rural and small-town South.

In cities, however, in the South as elsewhere, residential segregation made the job of school integration more difficult. Neighborhood schools in segregated neighborhoods meant segregated schools. In urban areas, the *Green* mandate to eliminate racially identifiable schools required more drastic action. The solution was busing, which the Supreme Court first approved in Swann v. Charlotte-Mecklenburg Board of Education, 402 U.S. 1 (1971).

In *Swann* and in every case thereafter, busing was justified as a remedy for past de jure segregation. Changing judicial attitudes made de jure segregation easier to prove, and busing spread to cities of the North and West. See, e.g., Keyes v. School District No. 1, Denver, Colorado, 413 U.S. 189 (1973). But in every case, the essential first step was proof of some official misconduct that triggered the affirmative obligation to desegregate. Where no such misconduct could be proved—this was called de facto segregation—racially identifiable public schools were not unconstitutional, and busing could not be required.

Busing, of course, was enormously controversial, both in the courts and on the streets. Unlike *Brown,* which even in the South came to be accepted as a hallmark of morality and justice, busing never enjoyed widespread popular support. Indeed in most instances it faced intense and sometimes violent local opposition. The ultimate threat to busing, however, came not from political opposition, but from the demographics of the American city. Even as more and more cities were required to bus, the changing population of those cities—especially the population of school-age children—made racial balance in public schools less and less realistic. Increasingly, there were not enough white students to go around. As minority enrollment in urban school systems rose from 50 to 60 to 70 per cent and higher, redistribution of students within those districts began to seem almost pointless.[a]

The initial response to the changing demographics of urban centers was interdistrict busing. Bringing suburban school districts, most of which were white and many of which were wealthy, into a metropolitan busing plan would combat resegregation in two ways. First, it would increase the pool of white students and make the goal of integration more achievable. Second, it would make white flight more difficult by extending the reach of the city schools into near-by suburbs. Early cases came from Richmond and Detroit. In both, district judges faced overwhelmingly black inner cities surrounding by a ring of white suburbs. Their solution was to divide the metropolitan areas into pie-shaped wedges and order the exchange of students between predominately black city schools and the predominately white schools in the adjacent suburbs. This sort of plan promised to achieve greater integration—but only by altering the jurisdiction of local governments.

In Milliken v. Bradley, 418 U.S. 717 (1974), the Supreme Court rejected this strategy. The Court reiterated that the only basis for ordering busing was to remedy de jure segregation. Racial separation that did not result from official misconduct was no cause for constitutional concern. From this premise, the Court reasoned that the scope of the busing remedy had to reflect the scope of the constitutional violation. If only the city were found guilty of de jure segregation, then only the city could be required to bus. If the city and suburbs collaborated in maintaining segregation, then both could be brought within one busing plan. In other words, interdistrict busing required proof of an interdistrict violation.

Exactly what constituted an interdistrict violation was not entirely clear. Perhaps the easiest case was where the boundaries between urban and suburban school districts had been gerrymandered to perpetuate segregation. An interdistrict remedy would also be proper where the district lines had historically been ignored to promote segregation,

---

[a] Whether and to what extent busing itself contributed to the resegregation of urban school systems are hotly disputed issues. "White flight" is the usual label for whites choosing to live in the suburbs or to send their children to private school in order to avoid busing. Critics of busing tend to exaggerate white flight in order to show the futility of a policy they oppose. Supporters of busing often discount the phenomenon. The empirical evidence is plagued by local variation and debate over methodology and often supports divergent interpretations. Most observers, however, would agree on at least two points.

First, the chief cause of the increasing minority enrollment in urban school systems was a large-scale demographic movement that pre-dated busing and that cannot plausibly be seen as a response to that policy. Second, busing often exacerbated that development, especially in the years immediately following a new court order. Thus, although it is not reasonable to see busing as the cause of its own defeat, it is fair to say that compulsory transportation as a means of desegregation was more problematic than was at first appreciated. For a review of the social science literature on these issues, see Christine Rossell, Applied Social Science Research: What Does It Say About the Effectiveness of School Desegregation Plans?, 12 J. Legal Studies 69 (1983).

see Newburg Area Council v. Jefferson County Board of Education, 510 F.2d 1358 (6th Cir.1974), or the government had acted to create and maintain racial segregation as between city and suburbs. See, e.g., Evans v. Buchanan, 393 F.Supp. 428 (D.Del.1975). Absent some version of an interdistrict violation, however, the courts were barred from ordering an interdistrict remedy. The result was that desegregation usually had to be accomplished within the political boundaries of a single school system. For many American cities, with large and increasing minority school populations, busing no longer held much prospect of success.

Civil rights activists began to seek an alternative remedy. Foreclosed by precedent and demography from further desegregation through busing, many began to attack the educational consequences of segregation rather than the racial distribution of students. *Brown* had said that separate educational facilities were inherently unequal. Attention now shifted from separateness to inequality. If racial separation were built into the demographics of the American city, inequality need not be. In many American cities, the chief issue became not how to redistribute the declining number of white students among predominantly black schools, but rather how to improve the education offered to black students.

Of course, the two goals were not inconsistent. Indeed, they were synergistic. If inner city schools were made better, whites might not be so anxious to leave them. To the extent that white flight reflected a fear of inferior education (as opposed to simple racism), perhaps it could be reversed if education were improved. Thus did magnet schools become part of the approach to desegregation. Court-ordered improvements to urban schools were justified, in part, as a way of attracting white students. But the rhetoric did not hide an important change in emphasis. Whereas busing sought to improve black education as a by-product of increased racial mixing, magnet schools (and similar remedies) tried to increase racial mixing as a by-product of improved black education. The immediate focus shifted from racial integration to quality education. The judicial authority to require quality education, however, still proceeded from the same source—that is, from an initial finding of de jure segregation by the affected school district.

2. History of the *Jenkins* Litigation.[b] The litigation in Kansas City recapitulates the story told above. At the time of *Brown,* Missouri schools were segregated by law. Within a few years, formal segregation was gone, but racially identifiable schools lingered in Kansas City. Efforts to address this problem within the confines of the KCMSD were at first inadequate and later futile. In 1958–59, the KCMSD enrollment was 22.5 percent black, and the system retained majority white

---

[b] The facts stated here are taken primarily from the extensive opinions of the Eighth Circuit. See Jenkins v. Missouri, 807 F.2d 657 (8th Cir.1986), and Jenkins v. Missouri, 855 F.2d 1295 (8th Cir.1988).

enrollment until 1970. During that time, school-by-school racial balance could have been achieved, but was not. As late as 1974, 80 per cent of black students in the KCMSD attended schools that were more than 90 per cent black. Redistribution of students and the closing of some predominantly black schools increased the mix, but these changes were undercut by steadily declining white enrollment. By 1983–84, white enrollment had dropped to less than one-third of the total, and the trend continued. No feasible plan for redistributing those students could hope to eliminate predominantly one-race schools in Kansas City.

The local response was a suit for interdistrict busing. In Kansas City, as in so many urban centers, the increasingly black inner city was surrounded by largely white outlying areas. If the suburbs could be made to exchange students with the KCMSD, racial balance could be achieved, and the political support of wealthy suburbs might be enlisted to help fund urban schools. The suit was filed by the KCMSD (and some students) seeking to establish misconduct by itself and others (the state, various federal agencies, and surrounding school districts in Missouri and Kansas) that would justify *inter*district busing. The allegation of *intra*district segregation was added only later, after the KCMSD had been realigned as a party defendant. Despite this realignment, it seems clear that, from the beginning, the interests of the KCMSD lay with the desegregation plaintiffs rather than with the other government defendants.

First and foremost, KCMSD wanted relief from the racial imbalance and economic isolation of the center city; it wanted metropolitan busing. This the District Court refused to order. It found the suburban school districts had eliminated all vestiges of segregation and had achieved unitary school systems within four years (usually within one year) of *Brown*. The Court also found that no action by the suburbs or by the other government defendants had caused significant continuing interdistrict segregation. The racial disparity between city and suburbs did not result in appreciable degree from government action, but from social and economic conditions for which the defendants were not directly responsible. In other words, there was no interdistrict violation. Therefore, there could be no interdistrict busing.[c]

Attention then turned to what could be done within the KCMSD to undo the lingering effects of the inferior education indigenous to segregated school systems. The magnet school plan and the capital improvements program were ordered to address that problem. The rationale was succinctly explained by the Eighth Circuit:

> "The District Court's remedial orders were based on the elementary principle that the victims of unconstitutional segregation must be made whole, and that to make them whole it

[c] For detailed discussion of the evidence and reasoning underlying this conclusion, see Jenkins v. Missouri, 807 F.2d 657 (8th Cir.1986).

will be necessary to improve their educational opportunities and to reduce their racial isolation. The foundation of the plans adopted was the idea that improving the KCMSD as a system would at the same time compensate the blacks for the education they had been denied and attract whites from within and without the KCMSD to formerly black schools. The long term goal of the District Court's effort was therefore: 'to make available to *all* KCMSD students educational opportunities equal to or greater than those presently available in the average Kansas City, Missouri metropolitan suburban school district.'"

On this rationale, the District Court's orders were approved.

3. Questions and Comments on *Jenkins*. By any estimate, the *Jenkins* order was far-reaching. The decision to create magnet schools for the whole system and the extent of new construction required are unusually aggressive remedies with predictably large price tags. Yet the Supreme Court specifically declined to review the validity of the order and agreed to hear only the question of how it might be enforced. This left the case in an unusual posture. The parties were invited to contest the property tax increase on the assumption that the underlying order was proper, but it is not clear that the two issues can so easily be kept separate. Would the dissenters have objected so vociferously to "judicial taxation" if they had not been concerned about the remedy?

Consider the issue on the facts of Griffin v. County School Bd. of Prince Edward County, 377 U.S. 218 (1964). *Griffin* involved the notorious decision by Prince Edward County, Virginia, to close its public schools rather than submit to integration. Various ways were found to funnel public money to private white academies, but black students were left without schools. It seems beyond any shadow of dispute that the federal courts could (as in fact they did) stop all forms of public money and assistance for the white academies. But could the courts also (as in fact they did) order the county to reopen the public schools, to provide the necessary money for their operation, and, if necessary, to raise taxes for that purpose? Is that the same issue presented in *Jenkins*? Would the dissenters have balked at judicial taxation in Prince Edward County? If so, would they be willing to curtail the enforcement of constitutional rights whenever there was a problem with money?

If "judicial taxation" would be proper on the facts of *Griffin,* what is the dispute in *Jenkins* all about? Is the case nothing more than a continuing debate about the limited grant of certiorari?

On the assumption that a federal court has the authority to raise local taxes, a subsidiary issue arises about the best way to do so. The majority disapproved the District Court's actions in setting new property tax rates and requiring issuance of bonds to finance the capital improvements. Instead, the District Court should have "authorized or required KCMSD to levy property taxes at a rate adequate to fund the desegregation remedy and [should] have enjoined the operation of state laws that would have prevented KCMSD from exercising this power." The majority insisted that the difference between direct judicial taxation and judicial coercion of local taxation was "far more than a matter of form." Is that true? If the court's authority to override state law in requiring higher local taxes is conceded, does it really matter just how that authority is exercised?

There is at least one more dimension of the *Jenkins* problem. Assuming that compelled local taxation is sometimes a permissible federal court remedy, for what kinds of constitutional violations might it be invoked? Could it, as the dissenters hypothesize, be ordered "in cases involving prisons, hospitals, or other public institutions, or indeed to pay a large damages award levied against a municipality under 42 U.S.C. § 1983"?

SPALLONE v. UNITED STATES
Supreme Court of the United States, 1990.
493 U.S. 265.

CHIEF JUSTICE REHNQUIST delivered the opinion of the Court.

This case is the most recent episode of a lengthy lawsuit in which the city of Yonkers was held liable for intentionally enhancing racial segregation in housing in Yonkers. The issue here is whether it was a proper exercise of judicial power for the District Court to hold petitioners, four Yonkers city councilmembers, in contempt for refusing to vote in favor of legislation implementing a consent decree earlier approved by the city. We hold that in the circumstances of this case, the District Court abused its discretion.

I

In 1980, the United States filed a complaint alleging, inter alia, that the two named defendants—the city of Yonkers and the Yonkers Community Development Agency—had intentionally engaged in a pattern and practice of housing discrimination, in violation of title VII of the Civil Rights Act of 1968 and the equal protection clause of the 14th amendment. The government and plaintiff-intervenor National Association for the Advancement of Colored People (NAACP) asserted that the city had, over a period of three decades, selected sites for subsidized housing in order to perpetuate residential racial segregation. The plaintiffs' theory was that the city had equated subsidized housing for families with minority housing, and thus disproportionately restricted new family housing projects to areas of the city—particularly southwest Yonkers—already predominately populated by minorities.

The District Court found the two named defendants liable, concluding that the segregative effect of the city's actions had been "consistent and extreme," and that "the desire to preserve existing patterns of segregation ha[d] been a significant factor in the sustained community opposition to subsidized housing in East Yonkers and other overwhelmingly white areas of the city." The District Court in its remedial decree . . . required affirmative steps to disperse public housing throughout Yonkers. Part IV of the order noted that the city previously had committed itself to provide acceptable sites for 200 units of public housing as a condition for receiving 1983 Community Development Block Grant funds from the federal government, but had failed to do so. Consequently, it required the city to designate sites for 200 units of public housing in East Yonkers. . . . Part VI directed the city to develop by November 1986 a long-term plan "for the creation of additional subsidized family housing units . . . in existing residential areas in east or northwest Yonkers." The court did not mandate specific details of the plan such as how many subsidized units must be developed, where they should be constructed, or how the city should provide for the units.

Under the charter of the city of Yonkers all legislative powers are vested in the city council, which consists of an elected mayor and six councilmembers, including petitioners. The city, for all practical purposes, therefore, acts through the city council when it comes to the enactment of legislation. Pending appeal of the District Court's liability and remedial orders, however, the city did not comply with Parts IV and VI of the remedial order. . . . The United States and the NAACP then moved for an adjudication of civil contempt and the imposition of coercive sanctions, but the District Court declined to take that action. Instead, it secured an agreement from the city to appoint an outside housing advisor to identify sites for the 200 units of public housing and to draft a long-term plan.

In December 1987, the Court of Appeals for the Second Circuit affirmed the District Court's judgment in all respects, and we subsequently denied certiorari. Shortly after the Court of Appeals' decision, in January 1988, the parties agreed to a consent decree that set forth "certain actions which the city of Yonkers [would] take in connection with a consensual implementation of Parts IV and VI" of the housing remedy order. The decree was approved by the city council in a five-to-two vote (petitioners Spallone and Chema voting no), and entered by the District Court as a consent judgment on January 28, 1988. Sections 12 through 18 of the decree established the framework for the long-term plan and are the underlying bases for the contempt orders at issue in this case. Perhaps most significant was § 17, in which the city agreed to adopt, within 90 days, legislation conditioning the construction of all multifamily housing on the inclusion of at least 20 per cent assisted units, granting tax abatements and density bonuses to developers, and providing for zoning changes to allow the placement of housing developments.

For several more months, however, the city continued to delay action toward implementing the long-term plan. [On June 13, 1988, the District Court entered an order] which provided greater detail for the legislation prescribed by § 17 of the decree. After several weeks of further delay the court, after a hearing held on July 26, 1988, entered an order requiring the city of Yonkers to enact on or before August 1, 1988, the "legislative package" described in a section of the earlier consent decree; the second paragraph provided:

> "It is further ORDERED that, in the event the city of Yonkers fails to enact the legislative package on or before August 1, 1988, the city of Yonkers shall be required to show cause at a hearing before this court at 10:00 a.m. on August 2, 1988, why it should not be held in contempt, and each individual city council member shall be required to show cause at a hearing before this court at 10:00 a.m. on August 2, 1988, why he should not be held in contempt."

Further provisions of the order specified escalating daily amounts of fines in the event of contempt, and provided that if the legislation were not enacted before August 10, 1988, any councilmember who remained in contempt should be committed to the custody of the United States Marshal for imprisonment. The specified daily fines for the city were $100 for the first day, to be doubled for each consecutive day of noncompliance; the specified daily fine for members of the city council was $500 per day.

Notwithstanding the threat of substantial sanctions, on August 1 the city council defeated a resolution of intent to adopt the legislative package, known as the Affordable Housing Ordinance, by a vote of four to three (petitioners constituting the majority). On August 2, the District Court [held both the city and the councilmembers in contempt.]

On August 17, the Court of Appeals stayed the contempt sanctions pending appeal. Shortly thereafter, the court affirmed the adjudications of contempt against both the city and the councilmembers, but limited the fines against the city so that they would not exceed $1 million per day. . . .

Both the city and the councilmembers requested this Court to stay imposition of sanctions pending filing and disposition of petitions for certiorari. We granted a stay as to petitioners, but denied the city's request. With the city's daily contempt sanction approaching $1 million per day, the city council finally enacted the Affordable Housing Ordinance on September 9, 1988, by a vote of five to two, petitioners Spallone and Fagan voting no. Because the contempt orders raise important issues about the appropriate exercise of the federal judicial power against individual legislators, we granted certiorari and now reverse.

II

The issue before us is relatively narrow. There can be no question about the liability of the city of Yonkers for racial discrimination. . . . Nor do we have before us any question as to the District Court's remedial order. . . . Our focus, then, is only on the District Court's order of July 26 imposing contempt sanctions on the individual petitioners if they failed to vote in favor of the ordinance in question.

Petitioners contend that the District Court's orders violate their rights to freedom of speech under the first amendment, and they also contend that they are entitled as legislators to absolute immunity for actions taken in discharge of their legislative responsibilities. We find it unnecessary to reach either of these questions, because we conclude that the portion of the District Court's order of July 26 imposing contempt sanctions against the petitioners if they failed to vote in favor of the court-proposed ordinance was an abuse of discretion under traditional equitable principles. . . .

In selecting a means to enforce the consent judgment, the District Court was entitled to rely on the axiom that "courts have inherent power to enforce compliance with their lawful orders through civil contempt." Shillitani v. United States, 384 U.S. 364, 370 (1966). When a district court's order is necessary to remedy past discrimination, the court has an additional basis for the exercise of broad equitable powers. See Swann v. Charlotte–Mecklenburg Bd. of Ed., 402 U.S. 1, 15 (1971). But while "remedial powers of an equity court must be adequate to the task, . . . they are not unlimited." Whitcomb v. Chavis, 403 U.S. 124, 161 (1971). "[T]he federal courts in devising a remedy must take into account the interests of state and local authorities in managing their own affairs, consistent with the Constitution." Milliken v. Bradley, 433 U.S. 267, 280–81 (1977). And the use of the contempt power places an additional limitation on a district court's discretion, for as the Court of Appeals recognized, "in selecting contempt sanctions, a court is obliged to use the 'least possible power adequate to the end proposed.'" United States v. City of Yonkers, 856 F.2d 444, 454 (2d Cir.1988).

Given that the city had entered a consent judgment committing itself to enact legislation implementing the long-term plan, we certainly cannot say it was an abuse of discretion for the District Court to have chosen contempt sanctions against the city, as opposed to petitioners, as a means of ensuring compliance. The city, as we have noted, was a party to the action from the beginning, had been found liable for numerous statutory and constitutional violations, and had been subjected to various elaborate remedial decrees which had been upheld on appeal. Petitioners, the individual city councilmen, on the other hand, were not parties to the action, and they had not been found individually liable for any of the violations upon which the remedial decree was based. Although the injunctive portion of that decree was directed not only to the city but to "its officers, agents, employees, successors and all persons in active concert or participation with any of them," the remaining parts of the decree ordering affirmative steps were directed only to the city.

It was, in fact, the city which capitulated. After the Court of Appeals had briefly stayed the imposition of sanctions in August, and we granted a stay as to petitioners but denied it to the city in September, the city council on September 9, 1988, finally enacted the Affordable Housing Ordinance by a vote of five to two. While the District Court could not have been sure in late July that this would be the result, the city's arguments against imposing sanctions on it pointed out the sort of pressure that such sanctions would place on the city. After just two weeks of fines, the city's emergency financial plan required it to curtail sanitation services (resulting in uncollected garbage), eliminate part-time school crossing guards, close all public libraries and parks and lay off approximately 477 employees. In the ensuing four weeks, the city would have been forced to lay off another 1100 city employees.

Only eight months earlier, the District Court had secured compliance with an important remedial order through the threat of bankrupting fines against the city alone. . . .

The nub of the matter, then, is whether in the light of the reasonable probability that sanctions against the city would accomplish the desired result, it was within the court's discretion to impose sanctions on the petitioners as well under the circumstances of this case.

In Tenney v. Brandhove, 341 U.S. 367 (1951), we held that state legislators were absolutely privileged in their legislative acts in an action against them for damages. We applied this same doctrine of legislative immunity to regional legislatures in Lake County Estates, Inc. v. Tahoe Regional Planning Agency, 440 U.S. 391, 404–05 (1979), and to actions for both damages and injunctive relief in Supreme Court of Virginia v. Consumers Union of United States, Inc., 446 U.S. 719, 731–34 (1980). The holdings in these cases do not control the question whether local legislators such as petitioners should be immune from contempt sanctions imposed for failure to vote in favor of a particular legislative bill. But some of the same considerations on which the immunity doctrine is based must inform the District Court's exercise of its discretion in a case such as this. "Freedom of speech and action in the legislature," we observed, "was taken as a matter of course by those who severed the Colonies from the Crown and founded our nation." *Tenney,* supra, at 372.

In perhaps the earliest American case to consider the import of the legislative privilege, the Supreme Judicial Court of Massachusetts, interpreting a provision of the Massachusetts Constitution granting the rights of freedom of speech and debate to state legislators, recognized that "the privilege secured by it is not so much the privilege of the house as an organized body, *as of each individual member composing it, who is entitled to this privilege, even against the declared will of the house.* For he does not hold this privilege at the pleasure of the house; but derives it from the will of the people. . . ." Coffin v. Coffin, 4 Mass. 1, 27 (1808). This theme underlies our cases interpreting the speech or debate clause and the federal common law of legislative immunity, where we have emphasized that any restriction on a legislator's freedom undermines the "public good" by interfering with the rights of the people to representation in the democratic process. The District Court was quite sensitive to this fact; it observed:

> "I know of no parallel for a court to say to an elected official, 'You are in contempt of court and subject to personal fines and may eventually be subject to personal imprisonment because of a manner in which you cast a vote.' I find that extraordinary."

Sanctions directed against the city for failure to take actions such as required by the consent decree coerce the city legislators and, of course, restrict the freedom of those legislators to act in accordance with their current view of the city's best interests. But we believe there are significant differences between the two types of fines. The imposition of sanctions on individual legislators is designed to cause them to vote, not with a view to the interest of their constituents or of the city, but with a view solely to their own personal interests. Even though an individual legislator took the extreme position—or felt that his constituents took the extreme position—that even a huge fine against the city was preferable to enacting the Affordable Housing Ordinance, monetary sanctions against him individually would motivate him to vote to enact the ordinance simply because he did not want to be out of pocket financially. Such fines thus encourage legislators, in effect, to declare that they favor an ordinance not in order to avoid bankrupting the city for which they legislate, but in order to avoid bankrupting themselves.

This sort of individual sanction effects a much greater perversion of the normal legislative process than does the imposition of sanctions on the city for the failure of these same legislators to enact an ordinance. In that case, the legislator is only encouraged to vote in favor of an ordinance that he would not otherwise favor by reason of the adverse sanctions imposed on the city. A councilman who felt that his constituents would rather have the city enact the Affordable Housing Ordinance than pay a "bankrupting fine" would be motivated to vote in favor of such an ordinance because the sanctions were a threat to the fiscal solvency of the city for whose welfare he was in part responsible. This is the sort of calculus in which legislators engage regularly.

We hold that the District Court, in view of the "extraordinary" nature of the imposition sanctions against the individual councilmen, should have proceeded with such contempt sanctions first against the city alone in order to secure compliance with the remedial orders. Only if that approach failed to produce compliance within a reasonable time should the question of imposing contempt sanctions against petitioners have been considered. "This limitation accords with the doctrine that a court must exercise '[t]he least possible power adequate to the end proposed.'" *Shillitani v. United States,* supra, at 371.

JUSTICE BRENNAN with whom JUSTICE MARSHALL, JUSTICE BLACKMUN, and JUSTICE STEVENS join, dissenting.

I understand and appreciate the Court's concern about the District Court's decision to impose contempt sanctions against local officials acting in a legislative capacity. We must all hope that no court will ever again face the open and sustained defiance of established constitutional values and valid judicial orders that prompted Judge Sand's invocation of the contempt power in this manner. But I firmly believe that its availability for such use, in extreme circumstances, is essential. As the District Court was aware:

> "The issues transcend Yonkers. They go to the very foundation of the system of constitutional government. If Yonkers can defy the orders of a federal court in any case, but especially a civil rights case, because compliance is unpopular, and if that situation is tolerated, then our constitutional system of government fails. The issues before the court this morning are no less significant than that."

The Court today recognizes that it was appropriate for the District Court to hold in contempt and fine the city of Yonkers to encourage the city councilmembers to comply with their prior promise to redress the city's history of racial segregation. Yet the Court also reprimands the District Court for simultaneously fining the individual councilmembers whose continuing defiance was the true source of the impasse, holding that personal sanctions should have been considered only after the city sanctions first proved fruitless.

I cannot accept this parsimonious view of the District Court's discretion to wield the power of contempt. Judge Sand's intimate contact for many years with the recalcitrant councilmembers and his familiarity with the city's political climate gave him special insight into the best way to coerce compliance when all cooperative efforts had failed. From our detached vantage point, we can hardly judge as well as he which coercive sanctions or combination thereof were most likely to work quickly and least disruptively. Because the Court's ex post rationalization of what Judge Sand should have done fails to do justice either to the facts of the case or the art of judging, I must dissent.

I

[Justice Brennan's detailed factual history is omitted.]

II

. . . The Court's disfavor of personal sanctions rests on two premises: (1) Judge Sand should have known when he issued the contempt order that there was a "reasonable probability that sanctions against the city [alone] would accomplish the desired result"; and (2) imposing personal fines "effects a much greater perversion of the normal legislative process than does the imposition of sanctions on the city." Because personal fines were both completely superfluous to and more intrusive than sanctions against the city alone, the Court reasons, the personal fines constituted an abuse of discretion. Each of these premises is mistaken.

A

While acknowledging that Judge Sand "could not have been sure in late July that this would have been the result," the Court confidently concludes that Judge Sand should have been *sure enough* that fining the city would eventually coerce compliance that he should not have personally fined the councilmembers as well. In light of the information available to Judge Sand in July, the Court's confidence is chimerical. Although the escalating city fines eventually would have seriously disrupted many public services and employment, the Court's failure even to consider the possibility that the councilmembers would maintain their defiant posture despite the threat of fiscal insolvency bespeaks an ignorance of Yonkers' history of entrenched discrimination and an indifference to Yonkers' political reality.

The Court first fails to adhere to our longstanding recognition that the "district court has firsthand experience with the parties and is best qualified to deal with the 'flinty, intractable realities of day-to-day implementation of constitutional commands.'" United States v. Paradise, 480 U.S. 149, 184 (1987) (quoting Swann v. Charlotte–Mecklenburg Board of Education, 402 U.S. 1, 6 (1971)). Deference to the court's exercise of discretion is particularly appropriate where, as here, the record clearly reveals that the court employed extreme caution before taking the final step of holding the councilmembers personally in contempt. Judge Sand patiently weathered a whirlwind of evasive maneuvers and misrepresentations; considered and rejected alternative means of securing compliance other than contempt sanctions; and carefully considered the ramifications of personal fines. In the end, he readily acknowledged:

> "I know of no parallel for a court to say to an elected official: 'You are in contempt of court and subject to personal fines and may eventually be subject to personal imprisonment because of a manner in which you cast a vote.' I find that extraordinary.
>
> "I find it so extraordinary that at great cost in terms of time and in terms of money and energy and implementation of court's orders, I have sought alternatives to that. But they have all been unsuccessful. . . ."

After according no weight to Judge Sand's cautious and contextual judgment despite his vastly superior vantage point, the Court compounds its error by committing two more. First, the Court turns a blind eye to most of the evidence available to Judge Sand suggesting that, because of the councilmembers' continuing intransigence, sanctions against the city alone might not coerce compliance and that personal sanctions would significantly increase the chance of success. Second, the Court fails to acknowledge that supplementing city sanctions with personal ones likely would secure compliance more promptly, minimizing the overall disruptive effect of the city sanctions on city services generally and long-term compliance with the consent decree in particular.

As the events leading up to the contempt order make clear, the recalcitrant councilmembers were extremely responsive to strong segments of their constituencies that were vociferously opposed to racial residential integration. Councilmember Fagan, for example, explained that his vote against the Housing Ordinance required by the consent decree "was an act of defiance. The people clearly wanted me to say no to the judge." Councilmember Spallone declared openly that "I will be taking on the judge all the way down the line. I made a commitment to my people and that commitment remains." Moreover, once Yonkers had gained national attention over its refusal to integrate, many residents made it clear to their representatives on the council that they preferred bankrupt martyrdom to integration. As a contemporaneous article observed, "[t]he defiance councilmen are riding a wave of resentment among their white constituents that is so intense that many insist they are willing to see the city bankrupted. . . ." N.Y. Times, Aug. 5, 1988. It thus was not evident that petitioners opposed bankrupting the city; at the very least, capitulation by any individual councilmember was widely perceived as political suicide. As a result, even assuming that each recalcitrant member sought to avoid city bankruptcy, each still had a very strong incentive to play "chicken" with his colleagues by continuing to defy the contempt order while secretly hoping that at least one colleague would change his position and suffer the wrath of the electorate. As Judge Sand observed, "[w]hat we have here is competition to see who can attract the greatest notoriety, who will be the political martyr . . . *without regard to what is in the best interests of the city of Yonkers*" (emphasis added). . . .

The Court, in addition to ignoring all of this evidence before concluding that city sanctions alone would eventually coerce compliance, also inexplicably ignores the fact that imposing personal fines in addition to sanctions against the city would not only help ensure but actually *hasten* compliance. City sanctions, by design, impede the normal operation of local government. Judge Sand knew that each day the councilmembers remained in contempt, the city would suffer an ever-growing financial drain that threatened not only to disrupt many critical city services but also to frustrate the long-term success of the underlying remedial scheme. Fines assessed against the public fisc directly "diminish the limited resources which the city has to comply with the decree," United States v. Providence, 492 F.Supp. 602, 610 (D.R.I.1980), and more generally curtail various public services with a likely disparate impact on poor and minority residents.

Given these ancillary effects of city sanctions, it seems to me entirely appropriate—indeed obligatory—for Judge Sand to have considered not just whether city sanctions alone would *eventually* have coerced compliance, but also *how promptly* they would have done so. The Court's implicit conclusion that personal sanctions were redundant both exaggerates the likelihood that city sanctions alone would have worked at all and also fails to give due weight to the importance of speed, because supplementing the city sanctions with personal sanctions certainly increased the odds for prompt success. At the very least, personal sanctions made political martyrdom a much more unattractive option for the councilmembers. In light of the tremendous stakes at issue, I cannot fault Judge Sand for deciding to err on the side of being safe rather than sorry. . . .

B

The Court purports to bolster its judgment by contending that personal sanctions against councilmembers effect a greater interference than city sanctions with the "interests of . . . local authorities in managing their own affairs." Without holding today that the doctrine of absolute legislative immunity itself is applicable to local (as opposed to state and regional) legislative bodies, the Court declares that the principle of legislative independence underlying this doctrine "must inform the District Court's exercise of its discretion in a case such as this." . . .

The doctrine of legislative immunity recognizes that, when acting collectively to pursue a vision of the public good through legislation, legislators must be free to represent their constituents "without fear of outside interference" that would result from private lawsuits. Supreme Court of Virginia v. Consumers Union of the United States, Inc., 446 U.S. 719, 731 (1980). Of course, legislators are bound to respect the limits placed on their discretion by the federal Constitution; they are duty-bound not to enact laws they believe to be unconstitutional, and their laws will have no effect to the extent that courts believe them to be unconstitutional. But when acting "in the sphere of legitimate legislative activity," Tenney v. Brandhove, 341 U.S. 367, 376 (1951)— i.e., formulating and expressing their vision of the public good within self-defined constitutional boundaries—legislators are to be "immune from deterrents to the uninhibited discharge of their legislative duty." Id. at 377. Private lawsuits threaten to chill robust representation by encouraging legislators to avoid controversial issues or stances in order to protect themselves "not only from the consequences of litigation's results but also from the burden of defending themselves." *Supreme Court of Virginia,* supra, at 732. To encourage legislators best to represent their constituents' interests, legislators must be afforded immunity from private suit.

But once a federal court has issued a valid order to remedy the effects of a prior, specific constitutional violation, the representatives are no longer "acting in a field where legislators traditionally have power to act." *Tenney,* supra, at 379. At this point, the Constitution itself imposes an overriding definition of the "public good," and a court's valid command to obey constitutional dictates is not subject to override by any countervailing preference of the polity, no matter how widely and ardently shared. Local legislators, for example, may not frustrate valid remedial decrees merely because they or their constituents would rather allocate public funds for other uses. More to the point here, legislators certainly may not defy court-ordered remedies for racial discrimination merely because their constituents prefer to maintain segregation. . . .

III

The Court's decision today that Judge Sand abused his remedial discretion by imposing personal fines simultaneously with city fines creates no new principle of law; indeed, it invokes no principle of any sort. But it directs a message to district judges that, despite their repeated and close contact with the various parties and issues, even the most delicate remedial choices by the most conscientious and deliberate judges are subject to being second-guessed by this Court. I hope such a message will not daunt the courage of district courts who, if ever again faced with such protracted defiance, must carefully yet firmly secure compliance with their remedial orders. But I worry that the Court's message will have the unintended effect of emboldening recalcitrant officials continually to test the ultimate reach of the remedial authority of the federal courts, thereby postponing the day when all public officers finally accept that "the responsibility of those who exercise power in a democratic government is not to reflected inflamed public feeling but to help form its understanding." Cooper v. Aaron, 358 U.S. 1, 26 (1958) (Frankfurter, J., concurring).

NOTE ON *SPALLONE v. UNITED STATES*

Jenkins and *Spallone* make an interesting pair. In *Jenkins,* the Court held it permissible for the District Court to raise local taxes to fund a desegregation decree. In *Spallone,* the Court held that it was error for the District Court to hold individual city officers in contempt for refusing to implement a court order. Are the two decisions consistent? If the trial court in *Jenkins* had required local officials to raise property taxes and if, contrary to the likely outcome there, they had refused, what could the District Court have done about it? Could the officials then have been held in contempt? If so, what is the problem with *Spallone*? If not, how else could the taxes be raised?

The majority in *Spallone* thought that there was an important difference between holding local officials in contempt and holding the local government itself in contempt. And they thought it better to act against the city than the individuals. Could a case be made that this is backwards? As the dissent argues, who suffers if city services are terminated because money is needed to pay the federal contempt fine? And if capitulation by the individuals is required in order to lift the contempt against the city, is it realistic to suggest that an important component of legislative independence has been preserved?

Would these problems be better addressed if the choice among remedies were left to the district and circuit courts to be worked out on the facts of each case? What is the Supreme Court's role in such matters? What did the Court actually accomplish in *Jenkins* and *Spallone*?

For wide-ranging discussion of remedies for federal constitutional violations, with particular focus on *Jenkins* and *Spallone,* see Barry Friedman, When Rights Encounter Reality: Enforcing Federal Remedies, 65 So.Cal.L.Rev. 735 (1992).

Chapter VII

STATE SOVEREIGN IMMUNITY AND THE 11TH AMENDMENT

Pages 697-98, add to footnote g:

For an argument that *Hans* should not be read to bar federal claims against the states in federal court because the case involved only the assertion of a common law contract claim that was held to be barred by common law sovereign immunity, see William Burnham, Taming the Eleventh Amendment Without Overruling *Hans v. Louisiana*, 40 Case Western Res.L. Rev. 931 (1989-90).

Page 700, add at the end of the last paragraph of Note 4(ii):

For extensive discussions rejecting the diversity interpretation, see William Marshall, The Diversity Theory of the Eleventh Amendment: A Critical Evaluation, 102 Harv.L.Rev. 1372 (1989), and Calvin Massey, State Sovereignty and the Tenth and Eleventh Amendments, 56 U.Chi. L.Rev. 61 (1989). For a reply, see William Fletcher, The Diversity Explanation of the Eleventh Amendment: A Reply to Critics, 56 U.Chi. L.Rev. 1261 (1989). See also Exchange on the Eleventh Amendment (between Calvin Massey, William Marshall, Lawrence Marshall, and William Fletcher), 57 U.Chi.L.Rev. 117 (1990); Suzanna Sherry, The Eleventh Amendment and Stare Decisis: Overruling *Hans v. Louisiana*, 57 U.Chi.L.Rev. 1260 (1990); Akhil Amar, *Marbury*, Section 13, and the Original Jurisdiction of the Supreme Court, 56 U.Chi.L.Rev. 443, 493-99 (1989).

Page 701, add to footnote *l*:

For an elaborate consideration of all three theories discussed above and a plea for paying more attention to the text of the 11th amendment, see Lawrence Marshall, Fighting the Words of the Eleventh Amendment, 102 Harv.L.Rev. 1342 (1989). To the opposite effect, see Vicki Jackson, The Supreme Court, the Eleventh Amendment, and State Sovereign Immunity, 98 Yale L.J. 1 (1988), and Gene Shreve, Letting Go of the Eleventh Amendment, 64 Indiana L.J. 601 (1989), both of which suggest replacing current 11th amendment doctrine with a fresh approach to state sovereign immunity. Jackson elaborately argues that "the articulation of sovereign immunity as a constitutional principle" is unjustified and for the "gradual evolution of a more focused and candid development of the law of remedies for governmental wrongdoing." Shreve dismisses the 11th amendment as "a historical artifact" whose "role in modern constitutional law should be only slightly greater than article I's denial to Congress of the authority to confer titles of nobility." See also Allen Easley, The Supreme Court and the 11th Amendment: Mourning the Last Opportunity to Synthesize Conflicting Precedents, 64 Denver U.L. Rev. 485 (1988), which explores the doctrinal inconsistencies in the Court's 11th amendment jurisprudence. Finally, for an article locating the 11th amendment in a wide-ranging examination of conflicting "federalist" and "nationalist" models in federal courts law, see Richard H. Fallon, Jr., The Ideologies of Federal Courts Law, 74 Va.L.Rev. 1141 (1988).

Page 727, add a footnote after the third line on the page:

a For recent consideration of the consent issue, see Port Authority Trans–Hudson Corp. v. Feeney, 495 U.S. 299 (1990). The Port Authority Trans–Hudson Corp. (PATH) operates an interstate railway system, among other facilities. It is a wholly owned subsidiary of the Port Authority of New York and New Jersey, an entity created in a bi-state compact in 1921. Two employees sued PATH under the FELA and several other related federal statutes. PATH sought dismissal of the suits on the ground that it enjoyed the 11th amendment immunity of its creating states. The Court held that the suits could go forward.

Justice O'Connor wrote the Court's opinion. She first assumed without deciding that PATH was a state agency for 11th amendment purposes. She then said that the "Court will give effect to a state's waiver of 11th amendment immunity ' "only where stated by the most express language or by such overwhelming implication from the text as [will] leave no room for any other reasonable construction." ' " The governing statutes provided that the Port Authority (and hence PATH) would be subject to suits "of any form or nature at law, in equity or otherwise." This, the Court said, was not enough: "Sensitive to the values underlying the 11th amendment, the Court has required that consent to suit in *federal* court be express and thus has construed . . . ambiguous and general consent to suit provisions, standing alone, as insufficient to waive 11th amendment immunity." (Emphasis added.) But here the consent provisions did not stand alone. It was provided that venue for such actions could be in a judicial district "established by one of [the] States or by the United States" within the Port of New York area. This venue provision indicated clearly enough an intention to consent to suit in federal court.

Justice Brennan, joined by Justices Marshall, Blackmun, and Stevens, concurred in the judgment. He thought the 11th amendment inapplicable because neither the Port Authority nor PATH was, in the language of the 11th amendment, "one of the United States." He also restated his view, developed in more detail below, that the 11th amendment is inapplicable in federal question cases.

Page 735, add a footnote at the end of the third line on the page:

b *Hutto* was applied in Missouri v. Jenkins, 491 U.S. 274 (1989), to approve enhancement of an award of fees against the state to account for delay in payment. The 11th amendment was found inapplicable to an award of fees incidental to prospective relief. Explicit authorization of enhancement for late payment was therefore unnecessary. Justice O'Connor, joined by Chief Justice Rehnquist and Justice Scalia, dissented.

Page 736, add a footnote at the end of Note 3:

c A decade later, the Court extended the result in *Quern* to a circumstance where the 11th amendment is technically inapplicable. Will v. Michigan Department of State Police, 491 U.S. 58 (1989), was a § 1983 action brought in state court, where the 11th amendment does not apply. The Supreme Court nevertheless held the action barred on the ground that "person" as that term is used in § 1983 does not include states or state agencies. For fuller treatment of this decision, see this Supplement at pages 3 and 41, supra.

Page 737, add to footnote d:

For similar decisions finding no clear statement of an intent to override 11th amendment immunity, see Dellmuth v. Muth, 491 U.S. 223 (1989) (Education of the Handicapped Act), and Hoffman v. Connecticut Dept. of Income Maintenance, 492 U.S. 96 (1989) (Bankruptcy Act).

Page 737, delete Note 5 and substitute for pages 737–52:

5. *Welch v. Texas Department of Highways and Public Transportation.* There is an obvious tension between *Atascadero* and *Parden v. Terminal Ry.,* discussed at page 727 of the Casebook. The dissenters in *Parden* recognized the *power* of Congress to abrogate the sovereign immunity of the states through the regulation of commerce, but suggested that "its intention to do so should appear with unmistakable clarity." For the majority, something less than "unmistakable clarity" was sufficient.

This tension was resolved in Welch v. State Department of Highways and Public Transportation, 483 U.S. 468 (1987). The Jones Act, 46 U.S.C. § 688(a), provides a cause of action for injured seamen. *Welch* was a Jones Act case against the state of Texas and its highway department arising from injuries that occurred to a highway department employee on a ferry dock in Galveston. The District Court dismissed the action as barred by the 11th amendment and the Court of Appeals affirmed, holding that the Jones Act did not speak to the 11th amendment point with unmistakable clarity. Justice Powell announced the judgment of the Court overruling *Parden* and affirming the dismissal.

Speaking for a plurality of four, Justice Powell first said that the Jones Act did not abrogate the state's sovereign immunity:

"We assume, without deciding or intimating a view of the question, that the authority of Congress to subject unconsenting states to suit in federal court is not confined to § 5 of the 14th amendment. Petitioner's argument fails in any event because Congress has not expressed in unmistakable statutory language its intention to allow states to be sued in federal court under the Jones Act." [e]

After observing that "*Parden* is relevant to this case because the Jones Act applied the remedial provisions of the FELA to seamen," he then confronted *Parden*'s continuing vitality:

"Although our later decisions do not expressly overrule *Parden,* they leave no doubt that *Parden*'s discussion of congressional intent to negate 11th amendment immunity is no longer good law. . . . In subsequent cases the Court consistently has required an unequivocal expression that congress intended to override 11th amendment immunity. [Citing *Atascadero* and *Quern v. Jordan.*] Accordingly, to the extent that *Parden* is inconsistent with the requirement that an abrogation of 11th amendment immunity by Congress must be expressed in unmistakably clear language, it is overruled." [8]

The fifth vote to overrule *Parden* came from Justice Scalia, whose concurrence in the judgment is reproduced below in full:

[e] Justice Powell had previously noted that no question of "waiver" or "consent" was before the Court.

[8] "[W]e have no occasion in this case to consider the validity of the additional holding in *Parden*, that Congress has the power to abrogate the states' 11th amendment immunity under the commerce clause to the extent that the states are engaged in interstate commerce."

"The petitioner in this case did not assert as a basis for reversing the judgment that Hans v. Louisiana, 134 U.S. 1 (1890), had been wrongly decided. That argument was introduced by an amicus, addressed only briefly in respondent's brief, and touched upon only lightly at oral argument. I find both the correctness of *Hans* as an original matter, and the feasibility, if it was wrong, of correcting it without distorting what we have done in tacit reliance upon it, complex enough questions that I am unwilling to address them in a case whose presentation focused on other matters.

"I find it unnecessary to do so in any event. Regardless of what one may think of *Hans,* it has been assumed to be the law for nearly a century. During that time, Congress has enacted many statutes—including the Jones Act and the provisions of the FELA which it incorporates—on the assumption that states were immune from lawsuits by individuals. Even if we were now to find that assumption to have been wrong, we could not, in reason, interpret the statutes as though the assumption never existed. Thus, although the terms of the Jones Act (through its incorporation of the FELA) apply to all common carriers by water, I do not read them to apply to states. For the same reason, I do not read the FELA to apply to states, and therefore agree with the Court that Parden v. Terminal Ry., 377 U.S. 184 (1964), should be overruled. Whether or not, as *Hans* appears to have held, article III of the Constitution contains an implicit limitation on suits brought by individuals against states by virtue of a nearly universal 'understanding' that the federal judicial power could not extend to such suits, such an understanding clearly underlay the Jones Act and the FELA."

Justice Brennan, joined by Justices Marshall, Blackmun, and Stevens, dissented. Justice Brennan not only defended *Parden* but argued at great length that *Hans* should be overruled. Justice Powell responded to these arguments at length in his plurality opinion, leaving the Court divided four to four—with Justice Scalia the only uncommitted vote—on the fate of *Hans.*

Note that Justice Powell went out of his way to refrain from addressing whether the *Fitzpatrick v. Bitzer* rationale was limited to § 5 of the 14th amendment or whether it or some similar rationale authorized Congress to abrogate 11th amendment immunity under the commerce clause. This issue was addressed, and Justice Scalia disclosed his position on *Hans,* in *Pennsylvania v. Union Gas Company,* the next main case.

PENNSYLVANIA v. UNION GAS COMPANY
Supreme Court of the United States, 1989.
491 U.S. 1.

JUSTICE BRENNAN announced the judgment of the Court and delivered an opinion of the Court with respect to parts I and II, and an opinion with respect to part III, in which JUSTICE MARSHALL, JUSTICE BLACKMUN and JUSTICE STEVENS join.

This case presents the questions whether the Comprehensive Environmental Response, Compensation, and Liability Act of 1980 (CERCLA), 42 U.S.C. § 9601 et seq., as amended by the Superfund Amendments and Reauthorization Act of 1986 (SARA), permits a suit for monetary damages against a state in federal court and, if so, whether Congress has the authority to create such a cause of action when legislating pursuant to the commerce clause. The answer to both questions is "yes."

I

For about 50 years, the predecessors of respondent Union Gas operated a coal gasification plant near Brodhead Creek in Stroudsburg, Pennsylvania, which produced coal tar as a by-product. The plant was dismantled around 1950. A few years later, Pennsylvania took part in major flood-control efforts along the creek. In 1980, shortly after acquiring easements to the property along the creek, the state struck a large deposit of coal tar while excavating the creek. The coal tar began to seep into the creek, and the Environmental Protection Agency determined that the tar was a hazardous substance and declared the site the nation's first emergency Superfund site. Working together, Pennsylvania and the federal government cleaned up the area, and the federal government reimbursed the state for cleanup costs of $720,000.

To recoup these costs, the United States sued Union Gas under § 104 and § 106 of CERCLA, 42 U.S.C. § 9604 and § 9606, claiming that Union Gas was liable for such costs because the company and its predecessors had deposited coal tar into the ground near Brodhead Creek. Union Gas filed a third-party complaint against Pennsylvania, asserting that the state was responsible for at least a portion of the costs because it was an "owner or operator" of the hazardous-waste site, 42 U.S.C. § 9607(a), and because its flood-control efforts had negligently caused or contributed to the release of the coal tar into the creek. The District Court dismissed the complaint, accepting Pennsylvania's claim that its 11th amendment immunity barred the suit. A divided panel of the Court of Appeals for the Third Circuit affirmed, finding no clear expression of congressional intent to hold states liable in monetary damages under CERCLA.

While Union Gas' petition for certiorari was pending, Congress amended CERCLA by passing SARA. We granted certiorari, vacated the Court of Appeals' opinion, and remanded for reconsideration in light of these amendments. On remand, the Court of Appeals held that the language of CERCLA, as amended, clearly rendered states liable for monetary damages and that Congress had the power to do so when legislating pursuant to the commerce clause. We granted certiorari and now affirm.

II

In Hans v. Louisiana, 134 U.S. 1 (1890), this Court held that the principle of sovereign immunity reflected in the 11th amendment rendered the states immune from suits for monetary damages in federal court even where jurisdiction was premised on the presence of a federal question. Congress may override this immunity when it acts pursuant to the power granted it under § 5 of the 14th amendment, but it must make its intent to do so "unmistakably clear." See Atascadero State Hospital v. Scanlon, 473 U.S. 234, 242 (1985). Before turning to the question whether Congress possesses the same power of abrogation under the commerce clause, we must first decide whether CERCLA, as amended by SARA, clearly expresses an intent to hold states liable in damages for conduct described in the statute. . . .

[Justice Brennan concluded: "We . . . hold that the language of CERCLA as amended by SARA clearly evinces an intent to hold states liable in damages in federal court."]

III

Our conclusion that CERCLA clearly permits suits for money damages against states in federal court requires us to decide whether the commerce clause grants Congress the power to enact such a statute. Pennsylvania argues that the principle of sovereign immunity found in the 11th amendment precludes such congressional authority. We do not agree.

A

Though we have never squarely resolved this issue of congressional power, our decisions mark a trail unmistakably leading to the conclusion that Congress may permit suits against the states for money damages. [Justice Brennan's summary of the prior cases is omitted. After detailed consideration of the rationale of Fitzpatrick v. Bitzer, 427 U.S. 445 (1976), upholding Congress' power to subject states to suits for money damages in federal court when legislating under § 5 of the 14th amendment, he continued:]

Like the 14th amendment, the commerce clause with one hand gives power to Congress while, with the other, it takes power away from the states. It cannot be relevant that the 14th amendment accomplishes this exchange in two steps (§§ 1–4, plus § 5), while the commerce clause does it in one. The important point, rather, is that the provision both expands federal power and contracts state power; that is the meaning, in fact, of a "plenary" grant of authority, and the lower courts have rightly concluded that it makes no sense to conceive of § 5 as somehow being an "ultraplenary" grant of authority.

Pennsylvania attempts to bring this case outside *Fitzpatrick* by asserting that "[t]he 14th amendment . . . alters what would otherwise be the proper constitutional balance between federal and state governments." The state believes, apparently, that the "constitutional balance" existing prior to the 14th amendment did not permit Congress to override the states' immunity from suit. This claim, of course, begs the very question we face.

For its part, the dissent casually announces: "Nothing in [*Fitzpatrick*'s] reasoning justifies limitation of the principle embodied in the 11th amendment through appeal to antecedent provisions of the Constitution." The operative word here is, it would appear, "antecedent"; and it is important to emphasize that, according to the dissent, the commerce clause is antecedent, not to the 11th amendment, but to "*the principle embodied in* the 11th amendment." But, according to part II of the dissenting opinion, this "principle" has been with us since the days before the Constitution was ratified—since the days, in other words, before the commerce clause. In describing the "consensus that the doctrine of sovereign immunity . . . was part of the understood background against which the Constitution was adopted, and which its jurisdictional provisions did not mean to sweep away," the dissent clearly refers to a state of affairs that existed well before the states ratified the Constitution. The dissent, therefore, has things backwards: it is not the commerce clause that came first but "the principle embodied in the 11th amendment" that did so. Antecedence takes this case closer to, not further from, *Fitzpatrick*.

Even if "the principle embodied in the 11th amendment" made its first appearance at the same moment as the commerce clause, and not before, the dissent could no longer rely on chronology in distinguishing *Fitzpatrick*. Only if it were the 11th amendment itself that introduced the principle of sovereign immunity into the Constitution would the commerce clause have preceded this principle. Even then, the order of events would matter only if the amendment changed things; that is, it would matter only if, before the 11th amendment, the commerce clause *did* authorize Congress to abrogate sovereign immunity. But if Congress enjoyed such power prior to the enactment of this amendment, we would require a showing far more powerful than the dissent can muster that the amendment was intended to obliterate that authority. The language of the 11th amendment gives us no hint that it limits *congressional* authority; it refers only to "the *judicial* power" and forbids "*constru[ing]*" that power to extend to the enumerated suits—language plainly intended to rein in the judiciary, not Congress. It would be a fragile Constitution indeed if subsequent amendments could, without express reference, be interpreted to wipe out the original understanding of congressional power.

The dissent attempts to avoid the pull of our prior decisions by claiming that *Hans* answered this constitutional question over 100 years ago. Because *Hans* was brought into federal court via the Judiciary Act of 1875 and because the Court there held that the suit was barred by the 11th amendment, the dissent argues, that case disposed of the question whether Congress has the authority to abrogate states' immunity when legislating pursuant to the powers granted it by the Constitution. This argument depends on the notion that, in passing the Judiciary Act, "Congress . . . *sought* to eliminate [the] state sovereign immunity" that article III had not eliminated. As the dissent is well aware, however, the Judiciary Act merely gave effect to the grant of federal-question jurisdiction under article III, which was not self-executing. Thus, if article III did not "automatically eliminate" sovereign immunity, then neither did the Judiciary Act of 1875. That unsurprising conclusion does not begin to address the question whether other congressional enactments, not designed simply to implement article III's grants of jurisdiction, may override states' immunity. When one recalls, in addition, our conclusion that "art[icle] III 'arising under' jurisdiction is broader than federal-question jurisdiction under § 1331," Verlinden B. v. Central Bank of Nigeria, 461 U.S. 480, 495 (1983), the dissent's conception of *Hans'* holding looks particularly exaggerated.

Our prior cases thus indicate that Congress has the authority to override states' immunity when legislating pursuant to the commerce clause. This conclusion is confirmed by a consideration of the special nature of the power conferred by that clause.

B

We have recognized that the states enjoy no immunity where there has been "'a surrender of this immunity in the plan of the convention.'" Monaco v. Mississippi, 292 U.S. 313, 322–23 (1934), quoting The Federalist, No. 81, p. 657 (H. Dawson ed. 1876) (Hamilton). Because the commerce clause withholds power from the states at the same time as it confers it on Congress, and because the congressional power thus conferred would be incomplete without the authority to render states liable in damages, it must be that, to the extent that the states gave Congress the authority to regulate commerce, they also relinquished their immunity where Congress found it necessary, in exercising this authority, to render them liable. The states held liable under such a congressional enactment are thus not "unconsenting"; they gave their consent all at once, in ratifying the Constitution containing the commerce clause, rather than on a case-by-case basis.

It would be difficult to overstate the breadth and depth of the commerce power. It is not the vastness of this power, however, that is so important here: it is its effect on the power of the states. The commerce clause, we long have held, displaces state authority even where Congress has chosen not to act, and it sometimes precludes state regulation even though existing federal law does not pre-empt it. Since the states may not legislate at all in these last two situations, a conclusion that Congress may not create a cause of action for money damages against the states would mean that no one could do so. And in many situations, it is only money damages that will carry out Congress' legitimate objectives under the commerce clause.

The case before us brilliantly illuminates these points. The general problem of environmental harm is often not susceptible of a local solution. We have, in fact, invalidated one state's effort to deal with the problem of waste disposal on a local level. See Philadelphia v. New Jersey, 437 U.S. 617 (1978). A New Jersey statute prohibited the treatment and disposal, within the state, of any solid or liquid wastes generated outside the state. Indicating that a law applicable to all wastes would have survived under the commerce clause, we held that the exemption of locally produced wastes doomed the statute. As a practical matter, however, it is difficult to imagine that a state could forbid the disposal of *all* wastes. Hence, the commerce clause as interpreted in *Philadelphia v. New Jersey* ensures that we often must look to the federal government for environmental solutions. And often those solutions, to be satisfactory, must include a cause of action for money damages.

The cause of action under consideration, for example, came about only after Congress had tried to solve the problem posed by hazardous substances through other means. Prior statutes such as the Resource Conservation and Recovery Act of 1976, as amended, 42 U.S.C. § 6901 et seq., had failed in large part because they focused on preventive measures to the exclusion of remedial ones. See Note, Superfund and California's Implementation: Potential Conflict, 19 C.W.L.R. 373, 376, n. 23 (1983). The remedy that Congress felt it needed in CERCLA is sweeping: *everyone* who is potentially responsible for hazardous-waste contamination may be forced to contribute to the costs of cleanup. Congress did not think it enough, moreover, to permit only the federal government to recoup the costs of its own cleanups of hazardous-waste sites; the government's resources being finite, it could neither pay up front for all necessary cleanups nor undertake many different projects at the same time. Some help was needed, and Congress sought to encourage that help by allowing private parties who voluntarily cleaned up hazardous-waste sites to recover a proportionate amount of the costs of cleanup from the other potentially responsible parties. If states, which comprise a significant class of owners and operators of hazardous-waste sites need not pay for the costs of cleanup, the overall effect on voluntary cleanups will be substantial. This case thus shows why the space carved out for federal legislation under the commerce power must include the power to hold states financially accountable not only to the federal government, but private citizens as well.

It does not follow that Congress, pursuant to its authority under the commerce clause, could authorize suits in federal court that the bare terms of article III would not permit. No one suggests that if the commerce clause confers on Congress the power of abrogation, it must also confer the power to direct that certain state-law suits (not falling under the diversity jurisdiction) be brought in federal court.

According to Pennsylvania, however, to decide that Congress may permit suits against states for money damages in federal court is equivalent to holding that Congress may expand the jurisdiction of the federal courts beyond the bounds of article III. Pennsylvania argues that the federal judicial power as set forth in article III does not extend to *any* suits for damages brought by private citizens against unconsenting states. We never have held, however, that article III does not permit such suits where the states have consented to them. Pennsylvania's argument thus is answered by Fitzpatrick v. Bitzer, 427 U.S. 445 (1976). The 14th amendment does not purport to expand or even change the scope of article III. If Pennsylvania were right about the limitations on article III, then our holding in *Fitzpatrick* would mean that the 14th amendment, though silent on the subject, expanded the judicial power as originally conceived. We do not share that view of *Fitzpatrick*.[5]

IV

We hold that CERCLA renders states liable in money damages in federal court, and that Congress has the authority to render them so liable when legislating pursuant to the commerce clause. Given our ruling in favor of Union Gas, we need not reach its argument that Hans v. Louisiana, 134 U.S. 1 (1890), should be overruled. We affirm the judgment of the Court of Appeals for the Third Circuit, and remand the case for further proceedings consistent with this opinion.

It is so ordered.

JUSTICE STEVENS, concurring.

It is important to emphasize the distinction between our two 11th amendments. There is first the correct and literal interpretation of the plain language of the 11th amendment. . . . In addition, there is the

---

[5] Since Union Gas itself eschews reliance on the theory of waiver we announced in Parden v. Terminal Railway of Alabama Docks Dept., 377 U.S. 184 (1964), we neither discuss this theory here nor understand why the dissent feels the need to do so.

defense of sovereign immunity that the Court has added to the text of the amendment in cases like Hans v. Louisiana, 134 U.S. 1 (1890). With respect to the former—the legitimate scope of the 11th amendment limitation on federal judicial power—I do not believe Congress has the power under the commerce clause, or under any other provision of the Constitution, to abrogate the states' immunity. A statute cannot amend the Constitution. With respect to the latter—the judicially created doctrine of state immunity even from suits alleging violation of federally protected rights—I agree that Congress has plenary power to subject the states to suit in federal court.

Because Justice Brennan's opinion in Atascadero State Hospital v. Scanlon, 473 U.S. 234, 247 (1985), and the works of numerous scholars [1] have exhaustively and conclusively refuted the contention that the 11th amendment embodies a general grant of sovereign immunity to the states, further explication on this point is unnecessary. Suffice it to say that the 11th amendment carefully mirrors the language of the citizen-state and alien-state diversity clauses of article III and *only* provides that "[t]he Judicial power of the United States shall not be construed to extend" *to these cases.* There is absolutely nothing in the text of the amendment that in any way affects the other grants of "judicial Power" contained in article III. Plainer language is seldom, if ever, found in constitutional law.

In *Hans v. Louisiana,* however, the Court departed from the plain language, purpose, and history of the 11th amendment, extending to the states immunity from suits premised on the "arising under" jurisdictional grant of article III. Later adjustments to this rule, as well as the Court's inability to develop a coherent doctrine of 11th amendment immunity, make clear that this expansion of state immunity is not a matter of 11th amendment law at all, but rather is based on a prudential interest in federal-state comity and a concern for "Our Federalism." The 11th amendment, as does article III, speaks in terms of "judicial power." The question that must therefore animate the inquiry in any *actual* 11th amendment case is whether the federal court has power to entertain the suit. In cases in which there is no such power, Congress cannot provide it—even through a "clear statement." Many of this Court's decisions, however, purporting to apply

---

[1] See, e.g., Marshall, Fighting the Words of the 11th amendment, 102 Harv.L.Rev. 1342 (1989); Jackson, The Supreme Court, the 11th amendment, and State Sovereign Immunity, 98 Yale L.J. 1 (1988); Amar, Of Sovereignty and Federalism, 96 Yale L.J. 1425 (1987); Lee, Sovereign Immunity and the 11th amendment: The Uses of History, 18 Urb.Law, 519 (1986); Shapiro, Wrong Turns: The 11th amendment and the *Pennhurst* Case, 98 Harv.L.Rev. 61 (1984); Gibbons, The 11th amendment and State Sovereign Immunity: A Reinterpretation, 83 Colum.L.Rev. 1889 (1983); Fletcher, A Historical Interpretation of the 11th amendment: A Narrow Construction of an Affirmative Grant of Jurisdiction Rather than a Prohibition Against Jurisdiction, 35 Stan.L.Rev. 1033 (1983); Tribe, Intergovernmental Immunities in Litigation, Taxation, and Regulation: Separation of Powers Issues in Controversies About Federalism, 89 Harv.L.Rev. 682 (1976).

the 11th amendment, do not deal with judicial power at all. Instead, the issue of immunity is treated as a question of the proper role of the federal courts in the amalgam of federal-state relations. It is in these cases that congressional abrogation is appropriate.

Several of this Court's decisions make clear that much of our state immunity doctrine has absolutely nothing to do with the limit on judicial power contained in the 11th amendment. For example, it is well established that a state may waive its immunity, subjecting itself to possible suit in federal court. Yet, the cases are legion holding that a party may not waive a defect in subject matter jurisdiction or invoke federal jurisdiction simply by consent. This must be particularly so in cases in which the federal courts are entirely without article III power to entertain the suit. Our willingness to allow states to waive their immunity thus demonstrates that this immunity is not a product of the limitation of judicial power contained in the 11th amendment.

Another striking example of the application of prudential—rather than true jurisdictional—concerns is found in our decision in Edelman v. Jordan, 415 U.S. 651 (1974). There, the Court inexplicably limited the fiction established in Ex parte Young, 209 U.S. 123 (1908), which permits suits against state officials in their official capacities for ultra vires acts, and concluded that the *Young* fiction only applies to prospective grants of relief. If *Edelman* simply involved an application of the limitation on judicial power contained in the 11th amendment, once judicial power was found to exist to award prospective relief (even at some monetary cost to the state, see, e.g., Milliken v. Bradley, 433 U.S. 267 (1977)), it is difficult to understand why that same judicial power would not extend to award other forms of relief. In Pennhurst State School and Hospital v. Halderman, 465 U.S. 89, 104–06 (1984), the Court made explicit what was implicit in *Edelman:* the *Young* fiction "rests on the need to promote the vindication of federal rights," while *Edelman* represents an attempt to "accommodate" this protection to the "competing interest" in "the constitutional immunity of the states."

. . .

The theme that thus emerges from cases such as *Edelman* [and] *Pennhurst* . . . is one of balancing of state and federal interests. This sort of balancing, however, like waiver, is antithetical to traditional understandings of article III subject-matter jurisdiction—either the judicial power extends to a suit brought against a state or it does not. As a result, these cases are better understood as simply invoking the comity and federalism concerns discussed in our abstention cases, although admittedly in a slightly different voice.[3] In my view, federal

---

[3] This understanding of our state immunity cases explains an additional anomaly. Over the years, this Court has repeatedly exercised article III power to review state-court judgments in cases involving claims that, under our post-*Hans* decisions, could not have been brought in federal district court. To the extent the 11th amendment is broadly construed to have removed all federal power to adjudicate claims against

courts "have a primary obligation to protect the rights of the individual that are embodied in the federal Constitution" and laws, Harris v. Reed, 489 U.S. 255, ___ (1989) (Stevens, J., concurring), and generally should not eschew this responsibility based on some diffuse, instrumental concern for state autonomy. Yet, even if I were convinced otherwise, I would think it readily apparent that congressional abrogation is entirely appropriate. Congress is not superseding a constitutional provision in these cases, but rather is setting aside the Court's assessment of the extent to which the use of constitutionality prescribed federal authority is prudent.

Because Congress has decided that the federal interest in protecting the environment outweighs any countervailing interest in not subjecting states to the possible award of monetary damages in a federal court, and because the "judicial power" of the United States plainly extends to such suits, I join Justice Brennan's opinion. Even if a majority of this Court might have reached a different assessment of the proper balance of state and federal interests as an original matter, once Congress has spoken, we may not disregard its express decision to subject the states to liability under federal law.

JUSTICE WHITE, with whom THE CHIEF JUSTICE, JUSTICE O'CONNOR, and JUSTICE KENNEDY join as to part I, concurring.

[In part I of his opinion, Justice White did not find in the two statutes the "unmistakably clear language" required to abrogate the 11th amendment immunity. Part II in its entirety reads:]

My view on the statutory issue has not prevailed, however; a majority of the Court has ruled that the statute, as amended, plainly intended to abrogate the immunity of the states from suit in the federal courts. I accept that judgment. This brings me to the question whether Congress has the constitutional power to abrogate the states' immunity.[8] In that respect, I agree with the conclusion reached by Justice Brennan in part III of his opinion, that Congress has the authority under article I to abrogate the 11th amendment immunity of the states, although I do not agree with much of his reasoning.

Accordingly, I would affirm the judgment of the Court of Appeals.

JUSTICE SCALIA, joined by THE CHIEF JUSTICE, JUSTICE O'CONNOR, and JUSTICE KENNEDY, as to parts II, III, and IV, concurring in part and dissenting in part.

the states regardless of whether or not the claim is one arising under federal law, it is difficult to justify our exercise of power in these cases. However, if our post-*Hans* state-immunity cases are instead understood as premised on a prudential balancing of state and federal interests, these cases are easily explained: a state-court decision defining federal law tips the balance in favor of federal review.

[8] As a preliminary matter, I reiterate my view that, for the reasons stated by the plurality in Welch v. Texas Dept. of Highways, 483 U.S., at 478–95, *Hans v. Louisiana* should not be overruled.

I

I join part II of Justice Brennan's opinion holding that the text of CERCLA, as amended by SARA, clearly renders states liable for money damages in private suits. . . .

Finding that the statute renders the states liable in private suits for money damages, I must consider the continuing validity of Hans v. Louisiana, 134 U.S. 1 (1890), which held that the 11th amendment precludes individuals from bringing damage suits against states in federal court even where the asserted basis of jurisdiction is not diversity of citizenship but the existence of a federal question.

II

Eight members of the Court addressed the question whether to overrule *Hans* only two terms ago—but inconclusively, since they were evenly divided. See Welch v. Texas Dept. of Highways and Public Transportation, 483 U.S. 468 (1987). Since the substantive issue was addressed so extensively by the plurality opinion announcing the judgment of the Court in that case (which I will refer to as the "plurality opinion"), and by the dissent, I will only sketch its outlines here.

. . . If [the] text [of the 11th amendment] were intended as a comprehensive description of state sovereign immunity in federal courts—that is, if there were no state sovereign immunity beyond its precise terms—then it would unquestionably be most reasonable to interpret it as providing immunity only when the *sole basis* of federal jurisdiction is the diversity of citizenship that it describes (which of course tracks some of the diversity jurisdictional grants in U.S. Const., Art. III, § 2). For there is no plausible reason why one would wish to protect a state from being sued in federal court for violation of federal law (a suit falling within the jurisdictional grant over cases "arising under . . . the laws of the United States") when the plaintiff is a citizen of another state or country, but to permit a state to be sued there when the plaintiff is a citizen of the state itself. Thus, unless some other constitutional principle beyond the immediate text of the 11th amendment confers immunity in the latter situation—that is to say, unless the text of the 11th amendment is not comprehensive—even if the parties to a suit fell within its precise terms (for example, a state and the citizen of another state) sovereign immunity would not exist so long as one of the other, *nondiversity* grounds of jurisdiction existed.

About a century ago, in the landmark case of *Hans v. Louisiana*, the Court unanimously rejected this "comprehensive" approach to the amendment, finding sovereign immunity where not only a nondiversity basis of jurisdiction was present, but even where the parties did not fit the description of the 11th amendment, the plaintiff being a citizen not of another state or country, but of Louisiana itself. What we said in

Hans was, essentially, that the 11th amendment was important not merely for what it said but for what it reflected: a consensus that the doctrine of sovereign immunity, for states as well as for the federal government, was part of the understood background against which the Constitution was adopted, and which its jurisdictional provisions did not mean to sweep away. . . .

The evidence is strong that the jurisdictional grants in article III of the Constitution did not automatically eliminate underlying state sovereign immunity, and even stronger that that assumption was implicit in the 11th amendment. What is subject to greater dispute, however, is how much sovereign immunity was implicitly eliminated by what Hamilton called the "plan of the Convention." We have already held that "inherent in the constitutional plan" are a waiver of immunity against suits by the United States itself and a waiver of immunity against suits by other states. The foremost argument urged in favor of overruling *Hans* is that a waiver of immunity against suits presenting federal questions is also implicit in the constitutional scheme. On this single point I add a few words to what was so recently said in *Welch*.

The inherent necessity of a tribunal for peaceful resolution of disputes between the Union and the individual states, and between the individual states themselves, is incomparably greater, in my view, than the need for a tribunal to resolve disputes on federal questions between individuals and the states. Undoubtedly the Constitution envisions the necessary judicial means to assure compliance with the Constitution and laws. But since the Constitution does not deem this to require that private individuals be able to bring claims against the *federal government* for violation of the Constitution or laws, it is difficult to see why it must be interpreted to require that private individuals be able to bring such claims against the *states*. If private initiation of suits against the offending sovereign as such is essential to preservation of the structure, it is difficult to see why it would not be essential at both levels. Indeed if anything it would seem more important at the federal level, since suits against the states for violation of the Constitution or laws can at least be brought by the federal government itself. In providing federal immunity from private suit, therefore, the Constitution strongly suggests that state immunity exists as well. Of course federal law can give, and has given, the private suitor many means short of actions against the state to assure compliance with federal law. He may obtain a federal injunction against the state officer, which will effectively stop the unlawful action, see Ex parte Young, 209 U.S. 123, 160 (1908), and may obtain money damages against state officers, and even local governments, under 42 U.S.C. § 1983; see Monell v. New York City Dept. of Social Services, 436 U.S. 658 (1978). I think it impossible to find in the scheme of the Constitution a necessity that private remedies be expanded beyond this, to include a remedy not available, for a similar infraction, against the United States itself.

Even if I were wrong, however, about the original meaning of the Constitution, or the assumption adopted by the 11th amendment, or the structural necessity for federal-question suits against the states, it cannot possibly be denied that the question is at least close. In that situation, the mere venerability of an answer consistently adhered to for almost a century, and the difficulty of changing, or even clearly identifying, the intervening law that has been based on that answer, strongly argue against a change. As noted by the *Welch* plurality, "*Hans* has been reaffirmed in case after case, often unanimously and by exceptionally strong Courts"; its reversal "would overrule at least 17 cases, in addition to *Hans* itself" and cast doubt on "a variety of other cases that were concerned with this Court's traditional treatment of sovereign immunity." Moreover, unlike the vast majority of judicial decisions, *Hans* has had a pervasive effect upon statutory law, automatically assuring that private damages actions created by federal law do not extend against the states. Forty-nine Congresses since *Hans* have legislated under that assurance. It is impossible to say how many extant statutes would have included an explicit preclusion of suits against states if it had not been thought that such suits were automatically barred. Indeed, it is not even possible to say that, without *Hans*, all constitutional amendments would have taken the form they did. The 17th amendment, eliminating the election of Senators by state legislatures, was ratified in 1913, 23 years after *Hans*. If it had been known at that time that the federal government could confer upon private individuals federal causes of action reaching state treasuries; and if the state legislatures had the experience of urging the Senators they chose to protect them against the proposed creation of such liability; it is not inconceivable, especially at a time when voluntary state waiver of sovereign immunity was rare, that the amendment (which had to be ratified by three-quarters of the same state legislatures) would have contained a proviso protecting against such incursions upon state sovereignty.

I would therefore decline respondents' invitation to overrule *Hans v. Louisiana.*

III

Justice Brennan's plurality opinion purports to assume the validity of *Hans*, and yet reaches the result that CERCLA's imposition of monetary liability is constitutional because Congress has the power to abrogate state sovereign immunity in the exercise of its commerce clause power. Justice White, who not merely assumes the validity of *Hans* but actually believes in it, agrees with that disposition. Better to overrule *Hans*, I should think, than to perpetuate the complexities that it creates, but eliminate all its benefits to the federal system. If *Hans* means only that federal-question suits for money damages against the states cannot be brought in federal court unless Congress clearly says so, it means nothing at all. We do not need *Hans* for the "clear statement" rule—just as we do not need to rely on any constitutional prohibition of suits against the federal government to require a similar rule for elimination of the sovereign immunity of the United States. As far as I can discern, the course the Court today pursues—preserving *Hans* but permitting Congress to overrule it—achieves the worst of both worlds. And it is a course no more justified by text than by consequences.

To begin with, *Hans* did not merely hold that article III failed to eliminate state sovereign immunity of its own force, without any congressional action to that end. In *Hans,* as here, there was a congressional statute that could be pointed to as eliminating state sovereign immunity—namely, the Judiciary Act of 1875, which gave United States courts jurisdiction over cases involving federal questions. . . . Thus, the distinction that the Court must rely upon is not one between cases in which Congress has assertedly *sought* to eliminate state sovereign immunity and cases in which in no such assertion is available; but rather the much more gossamer distinction between cases in which Congress has assertedly sought to eliminate state sovereign immunity pursuant to its powers to create and organize courts, and cases in which it has assertedly sought to do so pursuant to some of its other powers.

I think it plain that the position adopted by the Court contradicts the rationale of *Hans,* if not its narrow holding. *Hans* was not expressing some narrow objection to the particular federal power by which Louisiana had been haled into court, but was rather enunciating a fundamental principle of federalism, evidenced by the 11th amendment, that the states retained their sovereign prerogative of immunity. That is clear throughout the opinion, but particularly in the following passage:

> "Suppose that Congress, when proposing the 11th amendment, had appended to it a proviso that nothing therein contained should prevent a state from being sued by its own citizens in cases arising under the Constitution or laws of the United States: can we imagine that it would have been adopted by the states? The supposition that it would is almost an absurdity on its face.
>
> "The truth is, that the cognizance of suits and actions unknown to the law, and forbidden by the law, was not contemplated by the Constitution when establishing the judicial power of the United States."

This rationale is also evident from *Hans'* reliance upon the dissenting opinion of Justice Iredell in *Chisholm* —whose views, the Court said, "were clearly right,—as the people of the United States in their sovereign capacity [by ratifying the 11th amendment] subsequently decided." Iredell's only words addressed precisely to the constitutional issue were as follows:

> "So much, however, has been said on the Constitution, that it may not be improper to intimate that my present opinion is strongly against any construction of it, which will admit, under any circumstances, a compulsive suit against a state for the recovery of money. I think every word in the Constitution may have its full effect without involving this consequence, and that nothing but express words, or an insurmountable implication (neither of which I consider, can be found in this case) would authorise the deduction of so high a power."

Our later cases are similarly clear that state immunity from suit in federal courts is a structural component of federalism, and not merely a default disposition that can be altered by action of Congress pursuant to its article I powers. [Justice Scalia's discussion of the precedents is omitted.] The only attempt by either the plurality or Justice White to reconcile today's holding with the "broad constitutional principle of sovereign immunity" established by these precedents is the plurality's facile assertion that "in approving the commerce power, the states consented to suits against them based on congressionally created causes of action." The suggestion that this is the kind of consent our cases had in mind when reciting the familiar phrase, "the states may not be sued without their consent," does not warrant response.

The Court's conclusion is not only contrary to the clear understanding of a century of cases regarding the 11th amendment, but it contradicts our unvarying approach to article III as setting forth the *exclusive* catalog of permissible federal-court jurisdiction. When we have turned to consider whether "a surrender of [state] immunity [is inherent] in the plan of the convention," we have discussed that issue *under the rubric of the various grants of jurisdiction in article III,* seeking to determine which of those grants must reasonably be thought to include suits against the states. We have never gone thumbing through the Constitution, to see what *other* original grants of authority—as opposed to amendments adopted after the 11th amendment—might justify elimination of state sovereign immunity. If private suits against states, though not permitted under article III (by virtue of the understanding represented by the 11th amendment), are nonetheless permitted under the commerce clause, or under some other article I grant of federal power, then there is no reason why the other limitations of article III cannot be similarly exceeded. That article would be transformed from a comprehensive description of the permissible scope of federal judicial authority to a mere default disposition, applicable unless and until Congress prescribes more expansive authority in the exercise of one of its article I powers. That is not the regime the Constitution establishes.

The Court's error is clear enough from the embarrassing frailty of the case support to which the plurality opinion appeals. Justice Brennan . . . does not cite . . . a single Supreme Court case, over the past 200 years upholding (in absence of a waiver) the congressional exercise of the asserted power—or even a single Supreme Court case finding that such an exercise has *occurred.* How strange that such a useful power—one that the plurality finds essential to the achievement of congressional objectives—should never have been approved and rarely (if ever) have been asserted. . . .

Finally, the plurality opinion errs in relying on *Fitzpatrick v. Bitzer,* which upheld a money award against a state under title VII of the Civil Rights Act of 1964. The distinction, as we carefully explained in that opinion, is that the Civil Rights Act was enacted pursuant to § 5 of the 14th amendment. We held that "the 11th amendment, and the principle of state sovereignty which it embodies . . . are necessarily limited" by the later amendment, whose substantive provisions were "by express terms directed at the states" and " 'were intended to be, what they really are, limitations of the power of the states and enlargements of the power of Congress.' " Nothing in this reasoning justifies limitation of the principle embodied in the 11th amendment through appeal to antecedent provisions of the Constitution. The plurality asserts that it is no more impossible for provisions of the Constitution adopted *concurrently* with article III to permit abrogation of state sovereign immunity than it is for provisions adopted *subsequently.* We do not dispute that this is possible, but only that it happened. As suggested above, if the article I commerce power enables abrogation of state sovereign immunity, so do all the other article I powers. An interpretation of the original Constitution which permits Congress to eliminate sovereign immunity only if it wants to render the doctrine a practical nullity and is therefore unreasonable. The 14th amendment, on the other hand, was avowedly directed against the power of the states, and permits abrogation of their sovereign immunity only for a limited purpose.

IV

It remains for me to consider whether the doctrine of waiver applies here. . . . *Parden* is the only case in which we have held that the federal government can demand, as a condition to its permission of state action regulable under the commerce clause, the waiver of state sovereign immunity. Two terms ago, in *Welch,* we overruled *Parden* insofar as that case spoke to the clarity of language necessary to constitute such a demand. We explicitly declined to address, however, the continuing validity of *Parden*'s holding that the commerce clause provided the constitutional power to make such a demand. I would drop the other shoe.

There are obvious and fatal difficulties in acknowledging such a power if no commerce clause power to abrogate state sovereign immunity exists. All congressional creations of private rights of action attach recovery to the defendant's commission of some act, or possession of some status, in a field where Congress has authority to regulate conduct. Thus, *all* federal prescriptions are, insofar as their prospective application is concerned, in a sense conditional, and—to the extent that the objects of the prescriptions consciously engage in the activity or hold the status that produces liability—can be redescribed as invitations to "waiver." For example, one is not liable for damages to private parties under the federal securities laws, unless one participates in the activity of purchasing or selling securities affecting interstate commerce; and it is possible to describe that liability as not having been categorically imposed, but rather as being the result of a "waiver" of one's immunity, in exchange for federal permission to engage in that activity. At bottom, then, to acknowledge that the federal government can make the waiver of state sovereign immunity a condition to the state's action in a field that Congress has authority to regulate, is substantially the same as acknowledging that the federal government can eliminate state sovereign immunity in the exercise of its article I powers—that is, to adopt the very principle I have just rejected. There is little more than a verbal distinction between saying that Congress can make the Commonwealth of Pennsylvania liable to private parties for hazardous-waste clean-up costs on sites that the Commonwealth owns and operates, and saying the same thing but adding at the end "if the Commonwealth chooses to own and operate them." If state sovereign immunity has any reality, it must mean more than this.

* * *

The Court's holding today can be applauded only by those who think state sovereign immunity so constitutionally insignificant that *Hans* itself might as well be abandoned. It is only the Court's steadfast refusal to accept the fundamental structural importance of that doctrine, reflected in *Hans* and the other cases discussed above, that permits it to regard abrogation through article I as an open question, and enables the plurality to fight the *Hans* battle all over again—but this time to win it—on the field of the commerce clause. It is a particularly unhappy victory, since instead of cleaning up the allegedly muddled 11th amendment jurisprudence produced by *Hans,* the Court leaves that in place, and adds to the clutter the astounding principle that article III limitations can be overcome by simply exercising article I powers. It is an unstable victory as well, since that principle is too much at war with itself to endure. We shall either overrule *Hans* in form as well as in fact, or return to its genuine meaning.

I would reverse the judgment of the Court of Appeals on the ground that federal courts have no power to entertain the present suit **against** the Commonwealth of Pennsylvania.

JUSTICE O'CONNOR, dissenting.

I agree with Justice Scalia that a faithful interpretation of the 11th amendment embodies a concept of state sovereignty which limits the power of Congress to abrogate states' immunity when acting pursuant to the commerce clause. But that view does not command a majority of the Court, thus necessitating an inquiry as to whether Congress intended in CERCLA and SARA to abrogate the states' 11th amendment immunity. On that question, I join part I of Justice White's opinion. I also join parts II, III, and IV of Justice Scalia's dissenting opinion.

NOTE ON *PENNSYLVANIA v. UNION GAS COMPANY*

Had enough?[a]

[a] For further consideration of the meaning of the Eleventh Amendment in light of *Pennsylvania v. Union Gas Company*, see George D. Brown, Has the Supreme Court Confessed Error on the Eleventh Amendment? Revisionist Scholarship and State Immunity, 68 U.N.C.L.Rev. 867 (1990); Vicki C. Jackson, One Hundred Years of Folly: The Eleventh Amendment and the 1988 Term, 64 So.Cal.L.Rev. 51 (1990).

For an example of a statute enacted in November of 1990 in which Congress explicitly abrogated state 11th amendment immunity in the context of suits for copyright infringement, see 17 U.S.C. § 511 ("Any State, any instrumentality of a State, and any officer or employee of a State or instrumentality of a State acting in his or her official capacity, shall not be immune, under the Eleventh Amendment of the Constitution of the United States or under any other doctrine of sovereign immunity, from suit in Federal court by any person, including any governmental or nongovernmental entity, for a violation of any of the exclusive rights of a copyright owner provided by sections 106 through 119, for importing copies of phonorecords in violation of section 602, or for any other violation under this title.")

Page 773, add to Note 4:

Michael Wells, The Impact of Substantive Interests on the Law of Federal Courts, 30 Wm. & Mary L.Rev. 499, 520–23 (1989) (discussing *Pennhurst* in the course of a wide-ranging investigation of the unacknowledged influence of substantive interests on federal courts doctrine).

Appendix B

SELECTED FEDERAL STATUTES

Page B–3, delete 42 U.S.C. § 1981 and substitute the following:

§ 1981. Equal rights under the law

(a) All persons within the jurisdiction of the United States shall have the same right in every State and Territory to make and enforce contracts, to sue, be parties, give evidence, and to the full and equal benefit of all laws and proceedings for the security of persons and property as is enjoyed by white citizens, and shall be subject to like punishment, pains, penalties, taxes, licenses, and exactions of every kind, and to no other.

(b) For purposes of this section, the term "make and enforce contracts" includes the making, performance, modification, and termination of contracts, and the enjoyment of all benefits, privileges, terms, and conditions of the contractual relationship.

(c) The rights protected by this section are protected against impairment by nongovernmental discrimination and impairment under color of State law.

Page B–5, delete 42 U.S.C. § 1988 and substitute the following:

§ 1988. Proceedings in vindication of civil rights; attorney's fees

(a) The jurisdiction in civil and criminal matters conferred on the district courts by the provisions of this Title, and of Title "CIVIL RIGHTS," and of Title "CRIMES," for the protection of all persons in the United States in their civil rights, and for their vindication, shall be exercised and enforced in conformity with the laws of the United States, so far as such laws are suitable to carry the same into effect; but in all cases where they are not adapted to the object, or are deficient in the provisions necessary to furnish suitable remedies and punish offenses against law, the common law, as modified and changed by the constitution and statutes of the State wherein the court having jurisdiction of such civil or criminal cause is held, so far as the same is not inconsistent with the Constitution and laws of the United States, shall be extended to and govern the said courts in the trial and disposition of the cause, and, if it is of a criminal nature, in the infliction of punishment on the party found guilty.

(b) In any action or proceeding to enforce a provision of sections 1977, 1977A, 1978, 1979, 1980, and 1981 of the Revised Statutes [42 U.S.C. §§ 1981–1983, 1985, 1986], title IX of Public Law 92–318 [20 U.S.C. § 1681 et seq.], or title VI of the Civil Rights Act of 1964 [42

U.S.C. § 2000d et seq.], the court, in its discretion, may allow the prevailing party, other than the United States, a reasonable attorney's fee as part of the costs.

(c) In awarding an attorney's fee under subsection (b) in any action or proceeding to enforce a provision of sections 1977 or 1977A of the Revised Statutes [42 U.S.C. §§ 1981 or 1981a], the court, in its discretion, may include expert fees as part of the attorney's fee.

†